LIMITED CHOICES

LIMITED CHOICES

The Political Struggle for Socialism in Tanzania

Dean E. McHenry, Jr.

LYNNE RIENNER PUBLISHERS

BOULDER
LONDON

Published in the United States of America in 1994 by
Lynne Rienner Publishers, Inc.
1800 30th Street, Boulder, Colorado 80301

and in the United Kingdom by
Lynne Rienner Publishers, Inc.
3 Henrietta Street, Covent Garden, London WC2E 8LU

© 1994 by Lynne Rienner Publishers, Inc. All rights reserved

Library of Congress Cataloging-in-Publication Data
McHenry, Dean E., 1939–
  Limited choices : the political struggle for socialism in Tanzania
by Dean E. McHenry, Jr.
  Includes bibliographical references and index.
  ISBN 1-55587-429-0 (hc: alk. paper)
  ISBN 1-55587-556-4 (pb: alk. paper)
  1. Socialism—Tanzania—History. 2. Tanzania—Politics and
government—1964–   I. Title.
HX448.5.A6M35 1994
320.5'31'09678—dc20   94-14623
                                                      CIP

British Cataloguing in Publication Data
A Cataloguing in Publication record for this book
is available from the British Library.

Printed and bound in the United States of America

∞ The paper used in this publication meets the requirements
of the American National Standard for Permanence of
Paper for Printed Library Materials Z39.48-1984.

Contents

List of Tables and Figures	vii
Preface	ix
Acknowledgments	xi
Chronology	xiii
Map of Tanzania	xvi

1	Introduction	1
2	Tanzanian Socialism	15
3	Leadership and Socialism	29
4	Democracy and Socialism	47
5	Equality and Socialism	75
6	Agricultural Cooperatives and Socialism	105
7	Industrial Parastatals and Socialism	129
8	Self-Reliance and Socialism	159
9	Subnationalism and Socialism	189
10	Conclusion	215

Appendix	241
Bibliography	243
List of Abbreviations	263
Index	267
About the Book and Author	283

Tables and Figures

Tables

2.1	Distinctions Between Ideological and Pragmatic Socialists	18
3.1	Summary of Reasons Given by Regional Political Committees and Central Committee for Rejecting Possible Candidates for National Assembly in 1985 Elections	35
5.1	Changes in Tanzania's Minimum Wage	77
5.2	Changes in Producer Price of Maize and Cotton Compared with Changes in Consumer Price Index	79
5.3	Proportion of Primary School–Age Children in Primary School	85
6.1	Number of New Cooperatives, Number of Villages Included in Cooperatives, and Average Number of Villages per Cooperative, by Year Formed	115
7.1	Economic Activities Requiring Exclusive or Majority Public Ownership	132
7.2	Contribution of Manufacturing to Gross Domestic Product	140
7.3	Textile Production in Tanzania	141
8.1	Tanzanian National Debt and Ratios of Debt to Gross National Product and Debt Service to Exports	171
8.2	Tanzania's Exports, Imports, and Export/Import Ratio	171
8.3	Composition of Tanzania's Imports	172
8.4	Tanzania's Food Imports	172

9.1	Comparison of Historical, Cultural, and Political Features of Constituent Parts of Tanzania	192
A.1	Official Exchange Rate of Tanzanian Shilling	241

Figures

10.1	Gross National Product per Capita	227
10.2	Ratio of Private to Government Consumption	228

Preface

The concluding years of the twentieth century may be remembered as the period when socialism "died." Even if one does not accept the finality of the "triumph" of liberalism over socialism, one must accept the fact that the political face of the world has radically changed. Almost everywhere, socialism, as a form of social and economic organization, seems to be in disrepute. Although most scholarly attention has been given to the demise of socialism in the North, especially the radical changes in Eastern Europe and the collapse of the Soviet Union, there have been important changes within states committed to building socialism in the South as well.

One of the most significant cases is that of Tanzania, which formally initiated socialist construction more than a quarter of a century ago. Tanzanian socialism shared with socialisms of the North the criticisms of individualism and the praise of collectivism; the depreciation of private enterprise and the glorification of collective and state enterprise; the condemnation of inequality and the support for state efforts to bring education and health services to all; and the fear that unfettered individual liberties would retard the creation of the good society.

Independence was accompanied by a widespread feeling that much could be done to transform Tanzanian society. This optimism was reflected in the positive public reaction to Tanzanian socialism in the 1960s. It contrasted with the more cynical and sanguine attitudes toward socialism prevalent at the time in Eastern Europe and the Soviet Union. Twenty-five years later, though, disillusionment and cynicism had crept in. Although the formal commitment to socialism remained, many of the basic policies enacted to facilitate socialist construction were being reversed. An explanation of these changes and a prediction of whether they will lead to a complete abandonment of the goal of socialism will be sought in the pages that follow.

The sources of information used to address these issues are twofold. First, I have relied upon the work of many scholars who have sought to understand the changes that have taken place both in Tanzania and in other countries seeking to build socialism. Second, I have relied upon my own work in Tanzania, which spans a period of more than thirty years.

The challenges a researcher faces in Tanzania are both stimulating and daunting: understanding meanings in a context of cultural diversity and justifiable suspicion; interpreting scholarly writings whose authors have very strong and very different orientations; extracting an accurate picture of events from newspapers owned by the sole political party and/or the government; seeking countrywide generalizations where regional variations are substantial; and fighting diseases of various sorts or covering distances over roads that shake vehicles apart—all are a part of the undertaking. These do not excuse error, but they make modesty in presenting assertions imperative.

Although I have sought to view the struggle over socialist construction in Tanzania with detachment and objectivity, biases certainly will be found. My perspective is bound to be affected by feelings of admiration for Tanzanians, Tanzania, and the basic ideals of Tanzanian socialism. Yet I have sought to temper that orientation with objectivity and critical appraisal.

Finally, I accept the view that the scholarly aim should be to build general knowledge. Yet I do not see that ultimate aim to be contradicted by a focus on socialist construction in a single country. This work is organized to present data on issues of central importance to socialist undertakings regardless of the country in which they occur. It is my hope that this book will contribute both to an understanding of Tanzania's experiences and to the general process of socialist construction.

Dean E. McHenry, Jr.

Acknowledgments

This book is the result of the help of many people and many institutions. Spiritual support came from family, friends, and colleagues both in Tanzania and elsewhere. Intellectual support came not only from the scholars cited in footnotes but also from many others who have directly and indirectly provided knowledge and insights. Financial support of my Tanzanian research over many years came partly from the Midwest Consortium for International Development, the University of Dar es Salaam Research Council, the Fulbright Scholar Program, and the Fletcher Jones Foundation at Claremont Graduate School. Publishing support came from Lynne Rienner Publishers, whose staff provided helpful counsel, editorial assistance, and encouragement in the preparation of this manuscript. None of these sources of support is responsible either for what is said in the following pages or for how it is said. Nevertheless, I acknowledge with gratitude their contributions to this work.

D.E.M.

Chronology

1954	7 July: Tanganyika African National Union (TANU) is formed from Tanganyika African Association
1957	5 February: Afro-Shirazi Party (ASP) is formed from African and Shirazi Associations
1961	9 December: Tanganyika becomes independent
1962	22 January: Julius Nyerere resigns as prime minister of Tanganyika and Rashidi Kawawa replaces him
	1–5 November: Elections held in Tanganyika
	9 December: Tanganyika becomes a republic and Nyerere becomes its first president
1963	14 January: TANU's NEC decides to move to a one-party system
	8–11 July: Elections in Zanzibar give ZNP-ZPPP control of government, though ASP wins majority of votes
	10 December: Zanzibar becomes independent
1964	12 January: Zanzibar revolution takes place and ASP assumes control of government
	20–25 January: Army mutinies in Tanganyika
	26 April: United Republic of Tanganyika and Zanzibar is formed
	29 October: United Republic of Tanganyika and Zanzibar renamed United Republic of Tanzania
1965	5 July: Interim Constitution passed by National Assembly making Tanzania a one-party state with TANU being that part of the party on the mainland and ASP that part on the isles
	30 September: Elections held on mainland
1967	5 February: Arusha Declaration committing the state to socialist construction is published
	11 February: Nationalization of the "commanding heights" of the economy begins
	March: Nyerere's "Education for Self Reliance" is published
	September: Nyerere's "Socialism and Rural Development" is published
1969	24 September: Ruvuma Development Association is disbanded by TANU's Central Committee
1970	30 October: Elections are held on mainland
1971	21 February: "TANU Guidelines," 1971 are announced
1972	7 April: Zanzibar's Revolutionary Council Chairman Abedi Karume is assassinated
1973	6 November: Nyerere announces that it is an "order" for all peasants move into ujamaa villages by end of 1976
1975	2 June: Interim Constitution is amended to entrench party supremacy

1975 (cont)	26 October: Election is held on the mainland
	12 August: Villages and Ujamaa Villages Act is passed by National Assembly
1976	14 May: Cooperative unions are dissolved
1977	5 February: Chama cha Mapinduzi (CCM) is formed from a merger of TANU and ASP
	25 April: Permanent Constitution of Tanzania is adopted to replace Interim Constitution
1979	January: Tanzanian troops move into Uganda following Idi Amin's intrusion into Tanzania
1980	26 October: Elections are held on the mainland
1981	23 November to 7 December: *CCM Guidelines, 1981*, adopted by CCM's NEC
1982	28 June: Cooperative Societies Act, 1982, reestablishing cooperatives, is signed into law by Nyerere
1984	29 January: Zanzibar's President Aboud Jumbe resigns
	31 January: Ali Hassan Mwinyi is sworn in as interim chairman of the Revolutionary Council
	20 February: CCM's NEC removes chief minister of Zanzibar, Brig. Ramadhani Haji Faki
	12 April: Tanzania's Prime Minister Edward Moringe Sokoine dies in an auto accident
	19 April: Mwinyi elected to Zanzibar presidency
	24 April: Salim Ahmed Salim appointed Tanzania's prime minister
1985	20–21 February: NEC directed that production-oriented rural cooperatives be established to replace marketing-oriented ones
	15 March: New Constitution of Tanzania comes into effect, which contains a Bill of Rights
	27 October: Mwinyi elected president of Tanzania, replacing Nyerere; Idris Abdul-Wakil elected president of Zanzibar, replacing Mwinyi; and first elections to House of Representatives in Zanzibar take place
1986	August: IMF agreement is completed
1987	22–30 October: Third CCM National Conference adopts the Fifteen-Year Party Program
1988	26 January: Seif Shariff Hamad removed as Zanzibar's chief minister
	16 May: Hamad and associates are expelled from CCM
1989	10 May: Hamad is arrested in Zanzibar
1990	February: Nyerere opens multiparty debate in Tanzania
	28 October: Elections are held in Tanzania
1991	14 February: Leadership code is relaxed with proclamation of Zanzibar Declaration by the NEC
	23 February: Nyalali Commission to examine multiparty issue is appointed

1992 18–19 February: Extraordinary national conference of CCM agrees to the Nyalali Commission's recommendation of a multiparty system

April-May: National Assembly passes legislation to initiate a multiparty system

1 July: Formal start of the multiparty system

1993 25 February: National Assembly tables report of Parliamentary Constitutional and Legal Affairs Committee (Marmo Committee) that rules Zanzibar's membership in Islamic Conference Organisation (OIC) violates Articles of Union

22 August: National Assembly votes unanimously to move toward establishment of a separate government for mainland

14 October: CCM's NEC calls for a presidential commission to assess popular feelings about the form of union

Tanzania

1
Introduction

Uzoefu ndio mama wa maarifa.[1]
"Experience is the mother of knowledge."

The primary purpose of this book is <u>to provide a description and an explanation of Tanzania's inability to realize its vision of socialism</u>. Tanzania's predicament is one instance of a broader crisis facing socialism as the twentieth century closes. Because in this century the confrontation between socialism and its alternatives both within and among states has had a profound impact on the lives of people everywhere, the character of the twenty-first century is likely to be profoundly affected by the outcome of that crisis. There are conflicting theses regarding what that outcome will be.

On one side are those who proclaim socialism's "death." They argue that socialism will soon be abandoned by states throughout the world as a means of organization and a goal for aspiration. Evidence is everywhere. In the North: Eastern European socialist regimes collapsed one after another. The USSR fell apart and the independent republics initiated radical changes in the organization of their political economies. Both "socialist" and nonsocialist governments in the West embarked upon privatization of public enterprises, signifying a retreat from modest collective forms manifest in their societies. The response among opponents of socialism in both the East and the West was jubilation as they saw a long, unpleasant historical chapter at an end. In an obituary, Norberto Bobbio argued that the reason for the demise of "the greatest political utopia in history" was that it had "completely upturned into its exact opposite."[2] In the South: More than a decade before the collapse of Eastern European communism, China had broken from Maoism and embarked on reforms that have been described as "capitalist restoration."[3] The Jamaican experiment was abandoned in the late 1970s with the downfall of Michael Manley. In the late 1980s, the electoral defeat of the Sandinistas in Nicaragua led to a retreat from socialism. Socialist countries in Africa seemed to follow a similar path. By the early 1990s, those that had proclaimed themselves Marxist-Leninist were overthrown, as in Ethiopia; declared the abandonment of Marxism, as in Benin; or quietly moved away from the practices formerly undertaken in the name of Marxism-Leninism, as in Mozambique. Overall, the trend toward the demise of socialism in the South appears to parallel that in the North.[4]

On the other side are those who proclaim the transformation of socialism. They note that important elements of socialism are being retained despite the "death" of socialist regimes and despite the introduction of markets and other features of a liberal economy. When a country like China, for example, continues to proclaim socialism as the national objective, it is not a mere facade. Indeed, many have viewed this period of "dying" as a very creative one for socialism. Some see hybrid systems, social democracy, and the introduction of innovative means to old ends. They contend that reference to the death of socialism is simplistic and exaggerated.[5]

Whether one accepts the death thesis or the transformation thesis, there is common agreement that profound changes are taking place in socialist countries.

The Objectives of This Study

In the study that follows, I seek to comprehend the meaning of these changes. My broad objective is to contribute to an understanding of the possible future of socialism, particularly in the Third World, through the study of the experiences of a single country, Tanzania. My specific objectives, which I see as means to my broad objective, are three: First, I seek to describe what has happened in Tanzania since its leaders committed the country to socialist construction in 1967; second, I seek to evaluate the level of success achieved in its efforts; and third, I seek to account for the level of success achieved.

The Broad Objective

The utility of the case of Tanzania for addressing the broad issue of socialism's future, particularly its future in the Third World, can be argued on two general grounds. First, it has been a serious and significant example of an effort to build a socialist society. Those who lead the state have persisted in their formal commitment to build socialism for more than twenty-five years in the face of strong external and internal pressures to abandon the effort. And there is an extensive scholarly literature on Tanzania and its socialism that ranges between the extremes of great affection and optimism to great disaffection and pessimism. This pairing of observers' attitudes and predictions has been common. So intense were feelings about Tanzania among scholars that commentators began to write about afflictions they called Tanzaphilia and Tanzaphobia.[6] Broadly speaking, the former affected observers writing in the years immediately following Tanzania's commitment to build socialism—that is, from the late 1960s through the early 1970s; the latter affected observers writing from the late 1970s following the beginning of the economic decline. The attitudes derive in part from the ideological predisposition of scholars and in part from factors associated with the objective situation in Tanzania. The extent and intensity of debate over Tanzanian socialism suggest that it has been considered critical to the general debate over socialism in the Third World.

Second, Tanzania's socialism shares important traits with other Third World socialisms. These include both its volitional character and its troubled history. Most Third World socialisms, recognizing that the societies they seek to reconstruct are characterized by social formations very different from those that were the focus of Marx's analysis, deemphasize determinism. The same is true of Tanzania's socialism: It shares with the independence movement out of which it grew an optimism toward the capacity of human effort. In it the realization of a socialist society depended upon human will. As such, it challenged both traditional fatalism and the determinism of Marxism. Also, like many other Third World socialisms, it has had an increasingly troubled history.

Critics suggest socialism may have died already—if it ever lived. Their voices became particularly loud and persistent in the post-1979 period. For example, Susanne Mueller wrote in 1980 that Tanzanian socialism had become "the vehicle for pauperisation both at the economic and political level."[7] James Weaver and Alexander Kronemer declared the following year that it was a "miserable failure."[8] Zaki Ergas described it in a similar fashion, saying it had "utterly failed."[9] A shallow and flippant editorial in the *Wall Street Journal* identified Tanzania as

> a country that has been lurching along on an ever more weird and dictatorial path, building up an ever more socialist and bankrupt government, sucking in ever larger amounts of Western aid, and sinking still lower in the gutter.[10]

Michael Lofchie, a scholar with great knowledge about East Africa, described Tanzanian socialism as "a bitter disappointment . . . an economic failure of such calamitous proportions that meaningful recovery may well be impossible" and referred to Tanzania as "the sick country of Africa."[11] The *Economist* concluded, somewhat naively, that "Tanzania has been ruined by its own stable but misguided government, which by the early 1980s had brought hunger where almost anything can grow, and poverty where mineral wealth lies just under the ground."[12]

At an international conference reviewing almost twenty years of the Arusha Declaration held at Arusha in December 1986, paper after paper declared socialism's failure. Michael Okema, a political scientist at the University of Dar es Salaam, concluded that "Tanzania today is not building socialism by any standards."[13] P.J.A.M. Kabudi and S.E.A. Mvungi, also from the University of Dar es Salaam, argued that "Tanzania has never been on a socialist path of development."[14] Girish Chande, the chairman and managing director of the J.V. Group of companies, described the situation then existing in Tanzania as one of

> falling production in our industries and in agriculture, falling Government revenues, falling standards of living for the mass of our people, declining standards of health and education services, increased smuggling and other black market operations, unbridled theft or misuse of public monies, lowered morale and decreasing efficiency in the public services and rampant corruption.[15]

And Aggrey Mlimuka concluded that "capitalist elements are expanding at a very fast rate and at the same time there is an entrenchment of capitalist tendencies in our society."[16] Mlimuka's remarks summarize what seems to be a trend among socialist states not only in the Third World but elsewhere.

Despite the fact that the Tanzanian case involves a serious effort to build socialism and that it shares with other Third World socialisms important features, I do not claim that it can be taken as a surrogate for all countries seeking a socialist transition. Yet I do claim that its experiences will contribute to the building of a general understanding of the problems of socialist construction.

The Specific Objective

If one accepts that Tanzania is an important case of an effort to build socialism in the Third World, then a description, evaluation, and explanation of the country's experiences is important. Had existing works on Tanzania come to an agreement on what has happened, how it happened, and why it happened, there would be no need for an additional study. But any serious reader of studies about Tanzania will conclude that there is immense disagreement and controversy over almost every aspect of Tanzanian socialism and its implementation. The reasons are several.

First, ideological bias has significantly colored what has been written. It is hard to find two students of the Tanzanian scene with similar outlooks. There have been attempts to categorize authors who have written about Tanzania on a left-right continuum, but the differences in points of view are more than unidimensional.

Second, the paucity of empirical information has heightened ideological bias and controversy. Research by scholars at the University of Dar es Salaam is limited severely by a lack of funds both for daily survival and for research purposes. The government controls research clearance and access to information more than is the case in many other countries. Until the early 1990s, there was virtually no daily newspaper that was an alternative to those published by the party and the government.

Third, changes are often rapid and dramatic, and there is a time lag between the event and its incorporation into the scholarly literature. As I have described the evolution of studies, there may be increased ambiguities when studies mix accurate reports from different time periods.

Fourth, Tanzania is like the proverbial elephant in the story about a group of blind men, each of whom touched a different part of the creature's body and described the whole animal accordingly. A study in Tanga Region may claim to represent the reality of Kagera Region;[17] yet the country is large and diverse, and disagreements over what is seen in Tanzania may be more the result of regional variation than inaccurate observation.

There has been disagreement not only over descriptions of what has happened to Tanzanian socialism but also over explanations. Central to much of the discussion over the past decade has been the question of what has caused Tanzania's economic decline. The basic cleavage is between those who contend that Tanzanian socialism is the principal cause and those who attribute the decline to a variety of factors unrelated to Tanzanian socialism. Supporters of Tanzanian socialism have amassed a great list of specific causal factors that include those said to be out of the control of the party and government, like drought, insect infestation, the rise in the price of oil, worsening terms of trade with other countries, and the world recession; or said to be the result of adherence to principles not unique to the country's ideology that resulted in the war with Idi Amin, military support for Mozambique's struggle against the Mozambican National Resistance, and political support for liberation movements in southern Africa; or said to be a consequence of party and government errors, such as failing to rectify corruption, allowing public sector mismanagement to persist, embarking upon import substitution industrialization, and closing cooperatives and abolishing local government.

Opponents of Tanzanian socialism have laid the blame on the character of that socialism. Those attacking from the left have contended that a state bureaucracy has hijacked socialism in its own interest, that Tanzanian socialism is more populist than socialist, that it has not worked because it denied the rightful place of class struggle, that it overstressed distribution and understressed production. Those attacking from the right have contended that the real reasons it has been unable to deal with economic problems lie in the core assumptions of all forms of socialism, the denial of a leading role to private capital, an incentive system that tends to be insensitive to individual preferences, and an absence of individual freedom that adversely affects creativity. There is a need for a clearer picture of what has happened and why it has happened.

The Approach to This Study

In order to facilitate the achievement of this book's broad objective, I disaggregate the socialist project into aspects common to most countries seeking a socialist transition. Such an approach makes the findings directly relevant to categories of general knowledge about socialist construction. In order to facilitate the achievement of the book's specific objective, I describe, assess, and seek to explain Tanzania's experiences with each of these aspects of socialist development. I give particular attention to the impact of two explanatory factors that I feel have been given insufficient attention: political struggle among those formally adhering to socialist goals and the consequences of the "units of action" problem.

The Foci: Substantive Aspects

The substantive aspects of the socialist endeavor I address in this volume are the efforts to create leadership able to contribute to socialist construction; to secure democracy during the transition; to build social and economic equality; to use agricultural cooperatives and industrial parastatals as a means for socialist construction in rural and urban areas, respectively; to foster self-reliance in order to free the country from the constraints of the world system; and to contain subnationalism, which threatens the socialist project.

The role of leadership in socialist construction has been a subject of substantial dispute. Some Marxists claim that capitalism inevitably gives way to socialism, i.e., that leadership is irrelevant. Yet in Africa the capitalist mode of production is not well developed. As a result, Africans might have to wait centuries for its evolution and transformation even if this determinist view is correct. To expect such patience, according to other Marxists, is unrealistic. The major alternatives, skipping modes of production and revolution, require leadership. Indeed, Marxist experience implies that leadership plays a major role in socialist construction. For example, it is not possible to deny the impact of Lenin, Stalin, Khrushchev, and Gorbachev on the character of Soviet socialism; that of Mao on pre-1976 communist China; that of Castro on Cuban socialism; or that of Tito on Yugoslavian socialism.

There is less ambiguity in the position of Tanzanian socialists: Most have contended that leadership is extremely important to socialist construction. They note that Tanzania is not a society that can be divided neatly into capitalists and industrial workers: The overwhelming majority of the people are peasants. And Tanzanian socialism is not a determinist socialism but a voluntaristic socialism, i.e., one whose realization is to be achieved through human will. Indeed, Tanzania's effort to construct socialism has been a "top-down" undertaking; that is, leadership has been viewed as crucial for its realization. Where human will is the key to the socialist transition, leadership becomes critically important. In Chapter 3 I address Tanzania's experiences with leadership in socialist construction.

Democracy is implicit in the central notion of most socialisms, i.e., democracy interpreted as the primacy of group interest over individual interest. Yet there has always been a tension between socialist construction and democracy. In practice, many states whose leaders claimed a commitment to socialist construction became authoritarian. An array of rationalizations followed: Authoritarianism was necessary to thwart the undemocratic actions of opponents; it was required until popular "false consciousness" was overcome; it was a means to achieve more rapidly the socialist goal of economic development; and so on. This tension between socialist theory and practice characterizes Tanzania's experiences. Although Julius Nyerere and others have always said democracy was a necessary condition for socialism, the state's behavior has not been consistently in accord with the principle. In Chapter 4 I address Tanzania's experiences with promoting democracy in the building of socialism.

One of socialism's principal criticisms of the capitalist order has been the existence of immense inequalities in wealth and stature among individuals. As group-centered rather than individual-centered visions of the good society, socialisms have sought to bring about greater equality and a greater sense of equity within societies. The mechanisms are familiar: The wealth of the rich has been seized or highly taxed and distributed to the poor directly or indirectly through improved social services; the market for skills has been restricted to avoid what is deemed to be inequitable remuneration, and through control over wages and salaries the state has sought to reduce the gap between rich and poor; the stature of the poor is raised through the leveling process and through celebrations, awards, literature, and other nonpecuniary means. Through the first decade of Tanzanian socialism, Tanzania's success was widely touted, but the economic decline that began in the late 1970s had devastating consequences. In Chapter 5 I address Tanzania's experiences in promoting equality in socialist construction.

States seeking to build socialism have organized industrial and agricultural production separately. In rural areas, two forms of agricultural organization have been common: state farms and cooperatives. The emphasis has varied. In the Soviet Union, state farms, or *sovkhozy,* were seen as a higher form of socialist organization than cooperatives, or *kolkhozy.* In China emphasis was given, following a brief period of land reform, to cooperatives and communes rather than state farms. In agriculture-based countries, the success of socialism is dependent upon the success of such rural organizations. Tanzania decided to emphasize rural cooperatives rather than state farms. In Chapter 6 I address Tanzania's experiences with agricultural cooperatives in the socialist transition.

To many socialists, industrial organization is the key to socialist construction. Marxists saw socialism arising out of capitalist exploitation of industrial workers. The followers of Trotsky continue to emphasize the centrality of the industrial worker to the socialist transition. In Third World countries, though, there were few industrial workers. By 1967 industrial production contributed less than 10 percent of the gross domestic product (GDP) in Tanzania. Despite this fact, industry was still seen by many as a key to the future. Following the Arusha Declaration, the commanding heights of the economy were nationalized. Industrial parastatals became the heart of Tanzanian industry. Yet, by the late 1970s, rather than being in the forefront of the transition as some had predicted, parastatals became a serious drain on state finances. In Chapter 7 I address Tanzania's experiences with industrial parastatals in socialist construction.

The practical task of establishing socialism in one country "surrounded" by a hostile world made self-reliance an important socialist issue. The dependency school, arguing that the Third World lost when it allowed itself to be integrated into the world economy, had a significant impact on Tanzania. To a country seeking to build socialism, self-reliance seemed doubly important, for the world system was an especially hostile place for socialist construction. In Chapter 8 I address Tanzania's experiences with self-reliance in socialist construction.

Socialisms have tended to view subnationalism as the "group equivalent" of individualism, i.e., as fundamentally antisocialist. In multinational states, socialisms have confronted the national problem in two ways: through physical suppression and federal accommodation. Because the human and material costs of suppression are great, multinational socialist states often have adopted federalism as the preferred tool. It was viewed as a means of organizing a multinational state, such as the former Yugoslavia or the USSR, that eventually would lead to the natural demise of subnationalism. By the early 1990s, though, the federal "solution" had become the federal problem. Federalism, rather than providing proponents of socialism with access to a wider constituency, provided opponents with a subnationalist base. Subnationalism has not posed a major problem for Tanzania, with one important exception: that of Zanzibar. Whereas the union government in Tanzania rejects claims by many Zanzibaris that the country is a federation, Tanzania's history and structure suggest the contrary. Much as the Soviet republics used their limited autonomy to challenge the union government, during the 1980s Zanzibar became the center of the most vigorous opposition to the Tanzanian state. Zanzibari subnationalism seemed to combine with antisocialist ideas to form a potent brew. In Chapter 9 I address Tanzania's experiences with subnationalism and its federal "cure" in socialist construction.

The Foci: Explanatory Factors

I have noted previously that there is little agreement on the factors accounting for the growing challenge to the success of socialism in Tanzania.

The class in power, the world economy, the incentive system, poor management, a self-reliant peasantry, a stagnant party, and many other factors have been suggested. Although I review many of these causal factors in this study, particular attention is given to factional political struggle and what I identify as the "units of action" problem to account for what has happened to Tanzanian socialism. The former involves those who set policy, and the latter involves those who are affected by policy.

Political Struggle

Given the volitional character of Tanzanian socialism, that is, that its realization is determined by human action rather than by "invisible" forces, one might expect political struggle to be central to its realization. A focus on political struggle does not deny the impact of factors over which Tanzanians have little control. It merely assumes that an understanding of the progress of socialism in Tanzania is best attained by examining political struggle. Political struggle may be reduced in a crude fashion to other factors, and they, in turn, may be reduced in an even cruder fashion to still other factors. The objective reality, though, is that of a struggle among human actors over policy. It is especially in this struggle that I seek an understanding of the effort to build socialism in Tanzania.

Two broad approaches to the study of political conflict are represented among scholars of the Tanzanian scene: One borrows from the Marxist tradition and focuses on class struggles or class conflict, and the other borrows from the Western pluralist tradition and focuses on group struggles or group conflict, "group" being defined in terms other than class. Of the two traditions, the former is more widely employed among Tanzanian scholars. Yet in practice there is considerable blurring of the traditions. I contend that a focus on factional political struggle is not only accommodated within the pluralist tradition but also adds to the Marxist tradition. The former contention is uncontroversial; the latter requires elaboration.

Most class analysts argue along the lines of Issa Shivji's contention that a bureaucratic faction of the petty bourgeoisie has governed Tanzania at least since the formal commitment to socialism in 1967.[18] They would contend that this faction has become more classlike and may be referred to more appropriately as the state bourgeoisie or state class. If there has been any significant change in the character of the dominant class during this period, it has been in its increasingly friendly ties with the private bourgeoisie. The persistence of the same hegemonic class through the period suggests that significant policy changes are a consequence of something other than changes of the class in power. I suggest that factional political struggle will account for such policy changes.

Two rebuttals to this argument about the insufficiency of class analysis should be considered. First, one may argue that policy changes have not been significant. Because no real changes have occurred, there is no need to explain them. Second, although the hegemonic class remains the same, it has not been unchallenged. In an effort to strengthen its position when confronted by such class challenges, it has altered its policy. My view is that neither of these counterarguments is sufficient to obviate the need to view factional political struggle as a supplemental variable for explaining what has happened to Tanzanian socialism. The first counterargument is only true if one assumes that the effort to build Tanzanian socialism was a complete charade from the start. Such a claim is made by those who equate African socialism with defensive radicalism. Of course, it is likely that there were those who saw in Tanzanian socialism a cover for the pursuit of capitalism, but there is little evidence that the duplicity was general. Rather than assume universality, it is much more reasonable to view the current "return" to policies apparently contradicting Tanzanian socialism as victories of those who did not take Tanzanian socialism seriously or who preferred a route different from the route of those who initially plotted the course. The second counterargument implies a unity in the response of the hegemonic class that is as unrealistic as the uniform duplicity assumption was in the first counterargument. Surely it is more reasonable to suppose that there was more than one response proposed to challenges from other classes. If so, the policy decided upon must have resulted from factional struggle within the hegemonic class. Thus, I contend that the addition of a consideration of factional political struggle to class analyses is likely to improve their explanatory capabilities.

Although factions may shift in membership and in numbers from issue to issue, factional struggle may be examined effectively by simplifying reality into two, tendencies I identify as ideological socialists and pragmatic socialists. Although these tendencies have not been the focus of research, other writers have identified similar divisions. Joel Samoff, a scholar who has contributed much to the understanding of Tanzania, has referred to "the temporary dominance of capitalist and socialist tendencies" within the governing class as the basis for explaining "much of the apparent contradictory behavior of the Tanzanian government."[19] Dirk Berg-Schlosser and Rainer Siegler used the terms *radical* and *pragmatic* in a recent book to distinguish the groups involved in struggle.[20] The ideological socialists tend toward Marxism-Leninism; the pragmatic socialists tend toward liberalism. For the past quarter century, though, political struggle in Tanzania has determined the form the socialist middle path should take.

Units of Action

Virtually all the major objectives of Tanzanian socialism are unit specific; i.e., they take on different practical meanings within different groups. For example, democracy for the people of Kilimanjaro Region probably would mean the rejection of a tax on their coffee that was intended to support better health and education facilities elsewhere in the country; but for the people of the country as a whole, democracy probably would mean the acceptance of such a tax. Similarly, for the people of the country as a whole, the realization of self-reliance might require textile workers to spend more hours in the textile factory; but to such workers, self-reliance might require them to spend more time cultivating crops. The practical meanings of both concepts are group specific or group defined. Democracy has a different practical meaning to people in Kilimanjaro depending on whether it is defined relative to the region or to the country as a whole; self-reliance has a different practical meaning to textile workers depending on whether it is defined relative to the country as a whole or to the workers themselves. Thus, the same behavior in different units of action may be both a help and a hindrance to socialist construction.

The importance of units of action to socialist construction can be illustrated by other examples. First, a criticism of Nyerere's vision of a socialist society repeated over and over again in the literature was that it falsely claimed traditional society was socialist. What Nyerere was saying was that within the traditional family unit, there was common ownership of the means of production, people worked together for the good of all, and so on. That is, many of the features of Tanzanian socialism existed within the family unit. Yet if one picked the country as a whole as the unit within which to measure whether traditional society was socialist, one might agree with the critics. Family units tended not to cooperate for the good of all to the same degree that members of family units cooperated with each other. In other words, both Nyerere and his critics were right. The difference between them was that they were measuring socialism within different units. Ludwig Watzal, in a philosophical study of Tanzanian socialism, suggests that in the context of the family unit, there may be no "individual" individuality, making it socialist; but in the context of the country, there may be "family" individuality, making it nonsocialist.[21] In other words, the behavior of any subunit relative to the whole is likely to be individualistic, even though individuals within it behave in a socialist manner.

Second, the same reasoning helps explain ambiguous attitudes toward the role of cooperatives in the construction of socialism. Nyerere has observed that (a) they were socialist in content, but (b) they did not make a country socialist. What he was saying was that, among cooperators, socialism was manifested in those actions undertaken collectively; but within the country as a whole, cooperatives might compete in a very individualistic way with other marketing enterprises.[22]

Third, Susan Crouch points out the apparent contradiction between the selfless behavior implicit in socialism and the selfish behavior implicit in self-reliance.[23] The contradiction did produce confusion in implementation.

Yet, if interpreted as selflessness with regard to others within Tanzania and selfishness with regard to those outside Tanzania, behavior need not be in conflict. What these examples illustrate is a potential obstacle to socialist construction. This obstacle involves actions that at one level facilitate construction but at another level undermine it.

Conclusion

Socialism has been the primary alternative to individualism as the basis for organizing societies during the twentieth century. Yet the collapse of socialist regimes in the North has led to considerable doubt about the longevity of socialist regimes in the South—and about the future of socialism everywhere. This study involves an examination of the experiences of Tanzania with socialist construction. It accepts the claim of the familiar Swahili proverb, *Uzoefu ndio mama wa maarifa*—Experience is the mother of knowledge. It seeks both to describe and to explain those experiences in an effort to contribute to an understanding of the past and the future of socialism and of Tanzania. In the next chapter the form of socialism Tanzania has pursued is examined.

Notes

1. The proverbs at the start of each chapter in this book were derived from those found in Albert Scheven, *Swahili Proverbs, Nia Zikiwa Moja, Kilicho Mbali Huja* (Washington, D.C.: University Press of America, 1981).

2. Norberto Bobbio, "The Upturned Utopia," *New Left Review*, No. 177 (September/October 1989), p. 37.

3. Michel Chossudovsky, *Towards Capitalist Restoration? Chinese Socialism After Mao* (New York: St. Martin's Press, 1986).

4. Francis Fukuyama, in "The End of History?" *The National Interest*, No. 16 (Summer 1989), pp. 3–18, suggests a causal relationship between the collapse in the North and the increased rate at which socialism is being abandoned in the South.

5. Samuel Huntington, in "No Exit, The Errors of Endism," *The National Interest*, No. 17 (Fall 1989), pp. 3–11, argues against the idea of the death of socialism—at least insofar as it refers to a vision of societal organization. He contends that at the state level socialism may be, or may be about to become, effectively "dead," but that to argue that any body of ideas might become permanently irrelevant to the organization of society is unreasonable.

6. See Ali Mazrui, "Tanzaphilia: A Diagnosis," *Transition* (Kampala), No. 31 (June/July 1967), pp. 20–26; and James Karioki, *Tanzania's Human Revolution* (University Park: Pennsylvania State University Press, 1979), pp. 37, 38.

7. Susanne Mueller, "Retarded Capitalism in Tanzania," in Ralph Miliband and John Saville, eds., *The Socialist Register, 1980* (London: Merlin Press, 1980), p. 220.

8. James Weaver and Alexander Kronemer, "Tanzanian and African Socialism," *World Development*, Vol. 9, No. 9/10 (1981), p. 839.

9. Zaki Ergas, "The State and Economic Deterioration: The Tanzanian Case," *Journal of Commonwealth and Comparative Politics,* Vol. 20, No. 3 (November 1982), p. 290.

10. *Wall Street Journal,* 17 July 1981, p. 26. The *Journal* editorial endorsed the views presented by Kenneth Adelman, "The Great Black Hope, Richard II of Tanzania," *Harper's,* Vol. 263 (July 1981), pp. 14–19.

11. Michael Lofchie, "The Roots of Economic Crisis in Tanzania," *Current History,* Vol. 84 (April 1985), p. 159.

12. *Economist* (London), 20 June 1987, p. 3.

13. Michael Okema, "The International Response to the Arusha Declaration," a paper presented at the International Conference on the Arusha Declaration, Arusha, December 1986, p. 17.

14. Pala J.A.M. Kabudi and Sengondo E.A. Mvungi, "The Party System and Socialism in Tanzania: A Backlash of Populist Socialism?" a paper presented at the International Conference on the Arusha Declaration, Arusha, December 1986, p. 16.

15. Girish Chande, "Role of Private Capital in the Context of the Arusha Declaration," a paper presented at the International Conference on the Arusha Declaration, Arusha, December 1986, p. 3.

16. Aggrey Mlimuka, "The Party and the Arusha Declaration," a paper presented at the International Conference on the Arusha Declaration, Arusha, December 1986, p. 2.

17. For example, Michaela von Freyhold relies almost entirely on empirical observations of villages in Tanga Region for her book *Ujamaa Villages in Tanzania: Analysis of a Social Experiment* (New York: Monthly Review Press, 1979).

18. Issa Shivji, *Class Struggles in Tanzania* (Dar es Salaam: Tanzania Publishing House, 1976) and his "Introduction: The Transformation of the State and the Working People," in Issa Shivji, ed., *The State and the Working People in Tanzania* (Dakar: Codesria, 1985), pp. 1–15.

19. Joel Samoff, "Bureaucrats, Politicians, and Power in Tanzania: The Institutional Context of Class Struggle," *Journal of African Studies,* Vol. 10, No. 3 (Fall 1983), p. 86.

20. Dirk Berg-Schlosser and Rainer Siegler, *Political Stability and Development: A Comparative Analysis of Kenya, Tanzania, and Uganda* (Boulder: Lynne Rienner Publishers, 1990), p. 95.

21. Ludwig Watzal, "Ujamaa—The End of a Utopia?" (Munich, 1982), p. 15.

22. Julius Nyerere, "Socialism and Rural Development," in Nyerere, *Freedom and Socialism* (Dar es Salaam: Oxford University Press, 1968), p. 345.

23. Susan Crouch, *Western Responses to Tanzanian Socialism, 1967–1983* (Aldershot, United Kingdom: Avebury, 1987), p. 176.

2

Tanzanian Socialism

Chetu si changu.
"Ours is not mine."

The concept of Tanzanian socialism has been defined in the literature on Tanzania in two different ways: first, as the vision of the good society sought for Tanzania by those who have held political power, and second, as the reality of the society found in Tanzania at a given point in time. The semantic difference is a significant one in any evaluation of success. Those who have applauded and those who have criticized Tanzanian socialism often have been applauding and criticizing different things. The former tend to look at the vision, whereas the latter tend to look at the reality. Most Tanzanian leaders have used Tanzanian socialism to refer to the vision; they consider calling the reality Tanzanian socialism absurd. They contend that as long as the reality differs from the vision, it should not be identified by the same term. Nyerere has frequently said that Tanzania is *not yet* socialist, that the task is to *build* socialism, that to call the unfinished project by the same term as one would call the finished project is unreasonable. I concur. "Tanzanian socialism" properly refers to the vision alone. In this chapter I seek to answer the question, What is Tanzanian socialism? by exploring the *vision* of the good society it embodies. Subsequent chapters explore the efforts to change existing society so that it conforms with this vision; i.e., they examine what we refer to as socialist construction.

Tanzanian Socialism: Evolution

Socialism fit comfortably with the struggle for independence in most African countries. Nationalists saw it as the enemy of their enemies and friend of their friends. That is, most colonial governments had promoted capitalism and had fought socialism. And within Britain, France, and other colonial countries, European socialists were among the few who championed the right of colonized people to their independence. Furthermore, in collectivism African leaders found an idea that was more familiar to the societies in which they had been born than had been the idea of individualism. Thus, at independence the ideals of socialism had a head start over those of capitalism in the hearts of most Africans. Along with the affection for socialism, independence for most Third World countries brought a period of optimism. In Tanganyika, the ability of the nationalist leaders to unite the people of their country and win independence created a strong sense of self-confidence. The leaders of the new state believed they could decide the direction of change their country would take. All the ingredients for a socialism based on human volition were present in the early 1960s as country after country became independent. Tanganyika was not an exception.

In the early postindependence period, the idea of socialism was fostered in several ways. The constitution of the Tanganyika African National Union (TANU), the dominant political party, committed members to support socialism. And in 1962 Julius Nyerere published "Ujamaa—The Basis of African Socialism." In that essay, Nyerere claimed that a socialist was distinguished from a nonsocialist not by the amount of wealth he possessed but by his attitude of mind, that is, by how he used that wealth. Nyerere described a socialist society as one in which everyone worked and everyone cared for one another. Such a society, he argued, was much like precolonial, traditional African society.[1] These assertions about the character of socialism frustrated many Marxists, who contended that Nyerere had no understanding of true socialism.

What brought about the decision to commit the state formally to socialist construction is a matter of dispute. Ali Mazrui has emphasized the influence of Zanzibari socialists, who were made part of the union government to reduce Marxist pressure on the Zanzibari government, an issue I look at in more detail in Chapter 9.[2] Claude Ake has suggested it was an instance of "defensive radicalism," that is, an act that sought to make the masses think the ruling bourgeoisie was progressive in order to prolong the rule of that bourgeoisie.[3] Cranford Pratt, in the most thorough study of the period in which socialism was adopted, has suggested the commitment to socialist construction was due to Nyerere's concern with the growth of a privileged leadership.[4] Pratt has argued that the country's leadership accepted the commitment because of Nyerere's persuasive powers and because of the popular appeal of the accompanying nationalization measures. Indeed, there is general agreement among most scholars that Nyerere was the principal initiator and early propagator of Tanzanian socialism.

Initial Formulation

The most succinct and thorough outline of the package of ends Nyerere wanted Tanzania to attain is found in his introduction to *Freedom and Socialism,* the collection of his writings and speeches between 1965 and 1967.[5] He equates the word *ujamaa* with the Tanzanian version of socialism. This, he says, is a society in which people "are of equal account"; where human dignity is enhanced; where democracy is established; where everyone who is able works and receives "a return in proportion to his efforts and his contribution"; where there is no exploitation of one person by another; where "the tools of production and the mechanisms of exchange are firmly under the control of the people"; where there is an increase in the production of goods; and where the rule of law prevails. In more general terms, it would be a society seeking to enhance "man's cooperative spirit . . . not his personal aggressiveness"; it would encourage "service, not . . . personal acquisitiveness."[6] He stressed the fact that the realization of Tanzanian socialism was a task for Tanzanians: "By the use of the word 'ujamaa' . . . we state that for us socialism involves building on the foundation of our past, and building also to our own design."[7] This vision, this group of ends and means, is at the core of Tanzanian socialism.

Political Struggle for Changes in Initial Formulation

But Nyerere's vision is not the whole of Tanzanian socialism. As the body of ideas identified as socialism by those who have held state power in Tanzania since independence, Tanzanian socialism cannot be equated with Nyerere's ideas alone. Neither did Nyerere hold state power by himself, nor was there a unanimity of views on the issue among those who did hold state power.

From the time of the Arusha Declaration in early 1967 to the time multipartyism began in mid-1992, a formal commitment to socialism was required of everyone who participated in Tanzanian politics. What this meant was that the focal point of political struggle was not over *whether* socialism should be the goal but *how* socialism was to be achieved.

As has been noted, it is useful to differentiate between what I have called the ideological socialists and the pragmatic socialists. These factions are defined in terms of ideological tendencies associated with shifting coalitions of those who hold state power. Within each are gradations ranging between radical ideological socialists who differ little from Marxists to conservative pragmatic socialists who differ little from capitalists. An example of a relatively consistent ideological socialist would be Kingunge Ngombale-Mwiru, and an example of a relatively consistent pragmatic socialist would be George Kahama. Nyerere's ideas fall in the middle, though more on the pragmatic than on the ideological side.

The fundamental distinction lies in differing conceptions of the means to realize socialism: Ideological socialists tended to see a model in the experiences of Marxist regimes elsewhere in the world; pragmatic socialists tended to consider Tanzania's effort a relatively unique one, in which new thinking was required to surmount each obstacle. The similarities and differences can be described in terms of a variety of issues summarized in Table 2.1.

Table 2.1 Distinctions Between Ideological and Pragmatic Socialists

Issue	Ideological Socialists	Pragmatic Socialists
Collectivism versus individualism	Group welfare over individual welfare; less tolerant of individualism during socialist transition	Group welfare over individual welfare; more tolerant of individualism during socialist transition
Class struggle	Necessary condition; to be welcomed	Unnecessary condition; to be avoided
Role of workers and peasants	Central, but worker defined by position in relations of production	Central, but worker defined as one who works
Sectoral importance	More emphasis on industry	More emphasis on agriculture
Character of party	Vanguard with mass orientation	Mass with mass orientation
Ownership	Collective and state ownership with only temporary role for private sector in transition	Collective and state ownership with permanent role for private sector
Production	More enthusiastic support for collective production	Less enthusiastic support for collective production
Incentives	More emphasis on moral incentives	Less emphasis on moral incentives
Democracy	More supportive of popular democracy	Less supportive of popular democracy
Equality	More emphasis on equal access to resources	More emphasis on equal status
Industry	Greater emphasis on heavy industry	Less emphasis on heavy industry
Self-reliance	Less willing to compromise for foreign aid; less willing to allow at levels of action below state	More willing to compromise for foreign aid; more willing to allow at levels of action below state

Pragmatic socialists have tended to be more ready to compromise on *the route* to socialism than ideological socialists. The result of this difference was a creative tension. The success of the ideological socialists *within the party* helped rein in the extreme pragmatists, thereby maintaining at least some commitment to the socialist undertaking. And the success of the pragmatic socialists *within the government* helped rethinking about alternative paths, thereby maintaining the hope that socialism might be realized. From the time of the Arusha Declaration to the late 1980s, the ideological socialists within the party gradually brought Tanzanian socialism more into accord with their views, as shown by a review of party documents.

Changes in Initial Formulation

Party documents provide the best basis for an understanding of the evolution of the ideas of those who have dominated the state, for three reasons. First, the party has been the institution most closely associated with the initiation and elaboration of Tanzanian socialism. In point of fact, it was the party that formally committed the state to socialist construction. Second, party documents express the corporate resolution of institutional and factional debate better than can the words of any single individual or collection of individuals. They are the summary of deliberations by those who hold formal power in Tanzania. Third, the party has always claimed supremacy over other institutions in directing the state, a claim given constitutional backing following a decision of the party's National Executive Committee (NEC) made in Musoma in late 1974.

The Arusha Declaration of 1967

The proclamation of the Arusha Declaration on 5 February 1967 by the National Executive Committee of TANU is considered the formal start of the state's effort to build a socialist society. Written by Nyerere and revised slightly by the NEC, the declaration defined a socialist society in a manner consistent with Nyerere's ideas, i.e., as one without exploitation; with the major means of production and exchange under the control of the peasants and workers; with democracy; and with leaders and masses believing in, and committed to, the realization of such goals. To achieve such a society, the declaration argued, Tanzania must be more self-reliant, it must emphasize agriculture more than industry, and its people must work hard.[8]

Three documents adopted by the party the same year elaborated upon and clarified aspects of the declaration. Although not formally a part of the Arusha Declaration, they are considered by some writers to be a part of the Arusha "formulations." The first document was an elaboration on the declaration's call for public control of the commanding heights of the economy. Jeannette Hartmann describes it as "the second Arusha Declaration," for it was an important statement about the continuing need for private investment.[9] The other two formulations were written by Nyerere and focused upon the task of extending socialism to education and to rural areas: "Education for Self-Reliance" suggested ways the education system should be revised to produce socialist Tanzanians rather than capitalist Englishmen. "Socialism and Rural Development" spelled out how socialism might be brought to rural areas through the creation of socialist villages. Peasants would be persuaded to move into such villages and to live and work for the good of all.[10] These papers became the bases for two of the most significant policies to realize the socialist vision.

The 1971 TANU Guidelines

With the adoption by the NEC of the 1971 TANU Guidelines (*mwongozo*) four years after the Arusha Declaration, the ideas of more radical elements within the party first became a formal part of Tanzanian socialism. The 1971 guidelines were prompted by the overthrow of Milton Obote, the president of Uganda, following his adoption of policies that moved the country in a more socialist direction. The document was a declaration that the defeat of the Ugandan government's tentative steps toward socialism would not be allowed to spread to Tanzania. It attacked "imperialists" and "local puppets" for their role in seeking the defeat of socialism, and it stressed the importance of the masses in socialist construction, calling for a people's party and a people's army. Furthermore, the document criticized the tendency among leaders toward authoritarianism, which drove "a wedge between the Party and the Government on the one side and the people on the other."[11]

The 1981 CCM Guidelines

Although the suppression of consequent militant action by workers was a blow to the ideological socialists, they were decisive in the formulation of the 1981 guidelines, or *mwongozo,* approved by the NEC of Chama cha Mapinduzi (CCM)—the party formed in 1977 from a union of TANU and the Afro-Shirazi Party (ASP), the sole party on Zanzibar. This document expressed the need for a vanguard party, an extension of communal production, and greater mass control over the state, all issues that distinguished the ideological socialists from most pragmatic socialists. Regarding the vanguard party, the 1981 guidelines declared:

> It is true that fundamentally, socialism is the ideology of the peasants and workers and that it would be built on the basis of the unity of peasants and workers as a class. However, it is also equally true that without a core of fighters in the frontline, without a crackforce leading the struggle for socialist construction the desired objective would never be realised. . . . Members of Chama Cha Mapinduzi constitute the core of fighters in the frontline.[12]

The 1981 guidelines called for an extension of communal agriculture[13] and reiterated many of the principal objectives of the Arusha Declaration:

> The major objective of the Tanzanian revolution is to build a socialist state in which the exploitation of one man by another will be completely

eradicated; whose national economy will be owned and controlled by the mass of peasants and workers; in which production and social relations will be cordial, harmonious and on the basis of co-operation in the interest of the development of all and in which labour and work is accorded dignity as an activity in which every honourable and respectable person ought to participate.[14]

The 1981 guidelines came at a time when Tanzanian socialism was under great strain. Economic conditions were worsening. Observers abroad were proclaiming Tanzanian socialism's failure. Thus, in many ways, the guidelines were a reaffirmation of the commitment, a declaration of life. Yet the document was more than this, for it gave additional emphasis to the agenda of the ideological socialists.

The 1987 CCM Fifteen-Year Party Programme

The 1980s were years of great economic hardship. They might be divided into two halves, distinguished by how the state dealt with the problem. The first approach involved a more self-reliant attempt, i.e., one without International Monetary Fund (IMF) help; the second involved a less self-reliant attempt, i.e., one with IMF help. The former attempt failed to halt the decline. The latter brought ambiguous results: On the one hand, there was a marginal increase in per capita GDP; on the other hand, the national debt doubled, inequalities increased, and severe hardship continued. It was in this situation that the national conference of CCM in 1987 adopted the Fifteen-Year Party Programme, a document pushing Tanzanian socialism even further toward the views of the ideological socialists.[15]

Where Nyerere had argued that Tanzanian socialism sought to prevent the development of classes, the Programme declared that "the winning of state power by the revolutionary class is only the first stage of a social revolution."[16] Where Nyerere had seen a possible place for some private entrepreneurship, the Programme declared that "the concept of a 'mixed economy' is alien to socialism. It is a concept being advanced by sympathisers of capitalism in their efforts to distort the correct theory of socialism."[17] Where Nyerere had argued that there was no model to guide the construction of socialism in Tanzania, the Programme made reference to the historical lessons in the building of socialism to be learned from the examples of the USSR and Mongolia.[18] Where Nyerere had seen the necessity of a mass party, the Programme argued that in the transition period "the Party takes firm measures to strengthen its ideology, to purify its membership and leadership ranks."[19] Where Nyerere had made the peasantry central to the transition, the Programme expressed some doubt: It stated that the peasants, fishermen, and livestock keepers "are small-scale owners who are close to capitalists at least in their wishes and aspirations to develop and expand into capitalists."[20] And where Nyerere had argued that too much emphasis had been placed on industry and not enough on agriculture, the Programme argued that an industrial revolution was a necessary condition for an agricultural revolution: "That is the reason why we state that agriculture is the basis and industries the leader of the national economy."[21] Somewhat redefining Nyerere's idea of an ujamaa village, the Programme argued, "The central instrument for building a socialist and self reliant sector in agriculture and livestock-keeping is producer cooperatives in the rural areas." Yet it did not argue that "incorrect" production relations were the cause of production problems: "Non-application of science (the principles of better farming) and the use of inferior technology (implements) are the two factors which account for the poor performance of our agriculture."[22]

The 1991 Zanzibar Declaration

After twenty years of gradual radicalization of Tanzanian socialism, the tide began to turn in 1990 when CCM decided to draw up a new election manifesto, overturning an earlier decision to use the CCM Fifteen-Year Party Programme for that purpose. Then, in February of 1991, the participants in the NEC meeting in Zanzibar decided to limit significantly the scope of a core feature of the Arusha Declaration, its code of socialist ethics. Initially known as the leadership code, it had been formally renamed the code of ethics when it became applicable to all members. The code was a partial definition of socialist morality, i.e., it proscribed behavior that violated the tenets of Tanzanian socialism. For example, it forbade the renting of houses, earning two salaries, owning shares in private companies, serving on the board of directors of a private corporation, and other "capitalist activities." The Zanzibar Declaration eliminated many of these prohibitions for members, though it formally retained them for leaders. The specific changes will be addressed in Chapter 3. But, as the CCM secretary general, Horace Kolimba, said in a speech at the University of Dar es Salaam, what was important was "their collective impact in providing a sense of direction to the Party members and to the people of Tanzania as a whole."[23] He said the hope was that the relaxation of the code would "rescue our ideology of *Ujamaa* from being fossilised like it was in some of the East European countries with deadly consequence now visible to all."[24] To many ideological socialists, however, the Zanzibar decisions appeared to be the first significant steps toward the "undoing" of the Arusha Declaration, i.e., toward abandoning the commitment to socialist construction.

It is apparent from this brief review of major party documents that until about 1990 the ideology became increasingly radical; i.e., it came more and more into accord with the ideas of "leftist" elements among the ideological socialists. At the same time, the actions of the state became increasingly pragmatic; i.e., they came more and more into accord with the ideas of "rightist" elements among the pragmatic socialists. Examples of the latter ideas include trade liberalization and the acceptance of IMF and World Bank conditionalities. In other words, there were two opposing trends: a "pragmatization" of policy and a "radicalization" of ideology. The growing discrepancy represented by these two trends was legitimized by arguments that denied its existence. For example, one often heard explanations such as "Socialism does not mean poverty; the changes are necessary to overcome economic decline"; "Two steps forward and then one backward"; "The means may have changed, but the goals remain the same." As I will argue shortly, both the divergence and the recent convergence can be accounted for in terms of political struggle between the ideological and the pragmatic socialists.

Tanzanian Socialism: Classification

Is Tanzanian socialism really a form of socialism? I contend that it is because it shares with many socialist traditions a critique of individualism, an emphasis on communalism, an attack on capitalism, support for public ownership of the commanding heights of the economy, the goal of equality, the status accorded to workers and peasants, and a system of remuneration for work according to the labor contributed. Granted, it has not consistently supported ideas of some socialist traditions, such as class struggle, a vanguard party, and popular democracy. In sum, it belongs to the genus socialism but not to all its species.

The identification of the species of socialism to which Tanzanian socialism belongs has been the subject of dispute for a variety of reasons. Some observers have equated it with the Tanzanians' vision of socialism; others have seen it as the reality found in Tanzania. Some observers have categorized Tanzanian socialism as the ideas articulated in the Arusha Declaration; others have identified it as one of its subsequent forms. And some describe it as the function served by the vision, others the vision itself. Still, there are some uniformities among the observers' perceptions.

There is almost complete agreement that in the immediate post–Arusha Declaration period Tanzanian socialism was "utopian" as opposed to "scientific." Nyerere himself argues vigorously against the applicability of "scientific socialism" or Marxism.[25] Boesen, Madsen, and Moody write that "ujamaa could probably best be described as a type of idealistic, utopian socialism. Like the European classics, he [Nyerere] presumes certain basic principles as objectives and justification of human society."[26] P.F. Nursey-Bray calls ujamaa "utopian socialist theory that echoes Rousseau's romantic primitivism." He writes that it is "a socialist theory that is in essence idealist." And, he observes, "the Tanzanian experiment is the only genuine attempt on the Continent to put into practice the precepts of African socialism."[27] William Freund categorizes ujamaa similarly, but disparagingly:

> *Ujamaa* is utopian socialism in classic form; it was based on a vision in which the real class differences of Tanzanian society played no part. At its crudest, it was a blend of idealized pre-capitalist practice coupled to developmentalist goals and promises of state-given amenities.[28]

René Dumont and Marie-France Mottin also refer to ujamaa as "Utopian socialism" yet argue that such a label should *not* be viewed as disparaging.[29]

The most common classification of Tanzanian socialism within the utopian socialist tradition is that of social democracy. For example, A.F. Lwaitama suggests that "Nyerereism is only a Tanzanian version of world socialist democracy."[30] Abdul Babu says it parallels the social democracy of Western Europe, "a socialism of welfare, a socialism of social consumption but not of production."[31] Richard Sklar identifies Nyerere as a "participatory" socialist "in the democratic-corporatist tradition of G.D.H. Cole."[32] Cranford Pratt considers Tanzanian socialism to be of the democratic socialist variety.[33] Pala Kabudi and Sengondo Mvungi of the University of Dar es Salaam call it "Fabian inspired," a term that suggests a form of democratic socialism. They also call it "populist petit bourgeois socialism like that of Sismond and Russian Narodniks."[34]

Other scholars identify Tanzanian socialism as a form of populism. Susanne Mueller suggests it is similar to "the reactionary utopianism of Russia's Narodniks."[35] And, she writes,

> There is no point in speaking of socialism or the transition to socialism in Tanzania. To use the word "socialism" here is to empty it of all content. Furthermore, to invoke the euphemism of the "transition to socialism" and to analyse the existing situation in terms of setbacks and difficulties, incorrectly assumes that the process is still going on and that socialism in Tanzania is still on the agenda. Given the existing material and class forces and the implantation of Narodism, this was never the case.[36]

Gavin Kitching, equating Tanzanian socialism with populism, suggests that it has similarities with other utopian socialisms:

> Reduction of inequality between individuals, between regions and between town and country, a hardworking but spartan public service, decentralized to be nearer the people, serving a mass of small-scale, cooperatively organized, rural villages—this is Nyerere's vision of a socialist Tanzania. It would certainly have found favour with the Ricardian socialists, with Proudhon and with many of the populist and neo-populist thinkers of eastern Europe.[37]

Still others view Tanzanian socialism as a form of developmentalism. Indeed, there are significant parallels between a voluntaristic conception of development, i.e., one equating development with movement toward the achievement of goals set by the people of a country, and Tanzanian socialist construction. Nyerere himself has defined development in such voluntaristic terms.[38] Goran Hyden argues that in most of Africa "it is inevitable that socialist transformation and modernization must refer to essentially the same problematic."[39] Stephen Clarkson, in *The Soviet Theory of Development*, uses the two terms interchangeably. He writes that "development is defined squarely in terms of desired social, economic, and political progress towards socialism."[40] Thus, even those who identify Tanzanian socialism with populism and developmentalism tend to equate those terms with a form of utopian socialism.

Almost no attention has been given in the literature to the "radicalization" of Tanzanian socialism described above. Thus, the classifications of Tanzanian socialism refer to the set of ideas articulated by Nyerere and party leaders in the immediate post–Arusha Declaration period. When one looks at later developments, one must conclude that Tanzania had moved toward a form of "scientific socialism" or Marxism-Leninism by the 1987 CCM conference that adopted the Fifteen-Year Party Programme. Most Marxist scholars would disagree with this assertion, not because the content was less utopian and more "scientific socialist" but because the *function* of the ideology was not to promote the latter. For example, A.K.L.J. Mlimuka and P.J.A.M. Kabudi contend that the "leftists" in the party "have been used whenever the regime has felt it was in crisis." Citing the *1981 CCM Guidelines* as an example, the authors assert that

> when the ruling class has been rocked by crisis, it has utilised the services of the "leftists" in the party to salvage it. The "leftists" using their populist and progressive rhetoric that appeals to the sentiments of the people have temporarily made it popular. But after the ruling class has weathered the storms and securely consolidated its position it has unceremoniously discarded the "leftists."[41]

As a result, Mlimuka and Kabudi claim, "the Party 'leftists' in Tanzania have sustained and maintained the ruling class for all this time." Why did they perform this function?

> They have decided to work from within, thinking that they would be able to influence changes from within or "seize" an opportunity, when it comes, of capturing the state power. They have therefore ended in opportunism.[42]

Implicit in these comments is the view that *at the level of ideas* there had been considerable movement toward "scientific socialism" or Marxism-Leninism within the ideology by 1987, even if one still classified the socialism as utopian.[43] By the early 1990s, though, the ideology had moved much closer to its original form as outlined in the Arusha Declaration; i.e., it fell within the broad category of utopian and democratic socialisms. Indeed, such was the momentum to the right that many socialists were concerned that Tanzanian socialism was being replaced by liberal capitalism.

Conclusion

In this chapter I have sought to define and categorize Tanzanian socialism. I have argued three points. First, the fundamental goals of Tanzanian socialism—such as equality, human dignity, the end of exploitation, a gradually improving standard of living, and working for the collective good—are common to other utopian or democratic socialisms. Second, there has been a widespread misinterpretation of Tanzanian socialism as static, i.e., confined to the views of Julius Nyerere reflected in the Arusha Declaration. In reality, Tanzanian socialism was radicalized under the impact of ideological socialists for the first twenty years after the Arusha Declaration; then it was deradicalized under the impact of pragmatic socialists. Third, Tanzanian socialism might be classified as a utopian democratic form of socialism at the time of the Arusha Declaration, moving toward a Marxist-Leninist, scientific socialist form by the time of the Fifteen-Year Party Programme of 1987, and returning toward the former by the early 1990s. Human will was central to its realization as a utopian socialism throughout most of this period. Chapter 3 considers the exercise of human will through leadership.

Notes

1. Julius Nyerere, "Ujamaa—The Basis of African Socialism," in Nyerere, *Freedom and Unity* (London: Oxford University Press, 1967), pp. 162–171.
2. Ali Mazrui, "Socialism as a Mode of International Protest: The Case of Tanzania," in Robert Rotberg and Ali Mazrui, eds., *Protest and Power in Black Africa* (New York: Oxford University Press, 1970), p. 1144.
3. Claude Ake, *Revolutionary Pressures in Africa* (London: Zed Press, 1978), p. 93.
4. Cranford Pratt, *The Critical Phase in Tanzania, 1945–1968, Nyerere and the Emergence of a Socialist Strategy* (Cambridge: Cambridge University Press, 1976), pp. 230–231.
5. Julius Nyerere, *Freedom and Socialism* (Dar es Salaam: Oxford University Press, 1968), pp. 1–34.
6. Ibid., pp. 4–9.
7. Ibid., p. 2.
8. Julius Nyerere, "The Arusha Declaration," in Nyerere, *Freedom and Socialism*, pp. 231–250.
9. Jeannette Hartmann, "The Two Arusha Declarations," a paper presented at the International Conference on the Arusha Declaration, Arusha, December 1986.
10. Julius Nyerere, "Education for Self-Reliance" and "Socialism and Rural Development," in Nyerere, *Freedom and Socialism*, pp. 267–290 and 337–366, respectively.

11. Tanganyika African National Union, "TANU Guidelines on Guarding, Consolidating and Advancing the Revolution of Tanzania and of Africa," in Andrew Coulson, ed., *African Socialism in Practice: The Tanzanian Experience* (Nottingham: Spokesman, 1979), pp. 36–42.
12. Chama cha Mapinduzi, *The CCM Guidelines, 1981* (Dar es Salaam: Printpak for CCM, n.d.), p. 12.
13. Ibid., p. 28.
14. Ibid., p. 24.
15. Chama cha Mapinduzi, *Programu ya Chama cha Mapinduzi, 1987 hadi 2002* (Dodoma: CCM, 1987). An unofficial translation was published in the *Daily News* (Dar es Salaam) during January and February 1988.
16. *Daily News*, 5 January 1988, p. 4.
17. Ibid.
18. Ibid.
19. Ibid.
20. *Daily News*, 6 January 1988, p. 4.
21. *Daily News*, 14 January 1988, p. 4.
22. *Daily News*, 12 January 1988, p. 4.
23. *Daily News*, 18 March 1991, p. 4.
24. Ibid.
25. Nyerere, *Freedom and Socialism*, pp. 14–19.
26. Jannik Boesen, Birgit Storgard Madsen, and Tony Moody, *Ujamaa—Socialism from Above* (Uppsala: Scandinavian Institute of African Studies, 1977), p. 12.
27. P.F. Nursey-Bray, "Tanzania: The Development Debate," *African Affairs*, Vol. 79, No. 314 (January 1980), p. 55.
28. W.M. Freund, "Class Conflict, Political Economy and the Struggle for Socialism in Tanzania," *African Affairs*, Vol. 80, No. 321 (October 1981), p. 492.
29. René Dumont and Marie-France Mottin, *Stranglehold on Africa* (London: André Deutsch, 1983), p. 175.
30. A.F. Lwaitama, "Social Democracy and the Politics of the Arusha Declaration," a paper presented at the International Conference on the Arusha Declaration, Arusha, December 1986, p. 12.
31. A.M. Babu, "Twenty Years After Arusha," a paper presented at the International Conference on the Arusha Declaration, Arusha, December 1986, pp. 2, 7.
32. Richard Sklar, "Obituary of Chief Obafemi Awolowo," *ASA News*, Vol. 20, No. 3 (July/September 1987), p. 6.
33. Cranford Pratt, "Tanzania's Transition to Socialism: Reflections of a Democratic Socialist," in Bismarck Mwansasu and Cranford Pratt, eds., *Towards Socialism in Tanzania* (Toronto: University of Toronto Press, 1979), pp. 193–236.
34. Pala J.A.M. Kabudi and Sengondo E.A. Mvungi, "The Party System and Socialism in Tanzania: A Backlash of Populist Socialism?" a paper presented at the International Conference on the Arusha Declaration, Arusha, December 1986, pp. 11 and 9, respectively.
35. Susanne Mueller, "Retarded Capitalism in Tanzania," in Ralph Miliband and John Saville, eds., *The Socialist Register, 1980* (London: Merlin Press, 1980), p. 203.
36. Ibid., p. 221.
37. Gavin Kitching, *Development and Underdevelopment in Historical Perspective, Populism, Nationalism and Industrialization* (London: Methuen, 1982), pp. 63–70.
38. For example, when he introduced the second five-year development plan (1969–1974), Nyerere declared its purpose to be to "enable the nation to allocate

the resources it possesses in a manner which will bring the people as quickly as possible toward the goals they have set themselves." See United Republic of Tanzania, *Tanzania, Second Five-Year Plan for Economic and Social Development, 1st July 1969–30th June 1974, Vol. 1: General Analysis* (Dar es Salaam: Government Printer, 1969), p. x.

39. Goran Hyden, *Beyond Ujamaa in Tanzania, Underdevelopment and an Uncaptured Peasantry* (Berkeley: University of California Press, 1980), pp. 228–229.

40. Stephen Clarkson, *The Soviet Theory of Development* (Toronto: University of Toronto Press, 1978), p. 250.

41. A.K.L.J. Mlimuka and P.J.A.M. Kabudi, "The State and the Party," in Issa Shivji, ed., *The State and the Working People in Tanzania* (Dakar: Codesria, 1985), p. 80.

42. Ibid., p. 75.

43. Soviet observers have classified Tanzania as non–Marxist-Leninist but rather as a country with a "socialist orientation" or as one following "noncapitalist" development. See Francis Fukuyama, *Moscow's Reassessment of the Third World* (Santa Monica, Calif.: RAND, 1986), p. 84; Anatoly Gromyko, *Africa, Progress, Problems, Prospects (An Analysis of the 1960s and 1970s)* (Moscow: Progress Publishers, 1983), p. 80; and S.A. Sosna, *Public Enterprises in Developing Countries: Legal Status* (Moscow: Progress Publishers, 1983), p. 11.

3
Leadership and Socialism

Mshale usio na unyoya hauendi mbali.
"An arrow without a feather will not travel far."

Tanzanian socialism has often been described as "socialism from above."[1] The concept has a dual meaning. On the one hand, it refers to the effort of the party to get the masses to behave in accord with socialist policies; on the other hand, it refers to core leaders' work to get peripheral leaders to implement such policies. The two meanings are related: The latter is normally considered a prerequisite for the former. There are two approaches to assuring that peripheral leaders support socialist policies; one relies on obedience and the other on commitment. Reliance on obedience to directives alone is unworkable, for the situations leaders face are so variable and the decisions they make so numerous that enforcement is virtually impossible. Reliance on commitment poses a problem, too: How might leaders whose judgment is based on a commitment to socialism be distinguished from those whose judgment is not so based? The solution adopted in Tanzania was a set of personal behavioral guidelines called the leadership code.

The Leadership Code

A leadership committed to socialism means a leadership imbued with a socialist morality. To scientific socialists, socialist morality is the product of economic forces, and therefore it *is not* the driving force for the achievement of socialism. To utopian socialists, socialist morality is the product of individual moral choices, and therefore it *is* the driving force for socialist construction. Indeed, for utopian socialists the spread of socialist morality among leaders is a prerequisite for a socialist transition. The leadership code was a means of propagating a socialist morality.

According to Cranford Pratt, Julius Nyerere's decision to introduce a leadership code stemmed from his observation that leaders had begun to build houses for rent and in other ways to violate socialist principles that both he and the party publicly advocated.[2] Indeed, the Arusha Declaration was formulated partly as a vehicle for such a code. Part 5 of the declaration was titled "The Arusha Resolution." Section A of Part 5 came to be known as the leadership code. The first principle summarized the objective of the code; the second, third, fourth, and fifth principles specified ways the objective could be attained; and the sixth principle defined those to whom it was applicable. The six principles read:

1. Every TANU and Government leader must be either a peasant or a worker, and should in no way be associated with the practices of capitalism or feudalism.
2. No TANU or Government leader should hold shares in any company.
3. No TANU or Government leader should hold directorships in any privately owned enterprise.
4. No TANU or Government leader should receive two or more salaries.
5. No TANU or Government leader should own houses which he rents to others.
6. For the purposes of this Resolution the term "leader" should comprise the following:

    Members of the TANU National Executive Committee; Ministers; Members of Parliament; senior officials of organizations affiliated to TANU; senior officials of para-statal organizations; all those appointed or elected under any clause of the TANU Constitution; councillors; and civil servants in the high and middle cadres. (In this context "leader" means a man, or a man and his wife; a woman, or a woman and her husband.)[3]

The leadership code was by no means a complete statement of a socialist morality based on Tanzanian socialism; rather, it was a statement of *minimum* conditions of "right conduct" for leaders engaged in building socialism. These minimum conditions involved the avoidance of certain kinds of behavior deemed antisocialist. They served as a surrogate for a fully developed morality. Yet the code was an important practical step toward socialist construction, for it defined individual behavior, which could be monitored, rather than a professed attitude, which could not.

The acceptance of the code by the party's NEC was not without opposition, for it directly affected the activities of many leaders. According to Jeannette Hartmann, Nyerere "used nationalization of foreign capital, which he knew was popular with the Party activists, to pave the way for their acceptance of the conditions of the Leadership Code."[4] Its adoption symbolized to all Tanzanians that the party was serious about socialist construction. It was an important indicator of adherence to the ideals of Tanzanian socialism at the level of the individual.

The code had a remarkable longevity: The first *formal* retreat from it did not occur until early 1991. Yet it was often the subject of conflict between ideological and pragmatic socialists. The former tended to support an extension of its scope and intensification of its enforcement, whereas the latter tended to resist such an extension and intensification. Shortly after the code was announced, two "clarifications" were made that were supportive of the pragmatic socialist position. First, leaders were allowed

Leadership and Socialism 31

to transfer property into trusts for the benefit of their children. Second, the prohibition against employing labor, implicit in the first point of Section A of the resolution, was relaxed to allow the employment of "temporary" labor.[5]

Within a decade, the leadership code was entrenched constitutionally and its jurisdiction was extended substantially in accord with the wishes of the ideological socialists. By 1969, the code had become part of the TANU constitution; in 1977, it was made part of the CCM constitution and later the same year became part of the constitution of the United Republic of Tanzania.[6] In 1975, it was made applicable to all TANU members, and when it became part of the CCM constitution, it was extended to all Zanzibari members.

In the second decade after the Arusha Declaration, though, the ideological socialists fought more of a defensive battle as the code was increasingly ignored. This defensiveness spurred policy statements that stressed the importance of socialist morality among leaders. The *CCM Guidelines, 1981* states:

> The leader of Chama Cha Mapinduzi should firstly have the commitment of a socialist ideology, his actions and behaviour must demonstrate themselves to the followers, members and the general citizenry to be socialist. A leader's belief and commitment influences and reinforces that of those who are led. However, a leader who is discovered by his followers to be a hypocrite through his commitment and behaviour is a great enemy of the Party because he frustrates members, confuses citizens and creates a situation where the people start losing faith in fellow leaders and the Party in general. So the issue of Party leaders having a correct stand on ideology and in everyday life is of first priority for Chama cha Mapinduzi.[7]

Despite such pronouncements, though, the discrepancy between the leadership code and the behavior of leaders grew, especially during the 1980s.

By 1987, considerable alarm had arisen, especially among ideological socialists. The CCM Fifteen-Year Party Programme called for the party to take "firm measures to strengthen its ideology, [and] to purify its membership and leadership ranks."[8] It stated that "the main task of the Party in this period is to build a single ideology and leadership in Chama Cha Mapinduzi."[9] The intensification of demands for compliance by the ideological socialists paralleled the radicalization of Tanzanian socialism described in the preceding chapter—yet so did resistance to those demands.

The economic downturn created a quandary. When the question centered on the choice between maintaining the code and suffering serious economic hardship or modifying the code and suffering less serious economic hardship, the pragmatic socialists were more willing than the ideological socialists to modify the code. Nevertheless, the code *formally* remained in force throughout the second decade after the Arusha Declaration.

Part of the reason was the resolute support Nyerere gave the code. Nevertheless, pressures to relax the code grew in the late 1980s. In 1989, reacting to complaints about the hardships it was imposing, Nyerere argued that the code allowed work after office hours at things like poultry keeping and crafts, so that "being a socialist leader does not mean that you have to be a destitute."[10] By early 1990, though, he admitted that aspects of the code were "unrealistic in view of prevailing economic and social reality" and would have to be relaxed.[11] As described in Chapter 3, changes were announced at the NEC meeting held in Zanzibar in February 1991.

What became known as the Zanzibar Declaration significantly altered the code requirements for members of CCM who were not leaders. Such members henceforth would be allowed to rent one house; earn two salaries; own shares in the private company in which they were employed; own shares in parastatals, whether they worked in them or not; be directors of a company at which they worked; farm up to 20 hectares within the boundaries of a village; engage in small-scale commercial activities in the informal sector; and employ labor so long as labor laws were upheld.[12]

In describing the action, the CCM secretary general, Horace Kolimba, argued that the specifics of the individual changes were not so important as "their collective impact in providing a sense of direction to the Party members and to people of Tanzania as a whole."[13] Although the code remained in effect for party leaders, the "sense of direction" the changes implied was as clear to leaders as to members. Kolimba contended that the decisions sought to provide Tanzanians with a way out of "debilitating poverty." And, he argued, "This is the true spirit of the Arusha Declaration."[14] His justifications were those of the pragmatic socialists. Some ideological socialists would agree with a *Daily News* columnist who saw the decision as "the last straw which is bound to break the spinal cord of the Arusha Declaration."[15] Long before the Zanzibar Declaration, though, the leadership code had become unenforceable.

Securing Leaders Possessing Socialist Morality

The leadership code was directed at both party and government leaders, and its enforcement was assigned to both party and state institutions. The concern of this work is primarily with the party, for it has been the key to socialist construction. Unless the *political* leadership was committed, government leaders were unlikely to show much commitment. Three mechanisms—exclusion, education, and expulsion—were employed to obtain and maintain a committed political leadership.

Exclusion: Keeping Code Violators out of Leadership Positions

The party sought to enforce the leadership code through its review of possible candidates for party, parliamentary, and many other posts. Party review procedures to "weed out" those whose character and behavior seemed incompatible with party objectives actually began before the code was devised. What the adoption of the code did was provide an additional set of criteria intended to prevent those not adhering to the code's definition of socialist morality from contending for leadership positions.

Vetting of potential candidates for parliamentary seats has been the focus of most TANU and then CCM attention. In all parliamentary elections from 1965 to the present, vetting has taken place beginning at the district level and ending at the NEC. The intermediary levels involved in the vetting process have varied from election to election. A problem for scholars seeking to determine how rigorously the code was applied in the vetting process is that the reasons for a potential candidate's rejection have been kept secret.

The difficulty is exemplified by my study of the 1965, 1970, and 1975 elections. In the first two post–Arusha Declaration elections I found that the NEC increasingly overruled the district-level rank ordering of potential candidates.[16] Was this a consequence of an effort to keep out those not adhering to the code? Possibly—but there is no assurance that such an interpretation is correct. Rather, the NEC's rulings may indicate an effort to block challenges to existing patron-client systems, to thwart the rise of subnationalism, or to keep people with criminal records out of the National Assembly. Party assertions that ideological purity was the key could not be empirically verified.

Fortunately, the reasons for the rejection of possible candidates at two levels in the review process, the regional political committees (RPCs) and the Central Committee (CC) of the NEC, are available for the 1985 National Assembly election.[17] Although such data do not allow the observer to perceive trends over the whole post-Arusha period, at least it is possible to make some inferences regarding the importance of candidate vetting procedures for ensuring leaders' acceptance of socialist morality at a critical time.[18] There was serious economic hardship, and the socialist project was under heavier attack in 1985 than it had been in any preceding election. As a result, one might expect that the party would be especially careful to exclude "subversives," i.e., individuals who did not accept socialist morality as defined by the code.

In fact, the socialist commitment of potential candidates was of little concern to those involved in the vetting. Consider the data. Most of the reasons given by the RPCs and the CC for rejecting potential candidates in 1985 fall into five categories. The first category, and the most important to this study, is "lack of ideological commitment"; i.e., the potential candidate did not behave according to the tenets of the country's ideology. Examples from the Central Committee report are "He has capitalistic ambitions and has commercial projects" and "He is not reliable about our policy." Included in this category are all references to behavior not in accord with the code. The second category consists of "low personal moral standards"; i.e., the personal behavior of the potential candidate deviated from accepted norms. Examples are "The candidate is immoral and goes about with school girls" and "He is not truthful and is a drunkard." The third category comprises "uncooperativeness"; i.e., the potential candidate was divisive and uncooperative with current party leaders. Examples are "When he was the District Chairman . . . he participated in disputes between villages . . . and the town" and "He instigated trouble in . . . [a certain] Branch and threw his CCM card away." The fourth category consists of "lack of capability"; i.e., the potential candidate did not have the ability to perform the tasks required of a member of parliament. Examples are "His capability for the post is low" and "He is neither capable nor experienced." The fifth category involves "technical problems"; i.e., the potential candidate had not met formal rules governing eligibility. An example is "The candidate was sacked from the party in 1968 and procedures for pardon have not been followed." For each of these categories, the results are summarized in Table 3.1.[19]

At both the RPC level and the CC level a similar trend is evident: Lack of ideological commitment was the reason *least frequently* given for the rejections, whereas low personal moral standards was the reason *most often* given. There are two possible interpretations: Either more than 90 percent of the potential candidates lived up to the code or ensuring adherence to the code was not the principal function of the vetting process. The first possibility is unreasonable and is contradicted by more subjective evidence to be presented subsequently. The second possibility is more plausible, but it requires a more careful analysis of the vetting results.

Those results suggest that the vetting process functioned more as a forum in which to compete for patron or client ties than as a means of ensuring that the leaders would be committed to socialism. Of the forty-eight possible candidates rejected by RPCs, the CC sustained the rejections of only twenty-six of them.[20] When one compares the reasons given by the RPCs for rejecting those twenty-six whom the CC agreed should be rejected with the reasons the RPCs gave for rejecting the remaining twenty-two whose rejection the CC overruled, one finds that the CC accepted "lack of personal morals" in 71.4 percent of the cases, "uncooperativeness" in 35 percent, "lack of capability" in 42.3 percent, "technical problems" in 77.8 percent, and "other reasons" in 25 percent.[21] In other words, the CC deemed "uncooperativeness" and "lack of skill" less important to leadership than had RPCs. Also, of the twenty-two candidates whose rejection by RPCs was overturned by the CC, the CC justified its action on the grounds either that the RPC assessment was based on false information or that the RPC had failed to properly weight certain factors. The proportions of reasons given by the CC for overturning the RPCs' rejection of candidates were as follows: Candidate was popular, 39 percent; regional

Table 3.1 Summary of Reasons Given by Regional Political Committees and Central Committee for Rejecting Possible Candidates for National Assembly in 1985 Elections

	Grounds for Rejection[a] (Percentage)[b]						
Level of Vetting	Lack of Ideological Commitment	Lack of Personal Morals	Uncooperativeness	Lack of Capability	Technical Problems	Other	Total
Regional political committees	5.2	29.2	20.8	27.1	9.4	8.3	100
Central Committee	8.1	43.5	11.3	19.4	11.3	6.5	100

Source: CCM, "1985 Uchaguzi Mkuu, Mapendekezo ya Kamati Kuu Kuhusu Wagombea Nafasi ya Ubunge, Mkutano wa Halmashauri Kuu ya Taifa, Agenda," Nyongeza (UM) (9) (a) Uchambuzi wa Waombaji wa Ubunge Toka Majimbo ya Uchaguzi, Makubaliano ya Mapendekezo Kati ya Kamati ya Siasa ya Mkoa na Kamati Kuu ya NEC, and (UM) (10) (a) Kusigana Kati ya Mapendekezo ya Mkoa na Kamati Kuu Juu ya Wagombea wa Nafasi ya Ubunge, mimeo.

Notes: [a] Four other cases involved possible candidates rejected by regional political committees and the Central Committee for no reasons that were recorded in the above-mentioned source. [b] The percentages were calculated as follows: Each reason given for an individual's rejection was divided by the total number of reasons given for that individual, the results for all individuals were added, and the percentages falling into each category were calculated.

assessment was faulty, 30 percent; candidate was an officeholder, 18 percent; candidate might reform his ways, 12 percent.[22]

These data suggest that the leadership code did not play a significant role in guiding the decisions of the RPCs or the CC. It is not possible to determine the extent to which self-selection, the work of the annual district conferences, or the work of the district political committees may have accomplished the task of "cleansing" the group of potential candidates. Nevertheless, it is surprising to find virtually no invocation of ideological criteria by the CC or the RPCs in the vetting of candidates for the National Assembly. Such an absence suggests that, at least by 1985, a commitment to socialist morality may not have been a necessary condition for entry into leadership ranks. It suggests also that the vetting process involved a struggle over political clientelism. "Uncooperativeness" at the regional level may well have meant a refusal to be a good client. Cooperativeness is a crucial consideration in maintaining a clientelist system. Although the maintenance of such a system might assist some political leaders at the CC level, most would not be affected by "uncooperativeness" in any single region. Furthermore, nearly 20 percent of the reasons given by the CC for overturning the RPCs' recommendations were simply that the candidates rejected at the regional level were officeholders! Again, one might see this pattern as an effort to preserve an existing clientelist system where the CC members' clients or patrons were under attack. At the least, these data are suggestive.

At a minimum, the 1985 National Assembly election data show that by the mid-1980s the review procedures for an important group of prospective leaders did little to assure that they embodied a socialist morality.[23]

Education: Ideological Training to Prevent Violation

The leadership code was not only a set of rules to be imposed by gatekeepers but also an educational tool. It became part of ideological training. Such training was provided to both party members and leaders in a wide variety of settings, from schools to workplaces to ideological colleges. Although the code prescribed behavioral guidelines applicable to all, ideological and pragmatic socialists tended to differ over the degree of compliance required of leaders. The former tended to advocate more rigorous enforcement than the latter. The struggle for control over ideological training created ambiguities that undermined its effectiveness. The point can be illustrated by three examples.

First, there was conflict over whether ideological training should be mass or vanguard oriented. At the time of the Arusha Declaration, Kivukoni College was run by the party to train party members in skills they would need to perform party work. The formal commitment to socialist construction led to the college becoming the preeminent ideological institution in the country—yet its size allowed it to serve only select groups. Beginning in the 1970s, zonal colleges were established in various parts of the country to facilitate ideological training on a broader scale: at Murutunguru (1974), Lushoto (1974), Mahiwa (1974), Hombolo (1974), Ilonga (1976), Msaginya (1979), Zanzibar (1979), and Kiginga (1987). Despite the desire to broaden access to training implied by this expansion, the training facilities became the preserve of the ideological socialists, such as Kingunge Ngombale-Mwiru, who served first as a tutor and then as principal at Kivukoni. Two trends were apparent: Party headquarters tended to assume greater control over who was trained,[24] and Kivukoni College became even more a vanguard institution. As part of this process, in 1987 Ngombale-Mwiru announced that the policy of having a common curriculum for all the ideological colleges would be changed. Kivukoni College would have its own, "which would be commensurate with the status of being the highest ideological institution in the country."[25] The object appeared to be to develop a vanguard until the late 1980s. With the growing strength of pragmatic socialists within the party, the need to reduce the party's subsidies from the state, and the advent of multipartyism in the early 1990s, the zonal colleges were closed, and Kivukoni College ceased operating as an ideological institution for CCM.

Second, there was conflict over the role of external socialist models in ideological training. Nyerere fairly consistently contended that there was no single suitable external model for the development of Tanzanian socialism. Pragmatic socialists tended to see Tanzanian socialism as "homegrown" too. Ideological socialists were more prone to train people to look elsewhere in the world for models. As late as 1989, Ngombale-Mwiru, welcoming back a group of CCM leaders who had taken ideological training in the USSR, declared that it was important to learn from advanced socialist countries and to counter Western propaganda that socialism was being abandoned there.[26] Subsequent events in the USSR probably contributed to weakening the position of the ideological socialists in the early 1990s. But, more importantly, the variety of socialisms being imported by Tanzanians trained abroad and by expatriates from socialist countries brought about confusion in the minds of many over the appropriate form of a socialist morality.

Third, there was conflict over which view of Tanzanian socialism deserved what might be called the Nyerere mantle. Because Nyerere's association with Tanzanian socialism led to its increased popularity among most segments of Tanzanian society, both the ideological and the pragmatic socialists claimed that he supported their views of socialism. In fact, Nyerere seemed to find a creative tension in the struggle over the formulation of Tanzanian socialism. An example of the conflict over the Nyerere mantle occurred in the aftermath of the adoption of the CCM Fifteen-Year

Party Programme in 1987, i.e., the apogee of the ideological socialists' ability to shape Tanzanian socialism. A major seminar for tutors from the ideological colleges was organized, focusing on Nyerere's ideological contribution. An editorial on the seminar in the government newspaper described the near identity between Nyerere's ideas on socialism and those of the party. The writer joined the participants "in chanting our popular salutation: 'Long Live the Thoughts of the Chairman of Chama Cha Mapinduzi.'"[27] Although the editorial may have been an effort by ideological socialists to co-opt the popularity of Nyerere and direct it toward support of the Programme, an alternative interpretation is more appropriate. Given the contradictions between the Programme and Nyerere's vision of socialism, the likely consequence of such a seminar would be to enhance the position of the pragmatic socialist challengers. This is but one skirmish, but it is important because it is part of the shift in the relative positions of pragmatic and ideological socialists vis-à-vis the nature of Tanzanian socialism.

By the late 1980s, there was widespread evidence that the efforts to propagate socialist ideology, whether it be that of the Arusha Declaration or that of the Fifteen-Year Party Programme, were facing a crisis. A year and a half after initiating an effort to revive the CCM in late 1985, Nyerere expressed his frustration with the state of ideological awareness in the party. He said "that a good part of CCM membership knew very little or nothing about socialism and self-reliance" and that the "ideological level of CCM members was low."[28] Part of the reason may well have been the ambiguities created by ideological training conducted partly from the perspective of ideological and partly from the perspective of pragmatic socialists.

Expulsion: Removing Code Violators from Leadership Positions

To enforce the leadership code, two permanent commissions were created. Until the passage of the Commission Act No. 6 of 1973, enforcement of the code was solely the responsibility of the NEC. The 1973 act created the Commission for the Leadership Code and defined senior officials subject to the code as those Tanzanians earning at least TSh. 1,066.70 per month (TSh. = Tanzanian shilling).[29] In 1977, the commission was recognized in paragraph 78 of the state constitution that followed the merger of TANU and the Afro-Shirazi Party (ASP), the sole party on Zanzibar. The commission's stated objective was to "investigate the conduct and behavior of any Leader for the purpose of making sure that the rules of Leadership are being implemented as they should be."[30] Despite the code's extension to all members of TANU in 1975 and all members of CCM with the new party's formation in 1977, it was seldom enforced against anyone who did not hold a leadership position in the party or government. The second commission was the Control and Disciplinary Commission, created when the party secretariat was established in 1982.[31] Although the party constitution makes no reference to the commission's functions, its broad objective was to facilitate the work of the NEC in code enforcement.

The Commission on the Leadership Code issued a report on its activities during the first decade of its operation, 1974–1984, in which it asserted that during the decade it had accepted 2,125 complaints and confirmed and reported to the president 78 of them. That is, only 3.7 percent of the total were confirmed; i.e., fewer than 8 per year were verified. Of those, the president took some action on a total of only 60.[32] Thus, the agency with the specific function of weeding out leaders violating the leadership code was able to declare that 98 percent of the leaders were obedient to the code.

Nevertheless, its report described many loopholes, problems of interpretation, and uncertain jurisdiction that made this figure relatively meaningless as a measure of leaders' compliance.[33] For example, the commission was uncertain about the range of judgment left to it and complained that the Commission Act was not "amended to elaborate on what deeds at what level a leader does to be liable for breach of leadership code."[34] The commission also was uncertain about its role, given the many other institutions whose charges overlapped with it, including the Permanent Commission of Inquiry, anticorruption squads, and special squads for preventing smuggling. It was not until 1979 that the leadership commission was given recognition in the Zanzibar constitution for application to leaders there, and the procedures for reporting to the Zanzibari president were not spelled out. The leadership commission's report described how former leaders colluded with current leaders to obtain government tenders and operate businesses.[35] Clearly, the central organ for enforcing the code among leaders recognized the very severe limitations on its ability to be effective.

The NEC acted on its own to discipline members of the party both before and after the Commission on the Leadership Code came into existence.[36] Almost all such action has been justified on grounds other than the leadership code. Perhaps the most celebrated of all the NEC's actions came in 1968. Nine party members were expelled, including seven sitting members of parliament (MPs). None of the expulsions was for a direct violation of the code. In a study of the episode, H.U.E. Thoden van Velzen and J.J. Sterkenburg reported that the party newspaper accused the MPs of

> being contemptuous of Party Principles and Party ideology; . . . speaking with cynicism about Tanzania's socialist goals; . . . questioning whether Tanu should have any authority over them; . . . while "one even went so far as to suggest that we allow the formation of another Party."[37]

Most of the expelled MPs had argued for parliamentary rather than party supremacy. It was the challenge to the party, rather than its socialist ideology, that was the principal reason for their expulsion. In addition, one of the MPs was in detention for his role in the deaths of citizens involved with cattle thefts, and two others had charged a regional commissioner with using coercion to move people into villages. Of the two expelled who were not MPs, one was in exile abroad and one was in detention for reasons other than violating the code.[38]

The second-most-celebrated NEC actions were probably those on Zanzibar in late 1989, when several leaders in North Pemba, including the former chief minister of the isles, Seif Shariff Hamad, were expelled for "involvement in political agitation" of the wrong sort.[39] Once again, the issue had more to do with political power than with socialist vision.

The great majority of cases involved not the violation of the code but offenses to "right conduct" defined on other grounds. For example, in February 1987 three leaders were disciplined: One lost his position on a regional party executive committee because he had used his own farm illegally to win the "best village" award; another because he had stolen CCM branch funds; and the third for "altering a membership card for personal gain."[40] A casual review of other reports of expulsion gives the grounds as absenteeism, theft, excessive drinking, and indiscipline—i.e., issues not directly related to the code.[41] Thus, it seems appropriate to conclude that expulsion was rarely employed as a means of securing adherence to the leadership code.

Assessing the Success of the Effort to Secure Leaders Possessing Socialist Morality

Whether one assesses success of the leadership code through an examination of popular opinion, party pronouncements, or scholarly studies, there is general agreement that the enforcement mechanisms did not work well. The strongest evidence is what many empirical observers would say is the "softest." Virtually any knowledgeable Tanzanian can cite numerous examples of behavior of political leaders that has directly or indirectly violated the code—and the number of examples seemed to multiply through the 1980s. Such information is deemed soft because it is anecdotal and not easily verified. Yet an attempt to understand the dynamics of the effort to build socialism that rejects such data would be incomplete, for this information has played a major role in the growth of popular cynicism toward socialism. Furthermore, public, "sanitized" information can be found as corroboration.[42]

The party frequently expressed its frustration with its own leadership. Four years after the Arusha Declaration, committed leaders complained in the *TANU Guidelines, 1971* that "some leaders . . . disregard and cleverly avoid the leadership code," and they called for greater party commitment "to supervise the conduct and the bearing of the leaders."[43] A decade later, the authors of the *CCM Guidelines, 1981* called for the party to give greater "priority to the issue of a leader's commitment and ability."[44] In his speech at the opening of the CCM national conference in October 1987, Nyerere complained that the actions of some leaders were promoting a growing cynicism among the people. He gave the following example:

> If leaders retire, and immediately get the capital to begin a capitalist enterprise, they are not breaking the law; but it is not surprising if the people express some doubts about their previously expressed support for ujamaa, and ask themselves; how is it that in a socialist country they so quickly get all the money they need for such an enterprise? And it is this kind of thing which gives birth to cynicism about leaders who have not retired. Their commitment to building socialism and equality also begins to be questioned.[45]

Observers outside the party, especially Marxist and neo-Marxist scholars, have been similarly critical. For example, in the mid-1970s, Issa Shivji wrote of "numerous" breaches of the code.[46] A decade later Pala Kabudi and Sengondo Mvungi wrote of the leadership code being "discreetly overturned" and of leaders being "involved fully in proscribed activities."[47] Aggrey Mlimuka complained that the few code violators prosecuted "are always the small fish," whereas "the big fish who are real culprits are left free."[48] The views of Kabudi, Mvungi, and Mlimuka echo numerous stories, referred to previously, told by Tanzanians in private.

Why have the mechanisms to assure a leadership committed to socialism not worked better? Two categories of answers have been given, one situational and the other structural. Situational factors include economic hardship, limited skilled personnel, and the means used to instill socialist morality. First, economic hardship led to a lack of enforcement of and adherence to the code. This relationship was observed by Andrew Coulson during the economic slump of 1974,[49] and it affected enforcement and adherence in the 1980s. The 1991 Zanzibar Declaration, which excluded most CCM members from compliance, was brought about by continuing economic hardship. When the choice is between compliance and more economic hardship or noncompliance and less economic hardship, the latter is chosen. Second, running an effective government—or party—requires skilled manpower. Yet in a poor country such as Tanzania, skilled personnel have been in short supply. As a consequence, the code was sometimes compromised, and leaders who had failed to live up to it were "recycled." Critics of Nyerere suggested that he was too forgiving of those around him for code violations. Nyerere's behavior may be accounted for also by an understanding of the manpower constraints. Third, the principal method party leaders used to further socialist morality among fellow leaders was the seminar on socialist principles at ideological institutions or in the workplace. That a belief like Tanzanian socialism can be taught by seminar is unproven and doubtful.

Marxist and neo-Marxist observers have accounted for the failure in structural terms. Shivji has argued that the whole effort to build a democratic socialist society is fundamentally flawed. Enforcement of the code might move members of the state bourgeoisie out of the private sector, but this would do little either to end exploitation or to promote socialism.[50] Others have noted that Tanzania's neocolonial status precludes progress toward real socialism, no matter how effective the leadership code.[51] The claim of Shivji and his followers, that democratic socialism is fatally flawed, is based on a premise—challenged by most Tanzanian socialists—that those in power will not or cannot selflessly promote the well-being of the mass of people. Although such a premise is supported by much of Tanzania's experience, in comparison with the avarice of leaders in other parts of Africa that of Tanzania's leaders was of a much lower order—at least until the early 1990s.

The Contradiction: Public Commitment and Private Violation

The limited success of the leadership code contrasts with the major success of the party in maintaining a formal commitment to the socialist project. How can one account for the party's ability to maintain its commitment to socialism with the code's inability to maintain a socialist morality among leaders? The answer appears to lie in the development of a kind of patron-client system, a development alluded to in the review earlier in this chapter of the vetting of potential parliamentary candidates for the 1985 election. Those who have controlled the party have used it as the patron, and many of its more junior leaders are its clients.[52] For the privilege of having the party as their patron, they endorsed socialism and proclaimed it as the state's objective. They need not embody socialist morality, only clientelist loyalty. In such conditions, ideological commitment is not essential. More important becomes "cooperativeness," which means the act of behaving as a proper client.

Although the party persisted in its formal support of some form of socialism into the 1990s, society wavered. The indicators were everywhere, and those leaders committed to socialist construction expressed constant concern about it. They complained about the failure of the people to learn socialist ideology; they denounced the spread of private secondary schools; they bemoaned the growth of the black market; and they criticized the peasants for their failure to move rapidly into producer cooperatives. In response, the pragmatic socialists moved to relax the scope of the code's jurisdiction and to open the political arena to leaders of parties formally opposed to socialist construction. This movement had an impact on both the character of Tanzanian socialism and the relationship between the CCM leadership and civil society. It made the party more open to the influence of sentiments differing from those of existing Tanzanian socialism, and it made the leaders more sensitive to the need to reduce the gap between theory and practice among themselves.

Conclusion

The leadership code was established as an abbreviated statement of socialist morality. It was based on the view that the personal behavior of leaders had to be congruent with the socialist goals of the country for socialist construction to succeed. Although the code remained the same from its acceptance in the Arusha Declaration through the early 1990s, both its jurisdiction and aspects of Tanzanian socialism changed over the years, partly in response to the ideological socialist–pragmatic socialist struggle. Yet the code remained much more a part of the theory than of the practice of Tanzanian socialism. It was not central to decisions about who should be allowed to enter the leadership ranks or who should be forced out of those ranks.

As economic hardship increased starting in the late 1970s, the discrepancy between the tenets of the code and the behavior of leaders increased. In the opening address to the International Conference on the Arusha Declaration in December 1986, Hassan Mwinyi observed, "At some point . . . it may be necessary to review some of the provisions of the Arusha Declaration, especially the Leadership Code, so that current conditions can be taken into account."[53] "Current conditions" made it impossible to both adhere to the code and maintain an acceptable standard of living. Many among the ideological socialists feared that a retreat from the code would be a retreat from socialism, whereas many among the pragmatic socialists argued that if a definition of socialist morality made physical survival difficult, the definition was inadequate and needed to be revised. The Zanzibar Declaration of the NEC was not a complete victory for the pragmatists, since the ideological socialists managed to retain in theory the application of the code to leaders. Nevertheless, the declaration was an indication of the difficulty of maintaining a commitment to socialism in the conditions Tanzanians faced in the early 1990s.

Notes

1. This view is manifested in the titles of significant works on Tanzania. See Jannik Boesen, Birgit Storgard Madsen, and Tony Moody, *Ujamaa—Socialism*

from Above (Uppsala: Scandinavian Institute of African Studies, 1977), and Kjell Havnevik, *Tanzania: The Limits to Development from Above* (Sweden: Nordiska Afrikainstitutet, 1993).

2. Cranford Pratt, *The Critical Phase in Tanzania, 1945–1968, Nyerere and the Emergence of a Socialist Strategy* (Cambridge: Cambridge University Press, 1976), p. 235.

3. Julius Nyerere, "The Arusha Declaration," in Nyerere, *Freedom and Socialism* (Dar es Salaam: Oxford University Press, 1968), p. 249.

4. Jeannette Hartmann, "The Two Arusha Declarations," a paper presented at the International Conference on the Arusha Declaration, Arusha, December 1986, p. 7.

5. Pratt, *Critical Phase*, p. 239.

6. Tanganyika African National Union, *Katiba ya TANU, 1969* (Dar es Salaam: National Printing Co., n.d.), p. 6; Chama cha Mapinduzi, *CCM Constitution* (Dar es Salaam: Tanganyika Standard [Newspapers] Ltd., n.d.), pp. 6 and 7; and United Republic of Tanzania, "The Permanent Constitution, 1977" in Albert Blaustein and Gisbert Flanz, eds., *Constitutions of the Countries of the World* (Dobbs Ferry, N.Y.: Oceana Publications, 1979), p. 54.

7. Chama cha Mapinduzi, *The CCM Guidelines, 1981* (Dar es Salaam: Printpak for CCM, n.d.), p. 57.

8. *Daily News* (Dar es Salaam), 5 January 1988, p. 4.

9. *Daily News*, 2 February 1988, p. 5.

10. *Daily News*, 3 May 1989, p. 1.

11. *Daily News*, 22 February 1990, p. 1.

12. *Daily News*, 18 and 19 March 1991, p. 4.

13. *Daily News*, 18 March 1991, p. 4.

14. *Daily News*, 20 March 1991, p. 4.

15. *Sunday News* (Dar es Salaam), 26 May 1991, p. 8.

16. Dean E. McHenry Jr., "A Measure of Harmony/Disharmony in a One-Party State: Low-Level Party Leaders' Choices for Members of Parliament Compared with Those of Both High-Level Party Officials and the People in Tanzania, 1965–1975," *Journal of Developing Areas*, Vol. 17, No. 3 (April 1983), pp. 337–347.

17. Chama cha Mapinduzi, "1985 Uchaguzi Mkuu, Mapendekezo ya Kamati Kuu Kuhusu Wagombea Nafasi ya Ubunge, Mkutano wa Halmashauri Kuu ya Taifa, Agenda" (Dar es Salaam: CCM, n.d., mimeographed). Formally, the regional political committees were the political committees of the Regional Executive Committee, whose membership, according to the party constitution, included the regional chairman; the regional secretary; the regional commissioner; the members of the National Executive Committee, elected by the National Conference from the region; the national member of parliament, elected from the region; and members elected to the Political Committee by the Regional Executive Committee from among its membership (seven members in the case of a region in mainland Tanzania and four members in the case of a region in Zanzibar).

18. However, there are at least four limitations to the use of such data in inferring the success of the vetting process. First, the reasons are available for only two of five levels. The vetting process began at the Annual District Conference (ADC), where possible candidates were rank-ordered; the rank orders were then reviewed by the political committees at the district and regional levels; the regional recommendations were forwarded to the Central Committee of the NEC, which sent its recommendations to the NEC itself; and the NEC made the final decision on which two candidates should run for election. Second, the reasons are available

for only one of the five parliamentary elections held since Tanzania began socialist construction. Third, the position of candidate for parliament is only one of many leadership positions vetted by the party. Leaders of mass organizations, cooperative-union managers, and even the mayor of Dar es Salaam have been reviewed by the party before standing for election. Furthermore, some government leaders who do not come through the party may have undergone little or no screening. Fourth, the reasons available for the vetting decisions of the regional political committees and the Central Committee of the NEC may be incomplete or distorted by those who have compiled them. The reasons are derived from documents submitted to the NEC by the Central Committee to facilitate the final choice of candidates. Extracting the major reason or reasons for a decision from a discussion is difficult, and cross-checking those provided in the documents is not possible. Despite these limitations, the data provide the best available empirical basis for a judgment of the procedures for assuring a leadership committed to Tanzanian socialism.

19. See Dean E. McHenry Jr., "Socialist Morality: The Changing Character of Leadership in Tanzania," a paper presented at the annual meeting of the African Studies Association, Chicago, October 1988, Tables 1 and 2.

20. Five candidates accepted by the regional political committees were rejected by the Central Committee. No rejection was for lack of ideological commitment. Of the reasons given, four involved lack of personal morality and one lack of skill. See ibid., p. 11.

21. Ibid., Table 3.

22. Ibid., Table 4.

23. Nyerere seems to have recognized the problem. In the midst of the party consolidation program, initiated in 1985 to revitalize the party, he is reported to have told a group in Kilimanjaro Region

> that in future, good knowledge of . . . Party theory and socialist ideology would be a cardinal criterion for being considered for party leadership. He said it would no longer be enough to make a member a key Party leader on reasons that he is simply a "good fellow" (*mtu mwema*).

See *Daily News*, 21 September 1987, p. 1.

24. *Daily News*, 27 October 1987, p. 6.

25. *Daily News*, 26 November 1987, p. 1.

26. *Daily News*, 2 February 1989, p. 3.

27. *Daily News*, 26 November 1987, p. 1.

28. *Daily News*, 21 July 1987, p. 1, and 27 July 1987, p. 1, respectively.

29. This amounted to $152.39 at the time. Jamhuri ya Muungano wa Tanzania, Tume ya Tabia ya Viongozi, *Taarifa ya Miaka Mikumi, 1974–1984* (Dar es Salaam: Kiwanda cha Uchapaji cha Taifa, n.d.), p. 4.

30. United Republic of Tanzania, "The Permanent Constitution, 1977," p. 54.

31. Chama cha Mapinduzi, *The Constitution of Chama cha Mapinduzi, 1982* (Dar es Salaam: Printpak, n.d.), p. 7.

32. Jamhuri ya Muungano wa Tanzania, Tume ya Tabia ya Viongozi, *Taarifa ya Miaka Mikumi*, p. 16.

33. Ibid., pp. 17 and 18.

34. Ibid., p. 22.

35. Ibid.

36. The responsibility for expulsion has been shifting. In 1980, when disciplinary procedures were clarified, authority for actual expulsion was limited to the NEC; see *Daily News*, 8 August 1980, p. 1. In 1988, though, the party's secretary general, Rashidi Kawawa, contended that the regional party leadership should take

responsibility to remove ineffective branch leaders because higher levels of the party "did not know them and [were] likely to be misled by intrigues"; see *Daily News*, 18 April 1988, p. 1. This decentralization of disciplinary authority may have been caused by the increase in the number of cases, but it also may have been a response to growing regional diversity.

37. H.U.E. Thoden van Velzen and J.J. Sterkenburg, "The Party Supreme," in Lionel Cliffe and John Saul, eds., *Socialism in Tanzania. Vol. 1: Politics* (Nairobi: East African Publishing House, 1972), pp. 257–264.

38. Ibid.

39. *Daily News*, 13 October 1989, p. 1.

40. *Daily News*, 27 February 1987, p. 1.

41. *Daily News*, 2 January 1988, p. 3; 23 January 1989, p. 3; and 29 May 1990, p. 1.

42. Public cynicism is extensive, too. The CCM party is sometimes referred to as Chukua Chako Mapema, meaning "Take yours now!" Augustine Mrema, minister of internal affairs in the early 1990s, said CCM was sometimes alluded to as Chakula cha Meneja, or "the manager's food." See *Daily News*, 18 June 1991, p. 5.

43. Tanganyika African National Union, "TANU Guidelines on Guarding, Consolidating and Advancing the Revolution of Tanzania and of Africa," in Andrew Coulson, ed., *African Socialism in Practice: The Tanzanian Experience* (Nottingham: Spokesman, 1979), p. 38.

44. Chama cha Mapinduzi, *The CCM Guidelines, 1981*, pp. 57 and 58.

45. Julius Nyerere, *Address by Mwalimu J.K. Nyerere, Chairman of Chama cha Mapinduzi at the Opening of the National Conference, Dodoma, 22nd October, 1987* (Dodoma: Chama cha Mapinduzi, n.d.), p. 7.

46. Issa Shivji, *Class Struggles in Tanzania* (Dar es Salaam: Tanzania Publishing House, 1976), p. 95.

47. Pala J.A.M. Kabudi and Sengondo E.A. Mvungi, "The Party System and Socialism in Tanzania: A Backlash of Populist Socialism?" a paper presented at the International Conference on the Arusha Declaration, Arusha, December 1986, p. 10.

48. Aggrey Mlimuka, "The Party and the Arusha Declaration," a paper presented at the International Conference on the Arusha Declaration, Arusha, December 1986, p. 9.

49. Andrew Coulson, *Tanzania, A Political Economy* (Oxford: Clarendon Press, 1982), p. 198.

50. Shivji, *Class Struggles*, pp. 80–81.

51. A.K.L.J. Mlimuka and P.J.A.M Kabudi, "The State and the Party," in Issa Shivji, ed., *The State and the Working People in Tanzania* (Dakar: Codesria, 1985), p. 58.

52. Jan Kees van Donge and Athumani J. Liviga, in "In Defence of the Tanzanian Parliament," *Parliamentary Affairs*, Vol. 39, No. 2 (April 1986), p. 236, note that MPs receive many benefits as a consequence of their positions, including a good salary, allowances, and access to scarce resources.

53. Ali Hassan Mwinyi, "Opening Address by H.E. President Ali Hassan Mwinyi to the International Conference on the Arusha Declaration, 16-12-1986," mimeographed, p. 12.

4
Democracy and Socialism

Democrasi si domocrasi.
"Democracy is rule by the people, not by the mouth."

There is an apparent irony in Tanzanian socialism: On the one hand, it stresses the importance of leadership; on the other hand, it stresses the importance of democracy. The former emphasis implies that Tanzanian socialism is known at the top and propagated to the masses, whereas the latter implies that Tanzanian socialism is known at the bottom and propagated to the top.

Tanzanian leaders have claimed that there is no contradiction because the pursuit of socialism by the leadership is a response to the wishes of the masses. Indeed, the interconnection between democracy and socialism is a central theme of the struggle for Tanzanian socialism. Julius Nyerere's desire to eliminate the threat to democracy posed by oligarchic tendencies that had developed within the leadership led him to urge the adoption of the Arusha Declaration, according to Cranford Pratt.[1] The declaration itself contains the proclamation, "True socialism cannot exist without democracy also existing in the society."[2] Virtually every document defining Tanzanian socialism reiterates the commitment to democracy.[3] And virtually all policies implemented in the name of socialism were justified by claims that they would extend democracy.[4] This chapter describes and assesses Tanzania's experiences as it has pursued democracy and socialism.

The Pursuit of Democracy in Tanzania

Giovanni Sartori has observed that we live in an age of "confused democracy," that is, a period when there is little agreement on what constitutes a democratic society.[5] Political struggles are now fought less over whether a state should be democratic than over the meaning of democracy and how to achieve it. At a commonsensical level, there is agreement on the goal: Democracy refers to popular rule or rule by the people. But in the scholarly literature, two broad conceptualizations, one often called liberal democracy and the other popular democracy, are apparent. Liberal democracy is defined principally in terms of means, e.g., whether civil liberties, majority rule, political equality, and periodic elections exist.[6] Popular democracy is defined principally in terms of the end, i.e., whether the decisions of those who rule are in accord with the wishes of a majority of the people. Although popular democracy has been associated mainly with types of socialism and liberal democracy mainly with types of capitalism, both forms of democracy are found in polities pursuing utopian socialisms. The relationship between democracy and these socialisms is viewed by many authors as reciprocal; i.e., the former promotes the latter or the latter promotes the former.[7]

The arguments over whether democracy should take a liberal or a popular form resonated in the struggles over Tanzanian socialism. Nyerere has been the most articulate spokesperson. Initially, he accepted basic elements of the critique of liberal democracy, including the need for social and economic equality in order for true political equality to exist and the belief that organized opposition might be detrimental to true democracy. Yet he upheld other liberal democratic tenets, such as fair election procedures and open and free discussion before decisions are made.

Nyerere contended that "a political democracy which exists in a society of gross economic inequalities, or of social inequality, is at best imperfect, and at worst a hollow sham."[8] The criticism remained a central justification for the socialist undertaking. In mid-1990, Kingunge Ngombale-Mwiru complained that "theoreticians in capitalist countries only emphasised one aspect of democracy—political democracy—by parading democracy as the existence of more than one political party," thereby ignoring the underlying issues of economic and social justice.[9] The commitment to socialism was a consequence of this critique.

Nyerere's most publicized divergence from liberal democracy was his position on the relationship between organized opposition and democracy—a position he held from well before the Arusha Declaration until at least 1990.[10] He argued that only when there was disagreement over a "fundamental issue" was such an opposition necessary for democracy.[11] In Tanzania during the 1960s, he contended, there was no such disagreement. He accepted other aspects of liberal democracy such as "freedom of the individual, and the regular opportunity for him to join with his fellows in replacing, or reinstating, the government of his country by means of the ballot-box."[12]

Often Nyerere sought to show the absurdity of an organized opposition in Tanzanian situations. At one time he gave as an example a village where a hundred people sat and decided where a well should be dug, an example of democracy to him. Yet, he contended, to an "Anglo-Saxon" that would not be democracy because discussion was not properly organized into a "for" side and an "against" side.[13] At another time he likened the two-party system to a soccer game. Every few years competitors would play a game and the victor would rule the country. Yet, he asked, in a situation in which there was fundamental agreement, would it not have been better to disband the teams, let the electorate choose the best individuals from among them all, and let them meet in parliament "to discuss the details of the job and *cooperate in getting it done!*"[14]

Furthermore, Nyerere contended that organized opposition meant the imposition of some restrictions on members. Implicitly referring to the British system, he argued,

> It seems at least open to doubt . . . that a system which forces political parties to limit the freedom of their members is a democratic system and that one which can permit a party to leave its members their freedom is *un*democratic![15]

This critique was the basis for Tanzania's one-party system, adopted in 1965. For twenty-five years Nyerere maintained his contention that a one-party system was more conducive to democracy than a multiparty system. By 1990 conditions had changed. Nyerere initiated a debate that led to the introduction of a *multiparty system,* justified on the grounds that it would better promote democracy than would the one-party system. This change will be addressed later in this chapter.

Nyerere repeatedly argued that the tension between socialist leadership and democracy, referred to at the start of this chapter, was not a contradiction. He contended that "leadership cannot replace democracy; it must be part of democracy."[16] Leaders must help people "to understand both their own needs, and the things which they can do to satisfy these needs."[17] The leader was a facilitator whose task was to help people fulfill their own interests. "Teaching" socialism was seen in that context. To Nyerere, socialism was really the servant of democracy.

An Assessment of the Success of Democracy

Democracy in Tanzanian socialism placed the party in the position of critical intermediary between the people and the government. In theory, the party represented the collective interests of the people and made policy in accordance with popular will; the government carried out the policy according to the dictates of the party. There were two requirements for the system to work. First, the party had to be a democratic institution. Second, the government had to act in accordance with the wishes of the party. If these two requirements were met, then the government was in a democratic relationship with the people.

Assessments of democracy in Tanzania since 1967 have varied immensely. The variation appears to have depended upon a number of factors:

1. Whether the system was being judged in terms of liberal democratic or popular democratic definitions (judgments based on the former were more negative throughout than those based on the latter)

2. The ideological position of the writer (democratic socialists were more positive than Marxists)
3. When the study was done (earlier studies were more positive than later ones)
4. What parts of the "elephant" were examined (those who focused on the enhancement of equity as an indicator were more positive than those who focused on civil rights)
5. How much the theory influenced what was reported of the reality (those who based their understanding on the writings of Nyerere were much more positive than those who saw what was happening "on the ground")

These factors are often mixed, producing considerable confusion.

For the sake of simplicity, the assessments may be grouped into three broad categories: those of Marxist scholars, liberal scholars, and Tanzanian socialists.

Marxist scholars tended to ask the question, which class controlled the state? Initially, many felt that there was a chance for workers and peasants, who constituted the majority of Tanzanians, to dominate. By the mid-1970s, though, they saw clear evidence that this was not the case. As a consequence, they argued that liberal democratic procedures were needed to remove the bureaucratic bourgeoisie and empower workers and peasants.

Liberal democratic scholars deemed the country undemocratic from the establishment of the one-party state in 1965. They criticized Tanzania for not allowing opposition parties; for not allowing those who disagreed with the party's ideology to compete in elections; for transforming the legislature into a mere appendage of the party; and for limiting civil rights. Over the years, the criticisms were intensified as a result of the country's economic failures and the democratic "wave" in other parts of the world.

Tanzanian socialists recognized the drift from democracy, especially in the early 1980s. Party membership fell, meetings were not held, funding could not be obtained from members, and members increasingly seemed confused about the meaning of ujamaa. Furthermore, the party could not control the government.

A series of policy changes that seemed to defy the party's efforts to build Tanzanian socialism began with trade liberalization in the early 1980s and continued through the decade. Nyerere's party revitalization campaign following his retirement as the country's president in 1985 was largely unsuccessful. Both ideological and pragmatic socialists recognized the failure but seemed to call for different solutions. The former sought to transform the party into a vanguard institution to more adequately promote what it thought was the popular will; the latter sought reforms more in line with liberal democracy.

The three perspectives converged on the same assessment by 1990: One-party democracy was not working. To better understand what happened, let us turn to an examination of the three relationships in the one-party democratic system: between the people and the party, between the party and the government, and between the people and the government.

The People-Party Link

In 1991 CCM was put on trial before the Presidential Commission on the Party System. Many people spoke up to defend the one-party system, but a large proportion of them condemned CCM. "CCM should cleanse itself"; "'big shots' in the party and government were given new jobs after they were found to be corrupt or incompetent; they should have been taken to court"; "the party is being swayed by outside influences and weakening the Arusha Declaration"; and "CCM should open up" were comments made before the commission as reported by the government newspaper. The criticisms of CCM by those who called for a multiparty system were much harsher. Both friend and foe of one-party democracy were telling the commissioners that the party was no longer performing as the repository of the popular will.[18]

In theory, the democratic nature of the party was to be assured by open membership; the right of members to freely choose party leaders; the representation of nonmembers' views to the party through mass organizations; and the right of both party and nonparty members to choose those party members who would serve in the National Assembly. As those who testified before the commission asserted, weaknesses appeared in both theory and practice.

The Mass Versus Vanguard Issue

Historically, the party was at the heart of the national movement for independence. During that struggle, it had no serious rivals for the loyalty of Tanzanians. Its membership became a microcosm of Tanzania. This mass character was viewed by Nyerere and others as a necessary condition for the party to function as a democratic instrument. Then came the commitment to socialism. As long as socialism reflected popular preferences, its advocacy did not undermine the democratic character of the party or its leaders. The commitment of the party to build a socialist society, though, brought to the fore some leaders who sought to radicalize Tanzanian socialism, i.e., the ideological socialists. They played an important role within the party: Not only were they able to radicalize Tanzanian socialism, but they also added a vigor and commitment to the whole project that helped sustain it in the face of opposition. Indeed, it can be fairly said that the party's commitment to socialism might well have died in its infancy without the efforts of those classified as ideological socialists.[19] Their impact on the party posed problems, too.

Most ideological socialists saw the mass party as an obstacle to democracy because it allowed opposition elements to enter, enabling them to subvert the process of socialist construction. When ideological socialists talked of cleansing the party or weeding out bad elements in it, they meant removing those who were not fully committed socialists.[20] When pragmatic socialists talked of cleansing the party or weeding out bad elements, they meant removing corrupt or incompetent members.

The "openness" of the party became one of the chief battlegrounds in the struggle between pragmatic and ideological socialists. As has been noted, until about 1990 the trend had been for the ideological socialists to push the party toward greater ideological purity, i.e., toward a vanguard party. At that point a variety of factors combined to lead a trend back toward a mass party. First, popular support for the party had declined. By 1970 there were between 2.5 and 3 million TANU members.[21] This number is identical to the estimates for membership in CCM twenty years later, *after* TANU's union with ASP and *after* the population had doubled! The relative decline in party membership was partly due to the move toward vanguardism. Second, the party was unable to stem the serious economic decline that began in the late 1970s. Third, the party was unable to keep the government from adopting a series of policies during the 1980s that seemed to contradict its commitment to socialism. Although the economic hardships and government policies had little to do with vanguardism, pragmatic socialists used the apparent correlation to urge a return to a mass party. By 1991, several impediments to mass membership had been removed: The three-month period of ideological training and compliance with major aspects of the leadership code were abandoned as prerequisites for membership. Furthermore, the secretary general of the party was forcefully calling for a return to the party's mass character.

The Mass Organizations Issue

A similar cycle occurred with regard to the role of mass organizations. The theory of one-party democracy implied that all interests within the country should be represented in the party, yet the voice of any particular interest should be subordinate to that of the general will. As a result, the organizational autonomy of existing interests was replaced by a kind of corporatist arrangement linking them with the party. This change was perceived as a step toward democracy because it subordinated special interests to general interests. It denied the few the right to pursue their self-interest without placing that interest in the context of what was in the interest of the many. The party provided the context. Five mass organizations were recognized: the Union of Tanzania Workers (JUWATA), the Cooperative Union of

Tanzania (CUT), the Tanzania Youth Organization (VIJANA), the Tanzania Parents Association (WAZAZI), and the Union of Tanzanian Women (UWT).

In theory, mass organizations were to provide the party with the views of both members and nonmembers. The importance of such organizations for the representation of non–party members was emphasized by several leaders. For example, Seif Shariff Hamad said that when he was chief minister of Zanzibar, "non–party members were fully represented in the decision-making organs of the Party through their various mass organisations."[22] Rashidi Kawawa said that when he was secretary general of the party, mass organizations "provided fora for the articulation of ideas by Tanzanians who were not members of Chama Cha Mapinduzi and involved them in Party work."[23] An editorial in the *Sunday News* in the late 1980s said that "through the mass organisations—the eyes, ears and feelers of the Party among the people—the Party reaches every member of the society."[24]

This idea of the party having access to nonmembers through mass organizations incorporated a second aspect: Such organizations should serve not only as vehicles through which the people expressed their interests to the party but also as conduits of decisions made by the party to organization members. As ideological socialists pushed for a vanguard party, they viewed the mass organizations more as vehicles through which the national will would be realized than as vehicles for the representation of special interests. This view was expressed in an editorial in the *Daily News* in early 1988 that described the role of mass organizations as translating "into practice the aspirations of Chama Cha Mapinduzi."[25] During the 1970s and 1980s, the party asserted closer supervision over leadership of the organizations and turned them more into tools for the implementation of party policies than they had been initially.

The suppression of labor militancy, which arose in the early 1970s following the TANU guidelines of 1971, was an important contributor to the split between the ideological socialists within the party and the Marxists outside the party. Most of the former accepted the suppression as necessary both for one-party democracy and for socialist construction; most of the latter saw it as a stark reaffirmation that a worker-based socialism was not the intent of Tanzanian socialism. More importantly, the suppression marked the victory of those who saw mass organizations as mechanisms more for policy implementation than for popular representation. In effect, it was a further victory for those who advocated popular, rather than liberal, democracy.

Public expression of interest was discouraged or channeled into a form of supplication to the party. Yet, as economic hardships intensified, frustration with party-government policies increased. By the late 1980s, these frustrations were openly expressed. David Holela, secretary general of the Cooperative Union of Tanzania (CUT), complained that "matters affecting cooperatives' activities in the country were often decided upon unilaterally by the government in complete disregard of CUT rules."[26] And the minister of state in the Zanzibar chief minister's office complained in early 1990 that mass organizations "were currently closer to the party rather than their members."[27] As a consequence of these problems, Nyerere called for major changes in mass organizations in July 1990. He suggested the immediate granting of autonomy to JUWATA and WASHIRIKA and the eventual independence of the others.[28] By the middle of 1991, JUWATA and WASHIRIKA had become "affiliated" organizations with greater autonomy from the party; VIJANA, WAZAZI, and UWT continued their formal relationship, although with the prospect of increasing autonomy, too.[29] By late 1991 JUWATA had been replaced by a new labor organization, the Organisation of Tanzania Trade Unions (OTTU),[30] and by early 1993 WASHIRIKA had been replaced by the Tanzania Cooperative Alliance (TCA). Although the advent of multipartyism in 1992 led to a further increase in the autonomy of mass organizations in relation to CCM, government oversight and supervision remained strong.

The Elections Issue

The principle of liberal democracy that leaders should be chosen freely by followers was modified under Tanzania's one-party democracy. Two chief mechanisms restricted public choice.

The first mechanism was the candidate review procedure, which granted those who held office within the party power to deny individuals the right to compete for election. This modification of liberal democracy was justified on the grounds of popular democracy; i.e., it was necessary to avoid the subversion of the popular will by a few. During the ascendancy of the ideological socialists, the practice of party scrutiny of possible candidates was extended to virtually all elections, purportedly to enhance ideological purity within the party.[31] As noted in Chapter 2, ideological purity became progressively less important in the scrutiny process. Even for those who sought to employ it, the task of determining whether an individual's professed socialist "attitude of mind" was real or merely instrumental was extremely difficult. Rather than bringing about socialist *or* democratic representation, party scrutiny seemed to produce something that accorded with neither: a kind of patron-client system in which party leaders and their ideas were given support in return for the clients' opportunity to compete for office. As noted in Chapter 2, by 1985 the scrutiny process had become more a means of maintaining the patron-client system than of assuring a leadership committed to socialism.

The second mechanism that restricted public choice was an election manifesto produced by the party for each National Assembly election since that of 1975. The purposes of the manifesto were primarily education and control.[32] Formally, the purpose was "to ensure that the deliberations during campaigns centered on basic policy issues and on development instead of contestants accusing and mudslinging each other."[33] The 1985 manifesto stated quite clearly the subordinate position of members of parliament: "General elections offer Tanzanians an opportunity to . . . elect leaders who will oversee and implement the Party policy of Socialism and Self-Reliance."[34] Yet most of the manifestos appear to be like any party platform in a liberal democratic country, a compromise among various factions. The manifesto for the 1980 election included goals such as improved productivity, more self-reliance, improved agriculture and soil conservation, increased industrial production and capacity utilization, strengthened education, improved health services, and strengthened armed forces.[35] The 1985 manifesto was very similar, except for its advocacy of the newly declared policy of promoting producer cooperatives.[36] The result of these dual roles, demanding support for existing positions of the party *and* aspirations widely shared by Tanzanians, was ambiguity. The manifestos did not provide an effective mechanism either for "purifying" the party ideologically or for opening it up to represent everyone.

Party Consolidation

By the mid-1980s both ideological and pragmatic socialists were concerned about the party. Its inability to move toward the fulfillment of popular wishes and its growing separation from the people led to disillusionment both within and outside the party. At the December 1985 NEC meeting, four manifestations of the problem were identified: the lack of cell and branch meetings, the failure to pay monthly membership dues, a lack of decent party office space at the branch level, and the failure to complete the election of party leaders in many branches.[37] A party "consolidation" effort was initiated.

Early in 1962, Nyerere had resigned as prime minister and "returned to the party" to undertake a similar revitalization effort. When he returned to government service as president late in 1962, progress was apparent. In the 1980s, however, Nyerere was not able to repeat what he had done in the 1960s. By the end of the decade, he was clearly frustrated with the results of party consolidation. At the 1987 party conference, the problem of lack of quorums at the cell and branch levels was dealt with by reducing the size requirement from more than one-half to more than one-third of the eligible members.[38] The president spoke of a lack of accountability and the party "going to sleep."[39] Before he resigned as chairman in 1990, Nyerere basically admitted failure. His call for debate on a multiparty system and his comments on the inevitability of such a system indicated his judgment that the party was no longer serving as the democratic link between the people and the government.

Ironically, the multiparty debate seemed to accomplish what Nyerere had been unable to do for five years—it began to awaken the party. Party leaders seemed to realize that their survival depended on major reforms. A series of reforms was introduced, including reducing the number of meetings required of party bodies, cutting the number of departments in the secretariat, and requiring that leaders hold regular meetings with the public and report on them to the chairman of the party, Ali Hassan Mwinyi.[40] These steps were a clear admission that the party was *not* serving as the vital democratic link with the people—and they were also a reaffirmation of the belief that human will could set things right.

The Party-Government Link

The relationship between party and government in Tanzania has not differed markedly from that found in other single-party African states, with one exception: The party in Tanzania has sought with greater vigor to establish its supremacy. In theory, the two institutions are distinguished by their functions; i.e., the party makes policy and the government implements it. In other words, the former performs the political function and the latter the administrative one. But the reality is different. There has been a worldwide trend toward assumption of the political function by those who administrate. This trend was captured in the title of a well-known book, *The Bureaucratization of the World*.[41] One might expect the locus of power to have shifted even more toward government in the Third than in the First World. As Merilee Grindle wrote several years ago, policy outcomes in the First World appeared to be determined more by formal policymaking—the function of politicians—and in the Third World more by policy implementation—the function of administrators.[42]

This worldwide trend appeared to be interrupted by independence movements. Colonial administrators were pitted against nationalist political parties, and the latter won. This tendency was only a temporary setback for administrators. Soon after independence, the victors began to atrophy and administrations began to grow.[43] So pronounced had this phenomenon become in Africa by the mid-1960s that some observers suggested no-party states were developing.[44] Tanzania did not appear to follow this trend. In the 1960s, Immanuel Wallerstein contended that although the party was in decline throughout much of Africa, this was not the case in Tanzania.[45] Henry Bienen, in his seminal study of TANU, argued that the party's functions were not atrophying and its power and prestige were not gravitating to state agencies.[46] Crawford Young argued that only two countries in Africa had been able to shift from a mass party to a "revitalized mass party": Tunisia and Tanzania.[47]

What accounts for Tanzania's initial success in resisting the tendency toward party decline is in dispute. To many observers, the cause was the electoral system initiated for the one-party state in 1965. According to Young, "The 1965 elections remain a crucial moment of renewal and rebirth for the mass-party system in Tanzania. They compelled the elite to rebuild a link with the countryside."[48] Although the electoral system did not "provide a means whereby popular sovereignty can be expressed directly upon major issues," it gave people the sense that they might determine who governed them.[49] This conviction, in turn, provided the party with a legitimacy that limited the growth of bureaucratic power. To other observers, the key was Nyerere, who was able to transfer support for himself to support for the party. Still, Tanzanian exceptionalism did not last long.

Twenty years later, circumstances had changed. Cynicism about the party's ability to fulfill popular wishes was widespread. Nyerere expressed his frustration with what had happened to the party in early 1990, characterizing "TANU-era" leaders as those who were close to the people and who sought positions to serve the people, whereas "CCM-era" leaders were officebound and sought leadership positions for personal enrichment.[50] A change in public support accompanied the failure of the party to effect mechanisms of control over the government.

Party Efforts to Establish Supremacy

Party efforts to establish supremacy included the establishment of constitutional supremacy, the activities of the National Assembly, the practice of *kofia mbili* [two hats], and the creation of a secretariat.

Establishing constitutional supremacy. The NEC decided in late 1974 to make party supremacy a part of the constitution. In June of the following year the Interim Constitution was amended in accordance with the NEC's decision.[51] Although there was agreement that the purpose of the constitutional amendment was to strengthen the party's authority over the government, there was disagreement over how supremacy was to be realized. Such disagreement focused on the degree of involvement of the party in work traditionally assigned to the government. On one side were those who thought close involvement, verging on a merger of party and state, was appropriate; on the other side were those who felt a supervisory role that kept the institutions separate was appropriate. The issue does not appear to have divided pragmatic and ideological socialists from each other, but it did cause division within each. Some from both factions viewed close supervision as necessary to assure compliance, whereas others feared being co-opted by the government. The divisions within the party over the character of socialism and how it was to be imposed made government independence easier.

Using the National Assembly. In most Western democracies, in theory parliament has supremacy and in practice bureaucracies increasingly are challenging that supremacy. In Tanzania, the National Assembly has been subordinate to the party in theory and in practice. That subordination was manifest in the formal position of the assembly as a subcommittee of the national party conference; it was made clear in 1968 with the expulsion of "rebellious" members, discussed in the last chapter; and it was demonstrated in the scrutiny process for MPs and in the election manifestos. Virtually all observers note the National Assembly's policymaking impotence.[52] Under the theory of one-party democracy, the role of the assembly was supposed to be subordinate to that of the party in policymaking. Yet the assembly was to be a tool for controlling government.

Although some observers, such as Jan Kees van Donge and Athumani Liviga, contend that the assembly's role as a watchdog of the government has not been insignificant, more would agree with William Tordoff that the assembly has been a "residual" legislature whose power over government has been very limited.[53] Part of the reason for the assembly's ineffectiveness has to do with the dilemma of the MPs in that body. On the one hand, the MPs were "hired" as agents of the NEC to make sure the government implements its policies. On the other hand, they face many of those NEC members who are leaders of government. Although Tanzania may not have been a "party-state" because of the party's separation from the government, it has been a "part party-state" because of the party's links with the government. And government has tended to be a training ground for many pragmatic socialists in the party and a place where even ideological socialists were "pragmatized." Thus, in a sense, government was a separate institution for one faction within the party, the ideological socialists; but it was an extension of the party for the second faction, the pragmatic socialists. The assertion of power by the latter within the party has reduced tension between the government and the party.

Instituting kofia mbili. What is known locally as *kofia mbili*, i.e., the practice of party leaders holding joint party and government responsibilities, has been used in an attempt to strengthen the party relative to the government. The practice began with the appointment of party officials as ministers in the government. It was extended with the appointment of party secretaries who assumed the posts of regional and area commissioners as well. And it was extended further when the offices of chairman of the party and president of the country were combined (except for the period between 1985 and 1990, when Nyerere continued as chairman and Mwinyi assumed the presidency). Contrary to expectations, though, *kofia mbili* tended to result in an increase in the government's influence over the party rather than in the party's influence over the government. Nyerere spoke about this problem in a speech marking the tenth anniversary of the University of Dar es Salaam:

> At many levels we have given to one person two jobs at the same time: in the Party and in the Government. . . . And every time these two jobs are combined, that of the Government tends to overshadow that of the Party. So that in practice all of these people have become government persons first, and only secondly the spokesmen of the people's ideas, aspirations and complaints. They are so busy implementing government policy and defending government actions that they have little time to do purely Party work and to act upon—or even listen to—the proposals or complaints of the people. But the responsibilities of Government continue to be very attractive to Party leaders, and very often when they talk about Party supremacy a lot of Party leaders are in fact saying that all of them should have two jobs—and that the job in the Government should be the major one.[54]

Nyerere went on to argue that *kofia mbili* tended to separate the party from the people; that such a separation would mean "the death of the party"; and that

> without a live C.C.M., governed by the people themselves, we shall—under our existing Constitution—be governed by bureaucrats, University Graduates, and a few demagogues, and not by the people themselves or their representatives.[55]

In response to his urgings, the posts of area commissioner and district party secretary and of regional commissioner and regional area secretary were separated, whereas those at the village and national levels remained combined. When Nyerere accepted the CCM chairmanship once again in 1987, while Mwinyi continued as president, Nyerere justified his action in terms of the problems he had earlier cited with *kofia mbili*. He said,

> When the demands of these two responsibilities do clash, it is the party work which suffers. That is what happened when I was President of the country and Chairman of the Party. Despite my great wish to do the Party work, I found that I could not do so. There was no time. I spent much more time on government work. The result, as we all now recognize, is that the Party suffered.[56]

Nevertheless, ideological socialists argued against Nyerere's point of view, contending that key positions in the government should be occupied by committed party members to assure party supremacy and that the separation had not helped overcome the party's problems during the 1980s.[57] As a consequence, the regional and district posts were recombined in 1990. Two years later, though, in an effort to disentangle the party from the state following the decision to move to a multiparty system, the district and regional commissioners lost their party functions and became solely government officials.

Creation of the party secretariat. To counter the advantage of the government due to its control over expertise, the party gradually expanded its own bureaucracy. In 1982 it established a secretariat at its headquarters with seven departments and two commissions, partly to manage its own affairs and partly to develop its own expertise. Similar secretariats with five departments were established at regional and district levels. For a time, the secretariats may have served to strengthen the party relative to the government, yet the monetary costs were significant. In an effort to prepare for multipartyism and the end of the government's financial support, the number of departments was reduced to half in 1991 and still further in 1992.[58]

Nevertheless, the effort to control the government by creating the secretariat was like tilting at windmills. Inexorably, its efforts failed. This failure was partly due to the consequences of the struggle between ideological and pragmatic socialist tendencies within the party, which undermined their common agenda. But there were other factors. All the leaders of government were party leaders; as Nyerere argued in the discussion surrounding *kofia mbili,* in the competition between a "watcher" and a "doer," the latter always seems to win; the government was the intermediary with sources of outside aid; it had access to tax revenues; it funded 90 percent of the party budget; it had expertise; it had information. Thus, even if the party had been the democratic instrument of the people, it would have had difficulty controlling the government.

The People-Government Link

Under one-party democracy the government was to act in accord with the popular will as conveyed to it by the party. Yet over time the party seems to have increasingly alienated itself from the people and failed to control the government. Part of the reason for that failure was the fact that the pragmatic socialists, who were subordinate within the party, were dominant within the government. So the apparent inability of the party to control the government was really the inability of the ideological socialists to control the pragmatic socialists. The government "wing" of the pragmatic socialists supported its kin in the party by resisting implementation of policies with which it disagreed. Alternative tools for popular control of the government did not work well either.

Civil Rights

When one-party democracy was being debated, the TANU government opposed a bill of rights on the grounds that such a bill might prevent a government from acting in accord with the will of the people, i.e., that a bill of rights might undermine democracy. The government asserted that individual interests should be subordinate to the interests of the people as a whole, which were represented by the party. As a result, many individual civil rights—which are closely associated with liberal democracy—were not constitutionally protected. For example, the free flow of information was restricted by the Newspaper Act of 1976 and the Tanzania News Agency Act of 1976.[59]

By the early 1980s, the reasoning of those opposed to a bill of rights was severely undermined by the increasing inability of the party to represent the will of the people. The constitutional debate over democratizing Zanzibar, initiated in 1983, spurred a renewed demand for a bill of rights.[60] The Fifth Constitutional Amendments Act of 1984 incorporated such a bill into the constitution. Nevertheless, the state delayed implementation until March 15, 1988, ostensibly to give the government time to make necessary amendments to laws that might conflict with the individual constitutional rights guaranteed by the bill. Even after the bill went into effect, parliamentary acts were held superior to the civil rights specified in the bill.[61]

Despite the bill, on numerous occasions citizens' civil rights were violated.[62] The authoritarian relationship between many party and government officials and the peasants persisted. This relationship was exemplified by the use of orders issued by regional commissioners, district commissioners, regional party executive committees, regional party chairmen, and others in the late 1980s to ban dances, discotheques, and *ngomas* [parties] during weekdays and the drinking of traditional beer during working hours and to require such acts as planting famine crops and minimum acreages of cash crops.[63]

Accessibility

There was considerable ambiguity in party policies aimed at bringing government closer to the people. Local government and decentralization have a checkered history in Tanzania.

The problems with local government have been well described by Gelase Mutahaba. The original district councils established in 1962, the decentralized governmental system established in 1972, and the village governments established in 1974 were disbanded after a few years. Although they continued to exist, their powers were eroded. For example, starting in 1965, district council candidates were subject to vetting by TANU, and whoever was the TANU chair in a district would automatically become chair of the district council. In 1969 responsibilities for primary education, the larger health centers, and district roads were transferred to the technical ministries. And in 1970 the two major sources of funds, the local rate tax and produce tax, were abolished.[64] The ostensible reason given by the government for centralization was that local governments were not "democratic enough or effective instruments for the management of development."[65] Mutahaba added a reason related to the units of action problem: "It was also a result of the virtually inevitable clash between the drive for national integration with centrally determined development plans and the persistence of local desires for self-determined objectives."[66] Kingunge Ngombale-Mwiru complained in the mid-1980s that what really happened was that "the power aimed for the people had actually been hijacked by the bureaucrats."[67] Whatever the reasons and whoever was responsible, local government did not become an effective means by which people could gain control over their lives.

Through "decentralisation," initiated in 1972, Nyerere sought a new mechanism to make the government more accessible to the people. When introducing the policy, he argued that "we must face the fact that, to the mass of the people, power is still something wielded by others—even if on their behalf."[68] Yet this policy, too, failed in its ostensible purpose. An editorial in the *Daily News* asserted:

> Evaluation of the decentralisation period between 1972, when the first local governments were dissolved, up to 1984 proved that the bureaucrats in the districts and regions had hijacked the power of the people to decide on their affairs.[69]

The reestablishment of local government in 1984 was no more successful. The editorial quoted above went on to say that "the reintroduction of the local governments was, therefore, meant to correct this anomaly. However, the responsibilities placed under the newly-formed local governments were too immense."[70] Thus, the efforts to link the people directly to the government in a democratic way cannot be deemed to have been very successful.

Reformulating Democracy for Socialism

By 1990, the position of the ideological socialists within the party had changed. Even Nyerere had come to accept that his vision of how democracy might be best realized was not working. The popular democratic deviation from liberal democracy, often referred to as one-party democracy, was not functioning well. It was being pulled apart by the growing discrepancy between the ideology it espoused and the behavior of the leaders and the government. Either one-party democracy had to be revived or a new system had to be devised. In February 1990 Nyerere called for discussion of a multiparty system.

His reasoning became clear over the next several months: The purpose of the proposal was to make CCM more vigorous and sensitive to the people. He was reported to have said, "I don't propagate long live one-party system, but I do propagate long live CCM. I want it to live forever and crush all opposition parties that may crop up in the future."[71] He argued that it did not matter whether there were one or many parties. What was fundamental "was for Tanzanians to enjoy democracy."[72] Thus, to Nyerere, a multiparty system was a means to democratize what might remain virtually a one-party system.

Nine months later Kingunge Ngombale-Mwiru, the secretary for ideology, political education, and training, spoke in very similar terms. Unlike Nyerere, Ngombale-Mwiru was a key figure among the ideological socialists who had urged that CCM become a vanguard party in a single-party state in order to hasten the socialist transition. Perhaps for tactical reasons, he said,

> The one-Party system is not an ideological question for socialism. For us (CCM), the one-Party system is not one of the tenets or one of the component parts of the Arusha Declaration and the policy of Socialism and Self-Reliance. For a Socialist Party to successfully prosecute the struggle for socialism, the basic condition is the consent of the people concerned. To succeed, the Party must enjoy the confidence of the people, its policies actively supported by them because they deliver the goods, and its leadership respected and trusted by the people because of its honesty. Such a socialist Party can exist in a truly democratic one-Party system as well as a truly democratic multi-party system where the voice of the people is sovereign.

Ngombale-Mwiru noted also that "CCM is confident that it can be and is going to be an effective political player in any eventual Party system decided by the people."[73]

The initial reaction of leading party members was negative. In April 1990 Mwinyi asserted that the real need was a fairer international economic order and that a multiparty system would not affect that, but rather it would give rise to chaos.[74] In June, President Wakil of Zanzibar argued that a

> multi-party system will not provide solutions to economic problems Zanzibar is facing at the moment and will instead, wreck unity, peace and stability in the island. . . . Based on Zanzibar's turbulent history, parties which will be formed will be based along racial, regional and religious lines, something which is not healthy for the community.[75]

In July, when introducing Nyerere at a UWT meeting, the UWT chairperson, Sophia Kawawa, "denounced the suggestion of having many parties."[76] Although the critics were right that the introduction of a multiparty system was unlikely to improve the economy or change the international economic order directly, their reactions suggest the growth of a leadership more committed to pragmatism than to the democratic component of socialism.

Initial support for multipartyism came from former politicians, intellectuals, and professionals. They expressed a wide variety of grievances. Chief Abdallah Fundikira said he resigned as minister for justice in 1963 because he saw "a one-party system evolving." Kasanga Tumbo, the former Tanzanian high commissioner to Britain who had been jailed for three years and in 1967 banished to his village in Sikonge for ten years, said he fell out with the TANU government because of his opposition to a one-party state. Joseph Mbele of the University of Dar es Salaam said that, whereas he had been a member of the TANU Youth League (TYL), he was not a member of CCM "because he did not think the Party was serious in whatever it was saying it planned to do."[77] An Institute of Finance Management lecturer said CCM should allow other parties to coexist "because the culture of *ndiyo mzee* was no longer"[78]—that is, because the culture of authoritarianism was outdated.

President Mwinyi became concerned with the vehemence and extent of the grievances expressed. He sought to give the debate some direction in September 1990 by suggesting that when it was "exhausted" either a referendum would be held or a commission would be established to resolve the issue.[79] Nevertheless, the debate was far from exhausted when, two months later, Mwinyi announced his intention to form a presidential commission, similar to that which had been created when the one-party state was under consideration, to facilitate the collection and analysis of views.[80] In late February 1991 he appointed twenty members to the commission, half of whom were from Zanzibar and half from the mainland.[81] A month later he charged the commission to coordinate the expression of views by the people; advise on what should be done; assess the impact of any action on national unity; advise what should be done to ensure national unity; recommend ways of enhancing democracy; indicate necessary constitutional amendments; and assess the impact of possible changes on the place of Zanzibar in the union.[82] Judge Francis Nyalali was appointed chairman. At the time of his appointment, he contended that the commission could be impartial even though it was composed primarily of CCM members both because self-criticism was a tradition within CCM and because there were diverse views among party members on the issue.[83]

This channeling of the discussion was viewed by many as interfering with the process of debate. Indeed, leaders in the party and government repeatedly acted against those who sought to organize or voice their feelings in alternative forums. For example, when the unregistered steering committee chaired by Abdallah Fundikira sought to hold a "seminar" on multipartyism under the auspices of the registered Tanzania Legal Education Trust in March 1991, the government banned the latter organization on the grounds that it was engaging in political activity.[84] Although under international pressure the government allowed the steering committee to hold its seminar in June, organizations that evolved from it were refused registration, demonstrations were banned, demonstrators were arrested, and leaders were harassed.[85]

Multipartyism had become a focus of opposition to CCM and its government. Such opposition derived from a range of concerns not confined to the state's socialist objectives. At the steering committee's seminar in June 1991, complaints were raised about the treatment of student dissidents, foreign economic domination, the treatment of Zanzibar, violations of civil liberties, and the commitment to socialism. The resolution drafted by the steering committee at the conclusion of the seminar reflected this diversity of grievances and motives for multipartyism. It called for the release of Shariff Hamad, the detained former chief minister of Zanzibar; a pardon for political detainees; the right to peaceful demonstration and assembly without permits from the government; the repeal of laws that hampered free speech; an increase in aid from abroad for countries with many parties; the removal of the army from politics; the formation of a commission to draft a constitution from both within and outside the steering committee; and the establishment of a transitional government.[86]

A wide range of views was presented before the presidential commission. Of the more than 36,000 people who expressed their opinions, 77.2 percent favored continuation of the one-party state.[87] The most commonly expressed fear was that chaos would result from multipartyism. Although many severely criticized CCM, they distinguished between the misdeeds of individuals and the one-party state structure. Yet the commission did not consider its charge to be that of merely reporting popular sentiment. Among the voices it must have weighed more heavily than others was that of Nyerere.

In early December 1991, after nearly a year of public silence, Nyerere announced his support for multipartyism. In a press conference he said that although the majority of people supported CCM, there was a substantial minority who wanted pluralism. Although a sound opposition had not arisen, he believed there were "serious, patriotic people, some of them inside CCM, who could form a viable opposition party once the permission is given." He argued that the shift should be made soon: "We cannot remain an island. We must manage our own change—don't wait to be pushed." Furthermore, chaos might be checked by requirements that parties be national in scope and limited in number. He held that Mwinyi had to be serious about change; otherwise he would not have formed the presidential commission. "If the President didn't want change he could have used the excuse of a referendum in which the majority of people would vote for [a] one-party [structure]." Nyerere stated that the West was trying to install a new set of puppet leaders in the developing countries; that was why they dished out money to activists for democratic change. But, he noted, ironically, it was much harder to install puppets by democratic elections than by military coup.[88] In Mwinyi's New Year message given on the last day of 1991, he announced that a decision had been made to move to a multiparty system.[89]

It is ironic that a "democratic" decision would have resulted in the retention of the single-party system, deemed undemocratic by the tenets of liberal democracy, whereas an "undemocratic" decision was required to shift to a multiparty system, deemed democratic by the tenets of liberal democracy. The latter decision was legitimized as a democratic one by its approval at an extraordinary national party conference in February 1992.

What brought about this major change in the form of democracy in Tanzania? There were three major reasons. First, CCM had lost the ability to mobilize the population. Despite many years of effort to consolidate the party, it had moved a long way from the kind of democratic relationship with the people that TANU had had during the independence struggle. To intellectuals like Nyerere, CCM was not serving as a democratic vehicle to the extent necessary to advance the country politically and economically. Second, outside forces, supporting dissidents in their efforts and pressuring the government to change, had become increasingly active. Mwinyi had spoken of such forces in different ways. He contended that the late 1980s and early 1990s had been the "era" of multipartyism.[90] And, he said, "The wind of political change which started in Eastern Europe has engulfed the whole African continent. . . . This is a very strong force which leaders with rational minds cannot stand against."[91] Third, the internal costs of inaction were seen as greater than the internal costs of action. Mwinyi observed that the resistance of other African leaders to multipartyism had simply caused chaos and bloodshed.[92] He also stated, "We have resolved not to give our enemies a chance to disrupt our long cherished unity and peace on the excuse that they have been denied their democracy."[93] Furthermore, he argued, the fears of chaos under a multiparty system were unfounded because rules might be established that would meet the threat. Indeed, following the NEC approval, Mwinyi noted that "all the parties must be national. . . . They must draw supporters from both Zanzibar and Tanzania Mainland."[94] The secretary general of CCM at the time, Horace Kolimba, noted that the change was not unprecedented because Tanzania had made similar major changes in the past, like the movement to a single-party system and the formation of CCM.[95] Mwinyi observed that a multiparty system was not new to Tanzania.[96] Thus, multipartyism appeared to be a rational solution to many pressures facing Tanzania and Tanzanian socialism in the early 1990s.[97]

Multipartyism significantly altered the institutional mechanisms for democracy, shifting the locus from within the party to among parties. That shift opened up more space for opponents of Tanzanian socialism on both the left and the right. The immediate response of CCM leaders, fearing the challenge from the right more than from the left, was a retreat from the formal advocacy of socialism. Indeed, all the major opposition parties that formed in 1992 were to the right of CCM. Mwinyi began to use euphemism for the ideology. For example, he said, "The ideology of CCM and its forerunners—ASP and TANU—was and would continue to be the fight for the better welfare of Tanzanians."[98] Kolimba advised the mass organization JUWATA, shortly before it became OTTU, "to distance itself from defending theoretical socialism saying such an attitude will lead the society to economic stagnation."[99] Yet the retreat through euphemism and deemphasis of "theoretical socialism" was a tactical move.

If the party was able to revive its popular base through allowing competition, it would be better positioned to carry on an effective program to build socialism. Nyerere had long ago argued that democracy was a necessary condition for the realization of socialism. Multipartyism may be a necessary step for democracy, but that does not mean it is a sufficient one. Nor does it mean that it is a sufficient step for socialism. If, as Issa Shivji has suggested, the new political parties become merely tools of an elite, CCM may not be forced to become a tool of the masses to successfully compete.[100] By early 1993 many of the fears multiparty opponents had expressed to the Presidential Commission (commonly called the Nyalali Commission) about the potential for divisiveness appeared to be realized: Leaders of some of the new political parties were encouraging racial, religious, and regional animosities.

Conclusion

The effort to reformulate democracy by giving up a one-party state and moving on to a multiparty state was a two-edged sword: It might set back the socialist effort by encouraging individualism or it might provide the socialist effort with the popular support needed for its realization. In the situation Tanzania faced in the early 1990s, the gamble appeared necessary if the dream of a socialist society was to be kept alive. Yet within a year of the advent of multipartyism a serious rise in communal antagonism, spurred by some of the new party leaders, had occurred. Skepticism grew over whether democracy and the socialist project would be enhanced by multipartyism as such problems developed.

The tension between the leadership and democracy was partly a result of the participation by leaders in multiple levels of action. Most leaders had been chosen by constituencies that encompassed only a portion of the country's population. When the wishes of their constituents differed from those of the population as a whole, leaders had a choice: They might seek to further their constituents' interests, thereby acting in accord with democratic principles toward that subgroup of people, or they might seek to further the interests of the country's population as a whole, thereby acting in accord with democratic principles toward that group of people. Yet what was democratic behavior for the constituency unit was undemocratic behavior for the country unit, and vice versa. Only if the wishes of both the constituents and the people of the country as a whole were the same would leaders be able to behave democratically at both levels at the same time.[101] Despite the *potential* for tension between leadership and democracy, advocates of Tanzanian socialism initially thought it would not become real, for they saw no contradiction between socialism and the wishes of the majority of people both within each leader's constituency and within the country as a whole.

Notes

1. Cranford Pratt, *The Critical Phase in Tanzania, 1945–1968, Nyerere and the Emergence of a Socialist Strategy* (Cambridge: Cambridge University Press, 1976), p. 226.

2. Julius Nyerere, "The Arusha Declaration," in Nyerere, *Freedom and Socialism* (Dar es Salaam: Oxford University Press, 1968), p. 234.

3. Tanganyika African National Union, "TANU Guidelines on Guarding, Consolidating and Advancing the Revolution of Tanzania and of Africa," in Andrew Coulson, ed., *African Socialism in Practice: The Tanzanian Experience* (Nottingham: Spokesman, 1979), p. 41; Julius Nyerere, "Decentralisation," in Nyerere, *Socialism and Development* (Dar es Salaam: Oxford University Press, 1973), p. 349; Chama cha Mapinduzi, *The CCM Guidelines, 1981* (Dar es Salaam: Printpak for CCM, n.d.), pp. 44–45; Julius Nyerere, "Introduction" and "The Varied Paths to Socialism," in Nyerere, *Freedom and Socialism*, pp. 5 and 309, respectively. Most scholars concur; e.g., Idrian N. Resnick, *The Long Transition, Building Socialism in Tanzania* (New York: Monthly Review Press, 1981), p. 84; and P.F. Nursey-Bray, "Consensus and Community: The Theory of African One-Party Democracy," in Graeme Duncan, ed., *Democratic Theory and Practice* (Cambridge: Cambridge University Press, 1983), p. 98.

4. Nyerere, "Decentralisation," p. 349; Julius Nyerere, "President's Inaugural Address," in Nyerere, *Freedom and Unity* (London: Oxford University Press, 1967), p. 184; and Julius Nyerere, *Address by Mwalimu J.K. Nyerere, Chairman of Chama Cha Mapinduzi at the Opening of the National Conference, Dodoma, 22nd October, 1987* (Dodoma: Chama cha Mapinduzi, n.d.), pp. 11–12.

5. Giovanni Sartori, *The Theory of Democracy Revisited* (Chatham, N.J.: Chatham House, 1987), p. 6.

6. For a discussion of definitions of liberal democracy, see Samuel Huntington, "Will More Countries Become Democratic?" *Political Science Quarterly*, Vol. 99, No. 2 (Summer 1984), p. 195; Lawrence C. Mayer, *Redefining Comparative Politics: Promise Versus Performance* (Newbury Park, Calif.: Sage Publications, 1989), pp. 102–110; and William Riker, *Liberalism Against Populism, A Confrontation Between the Theory of Democracy and the Theory of Social Choice* (San Francisco: W.H. Freeman & Co., 1982), pp. xviii and 112.

7. Adam Przeworski argues that "the recurrent theme of the socialist movement . . . has been . . . [the] notion of 'extending' the democratic principle from the political to the social, in effect primarily economic, realm." See Przeworski,

Capitalism and Social Democracy (Cambridge: Cambridge University Press, 1985), p. 7. Bjorn Beckman argues that "bourgeois democracy" may facilitate the achievement of socialism. See Beckman, "Whose Democracy? Bourgeois Versus Popular Democracy," *Review of African Political Economy*, No. 45/46 (Winter 1989), pp. 84–97. Carol Gould argues that the extension of democracy facilitates the realization of the socialist goals of social cooperation and equality. See Gould, *Rethinking Democracy: Freedom and Social Cooperation in Politics, Economy, and Society* (Cambridge: Cambridge University Press, 1988), p. 3. Clive Thomas contends that "the struggle for political democracy is vital to the struggle for socialism" and that "one cannot exist without the other." See Thomas, *The Rise of the Authoritarian State in Peripheral Societies* (New York: Monthly Review Press, 1984), p. 99. Summing up these views, Frank Cunningham contends that, whereas socialism is necessary to make progress in democracy, democracy "furthers gaining and securing socialism." See Cunningham, *Democratic Theory and Socialism* (Cambridge: Cambridge University Press, 1987), pp. 25 and 137. David Held and John Keane consider the concepts virtually synonymous. See Held and Keane, "Socialism and the Limits of State Action," in James Curran, ed., *The Future of the Left* (Cambridge: Polity Press and New Socialist, 1984), p. 171.

8. Nyerere, "Introduction," p. 5.

9. *Daily News* (Dar es Salaam), 17 July 1990, p. 1.

10. Julius Nyerere, "The African and Democracy," in Nyerere, *Freedom and Unity*, p. 106. Benjamin Mkapa, the foreign minister in May 1990, argued similarly, contending that "there was no universal model for democracy and Tanzania did not necessarily need many parties for the country to be pluralistic." See *Daily News*, 16 May 1990, p. 1. It is interesting that the defense of this contention is deemed racist by several writers. For example, John Wiseman contends that scholars who justify African innovations in procedures to assure popular rule are really racist because such justifications are "based on the idea that different standards of behavior should be adopted in dealing with Africa and that what is unacceptable in Europe or America is quite acceptable for black people in Africa." See Wiseman, *Democracy in Black Africa, Survival and Revival* (New York: Paragon House, 1990), pp. 5–6. In a similar vein, Larry Diamond suggests that the application of criteria other than the procedures defining liberal democracy "demeans African people and cultures, for it implies that political freedom is somehow less important to them and organized political competition beyond their capacity to manage." See Diamond, "Sub-Saharan Africa," in Robert Wesson, ed., *Democracy, A Worldwide Survey* (New York: Praeger, 1987), pp. 74–75.

11. Julius Nyerere, *Democracy and the Party System* (Dar es Salaam: Tanganyika Standard Limited, n.d.), p. 8. An abridged version can be found in Nyerere, *Freedom and Unity*, pp. 195–203. In a speech he gave in the United Kingdom twenty years after the Arusha Declaration, he repeated much the same argument. See *Daily News*, 25 July 1987, p. 4.

12. Nyerere, "The African and Democracy," p. 106.

13. Ibid., p. 105

14. Nyerere, "Democracy and the Party System," p. 11.

15. Julius Nyerere, "The Principles of Citizenship," in Nyerere, *Freedom and Unity*, p. 127.

16. Julius Nyerere, "Freedom and Development," in Nyerere, *Freedom and Development* (Dar es Salaam: Oxford University Press, 1973), p. 62.

17. Ibid., p. 61.

18. A summary of the views presented to the commission can be found in Jamhuri ya Muungano wa Tanzania, Tume ya Rais ya Mfumo wa Chama Kimoja

au Vyama Vingi vya Siasa Tanzania, 1991, *Kitabu cha Pili: Majedwali ya Matokeo ya Uratibu wa Maoni ya Wananchi* (Dar es Salaam: National Printing Company [NPC]—Kiwanda cha Uchapaji cha Taifa [KIUTA], 1992).

19. As a result they were condemned by Marxist observers for sustaining a pseudo-socialism, thereby preventing the evolution of "true" socialism. See A.K.L.J. Mlimuka and P.J.A.M. Kabudi, "The State and the Party," in Issa Shivji, ed., *The State and the Working People in Tanzania* (Dakar: Codesria, 1985), p. 75.

20. For example, Joseph Mbwiliza, principal of Kivukoni College, spoke about tasks under the CCM Fifteen-Year Party Programme. See *Daily News*, 19 April 1989, p. 3.

21. Pius Msekwa, "Towards Party Supremacy: The Changing Pattern of Relationships Between the National Assembly and the National Executive Committee of TANU Before and After 1965," typescript, Department of Political Science, University of Dar es Salaam, M.A. program, 1973/74, p. 61.

22. *Daily News*, 12 December 1985, p. 3.
23. *Daily News*, 2 March 1988, p. 1.
24. *Sunday News* (Dar es Salaam), 17 April 1988, p. 4.
25. *Daily News*, 9 February 1988, p. 1.
26. *Sunday News*, 22 November 1987, p. 3.
27. *Daily News*, 24 March 1990, p. 1.
28. *Daily News*, 19 October 1990, p. 5.

29. *Sunday News*, 30 June 1991, p. 1. Mwinyi had argued that the mass organizations "have now come of age and should be freed from the mother's fold." Furthermore, he said that "the granting of autonomy to mass organisations was part of CCM's programme to further democratise the country's political system." See *Daily News*, 2 May 1991, p. 1. In August 1991 JUWATA voted to transform itself into and give way to the Organisation of Tanzania Trade Unions (OTTU); in December 1991 OTTU was formally launched following the passage of necessary legislation. See *Daily News*, 17 August 1991, p. 1, and *Sunday News*, 13 October 1991, respectively.

30. At a meeting at the University of Dar es Salaam, Issa Shivji said that under the legislation that was to inaugurate OTTU, the successor to JUWATA, the workers would have no powers and the president would have all powers. See *Sunday News*, 27 October 1991, p. 1.

31. Throughout the 1980s, the number of offices reviewed by the party increased. In 1988, the Central Committee began to review the candidates for Dar es Salaam city mayor, and after review by lower political bodies, the regional political committee would decide who the candidates for district and urban council chairmen would be. See *Daily News*, 7 October 1988, p. 1. The Central Committee also named candidates for regional chairman of the CUT and chairman of cooperative unions. See *Daily News*, 7 September 1987, p. 1, and 25 January 1991, p. 1, respectively.

32. *Daily News*, 2 August 1980, p. 1.
33. *Daily News*, 29 May 1990, p. 1.
34. *Daily News*, 25 October 1985, p. 4.
35. *Daily News*, 2 August 1980, p. 1.
36. *Daily News*, 25 October 1985, p. 4.
37. *Daily News*, 26 November 1988, p. 4.
38. *Daily News*, 29 October 1987, p. 1.
39. *Daily News*, 25 September 1990, p. 1.
40. *Sunday News*, 30 June 1991, p. 1.
41. Henry Jacoby, *The Bureaucratization of the World* (Berkeley: University of California Press, 1973).

42. Merilee Grindle, "Policy Content and Context in Implementation," in Grindle, ed., *Politics and Policy Implementation in the Third World* (Princeton, N.J.: Princeton University Press, 1980), p. 15.

43. Robert Rotberg, "Modern African Studies, Problems and Prospects," *World Politics,* Vol. 18, No. 3 (April 1966), p. 571.

44. The argument was discussed by Henry Bienen in "The Party and the No Party State: Tanganyika and the Soviet Union," *Transition* (Kampala), No. 13 (March–April 1964), pp. 25–32.

45. Immanuel Wallerstein, "The Decline of the Party in Single-Party African States," in Joseph La Palombara and Myron Weiner, eds., *Political Parties and Political Development* (Princeton, N.J.: Princeton University Press, 1966), p. 214.

46. Henry Bienen, *Tanzania, Party Transformation and Economic Development* (Princeton, N.J.: Princeton University Press, 1967), p. 221.

47. Crawford Young, "Political Systems Development," in John Paden and Edward Soja, eds., *The African Experience* (Evanston, Ill.: Northwestern University Press, 1970), p. 460.

48. Ibid., p. 463.

49. Pratt, *Critical Phase,* p. 207.

50. *Daily News,* 22 February 1990, p. 1.

51. For an excellent description of the process, see Bismarck Mwansasu, "The Changing Role of the Tanganyika African National Union," in Bismarck Mwansasu and Cranford Pratt, eds., *Towards Socialism in Tanzania* (Toronto: University of Toronto Press, 1979), pp. 169–192.

52. Raymond Hopkins, "The Influence of the Legislature on Development Strategy: The Case of Kenya and Tanzania," in Joel Smith and Lloyd Musolf, eds., *Legislatures in Development: Dynamics of Change in New and Old States* (Durham, N.C.: Duke University Press, 1979), p. 182; Edward Moringe Sokoine, *Public Policy Making and Implementation in Tanzania* (Pau, France: Université de Pau et des Pays de l'Adour, Centre de Recherche et d'Etude sur les Pays d'Afrique Orientale, 1986), p. 26; and Jan Kees van Donge and Athumani J. Liviga, "In Defence of the Tanzanian Parliament," *Parliamentary Affairs,* Vol. 39, No. 2 (April 1986), p. 235.

53. Van Donge and Liviga, "In Defense of the Tanzanian Parliament," pp. 230–240; and William Tordoff, "Residual Legislatures: The Cases of Tanzania and Zambia," *Journal of Commonwealth and Comparative Politics,* Vol. 15, No. 3 (November 1977), p. 235.

54. *Bulletin of Tanzanian Affairs,* No. 12 (March 1981), pp. 6 and 7.

55. Ibid., p. 7.

56. *Daily News,* 31 October 1987, p. 1.

57. *Daily News,* 28 February 1988, p. 1; *Sunday News,* 3 June 1990, p. 3.

58. In 1988 the departments in the NEC secretariat included Political Propaganda and Mass Mobilisation; Ideology, Political Education and Training; Administration; Social Services; Economic Affairs and Planning; and Organisation. See *Daily News,* 25 March 1988, p. 1. These were reduced by two in 1991, to Ideology, Propaganda and Mass Mobilisation; Finance and Administration; Social Services and Economic Affairs; and Organisation. In addition there were the commissions, such as the Control and Disciplinary Commission. See *Sunday News,* 2 June 1991, p. 3.

59. Sengondo Mvungi, "Freedom of Expression and the Law in Tanzania," a paper presented at a seminar held to commemorate twenty-five years of the Faculty of Law, University of Dar es Salaam, October 1986, p. 15.

60. Colin Legum, ed., *Africa Contemporary Record, 1984–1985* (New York: Africana Publishing Company, 1985), p. C29.

61. *Sunday News,* 15 November 1987, p. 8; L.X. Mbunda, "Limitation Clauses in the Bill of Rights," a paper presented at a seminar held to commemorate 25 years of the Faculty of Law, University of Dar es Salaam, October 1986, p. 1.

62. For example, see *Daily News,* 20 March 1991, p. 1; 20 June 1990, p. 3; and 2 August 1987, p. 4.

63. *Daily News,* 11 April 1991, p. 3; 6 January 1989, p. 3; 6 October 1987, p. 3; 26 September 1988, p. 3; 17 October 1988, p. 3; 8 February 1988, p. 3; 1 December 1987, p. 3; and 16 November 1987, p. 3.

64. G.R. Mutahaba, "Organization for Development: Tanzania's Search for Appropriate Local Level Organizational Forms," in Fassil G. Kiros, ed., *Challenging Rural Poverty* (Trenton, N.J.: Africa World Press, 1985), p. 127.

65. Ibid.

66. Ibid., p. 135.

67. *Daily News,* 18 August 1987, p. 3.

68. Julius Nyerere, *Decentralisation* (Dar es Salaam: Government Printer, 1972), p. 1.

69. *Daily News,* 23 February 1989, p. 1.

70. Ibid.

71. *Daily News,* 18 July 1990, p. 1.

72. *Daily News,* 19 July 1990, p. 1.

73. *Daily News,* 2 April 1991, p. 4.

74. *Daily News,* 11 April 1990, p. 1.

75. *Sunday News,* 3 June 1990, p. 1.

76. *Daily News,* 17 July 1990, p. 1.

77. *Daily News,* 29 September 1990, p. 1.

78. *Daily News,* 1 October 1990, p. 1.

79. *Daily News,* 25 September 1990, p. 1.

80. *Daily News,* 21 November 1990, p. 1.

81. *Daily News,* 24 February 1991, p. 1.

82. *Daily News,* 21 March 1991, p. 1.

83. *Daily News,* 22 March 1991, p. 1.

84. *Daily News,* 22 March 1991, p. 1, and 23 March 1991, p. 1.

85. *Daily News,* 5 September 1991, p. 1; 13 September 1991, p. 1; 14 November 1991, p. 1; and 21 November 1991, p. 1.

86. *Daily News,* 12 and 13 June 1991, pp. 1 and 5, respectively.

87. Jamhuri ya Muungano wa Tanzania, Tume ya Rais ya Mfumo wa Chama Kimoja au Vyama Vingi vya Siasa Tanzania, 1991, *Kitabu cha Pili: Majedwali ya Matokeo ya Uratibu wa Maoni ya Wananchi* (Dar es Salaam: National Printing Company–KIUTA, 1992), Table 1(a), p. 1. The proportion on the mainland was 79.7 percent in favor, and that on Zanzibar was 56.4 percent in favor.

88. *Daily News,* 14 December 1992, p. 1. Nyerere had noted a "levels of action" contradiction in the Western demand for multipartyism in a speech to the Council on Foreign Relations in New York three weeks earlier. He said,

> So I am putting before you these two questions. If lack of democracy is unacceptable within nations, and I do agree that it is unacceptable, why is it acceptable internationally? And if rule by One Party is not acceptable nationally (however democratic or otherwise the structures of that One Party), why is the rule by One Country—or One Party consisting of a small group of countries—acceptable internationally?

He contended, "In practice what exists internationally is the Law of the Jungle, where might is right." See *Daily News,* 6 December 1991, p. 4.

89. *Daily News*, 1 January 1992, p. 1.
90. *Daily News*, 3 January 1992, p. 1.
91. *Daily News*, 25 January 1992, p. 1.
92. Ibid.
93. *Daily News*, 4 February 1992, p. 1.
94. *Daily News*, 25 January 1992, p. 1. In response, a group called the Steering Committee for Free Political Parties in Zanzibar (Kamahuru) objected to the demand that parties be national. It claimed that "if this would happen there was a danger of relegating Zanzibar to the status of a region politically." See *Daily News*, 23 January 1992, p. 1.
95. *Daily News*, 25 January 1992, p. 1.
96. Ibid.
97. There were many parallels to the situation in Senegal in 1975, as described in Robert Fatton Jr., *The Making of a Liberal Democracy, Senegal's Passive Revolution, 1975–1985* (Boulder: Lynne Rienner Publishers, 1987).
98. *Daily News*, 4 February 1992, p. 1.
99. *Daily News*, 14 August 1991, p. 1.
100. *Daily News*, 4 January 1990, p. 4.
101. Nyerere suggested that compromise was a necessity: Individualism must be "tempered with" the good of society. The self-interest of an individual and a faction must be subordinate to the well-being of the community. How "the good of the community" is to be decided in a selfless society is not spelled out, yet it is a fundamental question that must be answered if socialist objectives are to be achieved. See Nyerere, "Democracy and the Party System," pp. 21–23.

5
Equality and Socialism

Aliye juu ni juu.
"He who is above is above."

Equality is a fundamental goal of most socialisms. According to Anthony Wright, "Among socialists who have taken values seriously, there has been wide agreement that equality should be regarded as a key socialist value, perhaps even *the* socialist value."[1] Tanzanian socialism is no exception. The primacy of equality has been widely affirmed—especially in Nyerere's writings. In the introduction to *Freedom and Socialism,* he identified "the first principle of socialism—the equality of man."[2] In "Socialism Is Not Racialism" he wrote, "Without the acceptance of human equality there can be no socialism."[3] In "The Varied Paths to Socialism" he held that "socialism is, in fact, the application of the principle of human equality to the social, economic and political organisation of society."[4] In "The Purpose Is Man" he stated, "The essence of socialism is the practical acceptance of human equality."[5] The first principle in the preamble to the TANU Constitution (the TANU Creed) declared belief in the equality of man.[6]

The practical implications of this commitment to equality are several. In Tanzanian socialism, human equality meant "every man's equal right to a decent life before any individual has a surplus above his needs; his equal right to participate in Government; and his equal responsibility to work and contribute to the society to the limit of his ability."[7] The pursuit of equality required that society be organized "in such a manner that it is impossible—or at least very difficult—for individual desires to be pursued at the cost of other people, or for individual strength to be used for the exploitation of others."[8] That meant that "economic, political, and social policies shall be deliberately designed to make a reality of that equality in all spheres of life."[9] Among those policies were ones assuring the rule of law and equality before the law; eliminating private control of the major means of production; strengthening of democracy; correcting "the glaring income differentials which we inherited from colonialism"; narrowing the gap between the incomes of factory workers and agricultural workers; enhancing equality of opportunity; and providing for the old and disabled.[10] Determining, and accounting for, the success of the pursuit of such a complex goal requires the examination of a wide variety of qualitative and quantitative data.

This chapter seeks to describe and assess the impact of policies affecting incomes, prices, taxes, services, ownership, production, and group status on the achievement of equality.

Income and Consumer Price Policies

The most direct mechanism for effecting equality of wealth has been to seek to close the gap in incomes. Because the primary source of income in urban areas differs from that in rural areas, the tools that the party and government have employed have differed. In the former, the party and government have sought to reduce the gap by establishing minimum wages for public and private employees and narrowing the range of wages and salaries paid to public employees. In the latter, they have set panterritorial prices, i.e., prices that were the same everywhere in the country, for major commodities crops. They sought greater equality, too, through control of consumer prices for the necessities of life.

Wages and Salaries

Although the figures vary from one source to another, there is general agreement that the gap in income between high and low wage and salary earnings narrowed, at least until the late 1980s. Nyerere contended in 1977 that within the public sector the ratio of maximum to minimum wages and salaries at independence after direct taxes was about 50:1; that it was about 20:1 in 1967; and that it was about 9:1 in 1976.[11] Richard Stren has asserted that by 1981 the gap had closed to 6:1.[12] Joel Barkan cited the ratio at the time of the Arusha Declaration as 30:1.[13] The minister of state in the Ministry of Finance, Economic Affairs and Planning in 1987 said that the ratio between high- and low-income earners had been about 20:1 in 1961 but was then 5.9:1.[14] These estimates vary because of differences in their calculation. Some take into account the impact of taxes and/or special salary supplements and privileges and some do not; some include all wage and salary earners and some only government-employed ones; some are based on salary schedules and some on income receipts. Yet the trend toward increasing equality, at least through the late 1980s, is widely acknowledged.[15]

This increase in equality, however, has been accompanied by a serious decline in the incomes of all wage and salary earners. Theodore Valentine argued that real disposable earnings of minimum-wage earners in 1980 were only 63 percent of what they were in 1969; those of middle-grade salary earners were only 37 percent; and those of top salary earners were only 21 percent![16] David Leonard has contended that between 1970 and 1980, minimum-wage earners' real wages and salaries had declined 21

Equality and Socialism

percent, and those of middle-grade civil servants fell 54 percent.[17] And the International Labour Organisation (ILO) calculated that between 1969 and 1980 the average wage earner's real income declined 47.6 percent.[18]

A comparison of changes in minimum wages with the consumer price index, as shown in Table 5.1, indicates that minimum-wage earners in the late 1980s were receiving in wages only about one-quarter of what they had received in 1967.[19] The proportion rose to about one-third in 1992.

The significantly greater declines in the higher salaries posed serious problems for the state. Skilled manpower went abroad, demoralization grew, and productivity declined. By the late 1980s, as the pragmatic socialists increasingly challenged the ideological socialists for control of

Table 5.1 Changes in Tanzania's Minimum Wage[a]

Year	Minimum Wage	Consumer Price Index (CPI)	Minimum Wage/CPI
1967	150[b]	5.2	28.8
1969	170	7.0	24.3
1972	240	8.2	29.3
1974	340	10.8	31.5
1975	380	13.6	27.9
1980	480	26.8	17.9
1981	600	33.6	17.9
1984	810	75.0	10.8
1986	1,055[c]	132.4	8.0
1987	1,370	172.1	8.0
1988	1,645	225.8	7.3
1989	2,075	284.1	7.3
1990	2,500	340.1	7.4
1991	3,500	415.9	8.4
1992	5,000	507.7	9.8

Sources: Minimum wage: International Labour Organisation, *Distributional Aspects of Stabilisation Programmes in the United Republic of Tanzania, 1979–84* (Geneva: ILO, 1988), Appendix I, Table Xa, p. 87; *Daily News* (Dar es Salaam), 2 May 1987, p. 1; 2 July 1987, p. 1; 7 November 1989, p. 1; 8 June 1990, p. 1; and 19 June 1992, p. 1. Consumer price index: International Monetary Fund, *International Financial Statistics Yearbook, 1992* (Washington, D.C.: IMF, 1992), pp. 674–675; and International Monetary Fund, *International Financial Statistics*, Vol. 47, No. 3 (March 1994), p. 526–527.

Notes: [a] By the late 1980s, variations from these minimum wages for civil servants became common. These variations included rural-urban differences, civil servant–parastatal differences, and differences among parastatals. For example, in 1987 the minimum wage for rural areas was set at TSh. 1,060 per month, i.e., TSh. 200 less than that for urban areas. In 1992 the minimum wage established for parastatals was raised to TSh. 5,230, i.e., TSh. 230 more than the minimum wage for civil servants. See *Daily News*, 4 July 1992, p. 1. In early 1992, Tanzania Electrical Supply Company (TANESCO) announced it was going to raise its minimum wage to TSh. 7,300, i.e., considerably higher than that of both civil servants and other parastatals. See *Daily News*, 6 April 1992, p. 1. [b] The minimum wage of TSh. 150 per month was established in January of 1963. [c] Formally, the minimum wage remained TSh. 810, though an "allowance" was added pending the report of a salary review commission.

CCM, steps were taken to ameliorate these problems. First, although the wage and salary changes continued to benefit the lower-paid workers more than the higher-paid ones in proportional terms, they did not in absolute terms. For example, in 1987 the minimum civil servant salary was set at TSh. 1,370, and all other salaries were increased, the increases ranging from 30 percent for the lowest paid to 10 percent for the highest paid.[20] Yet percentage increases do not mean the absolute gap is closing. Indeed, a 10 percent increase for someone earning TSh. 8,000 would be an increase of TSh. 800, whereas a 30 percent increase for someone earning TSh. 1,500 would be TSh. 450. Second, various fringe benefits were introduced to further offset the apparent equalization of income. Thus, by the late 1980s, both incomes and equity among wage and salary earners were in decline.

Those affected by minimum wage requirements and government salary schedules were a relatively small proportion of the total population. The total number of employees, including both regular and casual, rose from 2.8 percent in 1969 to 3.1 percent in 1974 to 3.9 percent in 1979 before it fell to 3.4 percent in 1984 and about 3.0 percent in 1989.[21] If one accepts the estimate by T.L. Maliyamkono and M.S.D. Bagachwa that the "second," or informal, economy grew from 9.8 percent of the GNP in 1978 to 31.4 percent of the GNP in 1986, actual employment may have been higher than hitherto estimated.[22] Yet many of those involved in the second economy are people who have been counted already as employees in the "first" economy. The IMF's effort to shrink public employment and expand private employment in the early 1990s is likely to have little impact on gross employment figures. Indeed, with the increase in population, a growth of employment beyond 3 percent of the population appears unlikely. Clearly, the party and government were unable to promote equality among a very large proportion of the population through this means.

Crop Prices

Most Tanzanians are dependent upon agriculture for their livelihood. A comparison of the prices paid for a food crop, maize, and a cash crop, cotton, with the cost of living index between 1967 and 1991, as shown in Table 5.2, indicates a fairly substantial decline for maize and a slight decline for cotton. Nevertheless, the overall decline has been less than that experienced by wage and salary earners.

This decline in real income from agriculture is illustrated by other figures as well. For example, the index of real producer prices between 1971/72 and 1985/86 starts at 160, rises to a peak of 179 in 1976/77, falls to a low of 91 in 1982/83, and rises to 108 in 1985/86. In constant prices, maize has declined in value from TSh. 2.55 per kilogram in 1979/80 to TSh. 1.65 in 1986/87. Also in constant prices, grade A cotton declined in

Table 5.2 Changes in Producer Price of Maize and Cotton Compared with Changes in Consumer Price Index[a]

Year	Maize Price[b]	Maize Price/CPI Ratio	Cotton Price[c]	Cotton Price/CPI Ratio	CPI
1967	27	5.2	92	17.7	5.2
1972	25	3.0	113	13.8	8.2
1977	85	5.2	230	14.2	16.2
1982	175	4.0	470	10.8	43.4
1987	820	4.8	1,945	11.3	172.1
1991	1,100	2.6	7,000	16.8	415.9

Sources: Crop prices: Peter Temu, *Marketing Board Pricing and Storage Policy, The Case of Maize in Tanzania* (Nairobi: East African Literature Bureau, 1977), pp. 48 and 69; United Republic of Tanzania, Ministry of Planning and Economic Affairs, Bureau of Statistics, *Statistical Abstract, 1982* (Dar es Salaam: Bureau of Statistics, 1983), p. 108; and, *Tanzanian Economic Trends*, Vol. 4, Nos. 3 and 4 (October 1991 and January 1992), Table 10 (a), p. 68, and Table 12 (b), p. 71. Consumer price index: International Monetary Fund, *International Financial Statistics Yearbook, 1991* (Washington, D.C.: IMF, 1992), pp. 674 and 675.

Notes: [a] The prices shown, beginning with those for 1977, were announced by the government in the first half of a season-year. Thus, the 1977/78 season prices are recorded here as the prices for 1977. The rationale for assigning the prices to the earlier year is that most of the crop is sold in that portion of the crop-year. The prices for 1967 and 1972 are an average of those paid to farmers during the year. [b] In Tanzanian cents per kilogram. [c] Grade A in Tanzanian cents per kilogram.

price from TSh. 7.66 per kilogram in 1979/80 to TSh. 5.99 in 1986/87.[23] Clearly, the income of the producers who market their crops declined. Was this decline more or less rapid than that of the predominantly urban wage and salary earners?

Although there is disagreement among observers, a comparison of the declines in wage and salary levels and in crop prices suggests that rural people have not suffered as much as urban people. According to David Leonard, in the period 1970–1979, farmers' income declined 46 percent, a figure slightly below the decline in income for middle-grade civil servants and considerably above that for minimum-wage earners noted above.[24] Joel Barkan, on the other hand, contends that the net effect of lower cash crop prices in the 1970s was a reduction of inequality within rural areas but an increase in inequality between rural and urban areas.[25] Yet the ILO study *Basic Needs in Danger* concludes that whereas the real income of wage earners declined 47.6 percent between 1969 and 1980, that of smallholders increased 8.5 percent.[26] The closure of the gap was not constant. According to the ILO, between 1969 and 1973/75 the gap widened; between 1973/75 and 1982 it narrowed sharply; after that, it stabilized.[27] Given the fact that per capita income in the urban areas has been greater than that in the rural areas and assuming that the figures in Tables 5.1 and 5.2 are accurate, it seems reasonable to conclude that rural-urban inequality has been reduced since the Arusha Declaration. Such a claim appears to contradict a widely held belief that government policy has favored urban over rural areas. Yet the apparent contradiction may not be a real one. The government may spend more per capita in urban than in rural areas while at the same time reducing inequalities between the two. The reason unequal expenditure may not prevent increasing equality lies in the fact that the cost of supporting an urban inhabitant is probably greater than that of supporting a rural inhabitant at an equivalent level. Thus, even though a transfer of wealth may have occurred between rural and urban areas, a decline in income inequality between most urban and rural dwellers probably occurred.

Consumer Prices

The government sought to control consumer prices so that the necessities of life would not be out of reach of the poor, especially the urban poor. For many years subsidies and price controls on essentials were used as mechanisms to promote equality. But serious budgetary problems, weakened state capacity, and increased IMF pressure during the middle and late 1980s brought either the mechanisms' formal abandonment, exemplified by the removal of the subsidy on *sembe* (maize meal) in 1984, or their informal abandonment, exemplified by the inability of the state to enforce what price controls remained in the late 1980s and early 1990s.[28]

Tax Policies

Taxation has two principal purposes: Taxes produce revenue for public uses and they are public policy tools. These two purposes sometimes come into conflict. Revenue generation may extract wealth from the poor; social policy may seek to provide wealth to the poor. Assessing the impact of taxation is complicated by the fact that taxation takes a variety of forms, some primarily concerned with revenue generation and others primarily concerned with social policy objectives. In general, tax policies in Tanzania have not promoted socialist equality.

Such a conclusion is supported by Amon Chaligha in a thorough review of the data and literature on Tanzania's tax system.[29] The evidence is of several kinds. First, within the categories of trade and sales taxes, Tanzania has not consistently taxed necessities less and luxuries more. Although luxuries like beer and cigarettes have been favorite items for increased taxation, neither customs nor sales tax has differentiated much between luxury and nonluxury items. For example, in 1987 during the budget debate, Cleopa Msuya, then the minister for finance, said he intended to amend the Customs Tariff Act of 1976 to raise duties 5 to 10 percent. He said that this would mean shoes would now be taxed at a 30 percent rate, instead of 25 percent; toys would be taxed at a 35 percent rate, rather than 25 percent.[30] And sales taxes, which were a flat 25 percent, would be increased to 30 percent in 1990. This affected tires for automobiles as well as those for bicycles.[31]

Second, within the category of income tax, Tanzania has taxed income from capital less heavily than income from labor, thereby benefiting those with wealth more than those without wealth.[32] This bias is shown through a comparison of the maximum tax rate for companies and individuals. Local companies paid a maximum tax of 40 percent in 1967; the tax rose to 45 percent in 1974 and to 50 percent in 1976. Individuals paid a maximum tax of 95 percent in 1967; the tax fell to 75 percent in 1973.[33] In addition, tax concessions have not been given as readily to individuals as to private businesses.[34]

Third, although the income tax on wage and salary earners has been very progressive—i.e., it has contributed to equality of income among such workers—it has not contributed to equality between them and other categories of Tanzanians. And, because wage and salary earners constitute only about 3 percent of the population, whatever equality is achieved among these workers cannot be generalized to the society as a whole. Their income is more accessible to the tax collector than that of other groups in the society. As a result, wage and salary earners have been forced to carry an inordinate proportion of the income tax burden.[35]

Fourth, the development levy was not as progressive a tax among those affected as was the personal income tax; i.e., in most, but not all, cases it did not contribute to equality. Prior to independence the British and German colonial governments had imposed hut and poll taxes to generate revenue and force Africans to engage in wage labor. These taxes were abandoned in 1969 but reintroduced in the early 1980s. Everyone, men and women, eighteen years of age and older had to pay what was known as the development levy. The amount of the levy, collected by district councils, varied around the country and over time. In rural areas it tended to be set as a flat rate.[36] In urban areas there was more variation: It sometimes involved a flat rate and sometimes a graduated one.[37] In some areas exemptions were allowed for hardship cases, though the numbers were not large.[38] Despite the efforts to graduate the tax and to provide exemptions, the development levy remained relatively insensitive to variations in wealth.

Fifth, the procedures applied for collecting the development levy tended to hurt the poor much more than the rich, thereby working against the objective of equality. Those unable to pay faced harassment in the form of fines, early morning raids, and demands for payment in foodstuffs.[39] For example, in 1988 the government news agency Shihata reported that "levy collectors were rounding up people who are on foot and shabby looking, leaving those who travel in cars."[40] When the poor still did not pay, they were imprisoned. In early 1989, the deputy minister for home affairs announced that over 2,000 people were in custody for failure to pay the development levy.[41] Rather than argue against the practice on equity grounds, opponents tended to argue against it on cost grounds. Nyerere, for example, pointed out that the incarceration simply meant that the government had to pay the defaulters' upkeep in prison and that it would be more rational to give them some kind of work to earn money to pay the levy.[42] In December 1990 the minister for home affairs, Augustine Mrema, ordered the release of all prisoners jailed for failing to pay the development levy. He observed that Isanga prison in Dodoma then held 309 people who had been given three months for failure to pay the TSh. 300 levy. Since it cost TSh. 3,000 per month to keep each prisoner, Mrema contended, "This is like exchanging a cow for a chicken." Instead, he argued, district councils should put levy defaulters to work repairing roads and the like.[43] It is interesting to note that work in lieu of tax had been a much-decried colonial policy.[44]

Thus, the taxation system has led to greater equity among those most accessible to the income tax, i.e., those who earn wages and salaries. Yet there have been so many deviations from principles of equity in the taxation system's general application that its contribution to socialist equality has been at best ambiguous.

Services Policies

A centerpiece in Tanzania's efforts to enhance equity has been its provision of public services. If inequality characterized tax collection, that inequality might be more than offset by a redistribution of funds to the people on an equitable basis through the provision of collective goods such as health, education, and other services. It is here that Tanzanian socialism gained much of its status in Africa and elsewhere.

Health

The socialist dream was a health service available to the many rather than the few and aimed primarily at providing good health care rather than making a profit.

Increased accessibility was sought by expanding free government health care. Although increases slowed as a consequence of the economic decline of the early 1980s, the number of government health delivery facilities and the number of government medical personnel serving the less affluent increased more rapidly than those serving the more affluent. For example, between 1976 and 1984 the number of hospitals increased from 147 to 152 (1.03-fold), and the number of dispensaries increased from

1,847 to 2,644 (1.4-fold). Even more significant was the fact that, whereas the number of medical doctors increased from 683 to 1,065 (1.6-fold), the number of rural medical aides increased from 1,049 to 4,601 (4.4-fold) and medical assistants from 770 to 2,383 (3.1-fold).[45]

Greater attention to care rather than profit was sought through the elimination of privately supplied health services. The Private Hospitals (Regulation) Act of 1977, enforced in 1980, required most private doctors to join the government service or to cease practicing medicine.[46] The minister of health at the time contended that only a small percentage of the population made use of such doctors anyway, so that the impact was more symbolic than real.[47] In the late 1980s, the minister for health and social welfare estimated that the few existing private hospitals treated only 3 percent of the patients in the country; those run by religious institutions treated 40 percent; government hospitals treated the rest.[48] The fees charged at the private hospitals were fixed by the government,[49] and the religious institutions were non–profit making. Thus, the health services had been expanded to reach a higher proportion of the population, and a high degree of government control had been established.

However, with the economic decline that began in the late 1970s, resources were insufficient to sustain the service. In 1989 the minister for health said there were only about TSh. 8 per Tanzanian available in the budget for health care. As a result, the government could no longer support free medical service for everybody.[50] The health minister said he was able to raise only about 10 percent of the amount required each year for drugs and medical equipment. Part of the gap was filled by donations from several European countries.[51] In 1990, President Mwinyi told an American donating medical equipment that "most Tanzanian doctors with expertise in their fields left the country to get 'job satisfaction' abroad simply because they lacked the necessary equipment in hospitals within the country."[52]

Those who stayed did so with great sacrifice. When in 1990 the president visited the largest hospital in the country, Muhimbili in Dar es Salaam, he was met by a wide variety of complaints. One doctor showed him an ad in the party newspaper, *Uhuru*, for a position paying TSh. 7,500 a month for a typist who could type forty words a minute; after six years working as a surgeon, the doctor said, he got only TSh. 6,600 a month. He said the World Health Organization (WHO) paid TSh. 200,000 to TSh. 600,000 per month, i.e., U.S.$1,000 to U.S.$3,000.[53] In 1991 the chief medical officer in Zanzibar contended that eighteen out of thirty-five local doctors had resigned because of pathetic conditions, including shortages of basic drugs and equipment, poor pay, and lack of incentives. "We have hung on all this time because of nationalist attitudes. . . . We have to attend fellow citizens under whatever circumstances."[54]

A crisis had been reached with regard not only to curative medicine but also to preventative medicine. To many, socialist and nonsocialist systems could be distinguished by the greater emphasis the former put on preventative medicine and the latter on curative medicine. By the early 1990s, preventative medicine seemed to have been reduced to authoritarian measures such as orders that toilets be built in houses.[55]

The government's lack of revenue was seriously undermining its efforts to provide health care for all. The principal response of the government was liberalization, i.e., the encouragement of private pharmacies and doctors. Although such encouragement may have made medical care more available to some, it did not make it more available to others. Thus, the growth of inequality was allowed.

Education

Of all the social services, education was given the most attention as a tool for socialist transition. It was the subject of Nyerere's first post-Arusha paper, "Education for Self-Reliance."[56] Nyerere told educators in 1988 at a symposium on twenty years of the Arusha Declaration, "As teachers you are among the front-line workers in the building of a socialist Tanzania as defined in the Arusha Declaration."[57] In his view, education was the gateway to the good life, making equal access critically important. Tanzania's post-Arusha adult education and Universal Primary Education (UPE) programs have earned praise around the world. In 1991, Mwinyi claimed in a speech at the University of Dar es Salaam that there had been real improvement since independence, with literacy rising from about 10 percent to a current 90 percent of the population and the proportion of school-age children in school increasing from 20 percent to 93 percent.[58] In reality, the levels Mwinyi referred to had been achieved a decade earlier and had declined through most of the 1980s.

Under Tanzanian socialism, equality was to be promoted by an emphasis on education for the many rather than the few. That meant emphasizing primary rather than secondary education. Throughout the 1970s, Tanzania made rapid progress in increasing the proportion of children in primary schools. Table 5.3 indicates that early success—and the failure that followed in the 1980s.[59]

In contrast, secondary school enrollments were kept low so that funds would be spent on education for the many rather than for the few. According to the ILO, only 2.4 percent of the estimated age group (fourteen through seventeen) were in government secondary schools in 1980, "one of the smallest [percentages] in the world."[60] The level was kept to between 3 and 4 percent during most of the 1980s, yet by 1990 it had jumped to 6.9 percent.[61]

The jump was due to two changes in government policy in the mid-1980s as a consequence of pressure from more advantaged groups. The government allowed private secondary schools to be established, and it began "double-sessioning" government secondary schools in the late

Table 5.3 Proportion of Primary School–Age Children in Primary School

Year	Percent
1970	34.0
1975	53.0
1976	70.0
1977	99.0
1978	96.0
1979	100.0
1980	93.0
1982	90.0
1983	87.0
1984	83.0
1985	72.0
1986	69.0
1987	66.0
1988	64.0
1989	63.0
1990	63.0

Source: World Bank, *World Tables 1992* and *World Tables 1993* (Baltimore: Johns Hopkins University Press for World Bank, 1992 and 1993), pp. 590–591 and pp. 590–591, respectively.

1980s. In 1988 the deputy minister for education estimated that there were 175 private secondary schools with 75,545 pupils, whereas there were 113 public secondary schools with 52,158 pupils.[62] In June 1990 it was estimated that the number of private secondary schools had increased to 210.[63]

The identification of a school as private simply meant that it was not run by the central government. Many organizations were involved in these schools' establishment, often public or semipublic institutions that were town, district, or regionally based.[64] These private schools were guided and regulated, though not funded, by the central government. It was the government that set the fees such schools were allowed to charge. The effect of the double-sessioning in public schools and this growth of private schools was to draw resources away from mass education toward more elite education.

University education has always been a "problem" for those seeking to build an equitable society. Very few students were able to attend.[65] Yet, in 1980, 31 percent of the ministry of national education's budget went to the University of Dar es Salaam, the sole university in the country at the time.[66] The elitism of the university was also reflected in the disdain students had toward fulfilling the charge in "Education for Self-Reliance" that they engage in productive activities to meet part of the cost of their education. At the university's tenth anniversary, Nyerere asked, "Can we say the University is playing a vanguard role in the question of education for self reliance? And since the answer is clearly in the negative, should not the University, like the rest of us, take a critical look at itself?"[67]

Although the University of Dar es Salaam has been an institution of the privileged that has not been accessible to the masses, it played an indirect role in furthering equality through the development and fostering of socialist ideas. Efforts were made to instill in students the ideals of Tanzanian socialism, including the goal of equality. Following the 1974 Musoma Declaration of TANU's NEC, male students had to have had work experience and the party's endorsement before admission to the university. A development studies course was introduced to acquaint students with socialist ideas. Though many went through such training as if it were a charade, others approached it with much more seriousness. In addition, the University of Dar es Salaam was home to many Marxists, neo-Marxists, and ideological socialists who engaged in debate about socialist ideas.[68] And, when the Faculty of Agriculture of the university became Sokoine University in 1984, its charge was to improve the well-being of poorer farmers. At times students from the university have challenged the government and party, usually when they felt that socialist ideals have been violated.[69] So, though elitist in many ways, the university has made indirect contributions to the pursuit of equality.

That goal involved not only achieving equal access to education but also achieving a high quality of education. Equal access to worthless education is meaningless. Given limited resources, the two goals varied inversely; i.e., as access to education grew, the quality declined. As the economic situation worsened, a variety of problems became evident. The skills acquired were unused. In 1987 the minister for labour told the National Assembly that "500,000 youths or 91 percent of the pupils who completed primary school under the Universal Primary Education (UPE) Programme in 1984 were idling in the rural and urban areas," and another half-million were being added to these numbers annually because they had not been properly trained to take up self-employment.[70]

The shortage of teachers grew. In 1988 the minister for education noted that "in some primary schools, there were one or two teachers per school with seven classes."[71] In 1989 he said he needed 4,000 graduate teachers, whereas he was getting only 300 a year.[72] The same year, the deputy minister for education suggested that only half the Grade A–trained (best-trained) teachers were actually teaching.[73] In 1990, the minister for education in Zanzibar said 30 percent of the teachers in primary schools were untrained, and 42 percent of those in secondary schools were "not qualified to do the job."[74] The shortage of qualified teachers was due in part to the problem of remuneration.

Shortages of equipment and supplies increased. Teachers were perpetually faced with insufficient desks, books, notebooks, and other supplies necessary for quality instruction. A senior lecturer in the Department of Criminal and Civil Law at the University of Dar es Salaam, summing up the sense of despair in the late 1980s, said that "the policy of education for self-reliance . . . aimed at preparing youngsters for village communal life, has totally failed to achieve the desired goal."[75]

The principal causal factors in the reversal of the trend toward increasing access to quality education were problems associated with funding. In the budget debate in 1987, the minister for education said, "The country's ability to support and promote education has been declining year after year for the past ten years."[76] The following year he contended that the decline in support for education was reflected in the proportion of the budget devoted to education: 1962/63, 19.6 percent; 1967/68, 13.7 percent; 1984/85, 6.5 percent; and 1988/89, 5.4 percent.[77] Teachers found it difficult at times both to get their salaries and to survive on them. An editorial in the *Daily News* in 1989 noted, "On countless occasions, we have carried reports by teachers that some district councils have used money meant for their salaries to pay for other administrative costs."[78]

Lack of funds meant insufficient supplies. In 1987, the minister for education claimed that the cost of adequate primary school materials was TSh. 1,056 per student per year, but the government could only afford TSh. 100.[79] Town and district councils sought to fill the gap in a very minor way by ordering materials from the sole supplier, Tanzania Elimu Supplies (TES), a government-owned company given a monopoly in educational materials to avoid possible profiteering by private companies. By March 1987 the district councils' debts to TES had reached TSh. 63 million. In response, TES limited credit to the district councils; the result was that education materials worth TSh. 172 million piled up in the supplier's warehouse. To avert the bankruptcy of TES and make supplies available to some, the government decided to allow TES to sell needed supplies to private shops at set prices.[80] Thus, privatization of the economy was furthered and those who could afford to buy supplies were advantaged.

The lack of public funds led to a further compromise, with the objective of using education as a means to promote equality: School fees, which had been abolished in 1973, were reintroduced in the mid-1980s.[81] The fees were raised almost every year to cover an increasing proportion of the cost of education.[82] Although formally government secondary school students were not supposed to be expelled because of their inability to pay school fees, they were not treated in the same manner as those who were able to pay. In 1990, the deputy minister for education admitted that 723 students had been "sent home" in 1987. Yet, he argued, they were not expelled; rather, they were directed to collect the fees. If their families could not pay, they were supposed to get the money from the village government or the district or town council.[83] Given the financial position of those bodies, the likelihood of obtaining funding from any of these sources was remote.

The financial problems the country faced also led to corruption, which further weakened education. An example was a major scandal that became public in October 1990 at the Ministry for Education headquarters in Dar es Salaam. Allegations included theft of TSh. 40,224,436 and a plot to burn the headquarters in order to hide the crime. One hundred and twenty-five workers were dismissed, eighty-six of whom were charged with crimes.[84]

The trends away from equal access to education for all became obvious to most Tanzanians in the 1980s. In late 1988, Nyerere expressed his frustration about the expansion of private secondary schools in the following way:

> Ten new Government secondary schools and thirty three new private secondary schools were opened last year with Government approval! Where do we get the teachers from? Already our Secondary School teachers have classes which are too big for proper teaching, and in some of the science subjects we often cannot provide any teachers at all. And many of these new private schools are the result of public collections supported by—or even initiated by—Party leaders and other prominent public figures! At the same time, public expenditure on education as a proportion of the Budget is decreasing not increasing.[85]

Nyerere was critical also of what had happened to the effort to make schools more self-reliant. In the same speech quoted above he said that, according to the Ministry for Education, the value of production in educational institutions "came to about 3 percent of the present very low recurrent budget for the Ministry of Education. This, 20 years after the policy was officially adopted!"[86]

Water

As a necessity, the supply of water became an important issue in the effort to enhance equality. In 1971 a twenty-year goal of providing clean and safe water within 400 meters of everyone's house was initiated. By 1985 water had been provided to only 42 percent of the households, instead of the targeted 89 percent.[87] In response to such difficulties, the minister for water announced in mid-1987 that not only had the "clean water for all" target been shifted to the year 2000, but also the responsibility for achieving it had been transferred "to the people" because "the truth is the Government can no longer afford" to assume the primary responsibility.[88]

Even those who were formally to be provided with water often did not get it. The minister for water estimated in 1988 that 60 percent of existing water supply schemes in the country had broken down "due to lack of maintenance and poor handling."[89] In December of that year, for example, Singida town entered its fourth week without water in the pipelines because there was no money for pumps and pipes were said to be rusted.[90] These are merely examples of trends that continued through the early 1990s.

Equality and Socialism

The rapid growth of towns posed particular problems. Dodoma's water supply was always considered problematic. In February 1990 demand was estimated at about 7 million gallons a day, whereas supply was about 6 million gallons.[91] The same month the branch manager of the National Urban Water Authority (NUWA) said that the present Dar es Salaam population required 80 million gallons a day but less than half of that was reaching the city.[92] The major sources were the Upper and Lower Ruvu projects. The Upper Ruvu project was built in 1959 to pump 18 million gallons a day but produced only 11 million; the Lower Ruvu was built in 1976 to pump 40 million gallons but pumped less than half that; and the Mtoni pumps installed in 1950/51 to supply 2 million gallons were reported in 1988 to be "dilapidated."[93] Efforts were being made to improve the pumping stations, but even a TSh. 2.12 billion Italian-funded rehabilitation project was only expected to raise levels to those that had been available in 1976.[94] Even if fully exploited, the Upper and Lower Ruvu maximum yield has been estimated to be only 84 million gallons a day.[95] Given the rapid growth of Dar es Salaam, the need to develop alternative sources is imminent. Yet the financial position of the government makes such development dependent upon external funding, over which Tanzania has little control.[96] Once again, the first decade following the Arusha Declaration was a period in which there was a significant advance toward equal access to a valued good; but that progress was stymied in the 1980s to a considerable extent by the economic decline.

Housing

Shelter is another necessity of life. Its provision to all is an implicit objective of the socialist enterprise. The task was more challenging in urban than in rural areas for a variety of reasons: Traditional construction materials were not as available in, or as appropriate to, urban areas; supportive social networks that assisted in the construction of houses were less developed in newly settled urban areas; appropriate land on which to build houses was not as readily available; and rates of urbanization and consequent need for housing rose substantially in the 1980s and 1990s. Yet government policies were able neither to come close to meeting the demand for housing nor to improve the degree of equality in its provision.[97]

The National Housing Corporation (NHC), established in 1962, had by 1989 constructed fewer than 15,750 houses. During the period between 1964 and 1989, demand was estimated to have increased from 20,000 to 400,000.[98] As an editorial in the government newspaper said, "The oftheard saying that in Dar es Salaam it is easier to secure a job than a house underlies the seriousness of the housing problem in our capital city, and indeed in other towns in the country."[99] By 1990, the NHC was unable to keep up the houses it had built and had accumulated a large debt owed to the Tanzania Housing Bank (THB).[100] More importantly, those who had NHC houses were among the privileged few. As in the case of countries not pursuing socialism, creditworthiness was demanded for THB loans. Villages and cooperatives were required "to have a bank account with THB, deposit 5 percent of the loan value, possess land title deeds and a certain amount of work done at the site in order to be considered for the bank's housing loan."[101] Richard Stren, who studied Tanzania's housing policies, noted that the complexity of procedures for loans favored those with more education and, consequently, more wealth.[102]

In the early 1970s, the inability of the government to supply a number of houses sufficient to match demand brought a "site and service" program closely linked with the THB. The idea was that the government would demarcate sites and develop services and that individuals would be responsible for building—often with THB loans. What seemed to happen as a consequence of costs and complicated procedures was that it was the more wealthy who took advantage of the program.[103] Stren found that of the 4,433 individual loans in 1979, 70.3 percent "went to those with incomes over twice the minimum urban wage; included in this figure are 10.5 percent to those with incomes ten times the minimum wage and more."[104]

A third public institution charged with providing housing was the Registrar of Buildings (ROB), established under the 1971 Acquisition of Buildings Act. All rented buildings and houses valued over TSh. 100,000 were taken over by the government as part of the effort to end exploitation, and they were placed under the control of the ROB. By the mid-1980s, the growing demand for housing, the government's lack of resources, and the consequent need for increased private investment in the sector led to a change of policy. The president's legal power to acquire buildings ended in 1985, and he was empowered to return property that had been nationalized. But by January 1990 he had returned only thirty-five houses.[105] The beneficiaries were the privileged few who were given the right to occupy ROB houses and buildings.[106] To provide for greater efficiency, the ROB was merged into the NHC in 1989. Few observers had any illusions about the likelihood that the merger would significantly improve the ability of these institutions to promote equal access to housing.

Finally, another tool used to promote equality in access to housing has been rent control. It is ironic that during the 1980s the struggles over rent pitted the government's NHC against the government's structures to protect renters, a phenomenon reflecting the political struggle over Tanzanian socialism. As the government sought to put NHC on a better financial basis and to accommodate rents to inflation, rent increases were sought. Yet before such increases could go into effect, they had to be approved by rent tribunals. The University of Dar es Salaam Legal Aid Society was active in helping tenants resist the increases, arguing before the tribunals that these would lead to eviction of low- and medium-income workers who would not be able to pay the new rates.[107] The tribunals and the minister for local government tended to be sympathetic.[108] Yet those occupying NHC housing tended not to be the very poor, so efforts at keeping their rents down did little to promote equality.[109]

In early 1990, President Mwinyi responded to growing disquiet over the decline of social services. He said "that the budget for the social services was grossly inadequate during the three-year Economic Recovery Programme (ERP) which ended last year" and that this was a mistake. He pledged that a higher proportion of the budget would go to water, education, and health services.[110] Yet the momentum in the opposite direction, coupled with the lack of resources at the disposal of the government, meant that there was no significant shift of resources into services in the early 1990s.

Ownership Policies

Partly to facilitate the pursuit of equality, ownership of natural resources was assumed by the state. Yet by the 1980s, ownership policies were being undermined by two trends: State employees increasingly used their custodial position over natural resources as a source of private wealth, and pressures were growing to assign private title to such resources. Tanzania's experiences with ownership of land and minerals are examples of these trends.

Land

Although land became public shortly after independence, "improvements" were private. This fact led to de facto ownership of land in many areas, since improvements could be bought and sold. The process took place much more quickly in urban than in rural areas.

At independence, most land in rural areas was held by Africans in accord with customary land law. Under this system, the power to allocate land for individual use was held by an authority such as a chief or headman. Following the abolition of chieftainship in the immediate postindependence period, the power to allocate rural land was assumed by a variety of agents ranging from regional commissioners to district development officers to committees formed by district councils. With "villagization" during the 1970s, the power of land allocation was given to the village.

Two kinds of problems arose: There were disputes about land within the recognized boundaries of the village, and there were disputes about the extent of land over which the village had authority. The latter problem developed when, in an effort to stimulate production in the early 1980s, the party and government encouraged large-scale private farming. But, to protect the villagers, the NEC directed that villages get titles to their lands. If they did not do so, Rashidi Kawawa noted, "Our villages will lose their land to individuals."[111]

The issuance of land titles, though, meant that the power of those government officers who had responsibility for issuing such titles increased. The process became "infected" with corruption. For example, during a tour of villages by Nyerere in 1987, villagers in one area complained that they had tried ten times to get a land title for the village but had failed. Yet, they claimed, an individual was given title over 100 acres within what they considered the perimeter of the village. Nyerere's response was to urge the villagers to stand up to these corrupt government officials: "Fight for your rights. Hold protest rallies if necessary. These people should not be given room; otherwise they will think that Socialism in Tanzania has no people to defend it."[112] The procedures required of villages and of individuals to get title deeds differed. The complexity of the former so delayed the process that individuals were advantaged.[113]

Disputes over land within villages also undermined collective control of land. According to Anthony Marwa, as villages grew, villagers tended to oppose further redistribution of land within the jurisdiction of the village because it meant that those occupying land would lose some of it. The result: In many areas village governments became ineffective as land redistribution agents. The consequence for some was landlessness. As the demand for land close to the villages increased, a kind of landlordism developed. The landless "borrowed" land in return for payment in the form of a part of the crop harvested. Because of these developments, Marwa thought customary tenure should be abolished.[114] The Land Tenure (Established Villages) Act No. 22 of 1992 sought to do just that, revoking customary tenure rights and formally transferring "ownership" to the village. Yet the issue remained contentious as individuals successfully challenged the act's intent.[115]

Competition for land in urban areas was even more intense. As population grew rapidly, so did the demand for land. As the scarcity of land increased, so did the susceptibility to corruption of the government officers responsible for plot allocation.[116] Urban land had become a commodity, which made it more accessible to the rich than to the poor.

Minerals

Mineral wealth was put under state ownership along with land. Resources that require substantial capital to exploit, such as iron and coal, have remained under government control, but those that individuals might exploit, such as gold and tanzanite, have shifted away from public control. A major impetus for privatization was the decline in mineral production. In 1989, the general manager of the State Mining Corporation (STAMICO) said that "despite the country's vast mineral potential, the sector's contribution to the Gross National Product (GNP) has plummeted over the last 29 years from 10 percent in 1960 to 0.5 percent today."[117]

As liberalization of trade led to an increased demand on the informal market for hard currency, the incidences of smuggling of minerals and private "illegal" mining activities rose. Gold was one of the major foci of such undertakings. The STAMICO general manager estimated in the late 1980s that 6,000 to 10,000 kilograms a year were being smuggled out of the country while perhaps 10 kilograms were properly sold.[118] The minister for energy and minerals estimated that the gold smuggled out of the country each year was worth TSh. 500,000,000.[119] So profitable was the smuggling that 40,000 people were estimated to have joined the gold rush to Shinyanga, Igunga, Kahama, and Nzega districts.[120] Why did individual miners become so important? A major part of the reason was pricing. In 1987, when the official price of gold was TSh. 200 per gram, the unofficial price was estimated to be TSh. 2,000 per gram.[121] In an effort to win back at least the marketing of gold, the government appointed a foreign company, Dar Tadine Tanzania (DTT), to purchase it. When that did not work, the government canceled the DTT contract, and in January 1989 it allowed the Mwanza Regional Miners Association to buy it.[122] And in early 1990, the Bank of Tanzania began to buy gold directly from miners as well.[123] Apparently, the government had given up hope of controlling production and was scrambling to get a part of gold sales.

These problems of mining and marketing were not confined to gold production. In 1971 Tanzania had nationalized tanzanite mines and placed them under a state corporation, Tanzania Gemstones Industries. Yet most of the tanzanite was produced by illegal miners and sold to smugglers who sold it across the border in Kenya.[124] Unable to control the illegal miners, the commissioner for mines announced in 1988 that tenders for plots for mining the mineral by private individuals were being issued.[125]

Unlike the case of gold and tanzanite, the state has been able to maintain its control of the iron and coal. The likelihood that it will provide collective benefits, though, has been a matter of dispute between ideological and pragmatic socialists over a period of many years. On the one hand, ideological socialists have tended to favor the exploitation of iron and coal, as evidenced by the call for the establishment of an iron and steel industry in CCM's 1987 Fifteen-Year Party Programme. On the other hand, pragmatic socialists have tended to contend that their exploitation would be uneconomical. Nevertheless, in 1988 the Kwira Coal Mine in Mbeya Region opened with Chinese assistance. The mine had a capacity of 150,000 tonnes a year and a life span of sixty-five years.[126] But a variety of problems arose, especially with marketing the product. For example, the Southern Paper Mills found that the quality was not up to what it needed and balked at its use. There is serious doubt that coal exploitation will appreciably benefit Tanzanians as a whole.

Iron ore exists in Tanzania, but its extraction has involved even more difficulties than has that of coal. In the mid-1980s, the estimated cost of developing the Liganga iron ore complex was U.S.$1.8 billion. If fully developed, the complex would produce 500,000 tonnes of steel annually. Studies had shown that the ore deposits would be depleted in less than ten years and that there would be a persistent glut of steel on the world market, making Tanzanian steel uncompetitive. Consequently, there were major problems in arranging foreign financing.[127]

Thus, in the case of gold and tanzanite, public ownership has not brought about equal benefit; similarly, public exploitation of coal and iron has not contributed meaningfully to the goal of equality.

Nationalization

In the immediate aftermath of the Arusha Declaration, nationalizations took place that sought to place the commanding heights of the economy in the hands of Tanzanians. It was argued that collective ownership would mean that the profits would be available for the many rather than the few. Although nationalizations were directed at banking, import-export firms, and industries, many expatriate farms and even selected small Tanzanian businesses were taken over. More will be said about the nationalizations in industry in Chapter 7. Suffice it to say that the initial reasons for nationalization have been undermined by experience. The sharing of profits often became the sharing of deficits; reasonably productive businesses or farms often became unproductive enterprises; the litany of problems prompted pragmatic socialists to push for private ownership in the late 1980s and early 1990s. Although many of the problems faced by the nationalized enterprises were due to factors other than state ownership, it is difficult to argue that the nationalizations did much to realize equality.

Production Policies

One of the principal arguments of Marxists was that equality would be realized through changes in the relations of production. Virtually no observer has argued that production relations were radically changed in the years since the Arusha Declaration. Much more attention was given to the tool of collective production for the realization of equality. Ideological socialists, in particular, stressed the utility of communal production. Working together and sharing whatever was produced according to the amount of work put in was a central socialist idea. It is the idea reflected in the maxim "Equal pay for equal work."

Although a central theme of ideological socialists, communal production often has been criticized by pragmatic socialists on empirical grounds. They argue that the two major efforts, in the form of ujamaa villages during the 1970s and production-oriented cooperatives during the 1980s, were unsuccessful. My concern is with the success of communal production in promoting equality rather than productivity.

The empirical evidence does not support the notion that such production contributed significantly either to equity or to the participants' well-being. In a study of communal production in a sample of villages in 1980, Paul Collier, Samir Radwan, and Samuel Wangwe found that 8 percent of land was farmed communally; an average household earned TSh. 28 from the communal farm and TSh. 2,260 from individual plots; the former absorbed 20 percent of the village labor yet produced less than 2 percent of agricultural output. Furthermore, they found that "work on the communal shamba [small farm] is done disproportionately by the poorer half of the community. It is therefore an example of regressive taxation."[128] They concluded that "as presently operated, the majority of communal shambas cannot be viewed as successful for they are probably causing a net loss of output and worsening income distribution."[129] They wrote, "Among poor households 28 percent of total labour time is devoted to this effectively unremunerated activity as compared with only 20 percent of labour time devoted by non-poor households. Communal agriculture is therefore apparently having an adverse effect on income distribution."[130]

The goal of equality and the goal of production seemed to conflict in communal production. There was always struggle over what should be done with the product of communal production. On one side were those who believed that any distribution to individuals was an expression of individualism and not collectivism. On the other side were those who felt that individuals should be rewarded for their participation. In a sense, this was the division between ideological socialists and pragmatic socialists. It was also the difference between the socialist principle of "to each according to his contribution" and the communist principle of "to each according to his need." Both principles argued for equity. The difference was that the former argument was based on the work contributed, whereas the latter was based on the need of people in the community. There was a third alternative, often advocated by party and government officials outside the village, that called for the product of communal production to be used as a collective good to fund village undertakings. Remuneration systems often combined all three principles in the distribution of the product of collective work, deemphasizing the return for work. What this meant was that those who worked more on the communal farm were being taxed more—certainly a disincentive for individuals not fully committed to socialist selflessness and a violation of the socialist principle of to each according to his work.[131]

Group Status Policies

In general, the income, price, tax, service, ownership, and production policies sought equality among individuals rather than groups of individuals. Action to achieve group equality appeared either unnecessary or likely to produce additional problems for the socialist project. First, it would foster the development of a kind of *group* "individualism," i.e., a particular concern for the well-being of a subunit of the whole, which had led to ethnic and religious conflict elsewhere in Africa. Second, it would tend to obscure the problem of within-group equality, which would allow significant inequality to persist. Third, had individual equality been achieved within Tanzania, a reasonable degree of equality would have been established among subgroups of Tanzanians. Yet an imperfectly operating set of policies seeking individual equality allowed the perpetuation of gender-, region-, ethnicity-, and religion-based inequalities. Despite the potential problems, two approaches to furthering group equality were attempted. One was an effort to ignore or suppress group identity. For example, TANU and CCM banned references to ethnicity or religion in elections and party debates. The other was an effort to devise policy solutions.

The most pervasive inequality and the most difficult to overcome has been that associated with gender. The NEC contended in the Arusha Declaration that rural women work much harder than rural men.[132] Nyerere asserted in "Socialism and Rural Development" that "women did, and still do, more than their fair share of the work in the fields and in the homes."[133] And the party creed stated that one of the objectives of the party was "to see that the Government and all public institutions give equal opportunity to all citizens, women and men alike, irrespective of race, tribe, religion or status."[134] Several corrective steps were taken, like the passage of a new marriage law, elimination of the two-year work requirement for entry to the University of Dar es Salaam, and the appointment of women to significant political and governmental positions.

There is a vast and insightful literature on gender inequality in Tanzania.[135] Janet Bujra has suggested that the literature may be categorized into two perspectives: one that finds the cause in a multiplicity of attitudinal factors and the other that cites capitalist relations of production and reproduction.[136] Both conclude that the corrective efforts have been overwhelmed by patriarchal tradition and the way socialist policies have been implemented.[137] Patriarchal tradition has remained pervasive despite efforts to change it. Socialist policies have tended to ignore women, giving rise to the units of action problem. Policies that treated a group like the peasantry as though it were "ungendered" have led to the perpetuation— and sometimes the intensification—of gender inequality. For example, the increase in prices for cash crops might increase production and thereby benefit the peasantry as a whole, but the costs and benefits probably would not be shared equally by men and women. Given the gender relations in rural Tanzania, women probably would do most of the increased work and men probably would reap most of the additional income. The bottom line is that the effort to achieve gender equality has been far from successful.

Conclusion

Almost every policy of the government has an impact on equality. Of those directly aimed at individual equality, the trend is relatively clear: Most worked to some extent during the first decade of Tanzania's attempt to build socialism, yet the economic decline from the late 1970s undermined them all. The search for equality and production came to be seen as contradictory; i.e., the pursuit of equality seemed to undermine production, and vice versa. In the latter half of the 1980s, the state shifted its policies from those emphasizing equitable distribution to those emphasizing increased production—under pressure partly from pragmatic socialists and partly from the IMF. As part of the new emphasis, individualization of state property was accepted for two reasons: (1) The state did not have the power or will to stop it, and (2) the state saw in individualization the possibility of increased production—and consequently of increased state revenues. Those policies directly aimed at group equality seemed to pass through a similar cycle, shifting from demands for more vigorous to less vigorous action. Despite the shift of priorities from equality to production, the party maintained its commitment to socialism—but the path was different from that of the 1960s and 1970s. The task of challenging the proverb *Aliye juu ni juu*—He who is above is above—had proven more difficult than expected. Chapter 6 considers the experiences of the most important rural institution in the struggle to build a socialist society, i.e., the cooperatives.

Notes

1. Anthony Wright, *Socialisms, Theories and Practices* (Oxford: Oxford University Press, 1986), p. 33.
2. Julius Nyerere, "Introduction," in Nyerere, *Freedom and Socialism* (Dar es Salaam: Oxford University Press, 1968), p. 30.
3. Nyerere, "Socialism Is Not Racialism," in Nyerere, *Freedom and Socialism*, p. 258.
4. Nyerere, "The Varied Paths to Socialism," in Nyerere, *Freedom and Socialism*, p. 303.
5. Nyerere, "The Purpose Is Man," in Nyerere, *Freedom and Socialism*, p. 324.
6. The TANU Constitution was the First Schedule of the Interim Constitution of Tanzania and can be found in William Tordoff, *Government and Politics in*

Tanzania (Nairobi: East African Publishing House, 1967), pp. 236–251. Its preamble, the first part of the Arusha Declaration, was known as the TANU Creed. See Julius Nyerere, "The Arusha Declaration," in Nyerere, *Freedom and Socialism*, pp. 231–232.

7. Nyerere, "The Arusha Declaration," pp. 324–325.

8. Nyerere, "The Varied Paths to Socialism," p. 303.

9. Julius Nyerere, "Education for Self-Reliance," in Nyerere, *Freedom and Socialism*, p. 272.

10. Nyerere, "The Varied Paths to Socialism" and "The Purpose is Man," pp. 303–304 and 324, respectively.

11. Julius Nyerere, *The Arusha Declaration, Ten Years After* (Dar es Salaam: Government Printer, 1977), p. 16.

12. Richard Stren, "Urban Policy," in Joel Barkan, ed., *Politics and Public Policy in Kenya and Tanzania*, revised edition (New York: Praeger, 1984), p. 252.

13. Joel Barkan, "Comparing Politics and Public Policy in Kenya and Tanzania," in Barkan, ed., *Politics and Public Policy*, p. 22. Nyerere in *The Arusha Declaration, Ten Years After* gave the ratio as 29:1.

14. *Daily News* (Dar es Salaam), 25 July 1987, p. 3. Enos S. Bukuku contends that the officially known income ratios before taxes went from 22.5:1 in 1974 to 10.5:1 in 1981 and after taxes from 15.6:1 in 1974 to 6.6:1 in 1981. See Bukuku, "Twenty Years of the Arusha Declaration: Issues of Equity and Income Distribution," a paper presented at the International Conference on the Arusha Declaration, Arusha, December 1986, p. 10.

15. Theodore Valentine, "Wage Adjustments, Progressive Tax Rates, and Accelerated Inflation: Issues of Equity in the Wage Sector of Tanzania," *The African Studies Review*, Vol. 26, No. 1 (March 1983), p. 63; International Labour Organisation, *Basic Needs in Danger: A Basic Needs Oriented Development Strategy for Tanzania* (Addis Ababa: Jobs and Skills Programme for Africa, ILO, 1982), p. 270.

16. Valentine, "Wage Adjustments," p. 61. Enos Bukuku suggests that "top salary earners have had real declines in their *officially known incomes* but they have been able to make up for these declines via a number of fringe benefits (which are untaxed)." See Bukuku, "Twenty Years of the Arusha Declaration," p. 11.

17. David Leonard, "Class Formation and Agricultural Development," in Barkan, ed., *Politics and Public Policy*, p. 163.

18. International Labour Organisation, *Basic Needs in Danger*, p. 258.

19. The cost of living index hides considerable variation in the changes of prices of different items. For example, in 1990 Malima told the National Assembly that for most mainland towns the index rose about 28.3 percent in 1988 and 23.8 percent in 1989. See *Daily News,* 8 June 1990, p. 1. Early in 1989, though, the governor of the Bank of Tanzania said that between September 1987 and September 1988, food prices increased by 42 percent, drinks by 27 percent, clothing by 40 percent, household goods by 25 percent, and recreation and entertainment by 57 percent. See *Daily News,* 30 January 1989, p. 1.

20. *Daily News,* 2 July 1987, p. 1.

21. For the number of employees, see United Republic of Tanzania, Ministry of Finance, Planning and Economic Affairs, Bureau of Statistics, *Statistical Abstract, 1984* (Dar es Salaam: Bureau of Statistics, February 1986), p. 51 (for 1969–1979); International Labour Organisation, *Distributional Aspects of Stabilisation Programmes in the United Republic of Tanzania, 1979–84* (Geneva: International Labour Organisation, 1988), p. 31 (for 1984). For the population, see World Bank, *World Tables, 1991* (Baltimore: Johns Hopkins University Press for World Bank, 1991), pp. 564–565 (for 1969, 1974, 1979, and 1984). The 1989

census found that there were only about 700,000 wage and salary regular employees out of a population of 23.1 million. A March 1988 census of government employees found there were 308,507 such employees. See *Sunday News,* 27 October 1991, p. 3.

22. T.L. Maliyamkono and M.S.D. Bagachwa, *The Second Economy in Tanzania* (London: James Currey, 1990), p. 147.

23. United Republic of Tanzania, Ministry of Agriculture and Livestock Development, Marketing Development Bureau, *Price Policy Recommendations for the 1985 Agricultural Price Review, Summary* (Dar es Salaam: Marketing Development Bureau, 1985), pp. 23, 41, and 42.

24. Leonard, "Class Formation," p. 163.

25. Barkan, "Comparing Politics and Public Policy," p. 26. Nevertheless, Barkan contends, in the early 1980s, because the salaries of civil servants and politicians were among the lowest in Africa, the country had achieved "symbolic equality"; i.e., the public did not see such employees as profiting at their expense. See Barkan, "Comparing Politics and Public Policy," p. 24.

26. International Labour Organisation, *Basic Needs in Danger,* p. 258.

27. International Labour Organisation, *Distributional Aspects,* p. 19.

28. Exemplifying the process of decontrol was the elimination in the 1987/88 budget of government-set prices on detergent powder, cotton yarn, blankets, decorative paints, plastic containers, salt, louvre frames, radio sets and radio recorders, cooking oil, and matchboxes. See *Daily News,* 19 June 1987, p. 1. Numerous violations of government-set prices were reported in the local press. See, for example, *Daily News,* 15 March 1988, p. 1; 9 January 1990, p. 3; 5 June 1990, p. 1; and 2 April 1991, p. 1.

29. Amon Chaligha, "Taxation and the Transition to Socialism in Tanzania," Ph.D. dissertation, Claremont Graduate School, Claremont, Calif., 1990.

30. *Daily News,* 31 July 1987, p. 3.

31. *Daily News,* 20 June 1990, p. 1.

32. Chaligha, "Taxation and the Transition to Socialism," p. 163.

33. Ibid., p. 168.

34. Ibid., pp. 177–178.

35. Ibid., pp. 180–181.

36. For example, in June 1990, Kigoma District Council raised the development levy from TSh. 300 per person to TSh. 400. See *Daily News,* 19 May 1990, p. 3. The Manyoni District Council raised its rate from TSh. 450 per person to TSh. 500 for the same year. See *Sunday News,* 7 January 1990, p. 1.

37. In 1988 in Dar es Salaam the development levy was graduated, ranging from TSh. 150 for those earning a minimum wage of TSh. 2,000 per month to TSh. 1,000 for those earning over TSh. 11,001 per month. See *Daily News,* 13 February 1988, p. 3. In 1989 the levy was TSh. 350 in Iringa Municipality. See *Daily News,* 20 June 1989, p. 3. Tanga introduced a graduated system in 1990, changing from a flat rate of TSh. 300 to one ranging between TSh. 300 and TSh. 2,000. See *Daily News,* 5 March 1990, p. 5.

38. In 1988, it was estimated that of the 450,000 people in Dar es Salaam from whom officials expected to collect the development levy, only 0.67 to 0.78 percent would be exempted. See *Daily News,* 13 February 1988, p. 3.

39. For example, see *Daily News,* 21 December 1987, p. 3; 31 July 1989, p. 5; 2 July 1987, p. 3; and *Sunday News,* 24 September 1989, p. 1.

40. *Daily News,* 16 April 1988, p. 3.

41. *Daily News,* 24 June 1989, p. 3.

42. *Daily News,* 17 July 1987, p. 1.

43. *Daily News,* 20 December 1990, p. 1.
44. Dean McHenry Jr., *Tanzania's Ujamaa Villages, The Implementation of a Rural Development Strategy* (Berkeley: Institute of International Studies, University of California, 1979), pp. 31–32.
45. United Republic of Tanzania, *Statistical Abstract, 1984,* pp. 220–221.
46. *Daily News,* 30 October 1980, p. 1, and 2 July 1980, p. 1.
47. *Daily News,* 2 July 1980, p. 1.
48. *Daily News,* 31 October 1988, p. 3.
49. For example, *Daily News,* 21 October 1987, p. 1.
50. *Daily News,* 5 July 1989, p. 3.
51. *Daily News,* 20 July 1989, p. 3.
52. *Daily News,* 7 July 1990, p. 1. Dr. Hubert Kairuki, president of the Association of Gynaecologists and Obstetricians of Tanzania, estimated in 1991 that whereas there were about 850 doctors in Tanzania, about 200 had left for "greener pastures." Given that only about 34 doctors were graduated each year, though President Mwinyi may have overstated the problem, the number is significant. See *Daily News,* 9 October 1991, p. 4.
53. *Daily News,* 9 May 1990, p. 1.
54. *Daily News,* 27 April 1991, p. 1.
55. *Daily News,* 19 May 1990, p. 3, and 9 June 1990, p. 3.
56. Nyerere, "Education for Self-Reliance," pp. 267–290.
57. *Daily News,* 15 September 1988, p. 4.
58. *Daily News,* 9 April 1991, p. 4. The lack of precision in Tanzania's statistical data on enrollment and public expenditure in education is explored by Joel Samoff in "The Facade of Precision in Education Data and Statistics: A Troubling Example from Tanzania," *Journal of Modern African Studies,* Vol. 29, No. 4 (December 1991), pp. 669–689.
59. In early 1993 the United Nations International Children's Emergency Fund (UNICEF) reported that almost half the school-age children did not complete "standard seven" (the first seven years of schooling) or did not attend school at all, a drastic change from a decade earlier. See *Sunday News,* 14 February 1993, p. 1.
60. International Labour Organisation, *Basic Needs in Danger,* p. 118.
61. The figures for 1965 and 1986 are from *Daily News,* 9 August 1989, p. 3; that for 1988 is from *Daily News,* 15 September 1988, p. 4; that for 1990 is from *Daily News,* 9 July 1990, p. 3.
62. *Daily News,* 29 October 1988, p. 3.
63. *Daily News,* 21 June 1990, p. 3.
64. For example, the Mufindi Education Trust, established in 1984, had by 1988 constructed six secondary schools that had increased the percentage of primary school leavers going to secondary school from 1.6 to 13 percent; the regional commissioner in Singida in 1988 urged the Singida Region Cooperative Union (SIRECU) to seek ways to build a secondary school in town; and the district authorities in Mbinga launched an Education Development Trust Fund to raise money to build private secondary schools. See *Daily News,* 24 December 1988, p. 1; 8 March 1988, p. 3; and 9 May 1990, p. 5, respectively.
65. The total enrollment at the University of Dar es Salaam in 1980/81 was 2,678; in 1983/84 it was 3,110. See United Republic of Tanzania, *Statistical Abstract, 1984,* p. 214.
66. *Daily News,* 30 August 1980, p. 5. Julius Nyerere argued that in 1979/80 it cost 188 times as much for a student at the University of Dar es Salaam as for a pupil at a primary school. Joel Samoff presented data for 1982 suggesting that the ratio was 109.6:1. See Samoff, "The Facade of Precision," p. 239.

67. *Daily News,* 30 August 1980, p. 5.

68. Magnus Blomstrom and Bjorn Hettne, *Development Theory in Transition* (London: Zed Books, 1984), pp. 145–155; Yash Tandon, ed., *The Debate* (Dar es Salaam: Tanzania Publishing House, 1982); and Issa Shivji, "Tanzania: The Debate on Delinking," in Azzam Mahjoub, ed., *Adjustment or Delinking? The African Experience* (London: Zed Books, 1990), pp. 49–68.

69. Most student action has been in support of positions more often taken by ideological socialists than by pragmatic socialists. The response of the government has been self-righteous but often inegalitarian. For example, when President Mwinyi dismissed the university students in 1990 over their strike, he justified his actions on the grounds that students delayed returning to classes for two days after he advised them to return. The government newspaper reported the following: "Explaining that an 'advice' by a senior to a junior was actually a directive, the President said the breach of his instruction was an act of insubordination." See *Daily News,* 8 May 1990, p. 1.

70. *Daily News,* 22 July 1987, p. 1.

71. *Daily News,* 21 September 1988, p. 3.

72. *Daily News,* 13 February 1989, p. 3.

73. *Daily News,* 9 February 1989, p. 3.

74. *Daily News,* 28 June 1990, p. 1. The previous year Idris Wakil had given the same figure of 30 percent for the proportion of teachers who had not been trained for the profession. See *Sunday News,* 24 September 1989, p. 1.

75. *Daily News,* 11 January 1989, p. 3.

76. *Daily News,* 15 July 1987, p. 1.

77. *Daily News,* 2 September 1988, p. 3.

78. *Daily News,* 4 January 1989, p. 1.

79. *Daily News,* 15 July 1987, p. 3.

80. *Daily News,* 20 July 1987, p. 3.

81. Joel Samoff, "'Modernizing' a Socialist Vision: Education in Tanzania," in Martin Carnoy and Joel Samoff, eds., *Education and Social Transition in the Third World* (Princeton, N.J.: Princeton University Press, 1990), pp. 241–242. This study by Samoff contains a fairly extensive review of Tanzania's experience with education.

82. Private secondary school fees were set by the government at rates considerably higher than those at government secondary schools. At the end of 1987, the fees were raised from TSh. 3,200 to TSh. 5,500 for day students and to "only" TSh. 8,400 for boarders in forms 1 through 4. See *Daily News,* 31 December 1987, p. 3. As of January 1, 1990, they were raised for private day students in forms 1 through 4 to TSh. 8,000 and in forms 5 and 6 to TSh. 8,500; they were raised for private boarders in forms 1 through 4 to TSh. 11,000 and in forms 5 and 6 TSh. 11,500. The rise in fees for government day secondary schools was to TSh. 2,500 and for boarding secondary schools TSh. 4,000—i.e., to between 30 and 36 percent of the private school rates. See *Daily News,* 6 December 1989, p. 1.

83. *Daily News,* 24 January 1990, p. 1.

84. *Daily News,* 19 October 1990, p. 1.

85. *Daily News,* 15 November 1988, p. 4.

86. *Daily News,* 15 September 1988, p. 4.

87. *Daily News,* 21 January 1988, p. 3. The proportion of the rural population within 400 meters of water remained at 42 percent into 1993. See *Daily News,* 27 February 1993, p. 13.

88. *Daily News,* 23 July 1987, p. 1.

89. *Daily News,* 27 October 1988, p. 3.

90. *Daily News,* 21 December 1988, p. 3.

91. *Daily News,* 2 February 1990, p. 3.
92. *Daily News,* 19 February 1990, p. 1.
93. *Daily News,* 8 March 1988, p. 1.
94. Ibid.
95. *Daily News,* 16 May 1989, p. 3.
96. The Swedish International Development Authority in 1993 indicated that 70 percent of all rural water supply projects and a major part of urban projects were funded by external donors. See *Daily News,* 27 February 1993, p. 13.
97. According to W.B. Kapinga of the University of Dar es Salaam law faculty, "By 1984 nearly 70 percent of the entire urban population of Tanzania was living in squatter dwellings." See *Daily News,* 26 September 1987, p. 1.
98. *Daily News,* 16 May 1989, p. 1.
99. *Daily News,* 17 May 1989, p. 1. Richard Stren identifies the source of this "oft-heard saying" as a writer for the *Nationalist* in 1970. See Stren, "Urban Policy," p. 244.
100. *Daily News,* 16 May 1989, p. 1, and 25 January 1990, p. 1. By January 1990 the NHC had a debt of TSh. 266,486,673 to the Tanzania Housing Bank.
101. *Daily News,* 20 November 1987, p. 3.
102. Stren, "Urban Policy," p. 251. Nevertheless, in the ten-year period between 1973 and June 1984, the loans contributed to the construction of 30,450 individual units and 3,427 cooperative and village units. See *Daily News,* 20 November 1987, p. 3.
103. Stren, "Urban Policy," pp. 250–251.
104. Ibid., p. 251.
105. *Daily News,* 25 January 1990, p. 1. At the end of 1987, 2,253 buildings were under the ROB's control. In addition, it had built 727 housing units. See *Daily News,* 17 December 1987, p. 3.
106. Government agencies were among the beneficiaries of the nationalization of buildings. By December 1986 the ROB was owed TSh. 123,083,734, mostly by the ministries of Health and Social Welfare, Communications and Works, and Labour and Manpower Development and by the Muhimbili Medical Centre and Tanzania Tourist Corporation. See *Daily News,* 17 December 1987, p. 3.
107. *Daily News,* 29 March 1988, p. 3.
108. For example, in response to the proposed increase of about 2,000 percent in Morogoro in 1977, the tribunal allowed increases from TSh. 350 to TSh. 1,000—i.e., of about 300 percent—provided that all the money was used for repairs (which had not been made at some buildings for twenty years). See *Daily News,* 26 September 1987, p. 3. And an effort to increase rents on Ubungo housing from TSh. 45 per month to TSh. 1,990 and from TSh. 120 to TSh. 7,190 per month in 1988 was suspended by the minister for local government and reset at TSh. 200 instead of TSh. 45 and at TSh. 600 instead of TSh. 125. See *Daily News,* 2 September 1988, p. 3.
109. In 1992 several public institutions, including the National Housing Corporation and the Tanzania Housing Bank, were exempted from provisions of the Rent Restriction Act of 1984 "so that they can charge economic rates without prior approval of the Housing Tribunal." See *Daily News,* 14 March 1992, p. 1. Given the privileged position of most of those occupying public housing, the exemption may do more to promote than to undermine equality.
110. *Daily News,* 3 February 1990, p. 1.
111. *Sunday News,* 12 March 1989, p. 1.
112. *Daily News,* 24 July 1987, p. 1.
113. In late 1987, Gertrude Mongela said that only 517 of the more than 8,000 villages had been surveyed, a step necessary before land title could be conferred on

the village. See *Daily News,* 16 November 1987, p. 3. The Shivji commission on the land issue claimed that by June 1990, the number of villages surveyed had increased only to 1,123. Furthermore, it asserted that each survey took one to two years and cost at the time TSh. 300,000 per village to prepare, making the system of land tenure unworkable. See *Daily News,* 3 March 1993, p. 5. At the same time, the right to land in villages was being challenged by those who had lost it during the "villagization" process. For example, in 1991 ninety people at Kambi ya Simba village in Mbulu District were served with notices to hand over their farms to individuals who had had the land before villagization. See *Daily News,* 1 July 1991, p. 1. The following year the prime minister, John Malecela, spoke against the acquisition of village land by individuals, and the High Court in Arusha told regional magistrates and judges to stop court proceedings involving land acquired by villages under the villagization program. See *Daily News,* 2 October 1992, p. 1.

114. *Daily News,* 21 July 1989, p. 4. A similar recommendation came from the Shivji commission on the land issue, which reported in late 1992, calling for a new land tenure system in the villages. See *Daily News,* 3 March 1993, p. 5.

115. *Daily News,* 10 October 1993, p. 3; and 9 November 1993, p. 1. In November 1993 a High Court judge ruled in favor of two individuals who sought the return of land they claimed under customary tenure, effectively repealing the 1992 act. The government appealed the decision.

116. *Daily News,* 27 July 1989, p. 3; 19 December 1989, p. 3; and *Sunday News,* 1 April 1990, p. 1.

117. *Daily News,* 10 November 1989, p. 1.

118. Ibid.

119. *Daily News,* 22 November 1989, p. 1.

120. Ibid.

121. *Daily News,* 2 November 1987, p. 3.

122. *Daily News,* 14 January 1989, p. 1.

123. *Daily News,* 30 March 1990, p. 1.

124. *Daily News,* 29 December 1987, p. 1.

125. *Daily News,* 28 October 1988, p. 1.

126. *Daily News,* 3 November 1988, p. 1.

127. *Daily News,* 7 October 1989, p. 1.

128. Paul Collier, Samir Radwan, and Samuel Wangwe, *Labour and Poverty in Rural Tanzania* (Oxford: Clarendon Press, 1986), pp. 115–116.

129. Ibid., p. 117.

130. Ibid., p. 120.

131. McHenry, *Tanzania's Ujamaa Villages,* p. 168.

132. Nyerere, "The Arusha Declaration," p. 245.

133. Nyerere, "Socialism and Rural Development," p. 339.

134. See Nyerere, "The Arusha Declaration," p. 233.

135. See, for example, Ophelia Mascarenhas and Marjorie Mbilinyi, *Women in Tanzania, An Analytical Bibliography* (Uppsala: Scandinavian Institute of African Studies, 1983); Louise Fortmann, "Women's Work in a Communal Setting: The Tanzanian Policy of Ujamaa," in Edna Bay, ed., *Women and Work in Africa* (Boulder: Westview, 1982), p. 197; and Janet Bujra, "Taxing Development in Tanzania: Why Must Women Pay?" *Review of African Political Economy,* No. 47 (Spring 1990), p. 44.

136. Bujra, "Taxing Development," p. 51.

137. Fortmann, "Women's Work," p. 197; Bujra, "Taxing Development," p. 44.

6
Agricultural Cooperatives and Socialism

Wapiganapo tembo wawili ziumiazo ni nyasi.
"When two elephants fight, it is the grass that suffers."

The rural population was critical to socialist construction in Tanzania, as Julius Nyerere argued in his second post–Arusha Declaration paper, "Socialism and Rural Development," in late 1967:

> For the foreseeable future the vast majority of our people will continue to spend their lives in the rural areas and continue to work on the land. The land is the only basis for Tanzania's development; we have no other. Therefore, if our rural life is not based on the principles of socialism our country will not be socialist, regardless of how we organize our industrial sector, and regardless of our commercial and political arrangements.[1]

At the time of the Arusha Declaration, rural marketing cooperatives had been formed throughout most of the country. Although the cooperatives were technically nongovernmental organizations, political leaders had long viewed them as a means to achieve state objectives. They became a key to socialist development in the countryside and, consequently, the focus of intense political struggle. Indeed, the cooperative experience in Tanzania demonstrates more vividly than any other how the struggle between pragmatic and ideological socialists was self-defeating; i.e., it undermined efforts to achieve the socialist goals they held in common. In the imagery of the proverb that began this chapter, the struggle over the control and use of cooperatives trampled not only the peasants but also the cause of socialism.

Cooperatives and Socialism

Cooperative principles are very similar to the principles defining Tanzanian socialism. They include mutual self-help, democratic decisionmaking, equitable distribution of profits, voluntarism, and the pursuit of social welfare.[2] It is this congruence that was emphasized in the Arusha Declaration. Its authors wrote, "To build and maintain socialism it is essential that all the major means of production and exchange in the nation are controlled and owned by the peasants through the machinery of their Government and their cooperatives."[3] They implied that cooperative and government control and ownership of the major means of production and exchange were equally conducive to socialist construction. This congruence was challenged by Nyerere within a year. In an often-quoted passage from "Socialism and Rural Development," he wrote,

> Although marketing co-operatives are socialist in the sense that they represent the joint activities of producers, they could be socialist institutions serving capitalism. . . . For a farmers' co-operative marketing society is an institution serving the farmers; if they are capitalist farmers, then the existence of a cooperative marketing society will mean that one group of capitalists—the farmers—are safeguarding their own interests, as against another group of capitalists—the middlemen. It is only if the agricultural production itself is organized on a socialist pattern that co-operative marketing societies are serving socialism.[4]

The differences in the perception of the relationship between cooperatives and a socialist society found in the Arusha Declaration and in "Socialism and Rural Development" are a result of the differences in the attention the two documents give to scope. It is ignored in the former and stressed in the latter. Nyerere recognized that, even though the goals of cooperatives and of socialism may be similar, the difference in the scope of their application has the potential of making the building of cooperatives an obstacle to the building of socialism. This is an instance of what has been called the units of action problem.

For the function of marketing the crops of members, cooperatives embody the principles of Tanzanian socialism. But there are many other functions and groups in society. What socialist construction involves is extending collective action to other tasks and to the society as a whole. Viewed from the perspective of the society as a whole, cooperatives may serve either to obstruct or to facilitate socialist construction.

The Struggle for Control and Use of Cooperatives

The importance of cooperatives in rural areas led to their involvement in political conflict long before the Arusha Declaration. In the immediate postindependence period there was a great expansion of the cooperative movement, widely attributed to two political objectives.

The first objective was strategic; i.e., it was an effort to undercut the power of those engaged in trade. Goran Hyden observes that "the motivation . . . was primarily political: to cut out the middlemen, particularly the Asian traders."[5] Issa Shivji explains the expansion as part of a class struggle between the petty bourgeoisie, mostly African, and the commercial bourgeoisie, mostly Asian. The government, he argues, sided with the petty bourgeoisie because it was the principal agent of its bureaucratic sector. The government couched the struggle in nationalist terms, he contends, to cloud the fact that it was aimed less at increasing peasant well-being than at weakening the commercial bourgeoisie.[6] Jeannette Hartmann blames the politicians rather than the government. She contends that government officials had frequently warned of the consequences of overexpansion of cooperatives without regard to "economic considerations."[7] Yet, she argues, the party acted because of its concern for redistribution and control of the economy "irrespective of their economic consequences."[8] The Special Committee of Enquiry into the Cooperative Movement and Marketing Boards, appointed to examine the causes of the faltering cooperative movement in 1966, argues that the expansion was due to a political decision made at independence in order to promote "control of the economy by the indigenous people rather than by expatriates and others non-African in origin."[9]

The second objective was personal; i.e., it was an effort to provide a source of resources for politicians. The Special Committee of Enquiry cites examples of political leaders "commandeering" tractors paid for by cooperative unions for what it identified as noncooperative schemes without compensation.[10] Shivji suggests that the private benefit some politicians received through the expansion of cooperatives was merely an outcome of the class struggle: The commercial bourgeoisie lacked political weapons, so "it resorted to economic sabotage, corruption and bribery."[11] So extensive was such corruption, he contends, that "the cooperative movement was a 'failure' for the petty bourgeoisie as a whole."[12] Cranford Pratt argues that party-government efforts to control cooperatives, whether motivated by the desire to end corruption or by the possible "threat" autonomous institutions posed to socialist construction, led to a curtailment of peasant participation and a consequent loss of much of the cooperatives' popular legitimacy.[13] I.R.E.M. Msanga goes even further, noting that by 1967/68 "the cooperative movement was wholly under the hands of the politicians" and that cooperatives belonged "more or less in the category of public enterprises rather than private."[14] The Arusha Declaration marked the beginning of a new struggle for the control and use of cooperatives, that between the ideological and pragmatic socialists. The fundamental, though by no means the only, explanation for the post-Arusha experiences of cooperatives lies in this political struggle.

Transition from Cooperatives to Villages, 1967–1975

In the Arusha Declaration the role of cooperatives in socialist construction was mentioned in only three sentences. First, as part of the TANU Creed, incorporated into the declaration, TANU committed itself "to see that the

Government actively assists in the formation and maintenance of cooperative organizations."[15] Second, under Part Two, titled "The Policy of Socialism," cooperatives are identified as a potential owner and controller of the major means of production and exchange, in a sentence previously quoted. Third, the party's National Executive Committee called upon cooperatives "to take steps to implement the policy of socialism and self-reliance."[16] As has been noted, "Socialism and Rural Development" was published several months after the Arusha Declaration, detailing the president's and the party's perception of the role of cooperatives. Nyerere's document argued that to make cooperative marketing societies serve socialism rather than capitalism, it was necessary to create ujamaa villages, villages in which people lived and worked together for the good of all. It declared that "the basis of rural life in Tanzania must be the practice of cooperation in its widest sense—in living, in working, and in distribution."[17] Two years later, the Second Five-Year Plan, July 1969–June 1974, spelled out in more detail what political leaders expected of cooperatives in achieving their transition to socialism:

> The movement of the Co-operative Movement toward Ujamaa will be achieved in two directions—
> (i) through the formation of production based multipurpose societies *de novo,* or from Ujamaa Villages or agricultural associations; and/or
> (ii) by orientating marketing based societies towards additional activities more directly affecting production (including the establishment of farming units).

It concluded:

> In summary, the Second Five-Year Plan will represent a transitional period during which the traditional marketing functions of the co-operatives will be made more efficient, for the benefit of the farmer, while new growth will be shifted sharply in the direction of production and multi-purpose primary societies.[18]

The purpose of these documents was to involve existing cooperatives in the creation of a new form of cooperative, the ujamaa village. In a sense, 1967 marked the transition from the struggle between private trader-capitalists and the politician-socialists to the struggle between the ideological and pragmatic socialists. Although the formal intention may have been the transformation of the cooperative movement, that became tantamount to its abolition.

In the post-Arusha period the government, at the behest of the party, intervened in two ways: First, it sought to "cleanse" the cooperatives of antisocialist personnel, i.e., to rid them of the domination of petty capitalist farmers, widely referred to in the literature as kulaks. The kulaks were accused by party and government officials of having hijacked the cooperatives for their own benefit, of using the cooperatives to exploit the peasantry, of engaging in dishonesty and corruption. Numerous cooperative officials were removed; unions were reorganized on a regional basis; government officials were placed into positions of authority within cooperatives; and audits and prosecutions were instituted to control cooperative personnel. Hyden has argued that the consequence of such actions at the union level was only "the replacement of one petty-bourgeois group by another"—that is, "the trader and kulak farmers who had their own local power base have been replaced by representatives of what Shivji prefers to call the 'bureaucratic bourgeoisie.'"[19] At any rate, the actions of the government did not lead to a high level of performance of the cooperatives and estranged some of the most productive sections of the peasantry.

Second, the government sought to change the structure of cooperatives to promote socialist interests. This change ranged from promoting multi-functionality to transforming the cooperatives into ujamaa villages. The promotion of multifunctionality involved getting existing cooperatives to engage in activities that would "socialize" more aspects of their daily lives.[20] Hyden put it somewhat differently: "Multifunctionality ideally tends to reduce exploitation as it limits the opportunities for private traders and such groups to dominate various fields of economic activity."[21]

The ujamaa village was seen as the ultimate in multifunctionality.[22] The party and government soon made it clear that ujamaa villages would replace cooperatives, that is, that all primary cooperatives would have to convert themselves into ujamaa villages.[23] In 1971 Derek Bryceson, who was then the minister of agriculture, food and cooperatives, in an often-quoted statement argued that ujamaa villages would become the sole cooperatives and that with the weakening of the old primary societies, unions would face the fate of other middlemen and die.[24] Initially, the Cooperative Union of Tanganyika (CUT), the apex organization, disputed the assertion and fought the prediction. But when Nyerere himself told CUT members in a general meeting that the old primary societies would die, though the fate of the unions was undecided, the full transformation of the movement seemed inevitable.[25] John Saul contended that there were opponents of the efforts to transform cooperatives into ujamaa villages who argued that the "cooperative structure represents the wrong kind of ideology and the cooperators (both petty bourgeois bureaucrats and 'progressive' farmers) the wrong kind of interests to be trusted"[26]—in other words, that such a transformation would not undermine kulak dominance.

Nevertheless, the party and government put strong pressures on the movement in the early 1970s to provide financial and material support to the new villages.[27] Indeed, substantial wealth was taken from the troubled movement to promote ujamaa villages. Prime Minister Kawawa declared in mid-1972 that "the major task facing cooperative unions is to preach socialism and help Ujamaa villages in their development programmes."[28] Hundreds of thousands of shillings were provided by the CUT, the Dodoma Cooperative Union, the Arusha Cooperative Union (ARCU), the Nyanza Cooperative Union, the Iringa Farmers Cooperative Union, and other cooperative bodies.[29] In an insightful study, Ngila R.L. Mwase noted that ARCU was "deeply involved in helping the sixty-four ujamaa villages in the region." He observed that there were opponents, but the opponents dared not speak for fear of government and/or party sanctions. He quoted the regional chairman of TANU at the general meeting of ARCU leaders in 1972 as saying, "It's not a question of the union *helping* the ujamaa villages, it's their duty." The help in the 1972/73 season included TSh. 30,000 for educational purposes, TSh. 7,200 for safes, and TSh. 200,000 for tractors. In addition, fertilizers, weighing equipment, education, advice, and many other types of help were given. There was dissatisfaction with ARCU's assistance by some, according to Mwase, who felt poor individual farmers should not fund people who might be rich or lazy simply because they claim to live in an ujamaa village.[30] In summary, the cooperative movement was bled to support its replacement.

In summarizing his views of what was causing problems for cooperatives during this period, Hyden wrote:

> These institutions, and particularly the unions, have been arenas on which a struggle for control over the peasants has been waged between different factions of the emerging bourgeoisie, one locally-based, the other based in TANU and the government. The outcome of this struggle has not yet produced any significant material benefits for the peasants but has left the cooperative institutions in an even weaker operating position than before.[31]

According to one observer, by the mid-1970s the party and government had simply "lost patience" with the resistance of the old cooperatives to engaging in production or involving themselves in other functions beyond that of marketing.[32]

The Closure of Cooperatives, 1975–1982

In 1975 the Villages and Ujamaa Villages Act was passed, banning the existing primary cooperative societies from operating within the jurisdiction of the new villages. Although some rural primary societies continued to function for a while, within a year they had been closed and their assets and liabilities distributed among other entities. In 1976 the existing cooperative unions were abolished and their assets and liabilities similarly distributed.[33] The actions were political, not economic.

A wide range of explanations and rationalizations was given for the abolition.[34] One argument was that primary cooperatives had not been abolished, only transformed into institutions that permitted a higher level of cooperation. As has been seen, such transformation had been sought by the party and government almost since the Arusha Declaration. The Villages and Ujamaa Villages Act declared that "a village and its various organs shall perform their functions as if the village were a multipurpose cooperative society."[35] In a sense, the former cooperatives had been made redundant by new ones.[36] Yet it should be noted that although the act introduced a distinction between villages and ujamaa villages based on the extent of cooperation practiced within them, no village ever reached the higher level of cooperation allowing it to be registered as an ujamaa village. Indeed, observers dispute the claim that the villages had much real cooperative content. Elizabeth Minde, following her research, concluded that

> cooperatives as such are difficult to trace in the villages. There is no cooperative content in the marketing arrangements, signs of producing together so far leave much to be desired. Management of the affairs in the villages still retains the producer in a desperate position in that he does not have much to say. The net result therefore is to confuse the whole question of co-operatives.[37]

Furthermore, the experiences of the villages with collective production were quite bad generally, as noted in Chapter 5.[38]

A second argument, related to the first, was that abolition of the cooperatives moved the country toward a higher form of socialism. An important part of this argument was that parastatal crop authorities would buy crops directly from the villages. Such state instruments were viewed as more socialist than cooperatives. The unions, which Bryceson had designated as middlemen, were eliminated. The minister of state in the prime minister's office, P. Kimiti, when he introduced the Cooperative Societies Act of 1982, argued that the abolition of cooperatives was required in order to put power "securely in the hands of public corporations such as crop authorities in order to advance the economy."[39] If the crop authorities were indeed a higher form of socialism, the unhappy experiences with them during this period may account for the weakening of the ideological socialists that led to the reintroduction of rural cooperatives in 1982.

A third argument was that cooperatives were abolished to promote democratization. A document from the prime minister's office stated, "The old principle of cooperatives serving and benefiting only a few is no longer compatible with the nature of development of the country."[40] There are two aspects to this assertion. On the one hand, all villagers technically had a voice in the village government, whereas only members had a voice in the old cooperative. In that sense, there was democratization. At the same time, voluntary membership was ended and power was taken away from producers. On the other hand, the crop levy formerly paid to the cooperative societies now went to the village. Indeed, this became the principal source of income for the villages. Theoretically, more people benefited from crop marketing under the new arrangement, interpreted by some as a kind of democratization. Ironically, the villagers were not given a choice of whether they wanted this form of democratization.

Behind each of these explanations one can perceive groups that might gain and others that might lose; i.e., the decisions were not politically neutral. Those who held state power used such decisions to weaken political rivals. Hyden contends that, in addition to some of the factors cited above,

> There is little doubt . . . that the closure of all co-operatives was also determined by the fact that the bureaucratic bourgeoisie were unable effectively to control the co-operative organizations. The leadership of the co-operative movement often had divergent views from party and government officials on matters relating to rural development. By virtue of their positions as leaders of organizations with a local power base, they could argue effectively with party and government leaders. Moreover, they could mitigate the pressures on the peasants by the party.[41]

The abolition of the cooperatives was more in accord with the views of ideological socialists than of pragmatic socialists and reflected their dominance within the party at the time. Within a few years, though, the economic consequences forced a political reassessment.

The Reestablishment of Cooperatives, 1982–1985

The new marketing structures proved to be a disaster. The crop authorities borrowed billions of shillings they were unable to return to the banking system.[42] Still, peasants often went unpaid or payment to them was delayed. And the prices set by the government for crops declined steadily relative to their prices on the international market.[43] As a result, crops that were sold went increasingly to a revived petty trading class operating illegally. Production of both cash and food crops declined seriously. Pragmatic socialists began calling for a return of cooperatives, a call the ideological socialists could do little to resist. Indeed, neither ideological nor pragmatic socialists appeared to benefit from the existing system—ironically, only the private traders did. Thus, there was little dissent when the government appointed a twenty-two-member commission in 1980 headed by a former secretary general of the CUT to look into the question of reestablishing cooperatives;[44] when in 1981, on the commission's recommendation, the government committed itself to reestablishing them; and when in 1982 a new Cooperative Societies Act was passed ushering in a return of rural cooperatives.[45]

The party and government sought to frame the act to limit the likelihood that a cooperative movement identical to that which had existed prior to its abolition in 1975/76 would arise. The shift is evident in its statement of objectives. In contrast to the Cooperative Societies Act of 1968, which described the objectives as simply "the promotion of the economic interests of its members in accordance with co-operative principles," the act of 1982 stated that the cooperative movement

> shall . . . strive in accordance with its democratic, socialist and co-operative outlook—
> (a) to accelerate the building of socialism by bringing about socialist development both in rural and urban areas;
> (b) to foster the development of co-operative farming in rural areas as a means of modernizing and developing agriculture and of eliminating exploitation in the rural areas;
> (c) to satisfy the cultural needs of its members, as well as to increase their social and political awareness;
> (d) to improve the material living conditions of its members;
> (e) to promote co-operative education among its members.[46]

Three clauses in the act later became the focus of considerable political struggle. The act specified that every cooperative society should be multipurpose; that each should be economically viable; and that societies should form unions and unions should form an apex organization. As the government began to implement the act and establish cooperatives, the ideological socialists became alarmed and, once again, intense political struggle ensued. This time the conflict followed institutional lines more precisely. Pragmatic socialists, principally in the government, were pitted against ideological socialists, principally in the party.

Political Struggle over the Apex Organization

The Cooperative Societies Act of 1982 said the cooperative apex organization was to be controlled by cooperative unions. Yet the party, acting in accord with the ideological socialists, successfully opposed the implementation of the relevant clause. The reason is clear: Power would be lost by the party. Following the abolition of rural primary societies and the unions in 1975/76, the tertiary organization, the CUT, was retained. Urban cooperatives, which were not abolished at the time, and villages were linked to it. When TANU and the Afro-Shirazi Party merged in 1977, the apex organization was designated a mass organization under CCM. To effect the reorganization, the Jumuiya ya Muungano wa Vyama vya Ushirika (Establishment) Act of 1979 was passed. The legislation applied to both mainland Tanzania and Zanzibar. The apex organization given legal status was called WASHIRIKA.[47] It was a party organization. According to the CCM Constitution, its performance was subject to the supervision and direction of the Central Committee of the National Executive Committee.[48]

The secretary general of WASHIRIKA was appointed by the National Executive Committee.[49] The first two qualifications for leadership in WASHIRIKA state:

> (1) Leaders of the cooperative union must be members of CCM at the national level.
> (2) Leaders at all levels in Washirika before taking office shall be confirmed by the Party to make certain they fulfill the conditions and possess qualifications for leadership.[50]

Furthermore, according to WASHIRIKA's own rules, its first "duty" was

> preparing peasants and other cooperative members mentally and ideologically in all matters related to the policy of Socialism and Self-reliance for the purpose of understanding Party policy and to participate fully in building a Socialist state.[51]

As Elizabeth Minde has noted, "Because of the supremacy of the party, the organization always dances to the tune of the Party."[52] The Cooperative Societies Act of 1982 formally repealed the 1979 act that gave legality to WASHIRIKA. Yet WASHIRIKA continued to function as though it were the apex organization despite its legal abolition and its failure to be registered as a cooperative by the registrar. The struggle over WASHIRIKA was temporarily resolved by legislation in 1990 making it the apex organization.[53] But, as we shall see, this did not end the struggle.

Political Struggle over Multivillage Cooperatives

The second dispute involved the relationship between the new cooperatives and villages. The Cooperative Societies Act of 1982 stressed the primacy of the principle of economic viability. Section 15 stated, "A primary society may be formed for two or more villages and where it is economically viable, it may be formed for one village."[54] As a consequence, most cooperatives were formed to include more than one village, as shown in Table 6.1.

The average number of villages per cooperative in the country at the end of 1985 was 3.6.[55] Yet party interests were adversely affected by multivillage cooperatives. Village chairmen were also CCM branch chairmen. The removal of an important village enterprise, crop collection; the loss of the most important source of village income, the crop levy; and the removal of the cooperative from the jurisdiction of any single village significantly reduced the power of the party branch chairman. In addition, the ideological socialists still had faith that the villages were critical rural institutions for the transition to their vision of socialism.

At the apex level the party sought to retain control, whereas at the primary level the party sought to reassert it. Meanwhile, at least some

Table 6.1 Number of New Cooperatives, Number of Villages Included in Cooperatives, and Average Number of Villages per Cooperative, by Year Formed

Year	Number of New Cooperatives	Number of Villages in Cooperatives	Average Villages per Cooperative
1983	990	3,745	3.8
1984	896	3,002	3.4
1985	58	245	4.2
Total	1,944	6,992	3.6

Source: Calculated from figures supplied by the Ministry of Local Government and Cooperative Development, Dodoma, December 1986.

sections of the government were busily establishing multivillage cooperatives and seeking an apex organization controlled by cooperators. During the 1980s, the cooperatives were the scene of a more intense political struggle than in any prior period.

Reorganization of the Cooperatives, 1985–1990

By early 1985 most of the work of reestablishing cooperatives had been completed. Yet, ironically, that was the time when the party decided that cooperatives should be reorganized. The directive was issued in April 1985 requiring the establishment of a single production-oriented cooperative in every village.[56] Since only one cooperative could exist in a given area, that meant the dissolution or reorganization of many of the new cooperatives.

On the basis of figures for the end of 1985, i.e., the last figures before major efforts were undertaken to implement the directive, 83 percent of the cooperatives established since the act came into effect (i.e., 1,609 cooperatives) would have to be disbanded or re-formed; 95 percent of the villages involved in cooperatives (i.e., 6,657 villages) would have to form new ones; and those villages not within cooperatives at the end of 1985 (i.e., 1,000 to 1,500 villages) would have to form them as well. What was demanded was tearing down nearly all the cooperatives built since cooperatives were reintroduced in 1982 and creating approximately four times as many as there had been before.

The formal justification for the directive was simply that village-based producer cooperatives were the only way socialism might be built and people's lives improved.[57] Of course, the truth of this assertion depends on one's vision of socialism. To many pragmatic socialists, it would not be true. That is, to them village-based producer cooperatives were not requisites for their vision of a socialist society. In reality, the post-1982 resurrected cooperative movement was an effort of the pragmatic socialists, whereas the party directive was a counterattack by the ideological socialists. The cooperatives were clearly a political battlefield.

The party was wary of relying on cooperative officers to implement the directive alone. To keep such officers "honest," it called party cadres into action. All party members were ordered to join the producer-oriented cooperatives in their villages. And the policy contended that the effort to create producer-oriented cooperatives was really a part of the ongoing effort to strengthen the party—that is, it equated building the party with building the ideological socialists' vision of a socialist society.

Section 15 of the 1982 act, which stated that a single village might form a cooperative only if it were economically viable, was amended to state simply, "A primary society may be formed for one village."[58] Almost the only obstacle that might thwart the directive was resistance by cooperative officials responsible for cooperative guidance and registration. Yet the head of the Department of Ideology, Political Education and Training of the party's secretariat and the man principally responsible for the directive, Kingunge Ngombale-Mwiru, was also the minister for local government and cooperative development.[59] He was an important leader of the ideological socialists, as has previously been noted.

The registrar of cooperatives' Circular No. 4 of 1985 contained the first significant response to the party directive. It accepted the decision of the NEC as binding. Yet it argued that the dissolution of cooperatives had to be lawful; i.e., it had to take place in accord with Section 139 of the Cooperative Societies Act of 1982.[60] The section required a decision at a general meeting with not less than two-thirds "of the members or delegates" present, prior notice of the intent of the meeting, a proposal for the distribution of assets and liabilities, and a determination by the registrar that "the proposed division is not against the interests of the members of the existing society or against the public interest."[61] Compliance would not be impossible, though it might be slow.

Indeed, it did not proceed quickly. As a consequence, during 1986 Ngombale-Mwiru took two steps to speed it up. First, in September he decentralized responsibility for registering cooperatives from the registrar to the regional cooperative officers, making reregistration simpler. Second, in October he ordered all existing rural cooperatives that contained more than one village dissolved and replaced by village producer cooperatives by December 31 of that year.[62] As the date approached, good faith efforts were made by cooperative officials to comply. Yet they were often faced with conflicting pressures, as the case of Kilimanjaro Region illustrates.

District officers there complained about being pulled in four different directions: First, the NEC wanted one village, one cooperative; the regional cooperative officers' informal view was that it would be better to strengthen existing cooperatives; the union argued that the size of cooperatives was unimportant compared with the viability and profitability; and the permanent secretary contended that the principal need was to reduce the size to make them more manageable, implying that village-level cooperatives were not the only alternative.[63] Nevertheless, the district officers were forced to act in accord with the party directive as formally conveyed by the registrar.

The officers hurriedly arranged cooperative meetings to discuss dissolution and re-formation. Their initial efforts were not very successful. In Hai District, for example, nineteen cooperative meetings were arranged; fourteen were unsuccessful because of the absence of a quorum or party official or someone else required; three cooperatives would not split; two cooperatives decided to split into their four and three constituent villages.[64] Although the December 31 deadline was not met, it had its probable intended effect: Cooperative officers acted.

Yet cooperative officers acted with limited enthusiasm. At a workshop on cooperative development attended by top cooperative officials in April 1987, resolutions were passed calling for a return to registration of cooperative societies on the basis of economic viability and in opposition to their imposition on people.[65] When leaders of the cooperative movement met in late 1987, they expressed similar views: The secretary general of WASHIRIKA complained that government (and, by implication, party) interference was a principal source of cooperative problems. Those assembled recommended that the 1982 Cooperative Societies Act be reviewed to enhance cooperative autonomy, that a new cooperative policy be formulated making clear "the relationship and roles of cooperatives on the one hand and those of the party and the government on the other, that the ambiguous role of the apex organization be regularized and that economic viability be reintroduced as the key criterion for cooperative registration."[66]

Failure to meet the December 31, 1986, deadline did not end the drive for village-based, production-oriented cooperatives.[67] At the end of March 1989, of the 5,051 registered primary cooperative societies, 4,299 were single-village ones and only 752 were multivillage. The latter accounted for a total of 3,936 villages.[68] But along with this reorganization was a growing opposition within the movement to the "outside" imposition it involved.

Cooperative officers were faced with a second problem during this period: growing corruption within the movement. Part of the cause was the repeated intervention of the government at the behest of the party. Such intervention undermined the cooperative leaders' dependence upon, and responsibility to, cooperative members. As a result, these leaders were more predisposed to corruption than they otherwise might have been. Ironically, the government intervened not only to promote one form of socialism or another but also to stop corruption. The major tool used for the latter was the authority granted the registrar of cooperatives under the cooperative societies acts to remove cooperative leaders. The absence of a resolution of the apex organization problem hindered such efforts.

A significant case arose when the registrar, Flavian Tuniga, ordered the dissolution of the management committee of the Morogoro Region

Cooperative Union (MRCU) on October 21, 1989. The committee, under Chairman Clement Barogo, filed suit five days later. In March 1990, the High Court quashed the suspension of the management committee. The judge said it was "glaringly ultra vires and invalid,"[69] and he quashed, also, the appointment of a caretaker committee to replace the management committee. The judge ruled that the registrar could only appoint the caretaker committee after dissolution of the management committee, yet that dissolution legally never occurred. According to the judge, the registrar had failed to consult the secretary general of the apex organization as required by law. The registrar had argued that since WASHIRIKA had not been created in accord with the Cooperative Societies Act of 1982, there was no one to consult. The judge contended that this merely meant that the registrar "could not appoint any Care-taker Committee until there was an apex organisation and until the Secretary General was appointed."[70]

As the 1980s came to a close, the party faced many problems: The effort to shift to village-based, production-oriented cooperatives had demoralized many cooperative officers and many participants in the movement; most cooperative unions had high levels of debt; corruption had become widespread; and a growing mood of independence among those associated with the movement had developed.[71] This independence was supported by many government officials associated with cooperatives.

Struggle over Autonomy, 1990–Present

The formal turning point in the struggle over autonomy came in 1990, when the National Assembly passed another amendment to the Cooperative Societies Act of 1982, reversing the changes brought by the 1985 party policy on producer-oriented cooperatives. Under the new arrangements, only viable cooperatives could be registered; a primary society might be formed of two or more villages; single-purpose cooperatives were allowed; and membership eligibility requirements were tightened. The chairman of the CUT, Philip Ndaki, said the amendments made clear that "cooperative societies must be created out of economic merits and not just to appease the people politically."[72] At the same time, the National Apex Organisation of Tanzania (Formation) Act was passed, temporarily giving legality to the CUT.

The following year the Cooperative Societies Act of 1991 was passed, continuing the trend back toward cooperatives that functioned as autonomous units. The new orientation was reflected in changes of wording in the law. For example, the definition of a cooperative society was changed from "an association of persons who have joined together" to "an association of persons who have *voluntarily* joined together" (emphasis added). And the first two objectives of the old act—those calling on cooperatives to promote socialism and communal farming—were dropped.[73]

The 1991 act repealed the National Apex Organization of Tanzania (Formation) Act, which had been passed only the previous year. In its place, it called for the unions in each economic sector to form their own apex organization. The purpose was threefold: (1) to give the apex organizations greater independence from the government and party; (2) to give unions greater authority over these organizations; and (3) to allow a greater degree of functional specificity, which, it was thought, would promote efficiency. The apex organizations were given the power to form a cooperative federation for the country as a whole. In accord with CCM's effort to provide mass organizations with greater autonomy, the party ended CUT's affiliation in February 1992. Yet not until early 1993, following a report by the Cooperative Audit and Supervision Corporation (COASCO) of major problems with the apex organization's accounts, was the government prompted to disband CUT.[74] Its assets were transferred to a single apex organization, the Tanzania Cooperative Alliance (TCA).[75] Still to be established were apex organizations for sectors other than crop marketing and a federation of such organizations.

The possibility that cooperatives would serve effectively as agents of socialist development was threatened not only by their growing autonomy but also by growing peasant disillusionment.[76] The ending of cooperatives' monopoly over the purchase of most crops and the entry of private traders, the restrictions on credit to most unions because of their severe debts and problems of corruption, and mismanagement at both union and society levels had contributed to a greatly weakened movement.

Conclusion

Although they had been heralded in such terms as "the main pillar and hope for the construction of socialism in the country," cooperatives were floundering by the early 1990s.[77] A report in late 1992 estimated the debt of the unions at TSh. 66 billion![78] Given the major economic problems facing the country in the early 1990s and IMF conditionalities, the party and government could not afford to sustain the cost. The explanations for what happened are several.

First, the cooperatives were trampled by the ideological and pragmatic "elephants" in a political struggle. In the pre-Arusha period they were encouraged to undermine Asian traders. In the post-Arusha period they were "milked" to nourish ujamaa villages, disbanded, reestablished, and torn apart as the ideological socialists sought to use them to promote collective production—and to block advances in other areas by the pragmatic socialists.[79] The ever-changing policies, reflecting the course of the ideological and pragmatic socialist battle, reduced the legitimacy and effectiveness of cooperatives.

Second, they were undermined by the units of action problem; i.e., what benefited cooperative members did not necessarily benefit society as a whole, and vice versa. The consequence was a destructive struggle over "ownership" of the cooperatives. Historically, cooperatives had evolved in Britain as membership organizations. When the first Cooperative Ordinance came into operation in Tanganyika in 1933, government was given responsibility for registering and supervising the organizations. Ever since, there has been a tendency by the state to view them as tools to facilitate the achievement of state objectives. Their use for this purpose often clashed with their use for purposes desired by their members. Deborah Bryceson has interpreted the fate of cooperatives in terms of the struggle among units. She argued that there were three stages in this struggle. Initially, local cooperative leaders enjoyed prestige that "derived from being affluent members of the rural community who had economic and political power to influence the welfare of less advantaged peasants." Then, as the state imposed greater controls on cooperatives, especially in the post-Arusha period, the "cooperative patrons' maneuverability" was restricted. In Bryceson's words, the state sought to assert the "nation's dominance over the cooperative patron's neighbourhood. But, as ensuing events suggest, the neighbourhood was a more organic social unit than the nation." She saw the reestablishment of cooperatives in 1982 as the reassertion of the power of "neighbourhoods." And, she concluded, "the nation may have to evolve from the neighbourhood after all."[80] As I have argued previously, one of the major problems of socialist construction is how to connect the small with the large unit in a way that does not undermine the aspirations of each.

Third, besides the problems of units and of political struggle, a myriad of other factors contribute to an explanation of why cooperatives did not work well as instruments of socialist construction. These include the following:

1. *The involvement of party and government officials in the operation of cooperatives.* In the words of Philip Raikes, "Regional cooperative unions increasingly became parastatal institutions at the command of central and regional state authorities."[81]
2. *The level of corruption.* In 1989, Rashidi Kawawa, then party secretary general, said that in 1985/86 and 1986/87 over TSh. 850 million were stolen by cooperative employees.[82] Jokes about the purchase of *mazao hewa* (literally "air crop," i.e., invisible, phantom, or fictitious crops) abound.
3. *A confusion of ideas from all over the world about the role of cooperatives.* This confusion led one observer to conclude, "We have borrowed too much, too often, too many models and philosophies of cooperative development from too varied sources and donors. It is time to sit down and sieve the useful from all the chaff."[83]

4. *The IMF conditionalities.* These included the demand for high interest rates, which seriously affected cooperatives, and limits on credit, which meant some unions were unable to get sufficient funds for purchasing inputs and crops.
5. *A host of problems related to Tanzania's low level of economic development.* Storage facilities were insufficient; transport was often unavailable; spare parts kept ginneries out of service; deconfinement introduced new competition; supervision was unpredictable.
6. *Legal disputes.* For much of the time the apex organization had no legal standing.

Indeed, the list is a long one.

By the early 1990s the major question had shifted: It was not *how* cooperatives might be used in the pursuit of socialism but *whether* cooperatives would survive as marketing institutions for the rural population.

Notes

1. Julius Nyerere, "Socialism and Rural Development," in Nyerere, *Freedom and Socialism* (Dar es Salaam: Oxford University Press, 1968), p. 346.

2. The ILO has defined a cooperative as "a body set up to ensure self-help through mutual help; it is an association of persons who have joined together to fulfill individual needs in a democratic decision-making organisation in which all members participate and have a proportional share of gains and losses." See International Labour Organisation, *Cooperatives, A Review of Cooperative Development in the African Region: Scope, Impact and Prospects,* Report III, Seventh African Regional Conference, Harare, November-December 1988 (Geneva: International Labour Organisation, 1988), p. 13. And the International Cooperative Alliance (ICA) has defined cooperatives as institutions adhering to six principles: "(i) voluntary and open membership; (ii) equal rights of voting for members, i.e. one member, one vote; (iii) limited interest on share capital, if any; (iv) equitable distribution of the economic results arising out of the operations of the society; (v) constitutional provisions for the education of members, officers, employees and the general public; (vi) cooperation between cooperatives." See ibid., p. 16.

3. Julius Nyerere, "The Arusha Declaration," in Nyerere, *Freedom and Socialism,* pp. 233–234.

4. Nyerere, "Socialism and Rural Development," p. 345.

5. Goran Hyden, "The Politics of Cooperatives," in Hyden, ed., *Cooperatives in Tanzania, Problems of Organisation Building* (Dar es Salaam: Tanzania Publishing House, 1976), pp. 11 and 12.

6. Issa Shivji, *Class Struggles in Tanzania* (Dar es Salaam: Tanzania Publishing House, 1976), p. 74.

7. Jeannette Hartmann, "Development Policy-Making in Tanzania, 1962–1982: A Critique of Sociological Interpretations," Ph.D. thesis, University of Hull, United Kingdom, April 1983, p. 175.

8. Ibid., p. 154.

9. United Republic of Tanzania, *Report of the Presidential Special Committee of Enquiry into Cooperative Movement and Marketing Board* (Dar es Salaam: Government Printer, 1966), p. 5.

10. Ibid., p. 71.
11. Shivji, *Class Struggles,* p. 74.
12. Ibid., p. 75.
13. Cranford Pratt, *The Critical Phase in Tanzania, 1945–1968, Nyerere and the Emergence of a Socialist Strategy* (Cambridge: Cambridge University Press, 1976), p. 193.
14. I.R.E.M. Msanga, "Cooperatives, Policy and Law in Tanzania with Special Reference to Multi-Purpose Cooperative Societies: The Case Study of Same District," LLM dissertation, University of Dar es Salaam, November 1981, p. 80.
15. Nyerere, "The Arusha Declaration," p. 232.
16. Ibid., p. 250.
17. Nyerere, "Socialism and Rural Development," p. 348.
18. United Republic of Tanzania, *Tanzania, Second Five-Year Plan for Economic and Social Development, 1st July 1969–30th June 1974, Volume I: General Analysis* (Dar es Salaam: Government Printer, 1969), pp. 32 and 33.
19. Hyden, "The Politics of Cooperatives," p. 17.
20. *The Standard* (Dar es Salaam), 6 April 1972, p. 5.
21. Hyden, "The Politics of Cooperatives," p. 18.
22. The official history of TANU states that Circular No. 4 of 1967 directed cooperative societies to raise the necessary capital to assist in village development. See D.Z. Mwaga, B.F. Mrina, and F.F. Lyimo, eds., *Historia ya Chama cha TANU, 1954 Hadi 1977* (Dar es Salaam: Chuo cha CCM, Kivukoni, 1981), p. 103.
23. There was an effort during this period to convert ujamaa villages into agricultural producer cooperatives. This may appear to be a countertrend, but it should be understood otherwise. Since ujamaa villages had no legal identity, they could not obtain loans. Registering them as cooperatives gave them a legal identity. Some among the pragmatic socialists may have seen registration as a means of delaying the replacement of the old cooperatives by new villages, but most government officials seemed to accept it as a pragmatic act to strengthen the efforts of ujamaa villages to obtain credit.
24. John Saul, "From Marketing Cooperative to Producer Cooperative," in Rural Development Research Committee, ed., *Rural Cooperatives in Tanzania* (Dar es Salaam: Tanzania Publishing House, 1975), p. 293.
25. Ibid., p. 294.
26. Ibid., p. 302.
27. In October 1971 the government directed that villages be registered as cooperative societies under the 1968 Cooperative Societies Act. Why? "The registration of villages as Cooperative Societies enabled them to get loans from the Rural Development Bank and the National Bank of Commerce. . . . Direct sale of products instead of selling them to primary cooperatives would enable them to reduce costs by avoiding deductions made to these societies when selling crops. The surplus money would be retained as village funds." Mwaga, Mrina, and Lyimo, eds., *Historia ya Chama cha TANU,* p. 104.
28. *Daily News* (Dar es Salam), 27 July 1972, p. 5.
29. Newspaper reports of such assistance included *Nationalist* (Dar es Salaam), 18 August 1971, p. 8; and *Daily News,* 7 October 1972, p. 3; 15 June 1972, p. 3; and 7 December 1972, p. 3.
30. Ngila R.L. Mwase, "Cooperatives and Ujamaa: A Case Study of the Arusha Region Cooperative Union Limited (A.R.C.U.)," in Hyden, ed., *Cooperatives in Tanzania,* pp. 86–89.
31. Hyden, "The Politics of Cooperatives," pp. 18 and 19.
32. L.H.K. Mlowe, "Multi-Purpose Cooperative Development in Tanzania, Prospects and Problems," a paper presented at the Annual Symposium, Coopera-

tive College, Moshi, October 1984, reprinted in 1986 with some adjustments, p. 27.

33. In a few cases, such as that of the Kilimanjaro Native Cooperative Union, unions were able to incorporate and operate as companies, thereby retaining their assets. In most cases, the assets and liabilities were distributed among public institutions in a difficult process.

34. Many involved with cooperatives and many pragmatic socialists thought the decision was unreasonable. The decision to abolish the unions followed a study that concluded that in general, "the most important thing at present is to maintain unions." See Jamhuri ya Muungano wa Tanzania, Ofisi ya Waziri Mkuu na Makamu wa Pili wa Rais, Kamati ya Kuchunguza Vyama Vikuu vya Ushirika Tanzania Bara (M.M. Massomo, chair), "Taarifa," Dar es Salaam: Office of the Prime Minister and First Vice President, May 1975, mimeographed, p. 175. Msanga said the Villages and Ujamaa Villages Act of 1975 suggested government confusion. He held that the villages were both government institutions and "deemed" multipurpose societies, i.e., societies assumed to be something they really were not. See I.R. Msanga, "The Impact of Cooperative Legislations on the Development of Cooperatives in Tanzania with Special Reference to the Cooperative Societies Act, 1982," Cooperative College, Moshi, n.d. (ca. 1986), mimeographed, p. 107.

35. Jamhuri ya Muungano wa Tanzania, Ofisi ya Waziri Mkuu na Makamu wa Pili wa Rais, *Sheria ya Kuandikisha Vijiji na Vijiji vya Ujamaa* (Dar es Salaam: KIUTA, 1975), p. 29.

36. Muungano wa Vyama vya Ushirika Tanganyika, Idara ya Elimu na Utangazaji, *Ushirika Wetu* (Dar es Salaam: CUT Press, 1977), p. 86.

37. Elizabeth M. Minde, "The Changing Nature of Cooperatives and the Law in Tanzania (Mainland)," LLM dissertation, University of Dar es Salaam, 1982, p. 86.

38. The evidence is extensive. See Dean E. McHenry Jr., *Tanzania's Ujamaa Villages, The Implementation of a Rural Development Strategy* (Berkeley: Institute of International Studies, University of California at Berkeley, 1979), pp. 153–203; Paul Collier, Samir Radwan, and Samuel Wangwe, *Labour and Poverty in Rural Tanzania* (Oxford: Clarendon Press, 1986), pp. 115–116; Louis Putterman, "Tanzanian Rural Socialism and Statism Revisited: What Light from the Chinese Experience?" a paper presented at the International Conference on the Arusha Declaration, Arusha, December 1986, p. 3; United Republic of Tanzania, Office of the Prime Minister, Ujamaa and Cooperative Development Department, "Report on Village Data System, 1980," Dodoma: Nordic Project for Cooperatives and Rural Development in Tanzania, December 1980, p. 42; Reginald Herbold Green, "Agricultural Crises in Sub-Saharan Africa: Capitalism and Transitions to Socialism," *Bulletin* (Institute of Development Studies, Sussex), Vol. 13, No. 4 (1982), p. 77; and Dharam Ghai, Eddy Lee, Justin Maeda, and Samir Radwan, eds., *Overcoming Rural Underdevelopment* (Geneva: International Labour Organisation, 1979), p. 66.

39. Jamhuri ya Muungano wa Tanzania, *Majadiliano ya Bunge, 27 Aprili–5 Mei, 1982* (Dar es Salaam: Mpiga Chapa wa Serikali, 1984), p. 368.

40. Jamhuri ya Muungano wa Tanzania, Ofisi ya Waziri Mkuu na Makamu wa Pili wa Rais, Idara ya Maendeleo ya Ujamaa na Ushirika, *Maendeleo ya Ujamaa na Ushirika Tanzania (*Dodoma: Office of the Prime Minister and First Vice President, June 1976), p. 18.

41. Goran Hyden, *Beyond Ujamaa in Tanzania, Underdevelopment and an Uncaptured Peasantry* (Berkeley: University of California Press, 1980), p. 133.

42. Deborah Fahy Bryceson, *Second Thoughts on Marketing Co-operatives in Tanzania, Background to Their Reinstatement,* Plunkett Development Series 5 (Oxford: Plunkett Foundation for Cooperative Studies, 1983), p. 21.

43. Frank Ellis reports that in 1970 peasant producers received about 70 percent of the export sales values of export crops, and in 1980 they received about 42 percent. And he argues that "the basic process of Tanzania's political economy during the 1970s was the impoverishment of the rural economy to the end of supporting a proliferating state and parastatal bureaucracy." See Ellis, "Agricultural Marketing and Peasant-State Transfers in Tanzania," *Journal of Peasant Studies*, Vol. 10, No. 4 (July 1983), pp. 218 and 235. John Shao argues that "the expropriation of value from the Tanzanian peasants has been carried out without any increase in accumulation for the development of industry or infrastructure." Rather, the wealth taken from peasant producers was consumed by the extreme inefficiency of marketing authorities. See Shao, "Politics and the Food Production Crisis in Tanzania," in Stephen Commins, Michael Lofchie, and Rhys Payne, eds., *Africa's Agrarian Crisis, The Roots of Famine* (Boulder: Lynne Rienner Publishers, 1986), p. 98.

44. Deborah Bryceson notes that twelve other members were former cooperative officials. Bryceson, *Second Thoughts*, p. 30.

45. In a review of the 1982 act, Job Savage, Newton Guderyon, and Harold P. Jordan concluded that it violated "at least three of the most important concepts (principles) of the cooperative form of business enterprise. These are (1) *individuals are to become members of a cooperative on a voluntary basis*, (2) *members are to control their cooperatives on a democratic basis*, and (3) *cooperatives are to be politically neutral.* Of the three, the first two are perhaps the most important." Despite these drawbacks, the authors concluded that because the act states that the minister or registrar "may" rather than "must" intervene in various ways, it "is adequate for the purpose drawn." See Job Savage, Newton Guderyon, and Harold P. Jordan, "Review of Cooperative Development in Tanzania as It Relates to Agriculture," Dar es Salaam: Agricultural Cooperative Development International, December 1982, mimeographed, p. A2. I.R. Msanga has been more critical of the act. He has contended, "It has been the problem itself and not a guide to the solution." See Msanga, "The Impact of Cooperative Legislations," p. 39.

46. United Republic of Tanzania, *Cooperative Societies Act, 1982* (Act No. 14 of 1982, dated 28 June 1982), Section 4 (published as Supplement to the *Gazette of the United Republic of Tanzania*, vol. 43, no. 30, 23 July 1982).

47. Jamhuri ya Muungano wa Tanzania, *Jumuiya ya Muungano wa Vyama vya Ushirika Act, 1979*, No. 9 (Dar es Salaam: Mpiga Chapa wa Serikali, 1979). The terminology used to refer to the apex organization from 1979 to 1993 varied. The act identified it as WASHIRIKA, yet the term was sometimes translated as "the Union of Cooperative Societies." Also, especially following the repeal of the Jumuiya ya Muungano wa Vyama vya Ushirika Act in 1982, the apex was referred to as the Cooperative Union of Tanzania (CUT). The latter borrowed the initials of the predecessor of WASHIRIKA, the Cooperative Union of Tanganyika (CUT).

48. Chama cha Mapinduzi, *The Constitution of Chama cha Mapinduzi, 1982* (Dar es Salaam: Printpak, n.d.), Clause 80 (4).

49. The party constitution was amended at the party conference in October 1987, ending party appointment of the secretary general of WASHIRIKA. Subsequently, the NEC of the party selected candidates from among its own members and forwarded their names to the General Council of WASHIRIKA, which was charged with selecting from the candidates the one it wanted. See *Daily News*, 27 October 1987, p. 1. As part of the changes resulting from the move toward a multiparty system in 1992, CCM's role in the appointment of the secretary general was formally ended.

50. *Daily News*, 27 October 1987, p. 4.

51. WASHIRIKA, *Kanuni na Muundo wa Jumuiya ya Muungano wa Vyama vya Ushirika* (Dar es Salaam: WASHIRIKA, 1983), p. 1.

52. Minde, "The Changing Nature of Cooperatives and the Law," p. 7.

53. It was not until 1987 that the NEC agreed to make unions the basic membership unit of WASHIRIKA to accord with the Cooperative Societies Act of 1982. See *Daily News,* 28 February 1987, p. 1. But it had no legal status as the apex organization until 1990. One of the stimuli for resolving the ambiguity was the case of the removal of the executive committee of the Morogoro union in 1989 by the registrar, as described later in this chapter. See *Daily News,* 24 October 1989, p. 1. Within a few months of the decision in the case, a bill that gave WASHIRIKA legal standing was passed.

54. United Republic of Tanzania, *Cooperative Societies Act, 1982* (Act No. 14 of 1982), p. 280.

55. This figure is very close to the average of 3.65 given in Jamhuri ya Muungano wa Tanzania, *Majadiliano ya Bunge, 20–25 Juni, 1984* (Dar es Salaam: Mpiga Chapa wa Serikali, 1984), pp. 561–564.

56. Chama cha Mapinduzi, Idara ya Uenezi wa Siasa na Ushirikishaji Umma, *Ushirika wa Uzalishaji Mali Vijijini, Utekelezaji wa Maamuzi ya Halmashauri Kuu ya Taifa* (Dar es Salaam: CCM, April 1985).

57. Ibid., p. 43.

58. United Republic of Tanzania, *Written Laws (Miscellaneous Amendments) Act, 1985* (Act No. 8 of 1985).

59. The title of those who headed the departments was changed from "head" to "secretary." See *Daily News,* 27 October 1987, p. 1. Ngombale-Mwiru retained his position as secretary of the Department of Ideology, Political Education and Training.

60. United Republic of Tanzania, Ofisi ya Waziri Mkuu, "Registrar's Circular No. 4 of 1985" (Dodoma: Registrar of Cooperatives, 1985, mimeographed), p. 1.

61. United Republic of Tanzania, *Cooperative Societies Act, 1982,* pp. 324–325.

62. *Daily News,* 19 November 1986, p. 1. Apparently, the regional cooperative officers were informed of the deadline at a meeting in Dodoma on October 27.

63. Interview with regional cooperative officers in Moshi, 20 December 1986.

64. Interview with the regional cooperative officer of Moshi, 22 December 1986.

65. *Daily News,* 11 April 1987, p. 1.

66. *Daily News,* 18 November 1987, p. 3.

67. Reports on the continued drive for the reorganization include *Daily News,* 16 March 1987, p. 3; 23 March 1987, p. 1; 8 April 1987, p. 1; 16 June 1987, p. 5; 2 July 1987, p. 1; 22 July 1987, p. 1; 1 August 1987, p. 5; 29 September 1987, p. 1; 21 December 1987, p. 3; 19 January 1988, p. 1; 4 March 1988, p. 3; 11 March 1988, p. 1; and *Sunday News,* 12 April 1987, p. 3.

68. *Daily News,* 14 June 1989, p. 3. The following year the number of village primary cooperatives had increased to 5,616. See *Daily News,* 11 July 1991, p. 1.

69. *Daily News,* 19 March 1990, p. 3.

70. Ibid.

71. In August 1990 the debts of cooperatives and marketing boards had reached TSh. 27,772,594,546, 38 percent of which was interest. See *Daily News,* 27 June 1991, p. 3.

72. *Daily News,* 20 July 1990, p. 3.

73. United Republic of Tanzania, *Cooperative Societies Act, 1991* (Act No. 15 of 1991), published as a Supplement to the *Gazette of the United Republic of Tanzania,* Vol. 72, No. 33, 16 August 1991, pp. 165–219; and *Cooperative Societies Act, 1982* (Act No. 14 of 1982).

74. The process reflected heightened tensions in society. Apparently, the International Cooperative Alliance (ICA) threatened to expel Tanzania unless CUT was really controlled by member unions, so there were international as well as national pressures toward the separation of the movement from the state. See *Sunday News*, 28 February 1993, p. 1. When a meeting was called by the registrar of cooperatives to discuss the audit report and consider CUT's fate, the apex organization appealed to the High Court to block it. See *Daily News*, 5 March 1993, p. 1. The apex organization asserted that it had reregistered as an association and so was not under the jurisdiction of the registrar. The High Court dismissed the case, the meeting was held, and a caretaker organization was set up by the unions to oversee the establishment of a true apex organization called the Tanzania Cooperative Alliance. See *Daily News*, 9 March 1993, p. 1. Yet the issue got caught up in the major constitutional dispute of early 1993 over the status of Zanzibar in the union. The chairman of CUT, Khamis Hassan Khamis, would not allow the caretaker organization to assume control of CUT because the five Zanzibari unions were not participants in the decision. See *Daily News*, 17 March 1993, p. 1. Although the new apex organization was established, its birth took place as the cooperative movement was in a period of decline.

75. *Daily News*, 16 July 1993, p. 1; and 3 August 1993, p. 5.

76. A report on the Cooperative College Symposium in August 1991 stated, "Participants were skeptical of the sincerity of the government's intention to give autonomous powers to cooperatives through the 1991 Cooperative Act." See *Daily News*, 16 August 1991, p. 5. Later that year, the CUT chairman, Philip Ndaki, denounced the conduct of some party and government leaders who were imposing union organizations on members contrary to the Cooperative Societies Act of 1991. See *Daily News*, 24 October 1991, p. 3.

77. Rashidi Kawawa, the secretary general of CCM, made this remark at a meeting of WASHIRIKA. See *Daily News*, 27 June 1989, p. 4. Because of auditing problems, the extent of economic difficulties is not known with exactitude, but indications support the conclusion that there are major problems. For example, in June 1990 the minister of state responsible for cooperatives gave the following figures: In 1984/85, of eleven unions audited, only one was profitable (Kagera); in 1985/86, of twenty-three audited, ten were profitable (Kagera, Kyela/Rungwe, Arusha, Mbeya, Singida, Vuasu, Shinyanga, Njoluma, Iringa/Mufindi, and Dodoma); in 1986/87, of nineteen audited, seven were profitable (Kagera, Kyela/Rungwe, Arusha, Kilimanjaro, Vuasu, Nyanza, and Njoluma); in 1987/88, of three audited, two were profitable (Arusha and Biharamulo). See *Daily News*, 12 June 1990, p. 1.

78. *Daily News*, 13 October 1992, p. 1.

79. The repeated calls by many at the Cooperative College, Moshi, in recent years for a national policy isolating cooperatives from political struggle reflect this reality. There seems little likelihood that such a policy would succeed.

80. Deborah Fahy Bryceson, "Household, Hoe and Nation: Development Policies of the Nyerere Era," a paper presented at the conference Tanzania After Nyerere, London, June 1986, pp. 6–8.

81. Philip Raikes, "Socialism and Agriculture in Tanzania," a paper presented at the conference Tanzania After Nyerere, London, June 1986, p. 16.

82. *Daily News*, 27 June 1989, p. 4. The debts of the cooperatives had become so great that they could not be paid, much as was the case with the national debt. Early in 1991 the governor of the Bank of Tanzania, Gilman Rutihinda, announced the establishment of a "capital and interest subsidy fund to bail out cooperative unions from liquidity problems caused by high bank interest rates." See *Daily*

News, 6 February 1991, p. 3. In April of the same year, almost TSh. 28 million of a debt of TSh. 61 million owed by the Central Region Cooperative Union was written off by the Cooperative and Rural Development Bank (CRDB). See *Daily News,* 17 April 1991, p. 3.

83. J.K. Buganga, "The Registration, Management and Development of Cooperatives in Tanzania Mainland: The Future of Their Past," a paper presented at the Annual Symposium, Cooperative College, Moshi, 29 September–4 October 1986, p. 11.

7
Industrial Parastatals and Socialism

Ukiona chungu kipya, usitupe cha zamani.
"If you find a new cooking pot, don't throw away the old one."

Virtually all Third World states, regardless of whether they pursue socialism, capitalism, or some combination of the two, seek industrialization and rely on government leadership in its pursuit.[1] Yet industrial policies have varied immensely among Third World countries.[2]

In Tanzania, the Arusha Declaration emphasized agricultural, rather than industrial, development. It declared,

> We have put too much emphasis on industries. . . . The mistake we are making is to think that development begins with industries. It is a mistake because we do not have the means to establish many modern industries in our country. We do not have either the necessary finances or the technical know-how. It is not enough to say that we shall borrow the finances and the technicians from other countries to come and start the industries. . . . We cannot get enough money and borrow enough technicians to start all the industries we need. And even if we could get the necessary assistance, dependence on it could interfere with our policy on socialism.[3]

This deemphasis of industrialization was more acceptable to pragmatic socialists than to ideological socialists. The latter argued that Tanzania's transition to socialism should be informed by the historical experiences of other socialisms that placed greater emphasis on industry. The 1987 Party Programme, reflecting the ideological socialists' position, called for adherence to "the basic principle that an industrial revolution is a basic condition for facilitating the revolution in agriculture." Slightly modifying an old Marxist slogan, it proclaimed with some ambiguity that "agriculture is the basis and industries the leader of the national economy."[4] Yet the struggle over the emphasis industrialization should receive was only one of a myriad of controversies and problems that confronted Tanzania's effort to industrialize.

Industry had grown rapidly immediately following independence and continued to grow until the late 1970s. The early 1980s were a period of significant decline in industrial production and repeated attempts to overcome problems. By the late 1980s, Tanzanian industrial parastatals were in disrepute. More than half of them were operating at a loss, costing Tanzanians billions of shillings a year to maintain. If industry was "the leader," the transition was clearly in jeopardy. Indeed, the early 1990s saw the initiation of privatization, i.e., of the retreat from the use of the industrial parastatal as a tool for socialist construction.

Parastatals

Parastatals are state-run enterprises found in virtually all countries, regardless of whether they are pursuing socialism. In countries pursuing socialism, though, they have played a more central role in the economy.[5] A theoretical distinction is normally made between cooperatives, which are member controlled, and parastatals, which are state controlled. Many theorists have contended that the latter are superior to the former as a mechanism for socialist construction because they are more fully dominated by the socialist-oriented state. In practice, the Tanzanian state has used both organizations and has found parastatals as difficult to use for socialist construction as cooperatives. The reasons for this dilemma will be addressed subsequently.

Tanzania has created parastatals to run a wide variety of enterprises, including industrial factories, agricultural estates, mining concerns, and even educational establishments. According to John Nellis, Tanzania had 400 public enterprises by 1981—more than twice as many as any other African country.[6] Nevertheless, their share of Tanzania's GDP amounted to only 12.4 percent.[7] Of the various forms of parastatals, those in industry have been the most significant to the development of socialism in Tanzania.[8] Thus, industrial parastatals are the focus of this chapter.

The Establishment of State Control of Industrialization

As I.K. Bavu has said, "The Arusha Declaration is not the parent of parastatals in Tanzania."[9] Indeed, public enterprises were established by the British prior to independence and rapidly multiplied in the pre–Arusha Declaration period. What the Arusha Declaration did was to call for an expansion of the public sector to include the major means of production and exchange, such as

> land; forests; minerals; water; oil and electricity; news media; communications; banks, insurance, import and export trade, wholesale trade; iron and steel, machine-tool, arms, motor-car, cement, fertilizer, and textile industries; and any big factory on which a large section of the people depend for their living, or which provides essential components of other industries; large plantations, and especially those which provide raw materials essential to important industries.[10]

The nationalizations that followed suddenly made the state the most significant force in the manufacturing sector. According to W. Edmund Clark, the largest segment of the assets acquired was that in the industrial sector.[11] Although the 1967 nationalizations were the most momentous, they were not the only ones. Industrial, agricultural, and commercial properties continued to be taken by the state until the mid-1970s. By 1974, Reginald Green estimated, 80 to 85 percent of large and medium-scale firms were in the public sector.[12]

The Role of the Private Sector Under Tanzanian Socialism

Although there was broad support for nationalization, there was opposition to the complete nationalization of the industrial sector. This opposition came both from those who opposed socialism and from some of those who favored it, in particular the precursors of the pragmatic socialists. They successfully argued that management agreements with multinational corporations for most of the newly acquired industries were appropriate and that there should be a place for the private sector under Tanzanian socialism. The reassurances to the private sector came in a presidential statement and a government paper.

The president's statement was delivered a week after the Arusha Declaration and the start of the nationalizations. Nyerere likened the nationalizations to what happens in a military struggle: "The key positions of the economy have been secured for the nation in the same way as, during a war, an army occupies the sites which dominate the countryside."[13] On the one hand, complete ownership was acquired in three sectors: banks, major trading companies, and food processing industries. Controlling interest was acquired in seven other firms: Kilimanjaro Brewery and Tanzania Brewery; British American Tobacco; Bata Shoe Company; Tanganyika Metal Box; Tanganyika Extract Company; and Tanganyika Portland Cement.[14] On the other hand, the president declared that no other industries would be taken over in full or in part.[15] He reassured private investors with the following words: "We have rejected the domination of private enterprise; but we shall continue to welcome private investment in all those areas not reserved for Government in the Arusha Declaration."[16]

Shortly thereafter, Government Paper No. 4, *Wages, Incomes, Rural Development, Investment and Price Policy,* was published. It reiterated, though in more emphatic terms, Nyerere's words:

> All existing private firms other than those in which the Government has already expressed its intention to acquire majority, rather than exclusive, ownership are assured that they may continue with their present ownership.[17]

The paper clearly specified the areas reserved for the public sector, as shown in Table 7.1. It declared, in addition, that "government may permit

Table 7.1 Economic Activities Requiring Exclusive or Majority Public Ownership

Activities Reserved Exclusively for Public Sector	Activities Requiring Public-Sector Majority Ownership
Large-scale processing of maize and paddy	Mining
	Oil
External and wholesale trade	Steel
Banking	Machine tools
Insurance	Motor cars
Arms	Fertilizer
Electricity	Cement
Posts	Breweries
Telecommunications	Textiles
Railways	Cigarettes
Radio	Shoes
Water	Metal containers
	Extracts

Source: United Republic of Tanzania, *Government Paper No. 4 (Wages, Incomes, Rural Development, Investment and Price Policy)* (Dar es Salaam: Government Printer, 1967), p. 22.

private majority ownership in those areas normally requiring public sector majority ownership in special circumstances."[18] Furthermore, it stated explicitly that government policy was to promote private investment:

> The private investor can be assured of a fair and equitable reward for his efforts and, by virtue of the Government's commitment in this regard, the full support of the Government and the people of Tanzania in his endeavors. . . .
> The Government will support private investment in the sectors allocated to it in a number of ways. Foreign investors are guaranteed repatriation of their earnings and capital under the terms of the Foreign Investment Protection Act. The Government reaffirms its assurance to foreign investors in those sectors allocated to private capital that their activities are welcome and their interests will be protected. The Government will continue through its provision of infrastructure, research and other services to assist and encourage the development of private initiative in the interest of the overall economic development of Tanzania.[19]

Its only requirement was a nationalist one:

> While the Government intends to encourage private investment both by Tanzanians and by foreigners, it must and will also vigorously seek to encourage the use of the resultant earnings in the further national interest.[20]

Despite these reassurances, for a decade public sector advancement was the focus of the state's attention. As an important private businessman stated, there was "a tremendous sense of insecurity in the private sector" in the period between 1967 and 1972, and "it was indeed a brave and lonely soul who contemplated any major private capital investment" in the 1973–1977 period.[21] Reginald Green, who was deeply involved in the nationalizations, has noted the shift from a policy that sought public dominance to one that sought the phasing out of much private economic activity.[22] Not only did nationalization go further than Government Paper No. 4 of 1967 implied at the state level, but also district and regional authorities took over some of the manufacturing and processing industries within their purview, contrary to the president's immediate post-Arusha assurances.[23]

Besides the growth of the parastatal sector through the nationalizations, the state initiated many new industries. The public sector's share in manufacturing value added went from 14 percent in 1967 to 56.8 percent in 1982, and its share in manufacturing employment went from 15.5 to 52.7 percent during the same period.[24] The World Bank reported in 1974 that half the value added in manufacturing and over 90 percent of new capital formation were accounted for by public corporations.[25] By 1981, of the 707 industrial establishments with ten or more employees, 28 percent were wholly or partially state owned. Yet the parastatals accounted for 66 percent of net fixed capital and 55 percent of production and value added by such establishments.[26] Although the state had established itself as the dominant force in the industrial sector in the decade following the Arusha Declaration, the private sector, harassed and subordinated, persisted.

The Role of Workers Under Tanzanian Socialism

The state's relatively successful struggle for ownership of the commanding heights of the industrial sector did not mean it succeeded in controlling industrialization. Control of industrial production required control of labor, too. Ironically, the effectiveness of workers in the struggle for independence led those whom they had helped put into power to fear them and, consequently, to enact legislation to control them. First, the new TANU government legislated that the sole central labor organization would be the Tanganyika Federation of Labour (TFL), restricted the right to strike, and banned civil servants from membership. Second, renaming the central union the National Union of Tanganyika Workers (NUTA), it placed NUTA under the control of TANU. Third, through the Security of Employment Act of 1964, it established workers' committees whose members were elected at the enterprise level in all public and private enterprises. Although the government presented workers' committees as means by which workers would be empowered, most did not function in that way. According to Pius Msekwa, "In practice . . . the primary function of the workers' committee has been seen by management as being limited to ensuring that workers' discipline is carried out."[27] Despite the pre-Arusha problems, many observers thought real empowerment of labor would follow the Arusha Declaration.

Indeed, two important steps were taken: First, in 1969 TANU amended its constitution to permit the establishment in industries of party branches (where there were at least 250 members) and sub-branches (where there were at least 50 members). The avowed purpose was to build worker consciousness. Msekwa argued it was quite successful in this endeavor in the early years.[28] Second, by Presidential Circular No. 1 of 1970, workers' councils were established with the purpose of engaging workers in management. The councils were to advise the boards of directors of the enterprises concerned. Nyerere complained in the circular that the traditional management-worker relations of capitalist enterprises had been retained in public enterprises. He contended that greater worker participation was needed to further socialist democracy, workers' sense of power, and economic efficiency. All members of workers' committees would be members of the workers' councils in addition to the enterprise general manager, the TANU branch chairman, a NUTA representative, and others.

Establishment of workers' councils was slow, because of opposition from management and suspicion from workers who had been conditioned to being controlled through a variety of state-introduced institutions. According to Msekwa, "In Tanzania, the Presidential Circular does not appear to have been a direct response to workers' or NUTA's demands for workers' participation."[29] But workers' frustration with the constraints placed upon them grew in the early 1970s, partly as a consequence of the efforts of ideological socialists within TANU.

An important spur to the development of worker consciousness and activism was the TANU Guidelines of 1971. Activists referred to three clauses in the document to justify their calls for more militant action by workers. First, Clause 13 criticized the "habit in which one man gives the orders and the rest just obey them." And, it declared, "If you do not involve the people in work plans, the result is to make them feel a national institution is not theirs."[30] Second, Clause 15 condemned the arrogance and oppressiveness of some leaders. It argued, "There must be a deliberate effort to build equality between the leaders and those they lead."[31] Third, Clause 33 condemned waste in the parastatals. It declared, "The Party must ensure that the parastatals do not spend money extravagantly on items which do not contribute to the development of the national economy as a whole."[32]

In the following two years there were brief strikes, factory seizures, and a euphoric sense among some ideological socialists that the real socialist revolution was at hand. The government's response was ambiguous, since it was being pulled one way by ideological socialists and the other way by pragmatic socialists. This upsurge of worker activism reached its peak in May 1973 with the worker takeover of the Mount Carmel Rubber Factory, a private company owned and managed by a man of Iranian origin.

There was precedent for the takeover: The previous month workers had taken over Rubber Industries, Ltd., and the seizure was recognized by both the government and the party.[33] The workers refused to cooperate with NUTA in settling the dispute over who should control the Mount Carmel factory, charging that NUTA was an agent of their employer. At first, government responded positively to the seizure. The principal secretary to the Ministry of Commerce and Industries directed that the National Development Corporation (NDC) should take over the company while compensation discussions were being held.[34] But, in the end, the government stepped in and blocked the workers' effort.[35] The workers lost not only the struggle to control the factory but also their jobs.

There are two contradictory explanations of what transpired at the Mount Carmel Rubber Factory relevant to the socialist project in Tanzania. On the one hand, many observers suggest that the incident shows that the party's claim that it is a party of workers is fraudulent. They argue that the suppression of workers would not have occurred if worker interests had been paramount. On the other hand, there are those who argue that there was no contradiction between the proclamation of worker supremacy over the party and the action of the state. They contend that industrial workers constituted a labor aristocracy, i.e., a privileged group within Tanzanian society. As such, they did not deserve additional power or privilege.[36] In other words, by suppressing the workers at the Mount Carmel Rubber Factory, the state was pursuing the interests of Tanzanian workers in general. It was another case of what I have called the units of action problem. The manner in which the worker-state confrontation was resolved fostered a division among ideological socialists into those who gave up on the party as a vehicle for the transformation of Tanzanian socialism into a more "scientific" form of socialism and those who continued to work within the party toward that end.[37]

By the late 1970s one observer wrote of "a most remarkable transformation of industrial relations in Tanzania."[38] Dudley Jackson contended that the transformation involved an exchange between workers and the state: In return for "the acquiescence of workers and their organisations in a policy which severely restricted the right to strike and the right to engage in 'free' collective bargaining," workers were given "new and substantial rights, ranging from greater financial and tenurial security to industrial democracy and workers' education."[39] This worker-state truce, according to Manfred Bienefeld, was not "resolved progressively in relation to a socialist objective."[40]

The suppression of workers' efforts to assume control of industries was more a victory for the pragmatic socialists than the ideological socialists. Subsequent worker acquiescence was a sign of resignation, not of satisfaction. The position of the workers was an extremely difficult one. As the economy worsened during the 1980s, there were substantial layoffs; as urbanization grew rapidly, competition for jobs increased; as the value of the currency declined, wages did not rise accordingly. Whether the workers would have been better off had they gained greater control of industry is an open question. Yet the pauperization of the working class from the late 1970s was not in accord with the vision of either ideological or pragmatic socialists.

Though the state's "victory" over the owners of, and workers in, the industrial sector placed the parastatals at the disposal of those who were formally committed to using them for socialist construction, there developed an intense debate over *how* they should be employed.

The Strategy for the Use of Industrial Parastatals

Positions in the debate over the use of industrial parastatals often corresponded to the points of disagreement between ideological and pragmatic socialists. These disagreements became manifest in the planning for industrialization, which can be divided into three phases: The first focused on increasing the capacity of consumer goods industries as part of an import substitution strategy; the second focused on increasing the capacity of capital and intermediate goods; and the third focused on increasing the utilization and efficiency of existing capacity.

Phase One: Increasing Consumer Goods Production

Critics of the Three-Year Plan (1961/62–1963/64) and the First Five-Year Plan (1 July 1964–30 June 1969) that preceded the Arusha Declaration charged that the "plans" did not really *plan*. The critics asserted, first, that both plans merely presented "shopping lists" of desired industries, leaving industrialization too much up to the whim of investors; and second, that the consequence of this "strategy" was to encourage the development of consumer goods industries rather than intermediate and capital goods industries.

Although the Second Five-Year Plan (1 July 1969–30 June 1974) was more explicit than previous plans about the importance of the industrial sector, noting that its development was a necessary condition for overall economic development, it did not significantly change industrial priorities.[41] It did call for greater self-reliance in industrial production; it did call for a shift from an emphasis on import substitution for consumer goods toward import substitution for capital and intermediate goods;[42] and it did call for the development of a long-term industrial strategy.[43]

But the core of the plan was a list of 385 projects with "industrial investment possibilities."[44] The plan called for 84 percent of the industrial investments to be in the parastatal sector and only 12 percent in the private and 4 percent in workers' and cooperative sectors.[45] And, in accord with the Arusha Declaration, it called for a decentralization of industrial projects.[46] Finally, the plan called for greater emphasis on small-scale industries than had been the case in the past. Perhaps the greatest impact of the Second Five-Year Plan was its call for the development of a long-term industrial strategy.

Phase Two: Increasing Intermediate and Capital Goods Production

Substantial political conflict developed between ideological and pragmatic socialists on the prioritizing of capital versus consumer goods industries. Virtually all industry in 1967 produced for immediate domestic consumption or processed agricultural products for export. Both ideological and pragmatic socialists sought an industrial sector able to produce capital, intermediate, and consumer goods, yet they disagreed on the best strategy to reach such a goal.

Ideological socialists contended that heavy industries should take precedence over consumer goods industries, and pragmatic socialists argued the reverse. There has been a long-standing Marxist view that "Department II" (capital goods industries) should be emphasized over "Department I" (consumer goods industries).[47] The argument holds that such industries would have more linkages—and thereby stimulate the formation of other industries more—than would consumer goods industries.

Although Reginald Green, a scholar who served as an economic advisor to the Tanzanian Treasury between 1967 and 1974, suggested it might be better to establish consumer industries that might be markets for the capital goods industries first, opposition from pragmatic socialists in the late 1960s and early 1970s was based principally on the grounds of expediency. They contended it was less costly and more practical to build import substitution industries for consumer products in the early phases of industrialization. Yet their voices were muted as the ideological socialists came to dominate discussion within the party. According to Barker et al., from the late 1960s only a few people were arguing against an industrial strategy that stressed capital and intermediate goods production.[48]

The success of the ideological socialists in initiating a study of the need for capital goods industries in the Second Five-Year Plan culminated in what became known as the Long-term Industrial Strategy (1975–1995) or the Basic Industrial Strategy (BIS), which was encompassed by the Third Five-Year Plan (1976–1981). It entailed a plan to put into action ideas publicized by scholars such as Justinian Rweyemamu and Clive Thomas, which called for the production of goods that might be used to produce other goods. Yet it distorted their concept of basic industries to include "those industries producing goods to meet the 'basic needs' or requirements of the people, i.e., consumer goods."[49] Thus, the BIS did not exclude encouraging the manufacturing of consumer goods, though it stressed the need to direct resources to the production of goods needed by such industries.[50] Basic industries were defined to include iron, steel, and metalworking industries; cotton textiles, leather, and sisal; chemical industries; food processing and beverage industries; paper and wood products; and nonmetal products (cement and other construction materials).[51] Many pragmatic socialists argued against the massive investments required in such basic industries as iron and steel or paper and pulp. Yet their success in changing the meaning of "basic" in the BIS meant that the thrust of the strategy was more ambiguous than its initial advocates had wanted.

To most ideological socialists, iron and steel manufacture was the heart of the BIS. It is a dream that has persisted despite economic difficulties and despite the arguments of pragmatic socialists and their allies. The 1987 Party Programme reiterated the call for its establishment. But pragmatists have resisted its realization. After assessing the history of the effort to establish such an industry, Rune Skarstein and Samuel Wangwe concluded in 1986 that "Tanzanian production of steel cannot be efficient in the foreseeable future, but it could frustrate seriously the development of essential subsectors within manufacturing industry as well as the economy as a whole."[52]

In contrast to the situation with iron and steel, the paper and pulp mill was built, but at great cost. Skarstein and Wangwe calculated that the original estimate of cost per ton of installed capacity in 1978 was "2.3 times higher than the highest investment cost in industrialized countries at the time."[53] And 77 percent of the cost was to be in foreign exchange. Exports would have to be subsidized by the government to compete in the world market.[54] They concluded by saying that the Southern Paper Mills (SPM) project "contains lessons and experiences that should be carefully taken into consideration in the planning of future large-scale industrial projects in Tanzania."[55] In other words, it was a waste of resources. And by the 1980s, most existing industries were starved of resources, forcing them to close or operate far below capacity.

Phase Three: Improving Capacity
Utilization and Efficiency

The economic decline that began in the late 1970s influenced the objectives of the subsequent First Union Five-Year Development Plan (1981/82–1985/86) and Second Union Five-Year Development Plan (1988/89–1992/93) and Tanzania's ability to fulfill the plans. The first union plan called for increasing the availability of consumer goods; the second, for greater utilization of existing industrial capacity. Stemming the decline, rather than moving forward, was a central theme of the plans. Furthermore, a series of supplemental plans was introduced to deal with the severe economic problems: the National Economic Survival Programme (NESP) in 1981; the Structural Adjustment Programme (SAP) in 1982; and the Economic Recovery Programme (ERP) in 1986. The plans bore little relationship to what actually happened. For example, the first union plan sought an 8.8 percent *positive* annual growth rate in manufacturing but got a 5.2 percent *negative* rate.[56] Thus, during the 1980s the government adopted a defensive strategy that aimed primarily at overcoming existing problems of capacity underutilization and inefficiency. The state was struggling to stop the downward spiral of industry. What had happened to the dreams of both ideological and pragmatic socialists?

The Performance of Industrial Parastatals

An assessment of the performance of industrial parastatals involves the answer to two distinct questions. First, how successful was the state in keeping parastatals functioning? Second, how successful was the state in effectively using parastatals in the pursuit of socialism? The two questions are interrelated: Unless parastatals were kept viable, they would be of no value to socialist construction. Yet unless they served socialist purposes, their survival would be of no value to socialist construction.

Parastatal Viability

The shift from seeking to increase industrial capacity in the first four plans to improving capacity utilization and efficiency in the last two plans is indicative of serious problems with industrialization, clearly evident since the late 1970s. Table 7.2 shows the rise and fall of the contribution of manufacturing to the GDP. The most serious decline occurred in the 1980s. A brief survey of the experiences of industrial parastatals in two manufacturing industries, textiles and shoes, during that decade illustrates at a micro level what Table 7.2 shows at a macro level.

Textiles

The increase in the production of textiles has been greater and its decline less than that of the manufacturing sector as a whole in the period since the Arusha Declaration, as shown by a comparison of the data in Table 7.2 with those in Table 7.3. Since the capacity of textile firms by 1980 was approximately 250 million square meters a year, these figures indicate that capacity utilization had fallen to about 25 percent early in the decade.[57] Illustrative of popular frustration with the ability of parastatal firms to

Table 7.2 Contribution of Manufacturing to Gross Domestic Product

Year	Percent of GDP
1967	8.5
1968	9.0
1969	9.9
1970	10.1
1971	10.7
1972	11.4
1973	11.0
1974	10.6
1975	10.4
1976	12.4
1977	12.8
1978	13.5
1979	12.0
1980	10.9
1981	10.2
1982	8.3
1983	8.0
1984	7.7
1985	6.9
1986	6.2
1987	7.4
1988	5.3
1989	4.5
1990	5.1

Sources: Jamhuri ya Muungano wa Tanzania, *Hali ya Uchumi wa Taifa Katika Mwaka, 1979-1980* (Dar es Salaam: Government Printer, 1981), pp. 9–10; United Republic of Tanzania, *The Economic Survey, 1982* (Dar es Salaam: Government Printer, 1983), pp. 16–17; Jamhuri ya Muungano wa Tanzania, *Hali ya Uchumi wa Taifa Katika Mwaka, 1984* (Dar es Salaam: Government Printer, 1985), pp. 12–13; and, Jamhuri ya Muungano wa Tanzania, *Hali ya Uchumi wa Taifa Katika Mwaka, 1990* (Dar es Salaam: Government Printer, 1991), p. 29.

produce sufficient textiles is the complaint of an MP in 1989 that "22 years after the Arusha Declaration, Tanzanians had been reduced to wearing second hand clothes while they had plenty of cotton and a firm foundation for the textile industry."[58]

The holding company for parastatals engaged in the textile industry was the National Textile Corporation (TEXCO). The cloth-producing mills under it included URAFIKI, POLYTEX, KILTEX, SUNGURATEX, MUTEX, and MWATEX. TEXCO also produced gunny bags and blankets. Virtually every parastatal under TEXCO faced severe problems, summarized by the low level of capacity utilization.

The underutilization of capacity meant billions of shillings in losses and many consequent problems:[59] Workers could not be paid, resulting in layoffs; electric bills could not be paid, resulting in power cuts; and the government sales tax and excise duty could not be paid, resulting in seized property.[60] In each case, factories were either closed or threatened with

Table 7.3　Textile Production in Tanzania (in millions of square meters)

Year	Production
1967	14
1968	29
1969	46
1970	58
1971	67
1972	74
1973	80
1974	86
1975	87
1976	83
1977	79
1978	73
1979	85
1980	93
1981	96
1982	86
1983	60
1984	57
1985	66
1986	62
1987	73
1988	65
1989	71
1990	63

Sources: United Republic of Tanzania, *Statistical Abstract, 1970* (Dar es Salaam: Bureau of Statistics, 1972), p. 129, for 1967–1969; Bank of Tanzania, *Tanzania: Twenty Years of Independence (1961–1981), A Review of Political and Economic Performance* (Dar es Salaam: Bank of Tanzania, n.d.), p. 299, for 1970–1976; United Republic of Tanzania, Ministry of Planning and Economic Affairs, Bureau of Statistics, *Statistical Abstract, 1982* (Dar es Salaam: Bureau of Statistics, 1983), p. 134, for 1977–1981; and *Tanzanian Economic Trends,* Vol. 4, Nos. 3 and 4 (October 1991 and January 1992), p. 73, for 1982–1991.

closure. The reasons those involved gave for the losses had little to do with the fact that the industries were parastatals.

The general manager of MWATEX attributed losses in 1987 to unstable water and power supplies.[61] The minister for industries and trade attributed the decline in 1988 to "power shortage, inadequate water supply and aging machinery."[62] The same year the managing director of TEXCO attributed losses to problems associated with the devaluation of the shilling, the high interest rates on National Bank of Commerce (NBC) funds, the increase in cotton prices, the lack of foreign exchange for the purchase of spare parts, and the lack of utilities.[63] Two years later Cleopa Msuya, then minister for industries and trade, attributed the problems to a lack of capital, aged mills, and interruptions in water and power supplies.[64] The general manager of URAFIKI attributed the severe difficulties to "lack of sufficient spare parts and dyestuffs, erratic supply of cotton due to transport problems from producing regions and power interruptions which forced the mill to reduce its shifts from three to two towards the end of the year" and to devaluation of the shilling.[65] Most of these reasons have little to do with the form of ownership. Although they are self-serving reasons—i.e., they place blame on factors other than the individuals who made the analyses, and they may be incomplete—it would be unreasonable to dismiss them as insignificant and/or inaccurate.

Shoes

Much as complaints were raised about clothing, so were they raised about shoes. In 1989 an MP complained that "it was a national shame that 28 years after Uhuru the people have reverted to wearing *'makatambuga,'* sandals made from worn-out car tyres."[66] The reason was not the absence of capacity, but problems related to capacity utilization.

There were two parastatals engaged in shoe production, Morogoro Shoe Company and Tanzania Shoe Company (BORA). Both were part of a public holding corporation, the Tanzania Leather Associated Industries (TLAI). The Morogoro Shoe Company was built partly with a TSh. 112 million loan from the World Bank and opened in 1980 with a capacity of 4 million pairs annually. It produced 81,000 pairs in 1984 and only 27,000 in 1988.[67] The Tanzania Shoe Company was a result of the nationalization of Bata Shoe Company in the immediate post–Arusha Declaration period. It was by far the larger of the two, producing 1,879,694 pairs in 1984 but only 594,630 in 1988.[68] The capacity utilization declined from about 60 percent in 1979/80 to 30 percent in 1982/83 to 10 percent in 1986/87, and by 1990 a debt of TSh. 7.9 billion had been accumulated.[69] In both cases, the declines reflected serious production difficulties that were brought about by a variety of factors culminating in severe liquidity problems.

By February 1989 the problems had become so serious that BORA entered into a twelve-month contract with a private company, Global General Merchandise, in order to obtain funds for purchasing raw materials. In return, BORA promised to deliver 88 percent of its finished goods to Global General.[70] At the same time, it continued to press the government for additional help. The government's reaction indicated both its frustration with money-losing parastatals and its desire to support parastatals only if they were economically viable—regardless of whether they contributed to the pursuit of socialism. In July 1989 the deputy minister for industries and trade responded by pointing out the help it had given to, or helped arrange for, BORA: numerous loans, overdrafts, and letters of credit; aid from the Netherlands of G1.5 million in 1987; import support from Italy valued at U.S.$1.5 million; and the waiving of customs and storage charges for BORA's imported raw materials.[71] Furthermore, the government complained that even though the company was operating at only 10 percent of capacity, it kept 1,500 workers on the payroll, and between May 1988 and

February 1989 twenty officials of BORA were paid TSh. 2.287 million in mileage allowance.[72] By September 1991, production had fallen to 7 percent of capacity.[73] Managers complained that though they had cleared imported materials, still they did not have the funds needed for purchasing local materials to sustain production.[74] In 1993 the deputy minister for industries and trade again responded by claiming that between 1987 and 1992 about TSh. 1 billion had been "pumped" into BORA and "all that was like pouring water down in a leaking tin."[75]

In 1990, the general manager of Morogoro Shoe Company announced that the company would close until "the government" found solutions to its chronic problems, which were much like those of BORA. Its workers and managers were put on unpaid leave.[76] The same year, creditors began to seize vehicles from BORA for its failure to pay its debts to the NBC, the Tanzania Investment Bank (TIB), and Tanzania Development Finance Limited (TDFL), which by then totaled over TSh. 1.5 billion. Other creditors followed suit. In mid-1991 the general manager of BORA was arrested when he failed to cooperate with the seizure of fourteen vehicles under the terms of a court order obtained by the commissioner of customs and sales tax allowing auctioning of the parastatal's property to get back TSh. 52 million owed.[77] Meanwhile, the World Bank had agreed to undertake a serious study of how the government might reactivate the company.[78]

The "solution" was privatization. In April 1993, after a year and a half of negotiation, a Dar es Salaam–based company acquired a 70 percent interest in Morogoro Shoe Company, with TLAI retaining 30 percent.[79] Privatization of BORA took longer. In June 1993, one major bidder dropped out, frustrated by the "never ending process of negotiations" and the indecision of the government over whether it wanted a joint venture or an outright sale.[80] Sale of the factory, though not of the outlet shops, was reported the following month.[81] The sale culminated a long and complicated process of privitization.[82]

Experiences of Other Parastatals

The experiences of the textile and shoe parastatals paralleled those of other parastatals. In 1987, for example, parastatals of all types lost over Tsh. 7 billion; by 1988, the loss had risen to Tsh. 11 billion.[83] Paul Rupia, principal secretary in the president's office in the late 1980s, told a meeting of the Tanzania Association of Parastatal Organisations (TAPO) in 1988 that these losses had led to public questioning of the rationale for the parastatals' existence.[84] The issue was one of tradeoffs: Was it more "socialist" to support parastatals than it was to slow the rapid rise in the level of indebtedness to other countries, to provide peasants with a better price for their crops, to supply dispensaries with medicines, to furnish people with schools, and so on?

Parastatal Utility

Governments in both capitalist and socialist-aspiring societies run industrial enterprises that are not profitable but are considered essential to the public good. The debate is less over *whether* there should be such enterprises than over *which* enterprises should be so run. In a sense, socialist-aspiring societies differ from capitalist societies in that their list of enterprises is longer. Even within countries seeking to build socialism, there often exists a debate over the appropriate extent of public ownership of industries. In Tanzania by the late 1980s, ideological socialists were more reluctant to support the contraction of the public sector than were the pragmatic socialists. That reluctance was based more upon the dream of what parastatals might become than the reality of what they had become.

Almost from the time of the Arusha Declaration, critics have pointed to the discrepancy between the Tanzanian socialist vision of what parastatals should be and what they were. That is the implicit meaning of Clark's observation that in the aftermath of the Arusha Declaration "most parastatals have adopted a very narrow definition of socialism."[85] It is the view of F.C. Perkins, who has asserted that

> despite the rhetoric, Tanzania's industrialization programme has, in general, promoted the establishment of enterprises using large-scale capital-intensive, often technically, and almost invariably economically inefficient techniques. Its technological choice policy in industry has in most instances failed to promote the achievement of major national development objectives, such as employment creation, economic self reliance, decentralization of development, rapid growth of output, conservation of scarce development capital and efficient allocation of resources.[86]

And it is the contention of Barker et al., who observed that

> the post Arusha period has been noted for industrial investments that are efficient principally for transferring surplus outside the national economy.... Choice of technology after 1967 was left more or less entirely with multinationals, with the result that the development of skills has been neglected.... The state, which might have incentives to improve the efficiency of production, has neither been able to control labour processes in the factory nor to control the indirect manoeuvres of international capital.[87]

In other words, there was a marked discrepancy between the goals of Tanzanian socialism and what was done by those charged with seeking to attain those goals. To many observers, Tanzanian parastatals were not functioning as mechanisms for socialist construction. Thus, two explanations are required: Why did parastatals become unviable, and why did they fail to become effective tools for building socialism?

Reasons for the Problems of Industrial Parastatals

No single cause can explain either the parastatals' lack of viability or their limited usefulness for the socialist project. The causal chains are long and often intertwined in a complex way. Most of them are familiar to those who have examined development in other Third World countries. For analytic purposes, the reasons may be divided into two groups, technical and political. The two are not entirely separable, for technical difficulties may be the result of political actions and political actions may be influenced by technical problems.

Technical Explanations

Technical explanations may be divided into those focusing upon production and those focusing upon marketing.

Production Explanations

A major factor contributing to underutilization of Tanzania's limited industrial capacity is a lack of foreign exchange to purchase the imports needed to sustain production. Like other Third World countries embarking on industrialization, Tanzanian industries depend upon many types of imports: machinery for virtually all factories; spare parts for such machinery; oil for transport and power; parts to be assembled; chemicals for many kinds of products; and expertise to implement newly imported technologies. The reason for the lack of sufficient foreign exchange is multifaceted.

On the one hand, agricultural production has declined. Rune Skarstein and Samuel Wangwe argue that

> the additional productive capacities which were created in the 1970s, required increasing imports of spare parts, components, and intermediate goods and materials. These categories of imports had to be financed by Tanzania's export earnings. Since manufacturing industries are still at an "infant stage", they cannot be expected to contribute considerably to the country's export earnings. In an economy such as Tanzania, agriculture therefore has to be the main source of export earnings.[88]

Michael Lofchie argues in a similar fashion that "the core of Tanzania's economic collapse is the near-catastrophic drop in the production of exportable and industrial crops."[89] Why did agricultural production decline? Again, the reasons are multiple: Government prices have served as disincentives for crop production;[90] there has been a lack of industrial products needed for both production, e.g., fertilizer or insecticides, and incentives to production, e.g., consumer goods; most available investment money has been channeled into industry rather than agriculture; the marketing system of cooperatives and marketing boards has been inefficient and frustrating for growers; and agricultural prices have fallen on the international market. Each constitutes a piece of the explanation for the decline of agriculture.

On the other hand, a myriad of other factors contributes to the shortage of foreign exchange, including the heavy requirements of the kind of import substitution industrialization (ISI) pursued in Tanzania;[91] the failure to use resources available locally;[92] the emphasis of ISI on production of consumer goods rather than of capital and intermediate goods;[93] management contracts that directly and indirectly allowed "transferring surplus outside the national economy";[94] and "the role of foreign finance in favouring capacity expansion" over capacity utilization.[95] The explanation of each of these would involve another causal chain.

In addition to the foreign exchange problem, there seems no end to the list of reasons given by scholars and practitioners for parastatal production problems: overstaffing, inappropriate technology, poor planning, lack of technical expertise, corruption, worker indiscipline, poor management, poor workmanship—it is a litany of lacks and insufficiencies that has no simple origin.

Marketing Explanations

Inappropriate prices have been set by the government, resulting in losses for industrial parastatals. For example, in 1987 when the Price Commission increased the price of fuel without increasing the price of cement, the Portland Cement Company at Wazo Hill, which consumed 160 tonnes of heavy fuel per day, was forced to cut production.[96] In 1988 the Price Commission allowed Southern Paper Mills (SPM) to raise its prices 21 percent but did not allow Kibo Paper Industries, Ltd. (which used SPM paper and made bags for cement) or the Twiga Cement factory (which used the bags Kibo Paper Mills produced) to do so simultaneously. The result: Kibo Paper Mills raised its price anyway; the Twiga Cement factory was unable to buy the bags to package cement and claimed a loss of TSh. 5 million a day in domestic sales of cement as a result.[97] The same year, the chairman of the board of Kilombero Sugar Company complained that there was a four-month lag between when the prices of most industrial goods were raised and when the price of sugar was raised, resulting in a loss to the company of about TSh. 80 million per year.[98]

Not only did the government control many prices, it also channeled sales to "socialist" institutions. Such institutions often accumulated debt and could not pay for what they received. As a consequence, the producers either had to "sell" goods without expecting a return, certainly an unviable alternative, or to seek alternative, usually private, markets. In 1987 the Mbeya-based Zana za Kilimo had a backlog of over TSh. 19 million worth of hoes following its decision to halt sales to regional trading companies (RTCs) and cooperatives because they had outstanding debts to the company of TSh. 21 million. Zana za Kilimo had to seek government permission in order to sell to cooperative shops, primary cooperatives, ujamaa villages, and private companies.[99] A similar situation arose in early 1990: Butchery owners complained that the Tanzania Hides and Skins Company owed them TSh. 5 million and requested permission to sell to private businessmen.[100] The inability of the government from the late 1970s to bail out indebted public institutions undercut the viability of those to whom the debt was owed. In other words, where markets were compulsory, the failure of one "buyer" to pay for the goods received could render insolvent a wide range of suppliers.

As a consequence, throughout the 1980s the pressures to move to a liberal market grew, and year by year the government acceded to those pressures. Policies were adopted to move away from planned prices, to liberalize the market, and to privatize parastatals. Nevertheless, industry has not recovered significantly despite the introduction of these liberal orthodox measures, suggesting that the causes are more complex than state ownership or market involvement.

Political Explanations

Most of the causal chains developed by successively asking why a technical problem arose at some point involve political factors. Such political explanations take both a macro and a micro form.

Macro Explanations

Issa Shivji's explanation of the political factors is that managers of industrial parastatals are a part of the state bourgeoisie, whose object is to use the state as a vehicle for extraction of surplus for the benefit of that class and not for the benefit of the workers and peasants. Yet such an explanation is insufficient. Though it may be rational for the bureaucratic bourgeoisie to keep parastatals from being instruments for socialist construction, it would not be rational for them to keep parastatals from generating a surplus. Quite the contrary, the self-interest of the state class would be served by the success of industrial parastatals. To account for their lack of viability, one must turn to technical problems, popular opposition, and external factors. According to Shivji, the world economic crisis that began with the second oil price increase in 1979 has weakened the position of the bureaucratic bourgeoisie and enhanced that of the private compradorial bourgeoisie.[101] To the compradorial bourgeoisie, the distribution of imported goods is a more profitable enterprise than industrial production would be. The economic crisis, then, empowers a local class that has little interest in industrial production. Such an interpretation would suggest that substantial improvement in industrial production is unlikely to occur in the foreseeable future.

Rwekaza Mukandala's explanation for the viability and utility problems of industrial parastatals is more specifically related to parastatals. He contends that they "have been used by the ruling coalitions to sort out their intra-coalitional struggles . . . neutralize their enemies . . . legitimise their rule . . . solidify popular support . . . engineer change according to their own preferences . . . solidify their economic base and ultimately, consolidate their hold on state power."[102] Much as I have argued that cooperatives were a battlefield on which pragmatic and ideological socialists fought, Mukandala sees parastatals as a battlefield. And, similarly, the battle has harmed the "field," in this case the parastatals. He argues that the

> struggle for control between the political strata and the managerial strata as well as efforts of the latter as well as other groups to circumvent tight and later unrealistic income control have resulted in the phenomenal hemorrhage of resources from parastatals. . . . Tanzanian parastatals have served as avenues of individual capital accumulation."[103]

Illustrating his argument, he contends that "efforts by the political strata to mobilize the working class on their side in their struggle with the managerial strata . . . for a while led to 'nonmanagement' in the sector."[104] He says efficiency and effectiveness of parastatals have been "a casualty of" the struggle between the political and managerial strata; that tight financial accounting has not been in the interest of management; that the struggle and its consequences have "definitely contributed to Tanzania's economic and political malaise, including the discrediting of socialism which in turn has led to a liberalization which threatens not only to de-industrialize the economy among other things, but also to de-parastatize it."[105] Yet the start of the decline of industrial parastatals preceded liberalization, so it cannot be said to be *the* cause. Once liberalization was begun, though, it eliminated many of the supports that sustained industrial parastatals, such as protected markets and controlled competition.

Shivji and Mukandala disagree in their central focus. Shivji sees a class that did not control state power, the compradorial bourgeoisie, challenging the class controlling the state, the state bourgeoisie, in a struggle that implicitly undermines industrial production. Mukandala sees two parts of the ruling coalition, parastatal managers and politicians, struggling in a way that destroys the parastatals. Mukandala's depiction of the political struggle is not markedly different than that characterized as a struggle between pragmatic and ideological socialists, the former involving some of

Mukandala's managers and the latter involving some of Mukandala's politicians.

Micro Explanations

At a more micro level, there is a delicate relationship between the pursuit of economic viability for industrial parastatals and their use by political leaders for socialist construction. Opponents of the socialist project contend that the two are incompatible, i.e., that a lack of economic viability is inevitable if parastatals are used for socialist construction. Proponents disagree. Two examples of political involvement that appear to have undermined viability—though they may have promoted socialist objectives—are illustrative. In 1989 an MP complained that "political interests" determined project locations that were often uneconomical. For example, he cited the tobacco processing plant that was established in Morogoro while "tobacco is rotting in godowns in Tabora because it cannot be transported to Morogoro."[106] In pursuit of the socialist goal of equality, there was an effort to decentralize industry even though such decentralization might affect the parastatals' viability. Indeed, the pursuit of socialism might be said to be the pursuit of "political interests." A year later, in response to a question in the Zanzibar House of Representatives, the trade and industries minister admitted that the Zanzibar Bottling Plant charged an extra fifty cents on every bottle of soft drink supplied to wholesalers to fund construction of the party regional headquarters, in accord with "a government directive to public institutions to assist the project."[107] There is a tradeoff: On the one hand, higher prices may mean fewer buyers and diminished production; on the other hand, the CCM regional headquarters facilitates the work of an organization formally committed to socialist construction.

Underlying the critics' words in these two cases is the implication that the siting of the tobacco factory and the charge for the CCM headquarters reduced profitability *and* really did not contribute to socialist objectives. Yet reduced profitability does not necessarily mean either that economic viability has been lost or that socialist objectives have not been furthered. Although both pragmatic and ideological socialists would deny that industrial parastatals are intrinsically flawed, they would agree that both technical and political mistakes have been made in their use.

Changes in Socialist Industrialization

The serious problems facing industrial parastatals during the 1980s led party and state to rethink their role. There were two stages to this process: Initially, reforms were sought without a change from public ownership; subsequently, privatization became the dominant policy.

Reform Without Privatization

The reform efforts took three paths. First, industrial parastatals were threatened with closure. In November 1985, President Mwinyi, in one of his first acts as the new president, declared that parastatals had two years to (a) bring their accounts up to date and (b) show a profit or face closure. He said he would use an "iron broom" to get rid of inefficient parastatals. The effort focused on the accounts, for without them no accurate assessment could be made of their profitability. There was little response. As the deadline approached, an editorial in the government newspaper stated,

> Even on the surface of it things have changed but little. There are still enterprises and institutions which play ostriches—digging their heads in the sand pretending that there are no problems. They are still wasting public funds but are still getting away with it.[108]

Although the number of parastatals whose accounts were in arrears declined from 170 in 1985 to 163 in 1986 to 141 in 1987, Mwinyi's first demand remained unattained by the deadline he had set.[109] In May 1988 the deadline was extended to December 31, 1989. By June 1989, though, the number that had submitted accounts had been reduced only to 103.[110] Mwinyi's threat of closure had not even succeeded in bringing accounts up to date so that profitability might be judged.

Second, in 1987 Mwinyi announced that parastatals would be given greater autonomy.[111] A common cry of many parastatal managers was that they were not given the autonomy they needed to become efficient. The claim and the policy were ironic, in a sense, for more than a hundred parastatals were so autonomous that they were able to flout a direct order of the president to update their accounts for over four years! Yet there were controls that undermined efficiency, some of which were meant to promote socialist objectives and others of which were not. Mwinyi's announcement presumably referred primarily to a reduction in the latter.

Calls for increased autonomy were often a defense against calls for privatization. For example, in 1990 Nyerere urged resistance to hasty privatization because the problems with parastatals—lack of sufficient capital and lack of freedom by managers to manage their own affairs—might be addressed by other means. He said that if both were given the parastatals and they die, that would be fine. "But, what is being done is to deny them capital and freedom and to say they must die—that is witch-hunting."[112] President Mwinyi's response reflected Nyerere's position: He urged that parastatals be given more autonomy to "enable them to give better service to clients in the prevailing competitive scenario."[113]

Others went much further and called for the elimination of all controls and for complete autonomy. For example, a Tanzanian economist working for the United States Agency for International Development (USAID) argued in early 1990 that all the major government institutions that regulated or had some control over parastatals should be scrapped, i.e., the Standing Committee on Parastatal Organisations (SCOPO), workers' councils, the Parastatal Management Services Agreement Committee (PMSAC), and the Price Commission.[114] Such observers reasoned that only with complete autonomy would industrial parastatals become profitable.

Third, competition among public producers was introduced. Nyerere argued in 1989 that this should be done and that those "who would prove incompetent should be let to die a natural death."[115] The underlying idea was to borrow from "free" enterprise systems, though without relinquishing state involvement.

Reform Through Privatization

The seriousness of industrial decline, the ineffectiveness of the reforms, and the pressures of the IMF brought about a major change in Tanzania's approach to socialist industrialization: the privatization of many parastatals.[116] The process of privatization moved slowly. In July 1990, the Tanzania Association of Parastatal Organisations (TAPO) presented a report to President Mwinyi on restructuring.[117] In early December of that year the vice chairman of the Planning Commission, Malima, said the government would restructure parastatals the following year according to the TAPO recommendations.[118] Two days later the finance minister, Steven Kibona, warned money-losing parastatals that the government would no longer support them, that all parastatals should "be thrown" to the market.[119] The process moved much more slowly than suggested by the words of leaders.

To avoid the conclusion that this process involved an abandonment of socialism, parastatals were "rhetorically" transformed from socialist to nationalist institutions. In May 1991 an editorial in the *Daily News* listed the "familiar" problems in the following words: "under 50 per cent capacity utilization, enormous revenue losses, accumulation of debts, labour redundancies, embezzlement of funds, negligent handling of equipment and raw materials, and so on." It stated,

> This trend transformed many parastatals from a blessing to a *national* burden because the government, wary of letting those potential pillars of *patriotic* achievement die, has been bailing them out with kisses of life. But the Government itself, hard-pressed for cash and other key resources, is no longer able to "kiss" ailing parastatals.

The editorial concluded with a threat: "The message to them, lately, has been: survive or die." That is, the parastatals had to become profitable or face either dissolution or privatization.[120]

At the end of the year the Presidential Parastatal Reform Commission (PSRC) was established to coordinate privatization.[121] Early in 1992 the

Public Corporations Act of 1992 was introduced into parliament to provide for privatization. But privatization was not envisioned as being in opposition to socialist construction. Indeed, 40 percent of the shares of privatized parastatals were to be sold "at minimum cost" to workers wherever possible.[122] In closing the debate, the minister for finance said that the disposition of the parastatals would be made on a case-by-case basis, but those commercial parastatals receiving a government subsidy would be subject to "phaseout" within two years should they not be able to exist without subsidy.[123]

Perhaps of greater impact than the hesitant moves toward privatizing parastatals was the implicit message. Private businessmen were to be given considerably more "leash."

Conclusion

Whether the changes in the state's relationship to parastatals imply a movement from or toward the goals of Tanzanian socialism is a matter of considerable debate. Many observers argue that the declining significance of the public sector is indicative of a transition away from socialism. Others argue that it is merely a tactical retreat; i.e., it is the step backward that will allow the two steps forward.

The pragmatic socialist argument goes something like this: Control of industry by the state is for a purpose, facilitating the achievement of socialist goals. When state ownership no longer serves that purpose, its continuation is irrational. For example, industries that continually incur substantial losses and have to be subsidized by the state interfere with the goals of extending education, health services, investments in roads and agriculture, etc. In other words, the pragmatic socialists accept the view that some industrial parastatals were more harmful than helpful to the socialist project.

The ideological socialists tend to argue either that the pragmatic socialist assessment weighted profit too heavily or that the difficulties with production were not due to ownership but to other problems such as poor management, declining terms of trade, corruption, and so on—many of which might be corrected.

The latter point of view led to policies of reform without privatization; the former to policies of reform through privatization. In fact, Tanzania's policies in the late 1980s and early 1990s were a mixture of the two. Yet, as parastatal industries continued to falter and external pressure for change of ownership continued to grow, the trend was for privatization to become a more important part of the mixture. The trend is an important one, for the downgrading of the industrial parastatal and the upgrading of private enterprise runs counter to the strategy of socialist industrialization pursued since the Arusha Declaration. Whether this change means a return to the pre-Arusha era, involving the end of Tanzania's formal pursuit of socialism, is a question of fundamental importance.

There are two aspects to this question of whether the situation in the early 1990s represents a return to the pre-Arusha situation: an objective one (involving what is being done) and a subjective one (involving people's attitudes toward what is being done). Objectively, privatization does not appear to be giving rise to a pattern of industrial ownership identical to the one that existed prior to the formal commitment to socialism. Unlike the pre-Arusha period, during which a few major industries owned by foreign investors dominated the industrial sector, the current period of privatization appears to be leading toward a more mixed form of ownership with some joint foreign-local, some worker, some local African, some local Asian, some cooperative, and quite a bit of parastatal ownership. Nevertheless, privatization is likely to transfer public investments disproportionately to those with resources to buy them. That means there will be a tendency toward greater Asian and foreign control of industry, though it is unlikely such control will ever reach pre-Arusha levels.

Subjectively, privatization has reopened social cleavages that had closed at least partially in the post-Arusha period. According to Cranford Pratt and many other observers, the nationalization of industries served an important function: It popularized socialism. Ironically, the appeal of the nationalizations was to an exclusive, rather than an inclusive, nationalism, i.e., to the belief that the nationalizations would shift control over some enterprises from Tanzanians of Asian origin and put them under a government run by black Africans. Yet the socialism to which most Tanzanians lent support stressed an inclusive nationalism that contributed to Tanzania's relatively high degree of unity in the twenty-five years following the Arusha Declaration. The beginning of privatization has brought a return of an exclusive nationalism. Since Tanzanians of Asian origin are more likely to have the capital to buy factories from the state, some African businessmen and politicians have stirred up animosity toward them as a means of rallying support for their economic and political objectives.[124] Thus, the problems of industrial parastatals adversely affected more than the economic objectives of Tanzanian socialism. Chapter 8 turns to evaluation of Tanzania's experiences with the pursuit of self-reliance.

Notes

1. The term *industrialization* is used here to refer to the process of increases in manufacturing; it deliberately excludes increases in "mining and the generation and distribution of electricity, gas and water" often included in a definition of the industrial sector. See United Republic of Tanzania, Ministry of Finance, Planning and Economic Affairs, Bureau of Statistics, *Statistical Abstract, 1984* (Dar es

Salaam: Bureau of Statistics, 1986), p. 130. For reviews on the universality of the goal of industrialization and the centrality of government's role, see Peter Burnell, *Economic Nationalism in the Third World* (Boulder: Westview, 1986), pp. 100–108, which expands upon this point. Also see Helen Hughes, "Industrialization and Development: A Stocktaking," in Pradip Ghosh, ed., *Industrialization and Development: A Third World Perspective* (Westport, Conn: Greenwood, 1984), p. 21.

2. See, for example, Colin Bradford Jr., "Policy Interventions and Markets: Development Strategy Typologies and Policy Options," in Gary Gereffi and Donald Wyman, eds., *Manufacturing Miracles, Path of Industrialization in Latin America and East Asia* (Princeton, N.J.: Princeton University Press, 1990), pp. 48–49.

3. Julius Nyerere, "The Arusha Declaration," in Nyerere, *Freedom and Socialism* (Dar es Salaam: Oxford University Press, 1968), p. 241.

4. *Daily News* (Dar es Salaam), 14 January 1988, p. 4.

5. Amon Nsekela has noted that the achievement of social objectives may be more important than the achievement of profits. Yet he has expressed concern that neither social objectives nor profits have been achieved by many of Tanzania's parastatals. See Nsekela, "The Role of Public Sector in Tanzania: Performance and Prospects," in *The Role of Public Sector in the Economic Development in Tanzania, Proceedings of a Workshop Held in Arusha, Tanzania, on 27th to 29th of September 1983* (Dar es Salaam: Economic Research Bureau and Friedrich Ebert Stiftung, January 1984), pp. 3–4.

6. John Nellis, *Public Enterprises in Sub-Saharan Africa* (Washington, D.C.: World Bank, 1986), p. 5.

7. Ibid., p. 7. The figure is for the period 1974–1977, the only one available.

8. W. Edmund Clark, *Socialist Development and Public Investment in Tanzania* (Toronto: University of Toronto Press, 1978), p. 126; and B.J. Ndulu, "The Role of the Public Sector in Tanzania's Economic Development," in *The Role of Public Sector in the Economic Development in Tanzania, Proceedings of a Workshop held in Arusha, Tanzania, on 27th to 29th of September 1983* (Dar es Salaam: Economic Research Bureau and Friedrich Ebert Stiftung, January 1984), p. 25.

9. I.K. Bavu, "Proliferation of Parastatals and the Efficacy of Government," a paper presented at the International Conference on the Arusha Declaration, Arusha, December 1986, p. 6.

10. Nyerere, "The Arusha Declaration," pp. 233–234.

11. The proportions were: 37 percent industrial, 33 percent agricultural, 27 percent financial, and 3 percent commercial. Clark, *Socialist Development*, p. 107.

12. Reginald Herbold Green, "A Guide to Acquisition and Initial Operation: Reflections from Tanzanian Experience, 1967–74," in Julio Faundez and Sol Picciotto, eds., *The Nationalisation of Multinationals in Peripheral Economies* (London: Macmillan, 1978), p. 19.

13. Julius Nyerere, "Public Ownership in Tanzania," in Nyerere, *Freedom and Socialism*, p. 256.

14. Ibid., p. 253.

15. Ibid., pp. 253–254.

16. Ibid., p. 254.

17. United Republic of Tanzania, *Government Paper No. 4 (Wages, Incomes, Rural Development, Investment and Price Policy)* (Dar es Salaam: Government Printer, 1967), p. 21.

18. Ibid., p. 22.

19. Ibid., p. 23.

20. Ibid.

21. Girish Chande, "Role of Private Capital in the Context of the Arusha Declaration," a paper presented at the International Conference on the Arusha Declaration, Arusha, December 1986, p. 7.
22. Green, "A Guide to Acquisition and Initial Operation," p. 18.
23. Two examples with which I am familiar are a small rice-hulling enterprise in Ujiji and a small soap-making factory just outside Kigoma. In both cases the industries were seized from Tanzanians of Indian origin, and in both cases the industries failed soon after they were seized.
24. Rune Skarstein and Samuel Wangwe, *Industrial Development in Tanzania: Some Critical Issues* (Uppsala: Scandinavian Institute of African Studies, 1986), p. 19.
25. C.E. Barker, M.R. Bhagavan, P.V. Mitschke-Collande, and D.V. Wield, *African Industrialisation, Technology and Change in Tanzania* (Aldershot, United Kingdom: Gower, 1986), p. 184.
26. *Daily News,* 23 August 1988, p. 1.
27. Pius Msekwa, "The Quest for Workers' Participation in Tanzania," in N.S.K. Tumbo, J.M.M. Matiko, A.P. Mahiga, Pius Msekwa, and Helge Kjekshus, eds., *Labour in Tanzania* (Dar es Salaam: Tanzania Publishing House, 1977), p. 73.
28. Ibid., p. 75.
29. Ibid., p. 77.
30. Tanganyika African National Union, "TANU Guidelines on Guarding, Consolidating and Advancing the Revolution of Tanzania and of Africa," in Andrew Coulson, ed., *African Socialism in Practice: The Tanzanian Experience* (Nottingham: Spokesman, 1979), p. 38.
31. Ibid.
32. Ibid., p. 42.
33. Paschal Mihyo, *Industrial Conflict and Change in Tanzania* (Dar es Salaam: Tanzania Publishing House, 1983), p. 177.
34. Ibid., p. 180.
35. Issa Shivji, *Class Struggles in Tanzania* (Dar es Salaam: Tanzania Publishing House, 1976), pp. 142–145.
36. Disagreements with this characterization are noted in Barker et. al., *African Industrialisation,* p. 190.
37. A.K.L.J. Mlimuka and P.J.A.M. Kabudi, "The State and the Party," in Issa Shivji, ed., *The State and the Working People in Tanzania* (Dakar: Codesria, 1985), pp. 73–75.
38. Dudley Jackson, "The Disappearance of Strikes in Tanzania: Incomes Policy and Industrial Democracy," *The Journal of Modern African Studies,* Vol. 17, No. 2 (1979), p. 219.
39. Ibid., p. 251.
40. Manfred Bienefeld, "Trade Unions, the Labour Process, and the Tanzanian State," *The Journal of Modern African Studies,* Vol. 17, No. 4 (1979), p. 591.
41. United Republic of Tanzania, *Tanzania Second Five-Year Plan for Economic and Social Development, 1st July 1969–30th June 1974, Volume I: General Analysis* (Dar es Salaam: Government Printer, 1969), p. 59.
42. Ibid., p. 62.
43. Ibid.
44. Ibid., p. 65.
45. Ibid., p. 67.
46. Ibid., pp. 67–68.
47. This view is discussed by A.M. Babu, *African Socialism or Socialist Africa?* (Dar es Salaam: Tanzania Publishing House, 1981), pp. 46–47.
48. Barker et al., *African Industrialisation,* p. 181.

49. Katabaro Miti, "Continuity and Change in Tanzania's Economic Policy Since Independence," E.R.B. Paper 81.2 (Dar es Salaam: Economic Research Bureau, University of Dar es Salaam, 1981, mimeographed), p. 35.
50. Bank of Tanzania, *Tanzania: Twenty Years of Independence (1961–1981), A Review of Political and Economic Performance* (Dar es Salaam: Bank of Tanzania, n.d.), p. 112; and Skarstein and Wangwe, *Industrial Development*, p. 253.
51. Skarstein and Wangwe, *Industrial Development*, p. 116.
52. Ibid., p. 114.
53. Ibid., p. 158.
54. Ibid., p. 167.
55. Ibid., p. 168. By 1993 the cost to the government to sustain even limited production became so great that the factory was closed for four months and at least partial privatization was actively sought. See *Daily News*, 3 September 1993, p. 3.
56. *Daily News*, 23 April 1987, p. 1.
57. The capacity figures vary from source to source and over time. In mid-1993 Msuya reported them at 223.45 million square meters, 70 percent of which was in the public sector and 30 percent in the private sector. See *Daily News*, 20 July 1993, p. 1.
58. *Daily News*, 22 July 1989, p. 3.
59. *Daily News*, 26 February 1988, p. 1, and 1 November 1988, p. 3.
60. *Daily News*, 4 July 1991, p. 5.
61. *Daily News*, 26 February 1988, 1.
62. *Daily News*, 1 November 1988, p. 1.
63. *Daily News*, 28 March 1988, p. 1.
64. *Daily News*, 7 July 1990, p. 1.
65. *Daily News*, 14 March 1988, p. 3
66. *Daily News*, 22 July 1989, p. 1.
67. *Daily News*, 19 July 1989, p. 3.
68. Ibid.
69. *Daily News*, 23 March 1993, p. 1.
70. *Daily News*, 5 May 1989, p. 3.
71. *Daily News*, 19 July 1989, p. 3.
72. Ibid.
73. *Daily News*, 4 September 1991, p. 1.
74. *Family Mirror* (Dar es Salaam), 17 August 1989, p. 1.
75. *Daily News*, 21 July 1993, p. 1.
76. *Daily News*, 2 April 1990, p. 5.
77. *Sunday News*, 14 July 1991, p. 1.
78. *Daily News*, 30 March 1990, p. 3.
79. *Daily News*, 24 May 1993, p. 3. The company was renamed the G.T. Shoe Company and was expected to restart production later in the year.
80. The bidder was Mac Holdings Company, whose managing director, Yogesh Manek, complained about the privatization process. See *Sunday News*, 20 June 1993, p. 3.
81. *The Express* (Dar es Salaam), 22–28 July 1993.
82. *Daily News*, 23 March 1993, p. 1.
83. *Daily News*, 1 April 1989, p. 1.
84. *Daily News*, 2 December 1988, p. 1.
85. Clark, *Socialist Development*, p. 125.
86. F.C. Perkins, "Technology Choice, Industrialisation and Development Experiences in Tanzania," *Journal of Development Studies*, Vol. 19, No. 2 (January 1983), p. 231.

87. Barker et al., *African Industrialisation*, pp. 193, 194, and 196.
88. Skarstein and Wangwe, *Industrial Development*, p. 270.
89. Michael Lofchie, *The Policy Factor, Agricultural Performance in Kenya and Tanzania* (Boulder: Lynne Rienner Publishers, 1989), p. 109.
90. Ibid., p. 114.
91. Kilonsi Mporogomyi, "Industry and Development in Tanzania: The Origins of the Crisis," in Michael Hodd, ed., *Tanzania After Nyerere* (London: Pinter Publishers, 1988), p. 55. Similarly, Clark found in the immediate post-Arusha period that "parastatal firms tended to be larger, more capital intensive . . . and *more import oriented*" than they had been before the declaration. (Emphasis added.) Clark, *Socialist Development*, p. 134.
92. Masette Kuuya, "Import Substitution as an Industrial Strategy: The Tanzanian Case," in J.F. Rweyemamu, ed., *Industrialization and Income Distribution in Africa* (Dakar: Codesria, 1980), p. 71; and Andrew Coulson, "The State and Industrialization in Tanzania," in Martin Fransman, ed., *Industry and Accumulation in Africa* (London: Heinemann, 1982), p. 74.
93. Reginald Green calls this the "dependence critique" and cites Ajit Singh as one of its proponents. See Green, "Industrialization in Tanzania," in Fransman, ed., *Industry and Accumulation in Africa*, p. 96. I have noted that this is a position common to most ideological socialists.
94. Barker et al., *African Industrialisation*, p. 193.
95. Samuel Wangwe, "Industrialization and Resource Allocation in a Developing Country: The Case of Recent Experiences in Tanzania," *World Development*, Vol. 11, No. 6 (1983), p. 491. In an earlier study, Wangwe found the constraints on capacity utilization to vary by industry and to range between a lack of water and transport to poor management and administration. See Wangwe, "Factors Influencing Capacity Utilisation in Tanzanian Manufacturing," *International Labour Review*, Vol. 115, No. 1 (January–February 1977), pp. 65–77.
96. *Daily News*, 3 October 1987, p. 1.
97. *Daily News*, 5 March 1988, p. 1.
98. *Daily News*, 23 February 1988, p. 1.
99. *Daily News*, 3 October 1987, p. 3.
100. *Daily News*, 10 February 1990, p. 3.
101. Issa Shivji, "Introduction: The Transformation of the State and the Working People," in Shivji, ed., *The State and the Working People in Tanzania* (Dakar: Codesria, 1985), pp. 4–5.
102. Rwekaza Mukandala, "The Nurture of Power and Torture of Parastatals in Africa," a paper presented at the annual meeting of the African Studies Association, Denver, November 1987, p. 1.
103. Ibid., p. 16.
104. Ibid., p. 18.
105. Ibid., p. 20.
106. *Daily News*, 9 August 1989, p. 3.
107. *Daily News*, 27 June 1990, p. 3.
108. *Daily News*, 14 October 1987, p. 1.
109. *Daily News*, 28 March 1988, p. 1.
110. *Daily News*, 24 March 1990, p. 1.
111. *Sunday News*, 15 February 1987, p. 3.
112. *Sunday News*, 12 August 1990, p. 1.
113. *Daily News*, 12 November 1990, p. 1.
114. *Daily News*, 4 January 1990, p. 3.
115. *Daily News*, 5 May 1989, p. 1.

116. It is interesting to note that worker reaction was not necessarily averse to privatization and demonstrated rational self-interest. For example, in 1988, when a group of NEC members visited parastatals in Morogoro, workers asked that unproductive industries be sold to private businessmen rather than be shut down. Their confidence in the ability of the parastatals to survive competition with private enterprise was minimal. They asked that private businesses not be allowed to compete with public ones because the latter would be "cannibalized." See *Daily News,* 19 December 1988, p. 3.

117. *Sunday News,* 15 July 1990, p. 1.

118. *Daily News,* 7 December 1990, p. 1.

119. *Sunday News,* 9 December 1990, p. 1.

120. *Daily News,* 2 May 1991, p. 1; emphasis added.

121. *Daily News,* 22 September 1993, p. 1.

122. *Daily News,* 23 January 1992, p. 3. The Public Corporations Act gave the president power to repeal or amend any law establishing a parastatal to facilitate closing unprofitable ones. One MP objected to the transfer of power, likening the move to the creation of a "King Henry the 8th." See *Daily News,* 24 January 1992, p. 3.

123. *Daily News,* 25 January 1992, p. 6.

124. For example, the African businessman Ali Sykes and the leader of the unregistered Democratic Party, Reverend Christopher Mtikila, have been active in rousing anti-Asian sentiments in the early 1990s. See, for example, Ruth Evans, "Pride and Prejudice," *Focus on Africa,* Vol. 4, No. 3 (July–September 1993), pp. 33–37.

8

Self-Reliance and Socialism

Achanikaye kwenye mpini hafi njaa.
"He who gets blisters from the hoe-handle will not die of hunger."

The Arusha Declaration called for socialism *and* self-reliance, implying that the two aspirations were inseparable.[1] In a sense, self-reliance was posited as the answer to the volitional question, "Who will create and maintain the socialist society?" Self-reliance answers, "We will!" The concept was empowering in that it said to individuals and groups, "You have the capacity to accomplish what you want to accomplish!" It reduced what was expected from the government by implying, "If you want a better life, it is up to you to make it better!" And, ironically, it encouraged help from others. Aid agencies seemed to be more willing to support those countries seeking to improve their well-being on their own than those seeking assistance from abroad.

Despite the recognition of the importance of self-reliance, the country has become more, rather than less, dependent since the proclamation of the Arusha Declaration. The impact of this decline in self-reliance varied over time. During the period up to the late 1970s, the effect of dependence was subtle and relatively benign. With the start of the long economic decline, the effect was obvious and significant. It led to the 1986 IMF agreement, which marked a major substantive and symbolic turning point. The conditionalities it imposed required the abandonment of many policies that had been central to socialist construction. This chapter seeks to determine how and why Tanzania's efforts to achieve self-reliance have faltered.

The Meaning of Self-Reliance

There is no aspect of Tanzania's socialist undertaking whose pursuit has been as complicated by conceptual ambiguity as that of self-reliance. This ambiguity is the result of a lack of agreement among Tanzanian leaders over the answers to three questions: How much autonomy is required? What units are involved? What purpose is served?

Autonomy: The Dispute over Autarky

Self-reliance was the logical successor to independence as a vehicle for sustaining the sense of nationalism that gave political leaders their power.

During the independence struggle, nationalists rallied the support of insiders, i.e., the indigenous population, to oppose outsiders, i.e., the British rulers. The nationalists claimed that the former had a right to make decisions for "the nation," whereas the latter did not. Colonialism was a manifestation of the antithesis of this view, for it gave outsiders power over insiders. Independence marked a victory of nationalism over colonialism. Yet it soon became evident that non-Tanzanians retained significant influence over the economy despite independence, a situation that came to be identified as *neo*colonialism. As popular demands for improvements in the standard of living outpaced the ability of the state to fulfill them, political leaders found it both reasonable and expedient to blame outsiders. The struggle for self-reliance against neocolonialism was the new form of the struggle between insiders and outsiders. A basic issue facing Tanzanians in this struggle was how much autonomy from outsiders was needed to provide the opportunity for them to determine their future.

There are two sides in the arguments about the degree of autonomy necessary for self-reliance to exist. On one side are those who consider most links with the outside world to be harmful and something close to autarky necessary to achieve self-reliance. They tend to identify a country or group as self-reliant when it produces what it consumes and consumes what it produces. Low levels of trade would be an indicator of such self-reliance. They tend to argue that participation in the capitalist world economy will ipso facto produce dependency, i.e., surrender sovereignty to those who control that economy. Furthermore, they tend to argue that dependence on the world economy is poisonous to socialist construction; the less "taken" of the "poison," the less harm it would do.

On the other side are those who make a distinction between harmful and helpful links and consider a more selective severance of ties necessary to achieve self-reliance. They tend to identify a country or group as self-reliant when it produces the value of what it consumes and consumes the value of what it produces. A balance of trade would be an indicator of such self-reliance. They contend that participation in the capitalist world economy may be harmful in some respects but helpful in other respects. The task is to maximize the beneficial effects and minimize the harmful ones.

The former are more suspicious of the world economy, whereas the latter are more resigned to it. These different views on the degree of autonomy required for self-reliance tend to correspond with the ideological socialist–pragmatic socialist distinction. Despite the differences, both agree that the more local production can substitute for imported production, the higher the level of self-reliance will be. And both agree that though the measure of self-reliance might be economic, i.e., the flow of goods and services into and out of the country, the significance of self-reliance is political, i.e., who has the power to determine policy.

Units: The Unit-Specific Character of Self-Reliance

Although the idea of self-reliance arose out of nationalism, its meaning has not been confined to a characteristic sought for a nation. Most dictionary definitions of self-reliance imply that the concept refers to a characteristic of an individual, e.g., "reliance upon one's own efforts, judgment or ability" (*Webster's Third New International Dictionary*); "reliance upon one's own capabilities or resources" (*American Heritage Dictionary*); "healthy confidence in one's own abilities" (*Chambers Twentieth Century Dictionary*). In Tanzania politicians called for its realization among individuals and various subnational aggregations of individuals; i.e., the idea of "self" in self-reliance took on a variety of meanings. Individuals, families, villages, cooperatives, schools, wards, districts, and regions, as well as the nation, were called upon to be "self-reliant."

For this reason, a meaningful definition of self-reliance requires the identification of the unit to which it refers. The number of possible units within a single country is huge, ranging from a single individual to a myriad of possible combinations among citizens. When one moves beyond a single country the possibilities increase even more. In reality, a simpler set of units of action, ranked according to the number of individuals of which they are composed, appears more manageable and more useful. One such set includes groups smaller than a nation, a nation, and groups of nations.[2]

As Tanzania's efforts to achieve national self-reliance have faltered, two divergent tendencies have appeared. One has been the tendency of Nyerere and other prominent leaders to emphasize the need for regional, or what Ann Tickner calls collective and regional, self-reliance, reflected in Nyerere's work as chair of the South-South Commission and the revival of interest in the East African Community. The other has been the tendency toward individual self-reliance, reflected in the growth of the second economy. Although most pragmatic socialists have maintained that a multilevel approach to self-reliance is the most likely to succeed, ideological socialists have often professed skepticism.

In addition to the disagreements over whether the concept should be measured in terms of commodities or values, whether individual self-reliance could be relevant to a socialist transition, and how aggregates should be catalogued, ambiguity also arises from the application of the characterization of one level to a different level; e.g., a strong sense of national control or identification with the nation appears incompatible with a strong sense of local control or identification with a locality.

It is precisely this point that underlies one of Goran Hyden's arguments in *Beyond Ujamaa in Tanzania*. He contends that development in a direction towards greater national self-reliance is improbable without a successful subordination of the peasantry to the demands of the ruling classes. . . . The latter can only reduce their dependence on the metropolitan bourgeoisie by forcing the peasants into more effective relations of dependence.[3]

A similar point was made in an International Cooperative Alliance study of Tanzanian cooperatives undertaken in the mid-1980s—except from the point of view of a primary cooperative society rather than of the nation. The study contended that the self-reliance of such societies was being undermined by the national policy of replacing economically viable rural primary societies with village-based production-oriented cooperatives.[4] At a less abstract level, the contradictions are more striking. If coffee production were shifted to food production to further the self-reliance of coffee growers, the consequent shortage of foreign exchange would reduce national self-reliance. Indeed, if the people of rural areas were fully self-reliant, the people of urban areas might starve. As has been noted previously, this is precisely the "units of action problem." Actions to promote the achievement of self-reliance at one level may undermine it at other levels.[5]

Implementation of national self-reliance, then, may require subordinate groups to act in ways that make them less self-reliant. This is a major problem for those charged with the task of achieving national self-reliance, for it involves getting people to behave in ways that violate the principle whose achievement is sought. An ideologue who sought to induce individuals to behave solely to achieve national self-reliance would find the task very difficult. A pragmatist who was willing to relax the principle at some levels to achieve it at other levels would be better positioned to succeed. In such a situation, the pragmatist becomes essential to the ideologue.

The cost is conceptual ambiguity; i.e., at different levels or in different situations the requisite behaviors to achieve national self-reliance will be different. Leaders seeking to encourage self-reliance did not like to admit the contradictions posed by different units of reference. Indeed, the Arusha Declaration contended that national self-reliance was the summation of the self-reliance of constituent groups. It stated,

> If every individual is self-reliant the ten-house cell will be self-reliant; if all the cells are self-reliant the whole ward will be self-reliant; and if the wards are self-reliant the District will be self-reliant. If the Districts are self-reliant, then the Region is self-reliant, and if the Regions are self-reliant, then the whole nation is self-reliant and this is our aim.[6]

This assertion of complementarity was a theme Nyerere stressed often.[7] Kingunge Ngombale-Mwiru argued with him over one point: He contended that socialist self-reliance "does not mean each individual merely relying upon his own resources." Rather, he argued, it "hinges upon the group." Like Nyerere, though, in claiming that socialist self-reliance "means making the fullest use of our life in society by co-operating in all our activities in the interest of all the individual members," he implied a complementarity among these levels.[8]

That the use by a community of its own resources and skills for its own benefit, as in community self-reliance, would simultaneously benefit other communities, as in national self-reliance, is not necessarily true—as indicated by the examples cited previously.

Purpose: The Strategy Versus Goal Controversy

The complications posed by the dispute over how self-reliance should be measured and the variety of units to which self-reliance should be applied are compounded by a dispute over whether the concept refers to a strategy and/or a goal and the nature of that strategy and/or goal. Its conjunction with socialism in the Arusha Declaration suggests it is either a strategy for socialist construction or an aspect of socialism, but self-reliance has been linked with other projects and other ends. In listing some of these, Andrew Coulson includes "willingness to exist without foreign aid," "a minimization of trade," "a refusal to employ foreigners," "rural development," and "non-alignment."[9]

Self-Reliance as a Strategy

Most often, self-reliance is referred to as a strategy.[10] Its treatment in the Arusha Declaration is primarily that of a means by which socialism might be achieved. The essence of the strategy is "do it yourself." But there is some diversity of opinion over what this implies. Political leaders have tended to describe a diverse set of individual and group behaviors that they consider to be associated with the strategy. For example, Nyerere identifies who is involved in the strategy when he asserts that

> self-reliance is a positive affirmation that we shall depend upon ourselves for the development of Tanzania, and that we shall use the resources we have for that purpose, not just sit back and complain because there are other things we do not have.[11]

Ngombale-Mwiru identifies some of the characteristics and behaviors of those who are involved when he lists such things as enhancing self-confidence, accepting responsibility, making the best use of meager resources, reforming institutions that do not contribute to other aims of self-reliance, and enlisting the participation of the broad masses.[12]

Scholars have tended to focus upon stages involved in a strategy for transforming the way Tanzania relates to other countries. The three primary ones involve withdrawal, restructuring, and reentry. Thomas Biersteker describes the strategy with the following expressions:

> selective disengagement from international transactions (trade, aid, investment, technology, information, and manpower exchanges), replaced by reliance on internal capabilities; . . . a conscious *restructuring* of basic economic and political relationships, values, and institutions . . . between the country pursuing self-reliance and other countries in the international system and . . . within the country pursuing self-reliance; and . . . reassociation, or partial reestablishment of previous economic and political . . . transactions with industrial countries on a changed basis.[13]

Idrian Resnick suggests five stages: a shift of resource allocation "toward the domestic, rural economy"; a relative decline in exports as a percentage of GDP; a relative decline in imports as a percentage of GDP; the "gradual and negotiated disengagement from the world economic order"; and a reengagement in trade with other Third World and socialist countries on terms of equality.[14] The Biersteker and Resnick descriptions are similar, though in the final stage the former emphasizes the reestablishment of ties with industrial countries, the latter with Third World and socialist countries.[15] Though self-reliance may be portrayed as a strategy, it also may be portrayed as a goal.

Self-Reliance as a Goal

Strategies and goals are interrelated. Self-reliance may be treated as a goal in two senses. First, the putting in place of the strategy is a goal. For example, Magnus Blomstrom and Bjorn Hettne argued that "one of the most important objectives of the Tanzanian development strategy was to achieve 'self-reliance.'"[16] Second, the object of the strategy is a goal. The broad underlying objective of self-reliance is the enhancement of the relative power of the unit involved. Yet a variety of purposes is served by such an increase in relative power.

One goal is development. The final stage in both Idrian Resnick's and Thomas Biersteker's descriptions of self-reliance as a strategy is a situation in which ties with other countries promote Tanzanian development.[17] Although Mary Baughman Anderson explicitly rejects the idea that self-reliance is a goal, she describes it as "a strategy *for* economic and social development"; i.e., its objective is development.[18] And William Mayer argues in the same vein that self-reliance "means that the allocation of resources for production is geared to meet domestic demand *so that* an integrated domestic economic system is promoted"; i.e., its objective is an economic system geared for development.[19]

A second goal is economic nationalism. Peter Burnell suggests that economic nationalism might be thought of as "the pursuit of the national economic interest, an interest identified in terms of economic welfare or the economic means to welfare."[20] As Tanzania became less and less self-reliant during the 1980s, Nyerere began speaking of self-reliance more as a nationalist than as a socialist. At the opening of a public-private sector seminar in Dar es Salaam, he argued that he would rather see independent capitalists in Tanzania than a "bunch" of socialists "who were totally dependent on others."[21] During the same period, capitalists who were able to produce goods in Tanzania that would otherwise require foreign exchange, such as replacement parts for cotton ginneries, were treated as heroes.

A third goal is independence, at the national level, or freedom, at the individual level. In Nyerere's speech to the last session of parliament in 1980, he said, "We greatly value our independence. But a vital basis for our independence is self-reliance. If we neglect this foundation, we endanger our independence."[22]

In Nyerere's discussion of a self-reliant individual, he said such an individual "lives on what he earns, whether this be large or small, so that he is a truly free person beholden to no one."[23] What is apparent about this brief list is that each of these goals is a part of the bundle of interrelated objectives defining Tanzanian socialism.[24]

The Relationship Between Self-Reliance and Socialism

There is a kind of irony in the relationship between socialism and self-reliance. On the one hand, self-reliance says to look inward, to think of yourself and your group first, whereas socialism says to look outward, to think of your fellow "family" members and other groups in society first. That is, socialism emphasizes working together and relying on others, and self-reliance seems to emphasize the opposite. At the individual level, self-reliance comes close to the notion of individualism characteristic of a capitalist system, rather than to that of collectivism characteristic of a socialist one. Indeed, by the mid-1980s the many public employees who had their own *miradhi* [projects] to earn additional money jokingly justified these capitalist endeavors in terms of self-reliance. On the other hand, most Tanzanians committed to socialist construction would contend that the concept of self-reliance they employed was a group-oriented one concerned about the well-being of all.

Virtually all Tanzanian political leaders have supported the view that self-reliance is a path toward socialism. They have disagreed, though, over whether it is a requisite condition. Ideological socialists tended to see it as necessary at the national level. They argued that Tanzania exists within a world economy that functions under the logic of capitalism. Lack of self-reliance transfers to those who control that economy power over the direction of Tanzania's evolution. Therefore, if Tanzania is to build socialism, it must end its dependence.

Pragmatic socialists did not disagree with such an argument, except for the "must" in the conclusion. They tended to argue that it was possible to receive aid and to trade without necessarily transferring the power to direct Tanzania's evolution. Furthermore, they argued that in the process of socialist construction, Tanzania faced many dilemmas. Compromise in one area like self-reliance might be necessary for advance in another area like improving standards of living. Failure to compromise, they contended, would mean stagnation. For example, Susan Crouch argued that in 1974 during a period of economic crisis, Tanzania was willing to become more dependent on Western aid rather than to slow progress toward socialist programs such as Universal Primary Education (UPE) and villagization.[25] And Cranford Pratt argued similarly,

> The leadership in Tanzania decided that the transition to socialism would be more likely to be threatened by the fall in living standards and the standstill in development that would follow any halt in foreign assistance than by the dependency implicit in remaining dependent on foreign capital assistance.[26]

Such a compromise was in line with the thinking of pragmatic socialists. The problem they continually faced was when to compromise and whether the compromise would do more good than harm to the socialist transition. Since such decisions were subjective and judgmental, they were often viewed by ideological socialists as "surrenders" to capitalism.

The Assessment of Success in Achieving Self-Reliance

An assessment of the success of self-reliance requires a two-fold evaluation. First, we need to determine the extent to which a strategy of self-reliance has been put into place. Second, we need to determine the extent to which such a strategy has facilitated the achievement of socialism. The two are interrelated. In figurative terms, if a possible cure for societal ills is not fully developed, its impact is unlikely to be very significant. Virtually all qualitative and quantitative data suggest that Tanzania has become increasingly less self-reliant.

It is impossible to assess the success of self-reliance for Tanzania and every group of which it is composed. Thus, for the sake of simplicity this assessment is divided into two parts. The first focuses on self-reliance at the national level, the second on self-reliance at the subnational level.

The Degree of Success at the National Level

Most discussion of self-reliance has focused on that of a country in the international system. Both qualitative and quantitative data suggest that Tanzania has been frustrated in its efforts to promote self-reliance. Forms of dependency have shifted, but dependency has intensified.

Most observers would agree with the broad outline of Issa Shivji's characterization of what has occurred in Tanzania. He described Tanzania in the immediate postindependence period as a "neo-colony." He contended that, whereas on foreign policy matters Nyerere's "personality and principle-guided outlook resulted in the country making certain decisions with considerable independence," on domestic policy issues foreign ownership of the major means of production meant high levels of dependence.[27] After the Arusha Declaration, he argued, Tanzania's status was "in a situation of flux," with the potential for disengagement from the world economy.[28] But in the mid-1970s certain external shocks such as the rise in oil prices, world recession, and drought "exacerbated the internal contradictions inherent in a neo-colonial economy" and constricted its "relative autonomy *vis-à-vis* imperialism." Donors were "able to exert even greater pressure and erstwhile imperialist agencies like the International Monetary Fund and the World Bank began to call the tune in no uncertain terms."[29]

It was the IMF accord in 1986 that was the symbolic turning point. Prior to that agreement, Tanzanians were able to make most of their own decisions regarding what should be done to build socialism. After that agreement, Tanzanians were forced to substantially change policies enacted to attain aspects of Tanzanian socialism. Thus, an understanding of Tanzania's experiences with the issue of self-reliance in socialist construction requires a description of this profound event.

The precursor of the agreement was the long economic slump that began in the late 1970s. The long delay in reaching the agreement was a result of the perception by Tanzanian leaders that the "strings" attached to IMF assistance would seriously undermine the transition to socialism. The scholar Ajit Singh argued,

> It is . . . not difficult to see that although the arguments are couched in technical terms, the IMF is using the present economic crisis to push Tanzania towards market-oriented, non-socialist development, in return for which the Fund would provide some economic assistance.[30]

The political leader Kighoma Malima argued similarly:

> What we are witnessing in Tanzania and other developing countries today is a new and even more pernicious form of colonialism. The carrot of very limited financial support is being dangled before countries in a

desperate economic situation. But concealed in that carrot is a denial of sovereignty. Thus, one developing country after another is put under immense pressure to abandon any kind of enlightened and equitable socioeconomic policies based on social justice, in favour of the privatisation of their economies.[31]

For years, Nyerere personally opposed the conditionalities the IMF had demanded.[32] At a meeting of the Royal Commonwealth Society in London in 1985, he said that the IMF "has become largely an instrument for economic and ideological control of poor countries by the rich ones."[33] Four years after the initial agreement, when the IMF sought to impose new conditionalities, Nyerere claimed the conditionalities were meant more to "destabalise poor countries" than "to solve problems clouding their economies."[34] Although changes were undertaken in the Tanzanian economy beginning in 1982 to bring the country more into line with the demands of the IMF, the agreement was not reached until Mwinyi had replaced Nyerere as president late in 1985.

Mwinyi acknowledged that the delays were due to the demand that the country bend its "socialist principles in return for subsidies from abroad."[35] Yet he concluded that circumstances required him to take the step:

> There was no foreign exchange, no food, and worse still, there was no oil. And without oil, the country was coming to a standstill . . . For the first time, it was realised in stark terms how important oil was to the life of the country. Hitherto . . . we took everything for granted until we were jerked to reality. . . . The oil crisis had reached an alarming situation after the country failed to honour its debt and credit commitment.[36]

Mwinyi contended that the consequent inflow of money was more helpful than the conditionalities were harmful to socialist construction.[37] In awkward analogies he has likened the IMF agreement to a medicine that would be very costly but was preferable to death[38] and to a choice between two "spears," both of which "would bring suffering to the people."[39] In other words, the agreement was the lesser of two evils; it was likely to harm socialist construction less than would failure to accept it.

But such an important decision could not be made without the support of CCM, a party dominated by ideological socialists opposed to the agreement. There are two principal explanations for party acceptance of the IMF accord. First, economic conditions within Tanzania had gotten so bad that swing members between the ideological and pragmatic socialist camps came to support the latter in preference to continuation of the status quo. Second, Nyerere was caught in a dilemma. Mwinyi had succeeded him as president only a few months previously. Had he thrown his weight against Mwinyi, stability and peaceful leadership succession would have been undermined. So, although known as a harsh critic of the IMF agreement,

Nyerere decided not to oppose it. As "point man" in the struggle to resist accepting the conditionalities and as chairman of CCM, his acquiescence carried enough support for party approval.

The decision was the first significant defeat for the ideological socialists at the hands of the pragmatic socialists. A couple of years later, when Tanzania was threatened with a freeze on disbursements of funds for its economic recovery program because it resisted further devaluation, the National Executive Committee of CCM met and called on "Party and Government leaders to implement the policy on self-reliance practically."[40] Mwinyi announced accession to the IMF demand the following day.[41] "Practically" had come to mean "in accord with the pragmatic socialist view."

Pragmatic socialists have defended the decision by arguing its advantages and depreciating its disadvantages. For example, Joseph Rwegasira, when he was the JUWATA secretary general, said "the workers organization supported the agreement with the IMF because JUWATA realised that if the difficult economic situation was left to exist unchecked, the nation's political, ideological and social life would be jeopardized." He added, "We realise that a patient could not select treatment."[42]

The IMF package required the abandonment or radical modification of a wide array of policies adopted to facilitate the achievement of socialist goals. As these conditionalities were translated into state actions, the package was defended on a "lesser of two evils" basis. For example, when President Mwinyi announced one of the currency devaluations in November 1988, he said that should he not act in accord with the IMF demand, no other lender would provide Tanzania with assistance and the economy would be set back to the 1982–1986 period of lines and scarcities.[43] The IMF agreement limited the freedom of Tanzanian political leaders in their choice of policies to promote socialism. To the ideological socialists, this was a major setback. The pragmatic socialists saw in the agreement the possibility of new and more effective policies.

The inability of Tanzania to free itself from dependence is illustrated by aid and trade data. Aid to Tanzania has been substantial, yet it has had a pernicious effect.[44] Grants have led to projects that cost Tanzania more than they benefited the country. Loans have significantly limited Tanzania's choices. Unless they are paid back or there is an agreement on conditions donors feel will allow them to be paid back, further aid is unlikely.[45] The IMF accord is the most significant consequence of dependence on external sources of funds. Tanzania has been fortunate in that several First World countries have written off debts, but even this process has been subject to "strings" that affect the country's sovereignty. For example, when the United States agreed to write off about $80 million in debts in March 1990, it did so with the proviso that Tanzania continue its economic reforms.[46]

Quantitative data on outstanding debt do not show the nature of the strings attached. For example, they do not distinguish between the period of relatively benign assistance and that following the IMF accord. Nevertheless, the total debt, total debt-to-GNP ratio, and the debt service ratio constitute crude indicators of the degree of economic dependence, the larger figures implying the greater dependence. These are provided in Table 8.1.

Tanzania's total debt burden and debt-to-GNP ratio have grown at a rapid rate, especially since 1985. The cost, as has been noted, has been acceptance of IMF conditionalities and their attack on the path Tanzanians had chosen to pursue socialism.

A second quantitative measure of dependence that is slightly more refined than debt is the ratio of exports to imports. In a Third World situation, the higher this ratio, the higher the level of self-reliance. At the least, a high ratio indicates that the country is better able to balance what it sells abroad with what it buys from abroad than a country with a low ratio, thereby avoiding the dependency consequences of debt. Table 8.2 shows the serious imbalance in trade that has characterized Tanzania for many years. The trade ratio indicates that Tanzania has become less able to produce what it consumes and consume what it produces since the adoption of the Arusha Declaration; i.e., it has become less self-reliant.

The character of this dependence, however, has shifted. Tanzania has managed to decrease its dependence upon finished products and increase its dependence on intermediate and primary goods—though a reversal of this trend is shown in the early 1990s. Table 8.3 shows the character of Tanzania's imports.

There is a difference in the degree to which particular imported items are essential to survival. The more essential an item, the greater the power of those who control its distribution. Two key goods are food and fuel. The more a country depends on others for these, the lower its level of self-reliance.

Obviously, food is the most essential good. Those who need it will do what those who have it to offer ask, even if its acquisition undermines other goals. For example, during Peasants Day celebrations in 1980 Nyerere said,

> If I were told that Tanzania had no shoes, and the only place I could get them was South Africa, I would not order any. But, if I were told that Tanzania had no food, and that I could not get it from anywhere else except from South Africa, I would buy it.[47]

In President Mwinyi's first state of the nation speech in 1985 he declared that Tanzania could not be "a free and independent nation if we depend on foreign countries for our essential commodities such as food."[48]

Self-Reliance and Socialism 171

Table 8.1 Tanzanian National Debt and Ratios of Debt to Gross National Product and Debt Service to Exports

Year	Total External Debt (U.S.$ million)	Debt/GNP (ratio)	Debt Service/Exports (ratio)
1970	265.3	20.7	5.3
1973	509.5	27.3	7.2
1976	1,341.7	46.6	4.4
1979	2,196.6	49.2	9.0
1982	2,985.4	47.8	23.8
1985	3,867.1	56.8	22.5
1988	5,138.9	175.6	20.7
1991	6,459.0	250.8	24.6

Sources: World Bank, *World Debt Tables, 1988–89, Vol. 3 (Country Tables, 1970–79)* (Washington, D.C.: World Bank, 1989), pp. 214–215, for 1970–1979 figures; World Bank, *World Debt Tables, 1990–91, Vol. 2 (Country Tables)* (Washington, D.C.: World Bank, 1990), p. 358, for 1980–1988 figures; World Bank, *World Debt Tables, 1992–93, Vol. 2 (Country Tables)* (Washington, D.C.: World Bank, 1992), p. 398, for 1991 figures except for debt service/exports; and World Bank, *World Debt Tables, 1993–94, Vol. 2 (Country Tables)* (Washington, D.C.: World Bank, 1993), p. 442, for 1991 debt service/exports figure.

Note: Approximate trends are illustrated by these figures, though the World Bank figures reported for various years vary greatly from edition to edition of the *World Debt Tables* and also vary from the export and production figures prepared by the Tanzanian government.

Table 8.2 Tanzania's Exports, Imports, and Export/Import Ratio

Year	Exports (U.S.$ million)	Imports (U.S.$ million)	Exports/Imports (ratio)
1967	232.4	228.2	101.8
1970	258.3	317.3	81.4
1973	376.0	501.7	75.0
1976	464.9	640.1	72.6
1979	542.5	1,097.6	49.4
1982	415.4	1,112.8	37.3
1985	285.6	999.2	28.6
1988	372.0	1,185.0	31.4
1991	422.4	1,390.8	31.1

Sources: Calculated from Tables 8, 9, and 22, Bank of Tanzania, *Tanzania: Twenty Years of Independence (1961–1981), A Review of Political and Economic Performance* (Dar es Salaam: Bank of Tanzania, n.d.), pp. 278, 279–280, and 296, respectively, for 1967–1979; and Economic Research Bureau, *Tanzanian Economic Trends, A Quarterly Review of the Economy,* Vol. 2, No. 1 (April 1989), p. 43, for 1982–1988, and Vol. 4, Nos. 3 and 4 (October 1991 and January 1992), pp. 62 and 63, for 1991.

So food imports indicate the severity of dependence and the lack of self-reliance. Table 8.4 indicates the extent to which Tanzania has been dependent on food imports. Although there is considerable variation from year to year, the general trend appears to be up until 1988. From 1988 through 1991, imports of food appear to have declined substantially.[49] Whether that decline will continue is uncertain, for the table indicates considerable instability.

Table 8.3 Composition of Tanzania's Imports

Year	Capital Goods (percent)	Intermediate Goods (percent)	Consumer Goods (percent)
1967	24.0	41.0	35.0
1970	29.6	40.4	30.0
1973	25.1	45.0	29.9
1976	29.8	49.4	20.8
1979	45.0	40.4	14.6
1982	43.7	39.0	17.3
1985	43.6	40.2	16.3
1988	35.0	42.0	23.0
1991	51.6	25.7	22.7

Sources: Compiled by Amon Chaligha from United Republic of Tanzania, *The Economic Survey, 1974–75* (Swahili version), p. 25; *1982* (English version), p. 31; and *1984* (Swahili version), p. 25, for 1967–1973; Jamhuri ya Muungano wa Tanzania, *Hali ya Uchumi wa Taifa Katika Mwaka 1985* (Dar es Salaam: Mpigachapa wa Serikali, 1986), p. 21, for 1976 and 1979; and Economic Research Bureau, *Tanzanian Economic Trends, A Quarterly Review of the Economy,* Vol. 4, Nos. 3 and 4 (October 1991 and January 1992), p. 63, for 1982–1991. The 1991 figures are provisional.

Table 8.4 Tanzania's Food Imports

Year	Value of Food Imports (U.S.$ million)	Value of Food Imports per Capita (U.S.$)
1967	12.7	1.07
1970	24.5	1.90
1973	39.6	2.83
1976	63.5	3.87
1979	37.2	2.07
1982	108.6	5.48
1985	78.0	3.59
1988	105.4	4.54
1991	1.1	0.04

Sources: Imports calculated from Tables 9 and 22, Bank of Tanzania, *Tanzania: Twenty Years of Independence (1961–1981), A Review of Political and Economic Performance* (Dar es Salaam: Bank of Tanzania, n.d.), pp. 279–280 and 296, for 1967–1979; Economic Research Bureau, *Tanzanian Economic Trends, A Quarterly Review of the Economy,* Vol. 4, Nos. 3 and 4 (October 1991 and January 1992), p. 63, for 1982–1991. Population figure used in calculations from: United Republic of Tanzania, *Quarterly Statistical Bulletin,* Vol. 26. No. 1 (June 1975), Table 1, for 1967–1973; United Nations, *Demographic Yearbook, 1985* (New York: United Nations, 1987), p. 151, for 1976; United Republic of Tanzania, *Statistical Abstract, 1982* (Dar es Salaam: Bureau of Statistics, 1983), p. 64, for 1979–1982; United Republic of Tanzania, *Statistical Abstract, 1984* (Dar es Salaam: Bureau of Statistics, February 1986), p. 29, for 1985; *Daily News,* 15 March 1989, p. 1, for 1988; and World Bank, *World Tables, 1993* (Washington, D.C.: Johns Hopkins University Press for World Bank, 1993), p. 589 for 1991.

Fuel has been an essential commodity to the Tanzanian economy and to every "developed" and "developing" economy. Without oil, industry, transportation, trade, and virtually every other aspect of the economy would be unable to function. As has been noted, a major reason for the acceptance of IMF conditionalities in 1986 was the country's inability to obtain oil. Substantial investments and major concessions to foreign countries have been made in the search for oil in Tanzania, without significant success. In an editorial in the *Daily News* urging greater use of coal, the dependence on oil was starkly described:

> In 1972, Tanzania spent 230.7m on oil while its total foreign earnings were 2,277m. In 1980 it spent 2,223.4m, which is an equivalent of 45 per cent of the country's total expenditure. But since the mid 1980s, the oil bill has sharply risen to 60 per cent of the total foreign earnings.[50]

In sum, the quantitative data support the same conclusion as did the qualitative data: One of Tanzania's greatest failures has been its inability to increase its national self-reliance. It has had a parallel experience at the subnational level.

The Degree of Success at the Subnational Level

The Arusha Declaration envisioned national self-reliance as the summation of the self-reliance of lesser units. I have argued that there is not an additive relationship between the self-reliance of lesser and greater units and that in many cases the self-reliance of the former has undermined the self-reliance of the latter. Part of the reason there were so few cases of subnational self-reliance was the threat they posed to national leaders and their objectives and the consequent action by such leaders to contain the threat. A lack of self-reliance characterized almost every group.

CCM

CCM itself has been "dependent" upon financial grants from the government for decades. Although it has had constitutional supremacy over the government, it has always claimed a separate identity. Yet it could not exist in the form it had through the twenty-five years following the Arusha Declaration without a government subvention. According to TANU annual reports, the government supplied 95.0 percent of party expenditures in 1968, 95.5 percent in 1969, and 96.8 percent in 1971.[51] In the early 1990s, the party sought to become less dependent on such subsidies. Under CCM's 1990/91 budget, it claimed to be 27 percent "self-reliant"; i.e., 73 percent of its expenditures derived from government sources; in 1991/92 it sought to be 40 percent self-reliant; and by 1994/95 its goal was to be 75 percent self-reliant.[52] One spur to such self-reliance at the time was the possible shift to a multiparty system, which would eliminate CCM's constitutional supremacy and its complete freedom to allocate itself government funds.

Banks

The banks were national institutions, yet they were not permitted to function autonomously. They were not permitted by the party and government to become self-reliant. The reason was that their self-reliance would jeopardize national self-reliance. For example, Amon Nsekela, the chairman and managing director of the National Bank of Commerce, has complained about the fact that the bank had been compelled to lend to industrial parastatals to keep them in operation and "to provide adequate credit facilities to cooperative unions to enable them to purchase crops from peasantry."[53] The expansion of unsecured credit undermined the bank's self-reliance, yet it was essential to sustain industrial parastatals, to feed people who lived in urban areas, and to earn the foreign exchange upon which industry and transportation relied. In other words, the bank's self-reliance was sacrificed in order for the nation to be more self-reliant.

Parastatals

Although repeatedly called upon to be self-reliant, many parastatals amassed debts year after year. Industrial parastatals were sustained because the government viewed industrialization as necessary for national self-reliance. But the cost was to undermine the self-reliance of many other institutions with which the parastatals conducted business. When those other institutions sought to become self-reliant by demanding that debts be paid, industries floundered and national self-reliance was undermined further. For example, by June 1988 the textile holding company, TEXCO, had debts to the banks of over TSh. 1.5 billion and additional debts to its suppliers. One of those suppliers, the Tanganyika Electrical Supply Company (TANESCO), eventually cut power to one of TEXCO's subsidiaries, KILTEX, in April 1990 to force payment or reduce its costs. The result was that workers were laid off and production ceased.[54] Similarly, by late 1988, the Mbeya Ceramic Company had amassed a debt of TSh. 1.1 billion for electric power alone; TANESCO cut its power; and, the ceramics company claimed, it lost TSh. 800,000 in its first month of suspended production. TANESCO's response was to assert that its objective was self-reliance, or to "maximise the company's revenue," and that the lost production of another parastatal was not its concern.[55]

Numerous other examples might be cited of both the ripple effect of the failure of self-reliance by one institution or unit on another or others and the difficulties such failures posed to the nation's effort to build socialism. The Dodoma Wine Company (DOWICO), long a subsidiary of the National Milling Corporation (NMC), is a case in point. It owed over TSh. 273 million in late 1987 to growers, suppliers of raw materials, banks, and the government for taxes of various sorts. When other institutions demanded payment or halted subsidies, DOWICO became unable to bottle a million liters of wine worth around TSh. 100 million because it could not get the money it needed to purchase the empty bottles.[56]

Thus, most parastatals were not self-reliant; i.e., their expenditures did not match their incomes. When they sought to become self-reliant, they often undermined the self-reliance of others.

Ujamaa Villages

The most significant policy implemented in an attempt to build socialism in rural Tanzania was the movement of most of the rural population into villages in the decade following the Arusha Declaration. Yet the villages were pulled in two directions: toward self-reliance and away from self-reliance. Many saw villages as ways groups of people might become self-reliant by working together for the good of all. As self-reliant entities they might withstand the demands from the outside and those from inside that sought to undermine the goals they set for themselves. Indeed, villages were called upon to be self-reliant. They were urged to create their own welfare system, build their own schools, and fund other projects.

Others saw the villages as sources of resources for the self-reliance of the nation. There was no more criticized act by outsiders than the "takeover" by the state of the Ruvuma Development Association because of its separate orientation. The central party and government sought in a variety of ways to diminish the independence and self-reliance of villages. The party and government extracted wealth from them; determined the form of their government; sent central government agents into them to supervise implementation of party-government policies; and sought to "penetrate" them in order to achieve an assessment of the country's popular will.

These two opposing views did not neatly parallel the pragmatic versus ideological socialist division. Many within both groups wanted local units subordinated in such a way that they could be coordinated to achieve national self-reliance. Subsequent action had contradictory results. As banking institutions began to strive for self-reliance, their demand for villages to repay debts led to their seizure of village property. For example, in 1988 the Cooperative and Rural Development Bank (CRDB) began to take milling machines from villages in Dodoma Rural District for failure to pay loans.[57] Although this action may have increased the bank's self-reliance, it made it more difficult for the villagers to consume what they produced.

Local Government

When local governments were reestablished in 1983/84 following an eleven-year hiatus, during which most of their functions were turned over to the villages, they too found self-reliance difficult to attain. Again, a long list of detrimental consequences could be described, but the point can be made with an illustrative case. In 1989 the Korogwe District Council failed to pay a TSh. 2.5 million debt to TANESCO. As a result, TANESCO disconnected the Kilole water pumping station, which supplied water to the town.[58] The social and political consequences were unlikely to further socialist objectives. The debts of local governments were almost always a consequence, in part, of debts owed them.

A case in point was the Moshi Municipal Council. In 1989 the council sought to collect unpaid taxes in order to become more self-reliant itself. It seized the staff bus of Tanzania Tanneries, Ltd., and two typewriters from the Tanzania Housing Bank in an effort to get almost TSh. 20,000 plus a year's interest owed.[59] Needless to say, the impact on those institutions was to reduce their ability to contribute to socialist construction.

Cooperatives

The ability of cooperatives to become self-reliant institutions was undermined by state activities. As I have shown, they were bled in order to fund the new ujamaa villages; then they were closed by the state; then they were reopened by the state; then they were told to reorganize as production-oriented cooperatives on a village basis; and then they were told to be independent. But the state has found it very difficult to let them be self-reliant.[60]

An advisory group from the International Cooperative Alliance (ICA) in 1986 chided the state for its actions, arguing that

> because cooperatives are self-help organisations special care is needed to ensure that any assistance requested or offered contributes to the attainment of self-reliance rather than erodes their independence, or perhaps leads to a situation in which an activity can only be sustained by a continuous drip-feed of external aid.[61]

But the state still found it difficult to allow the cooperatives autonomy. Normally, it argued, "autonomy" tended to mean rule by corrupt managers or a rural elite. Defenders of state "interference" contended that the state's desire to sustain the organization caused it to act against corruption, and its desire to promote democratic control caused it to act against a rural elite leadership. Furthermore, the state had to provide funding to the cooperatives for purchases of inputs and crops. Once that was done, it had to assure that the funds were repaid or the banking institutions would be threatened.

In the late 1980s the National Bank of Commerce (NBC) and the CRDB delayed providing loans to cooperative unions until certain conditions were met, a vivid parallel with the conditionalities of international aid organizations.[62] Cooperatives were affected in other ways by the debts they accumulated: Some unions were unable to provide farm inputs of seeds, fertilizers, and insecticides.[63] Some had their property seized by CRDB.[64] Some had to halt purchasing crops.[65] Several union general managers were called before the CCM National Executive Committee at the end of 1989 to explain why their cooperatives should not be closed because of debts.[66] One response to these problems was to disparage the national institutions such as NBC to which debt was owed. At a Cooperative Union of Tanzania seminar in 1988, a participant, reflecting broad sentiment, referred to the NBC as a "peasant death dose."[67]

The consequence of the cooperatives' lack of self-reliance was a reduction in the self-reliance of members. In several cases, members were not paid for crops delivered.[68] In other cases, they had deductions taken from the payment for their crops to help cover the debt.[69] In still other cases, the property of those indebted to the union was seized. For example, in early 1990, the Singida union seized cattle, goats, sheep, a plow, and a house, which were to be auctioned to recover money owed the union.[70]

Cooperatives themselves were owed substantial sums. In April 1989 the Ministry of Local Governments, Community Development, Cooperatives and Marketing listed debts from marketing bodies to unions totaling over TSh. 3 billion.[71] Clearly, self-reliance was a rare characteristic at the local level.

Labor Unions

The autonomy of labor unions has not been allowed, though recent changes have pushed them in that direction. In 1991, as part of the reform of CCM, the mass labor organization, JUWATA, was replaced by the Organisation of Tanzania Trade Unions (OTTU). The parliamentary debate over OTTU suggested that autonomy is something that the party and government are finding it hard to allow, just as they are finding it hard to allow cooperatives similar autonomy. Once again, the self-reliance of a subnational unit has remained minimal.

One could go on and on describing the lack of self-reliance among subnational units and the impact such a lack of self-reliance has had on the self-reliance of other groups. Early in 1989 Mwinyi summarized the problem of an absence of self-reliance in the form of debt as "a 'cancer' in almost every institution, including the central government" and noted there was a "chain" of institutions that had failed to pay one another.[72]

Thus, the experience at the local level has not been much different than that at the national level. In both cases the forces working against self-reliance and autonomy appear to have prevailed. Why?

Reasons Self-Reliance Has Not Succeeded

There are several ways to account for the failure to achieve a high level of self-reliance at the national and subnational levels. The reasons can be divided into those primarily external to the unit seeking self-reliance and those primarily internal to such a unit. Many of the external reasons are related to the units of action problem, and many of the internal reasons are related to the struggles between the pragmatic and ideological socialists.

External Factors: The Units of Action Problem

Many observers have argued that the world system is inhospitable for socialism, i.e., that it is a kind of poison that brings either "sickness" or "death" to efforts to build socialist societies. The impact of the world system on socialist construction has long been a subject of debate.

The effect of the world system was at the core of a long-standing disagreement among Marxists over whether socialism in one country was possible. Many Marxists thought the world system was so hostile that socialism could not be constructed in a single country; others disagreed. For example, Friedrich Engels and Leon Trotsky thought socialism in one country was impossible. The utopian socialists, though, disagreed. Vladimir Lenin both agreed and disagreed; Joseph Stalin at first said it was impossible but later argued it was possible.[73] The absence of a consensus on the issue was due in part to honest disagreement over the impact of the world system and in part to the need of socialist leaders to assure followers of the feasibility of the venture they were undertaking.

More recently, Christopher Chase-Dunn has argued that socialism in one country was "unlikely as long as the political-economic forces of the capitalist world-economy remain strong."[74] What is apparent in such general literature is the notion that the world system *is* inhospitable to socialism, though debate continues over whether it is a sufficient cause for socialism's demise.

The responsibility of the world system for Tanzania's difficulties has been the subject of controversy, too. Michael Lofchie has argued that the world system "represents an environment that is deeply inhospitable to the developmental prospects of small agricultural countries." But, he contends, it does not make progress impossible.[75] Nyerere saw it as more of an impediment. Admitting that Tanzania made many policy mistakes, he contended that "our mistakes have made an impossible situation worse: they do not account for the situation itself." The real problems, he argued, arose from the unequal distribution of wealth in the world, patterns of world trade, worsening terms of trade, sudden price fluctuations, debt and interest payments, lack of foreign investment, IMF conditionalities, etc.[76] The impact of the world system on one country like Tanzania is in reality an instance of a more general phenomenon involving the impact of one unit of action on another.

There appears to be a kind of tendency or "law" that can be stated as follows: The larger the social unit, the more it determines the behavior of smaller constituent units. Thus, the international system operates in a way that undermines national autonomy and self-reliance, and the national system operates in a way that undermines subnational autonomy and self-reliance.

Many examples of this tendency, some of which have already been described, corroborate such an observation. Three are illustrative. First, under IMF conditionalities, the Tanzanian government agreed to reduce the money supply. Yet if money was not available to purchase crops, the country would become more dependent on the "outside" world. Thus, the government, acting in accord with the wishes of CCM, repeatedly ordered the NBC to make money available for crop purchases. This action adversely affected continued IMF support and the assistance of other multilateral and bilateral donors who followed the IMF lead. In his budget speech in 1989, Cleopa Msuya, the minister for finance, asserted that the greatest failure in the nation's economic recovery program was its high level of credit expansion caused by credit defaults of cooperatives and marketing boards.[77] Had the money lent to purchase crops been recovered, the government would have been able to meet the IMF demand for a contraction of the money supply. Consequently, the government did institute action to recover loans but in so doing made self-reliance more difficult for those groups and individuals from whom money and equipment were seized.

Second, beer had been made and consumed in Tanzania for many years prior to the establishment of colonialism. Nevertheless, the government has encouraged the consumption of beers familiar to those in the West partly because of the ease with which taxes can be levied on the product. Unlike traditional beer, though, imported raw materials for Western-style beer (brewed by Tanzania Breweries) account for 85 percent of the total brewing cost! A failure to import such raw materials provokes not only popular discontent but also a decline in state revenue. The result: more imports and a diminution of Tanzania's self-reliance.[78]

Third, when the Tanzanian police were unable to control violence and robberies beginning in the 1980s, self-reliant law enforcement groups, most often called *sungusungu,* were formed around the country. At first they were threatened by the central government directly; then they were co-opted. In some areas, participation was made mandatory. For example, in mid-1991 the CCM district executive committee in Zanzibar Urban District declared that those refusing to participate in *sungusungu* operations would have legal action taken against them.[79] In other words, their autonomy and self-reliance were quickly subverted.

Is this tendency or "law" I have described and illustrated a condition sufficient to account for the defeat of self-reliance efforts? In other words, can a smaller unit successfully resist its loss of autonomy to a larger unit of which it is a part? Clearly, we are dealing with a statistical "law," i.e., one that is true most but not all of the time. If leaders of the subunit are able and willing to pay the price, they may resist. Indeed, the pursuit of self-reliance, explicitly spelled out in the Arusha Declaration, was a direct consequence of leaders' resistance to demands for subordination by major Western powers in the mid-1960s. For six years, Tanzania resisted pressure to subordinate itself to IMF conditionalities. Nevertheless, the costs of autonomy have severely limited the opportunities for resistance at both national and subnational levels.

Internal Factors and the Pragmatic Socialist–Ideological Socialist Struggle

Many internal factors contribute to the failure to become more self-reliant, i.e., to resist the tendency of larger units to impose their will on smaller constituent units. The most frequently cited of these has to do with policy errors. Despite Lofchie's recognition of the inhospitality of external factors, he contends that Tanzania "offers a perfect example of the ways in which inappropriate agricultural policy can produce disastrous economic results."[80] In other words, he contends that inappropriate policy has prevented Tanzania from becoming self-reliant in agriculture.

Now, the "bottom line" in the determination of whether a policy is appropriate or inappropriate is whether the outcome is in accord or not in accord with the wishes of a group of people. That group of people may be considered the population of a country or a subset of the population. A policy may be inappropriate for the former but appropriate for the latter; i.e., it may not yield benefits for the population as a whole but may yield benefits for a part of the population. The appropriateness of a policy is dependent upon the perspective of the group by which it is assessed.

An example is the policy toward the use of tractors. Political leaders in Tanzania often warned against the dangers of tractors. In his Peasants Day speech in 1980, Nyerere observed that the "moment you want a tractor from abroad, you are giving up yourself to exploitation."[81] The policy document "Politics Is Agriculture" similarly warned against the use of tractors unless on a large farm where resources and knowledge were substantial: "Without these things, a tractor can be a disaster, can ruin the peasants and destroy the land."[82] And the authors of the document urged that animal power be used for plowing instead. Finn Kjaerby has observed that the "need to develop animal traction has been stressed over and again by the political leadership." Yet he found that financial resources have been concentrated on the foreign exchange-demanding and capital intensive state farm sector running considerable economic losses while the very basis of the national economy, the peasant sector, has been relatively starved of directly productive financial support.[83]

Why was this inappropriate technology, which reduces Tanzania's self-reliance, bought? Kjaerby blamed World Bank encouragement and "political interests."[84] He suggested that most tractors tended to be used on state farms, and state farms were a means of transferring wealth to urban areas. Now, ideological socialists tended to dominate the party in the period to which Kjaerby referred and to favor urban workers over the rural peasantry, but pragmatic socialists tended to be more willing to encourage large-scale private production, which might require tractors, too. Thus, the encouragement of the use of tractors does not seem to be a policy distinguishing these two factions. The groups each faction sought to support by the importation of tractors did differ, though. Nevertheless, the consequences of importing tractors and encouraging their general use were increased debt and reduced self-reliance of the country as a whole.

A second example is the impact of the demand for rapid modernization. Susan Crouch concluded her study of Western responses to Tanzanian socialism by arguing that the West did undermine the socialist transition by its large aid disbursements. Yet the impetus for such disbursements was internal pressure for quick modernization, which led to a "style of policy-making" not conducive to success.[85] It was the pragmatic socialists who were most responsive to demands for rapid modernization. Crouch concluded that the decisions taken to hasten development often compromised the objective of self-reliance.

Among those decisions was the tendency to emphasize consumer goods industries rather than producer goods industries. A.M. Babu has written that this fact is the reason "we are backward economically, culturally and politically," for this prioritization condemns "us to be permanently dependent, permanently underdeveloped and permanently victims of external pressures and influences."[86]

Ideological socialists have not been blameless in the argument over causes of the lack of self-reliance. Samuel Wangwe has argued that the Ministry of Finance and the Central Bank through its use of foreign exchange sought to encourage the importation of capital over intermediate goods, resulting in idle industries.[87] And idle industries mean less revenue for the government and fewer locally produced goods, both undermining self-reliance.

Perhaps a more significant cause of Tanzania's inability to become self-reliant than the policies traceable to either faction has been the inconsistency of policy or the half-heartedness of policy that has resulted from this factional struggle. As the gatekeepers fought among themselves, the ability of external forces to impose their will increased.

Conclusion

Dependency does not necessarily lead to the demise of socialism. What it does is to transfer some sovereignty to "outsiders," who may or may not act to block socialist construction. As noted, in the first post-Arusha decade its effect was relatively benign. It became a significant negative factor only at the time the IMF and World Bank demanded major policy changes with the 1986 accord. Why did a relatively benign dependence turn into a detrimental dependence? The reasons given by the international aid gatekeepers were, basically, that many of the policies taken in the name of socialist construction had not promoted economic advance and that the policy changes would produce such advance. This is not an antisocialist position, for economic advance is a socialist goal, too. Nevertheless, the implications of the IMF conditionalities for socialist construction are important. First, the room to maneuver for those wishing to build a socialist system was probably less than those who proposed Tanzanian socialism had assumed—and it has shrunk since. In other words, the constraints of the world system on Tanzania's ability to build a utopian or volitional socialism are greater than most ideological and most pragmatic socialists thought. Second, the situation of Tanzania in the world system hinders ideological socialists and favors pragmatic socialists. And among pragmatic socialists it favors those more willing to play the role of comprador.

Notes

1. The subtitle of the English version of the Arusha Declaration is "Socialism and Self-Reliance." See Julius Nyerere, *Freedom and Socialism* (Dar es Salaam: Oxford University Press, 1968), pp. 231–250. Parts 2 and 3 of the declaration are titled "The Policy of Socialism" and "The Policy of Self-Reliance." Seventy-five percent of the declaration lies in Part 3 describing self-reliance!

2. Roy Preiswerk has distinguished "individual" self-reliance from "collective" self-reliance and developed a tripartite classificatory system consisting of "local self-reliance," e.g., within an ethnic group, village federation, commune, or family; "national self-reliance"; and "regional self-reliance," e.g., transcontinental (Third World), continental, and subcontinental. See Preiswerk, "Introduction," in Johan Galtung, Peter O'Brien, and Roy Preiswerk, eds., *Self-Reliance, A Strategy for Development* (London: Bogle-L'Ouverture Publications, Ltd., for Institute of International Development Studies, Geneva, 1980), p. 14. Although Ann Tickner does not separate "individual" from what Preiswerk calls "collective" self-reliance and she uses the latter term to refer to what Preiswerk calls "regional" self-reliance, Tickner employs a fairly similar categorization system, distinguishing

"individual and local self-reliance," "national self-reliance," and "collective and regional self-reliance." See Tickner, *Self-Reliance Versus Power Politics* (New York: Columbia University Press, 1987), pp. 16–17. Clearly, these are gross categories, distinguished by the number of individuals within them. Under "individual and local self-reliance" a wide variety of aggregates in addition to those suggested by Preiswerk might be included, such as village and cooperative. Under "national self-reliance" one might distinguish between the corporate self-reliance of all people in the country and the class self-reliance of those who dominate the state. And under "collective and regional self-reliance" various groupings of dominant classes and nations might be distinguished.

3. Goran Hyden, *Beyond Ujamaa in Tanzania, Underdevelopment and an Uncaptured Peasantry* (Berkeley: University of California Press, 1980), p. 232.

4. International Cooperative Alliance, "A Report of the ICA/FAO/ILO Interagency Mission to Tanzania in Support of Cooperative Development" (Moshi: ICA, May 1986, mimeographed), pp. 28–29. The mission's team leader was Charles Gashumba, acting regional director of ICA. In a discussion I had with Kingunge Ngombale-Mwiru during the International Conference on the Arusha Declaration in December 1986 in Arusha, he argued that the economic viability of primary cooperatives was a "nonissue." My interpretation was that in this case he felt self-reliance conflicted with the ideological socialists' view of socialist construction.

5. Johan Galtung has argued that higher-level self-reliance is insufficient for lower-level self-reliance and the reverse in "The Politics of Self-Reliance," in Galtung, O'Brien, and Preiswerk, eds., *Self-Reliance,* pp. 361–368.

6. Julius K. Nyerere, "The Arusha Declaration," in Nyerere, *Freedom and Socialism,* p. 248.

7. For example, see Julius K. Nyerere, "After the Arusha Declaration," in Nyerere, *Freedom and Socialism,* pp. 390–391.

8. Kingunge Ngombale-Mwiru, "The Policy of Self-Reliance," in Lionel Cliffe and John Saul, eds., *Socialism in Tanzania: Vol. 2, Policies* (Nairobi: East African Publishing House, 1973), p. 66.

9. Andrew Coulson, *Tanzania, A Political Economy* (Oxford: Clarendon Press, 1982), p. 288.

10. Tickner, *Self-Reliance Versus Power Politics,* p. 9; and Mary Baughman Anderson, "Self-Reliant Development: A Comparison of the Economic Development Strategies of Mohandas Gandhi, Mao Tse Tung and Julius Nyerere," Ph.D. thesis, Department of Economics, University of Colorado, Boulder, 1978, p. 90.

11. Nyerere, "After the Arusha Declaration," p. 388.

12. Ngombale-Mwiru, "The Policy of Self-Reliance," pp. 66–70.

13. Thomas Biersteker, "Self-Reliance in Theory and Practice in Tanzanian Trade Relations," *International Organisation,* Vol. 34, No. 2 (Spring 1980), pp. 235–236.

14. Idrian N. Resnick, *The Long Transition, Building Socialism in Tanzania* (New York: Monthly Review Press, 1981), p. 93.

15. Johan Galtung refers to the stages or phases in more abstract terms, as "consciousness-formation, mobilization, confrontation, struggle proper and transcendence." See Galtung, "The Politics of Self-Reliance," p. 359. Galtung elaborates on these ideas in his book *The True Worlds: A Transnational Perspective* (New York: Free Press, 1980), pp. 139–149.

16. Magnus Blomstrom and Bjorn Hettne, *Development Theory in Transition* (London: Zed Books, 1984), p. 154.

17. Resnick, *The Long Transition,* p. 93; and Biersteker, "Self-Reliance in Theory and Practice," p. 230.

18. Anderson, "Self-Reliant Development," p. 90. Emphasis added.
19. William P. Mayer, "Planning for Self-Reliance," *Taamuli, A Political Science Forum*, Vol. 4, No. 2 (July 1974), p. 31. Emphasis added.
20. Peter Burnell, *Economic Nationalism in the Third World* (Boulder: Westview, 1986), p. 25.
21. *Daily News* (Dar es Salaam), 4 May 1989, p. 1.
22. *Daily News*, 23 July 1980, p. 4.
23. Nyerere, "After the Arusha Declaration," pp. 390–391.
24. Fred Riggs has noted the interrelationship among many of these concepts in "Development," in Giovanni Sartori, ed., *Social Science Concepts, A Systematic Analysis* (Beverly Hills, Calif.: Sage, 1984), pp. 125–203. Riggs noted that the most frequent concept used to define development was "choice: increasing capacity to make decisions." See ibid., pp. 161–162. He continued, "The concept is relevant also to the growing concern of many scholars that in an interdependent world system, most Third World countries have very little freedom of action. For them a more important goal is 'liberation' from the restraints imposed by dependency." See ibid., p. 166.
25. Susan Crouch, *Western Responses to Tanzanian Socialism, 1967–1983* (Aldershot, United Kingdom: Avebury, 1987), p. 176.
26. Cranford Pratt, "Tanzania's Transition to Socialism: Reflections of a Democratic Socialist," in Bismarck Mwansasu and Cranford Pratt, eds., *Towards Socialism in Tanzania* (Toronto: University of Toronto Press, 1979), p. 224.
27. Issa Shivji, "The Silent Class Struggle," in *The Silent Class Struggle*, Tanzanian Studies No. 2 (Dar es Salaam: Tanzania Publishing House, 1973), p. 20.
28. Ibid., pp. 22 and 38.
29. Issa Shivji, "Introduction: The Transformation of the State and the Working People," in Shivji, ed., *The State and the Working People in Tanzania* (Dakar: Codesria, 1985), pp. 4–5. A similar view of the continued neocolonial status of Tanzania is described by L. Mushokolwa in "The Political Economy of Tanzania," *Maendeleo* (Institute of Development Studies, University of Dar es Salaam), No. 1 (January 1985), pp. 37–43. And George W. Shepherd Jr. has described Tanzania as part of a "subimperial tributary system." Noting that Tanzania "obviously" has not succeeded in becoming self-reliant, he wrote that he nevertheless considered it "the most important example of the attempt to break out of the tributary relationship with the great powers of the world." He claimed Tanzania has made a start and even in the late 1980s seemed to remain optimistic by asserting that "if it succeeds, then a Third World alternative to tributary subservience will exist." See Shepherd, *The Trampled Grass, Tributary States and Self-Reliance in the Indian Ocean Zone of Peace* (Westport, Conn: Greenwood Press, 1987), pp. 104–105 and 107–108.
30. Ajit Singh, "Tanzania and the IMF: The Analytics of Alternative Adjustment Programmes," *Development and Change*, Vol. 17 (1986), p. 450.
31. Kighoma Malima, "The IMF and World Bank Conditionality: The Tanzanian Case," in Peter Lawrence, ed., *World Recession and the Food Crisis in Africa* (London: Review of African Political Economy and James Currey, 1986), p. 137.
32. *Daily News*, 21 May 1987, p. 1, and 6 July 1987, p. 1.
33. Julius Nyerere, *Africa—Hunger and Debt* (an address given at the Royal Commonwealth Society in London, 20 March 1985, pamphlet), p. 12. He described Tanzania's predicament vis-à-vis the IMF as follows:

> Tanzania's exchange difficulties began to become serious in 1978; yet between 1978 and 1984 Tanzania has made a *net* foreign exchange payment to the I.M.F. of 50.2 million S.D.R.s. It cannot even get into arrears on these payments—they have to take priority over purchases even of food

or minimum oil requirements. For if payments are not made when due, continued negotiation about a new Agreement is suspended, and also it is designated as bankrupt by all other trading and financial partners.

See ibid., p.13.

34. *Daily News*, 3 July 1990, p. 1.
35. *Daily News*, 1 March 1989, p. 1.
36. *Daily News*, 19 August 1987, p. 1.
37. *Daily News*, 4 May 1989, p. 1.
38. *Daily News*, 5 November 1988, p. 1.
39. *Daily News*, 23 November 1988, p. 1.
40. *Daily News*, 4 November 1988, p. 1.
41. *Daily News*, 5 November 1988, p. 1.
42. *Daily News*, 2 May 1987, p. 1. Several observers suggest that the "doctor" was not simply the IMF, that the accord had adherents within the government. Howard Stein suggests that the central IMF demand was a shift from a directive-passive market approach to a liberal-active market approach and that "Nyerere, Kawawa, Malima and the late Sokoine have been usually identified with the more directive solutions while Msuya, Salim and to some extent Mwinyi have preferred more active markets." See Stein, "The Economics of the State and the IMF in Tanzania," a paper presented at the annual meeting of the African Studies Association, Chicago, October 1988, p. 19. Werner Biermann attributes the acceptance of the conditionalities to a "technocracy," suggesting that the technocratic stratum's gradual changes "had been carefully observed and enhanced by the IMF, less midwife than godfather." See Biermann, "Tanzanian Politics Under IMF Pressure," in Michael Hodd, ed., *Tanzania After Nyerere* (London: Pinter Publishers, 1988), p. 182. Although using a different terminology, I contend that at this stage in the effort to build socialism, supporters of what Stein calls the liberal-active market and the group Biermann calls the technocracy were what I have identified as pragmatic socialists. A columnist for the *Daily News*, Joatham Kamala, asserted, perhaps facetiously, that the IMF agreement should not be compared with the Brest-Litovsk Treaty. See *Daily News*, 19 August 1987, p. 4.
43. *Sunday News*, 6 November 1988, p. 1.
44. Andrew Coulson has described the negative impact of several aid projects. See Coulson, "The Silo Project," "The Automated Bread Factory," and "Tanzania's Fertilizer Factory," in Coulson, ed., *African Socialism in Practice, The Tanzanian Experience* (Nottingham: Spokesman, 1979), pp. 175–178, 179–183, and 184–190, respectively. A personal note: In 1980 I was asked to testify before the U.S. House of Representatives Subcommittee on Africa on the allocation of aid to Tanzania. After considerable discussion, Rep. Stephen Solarz asked me how much more aid the United States should provide. My contention was that the question was unanswerable without an identification of how it would be allocated. As far as Tanzania was concerned, some aid hurt and some aid helped. Its desirability depended on whom within Tanzania we wanted to help and what the money was for. His question was straightforward. I believe the committee felt that I was unnecessarily complicating what members saw as a simple correlation between the provision of money and the provision of help. The idea that "aid" might hurt seemed contradictory.
45. This situation was a major precipitant of the IMF accord. But even the debt rescheduling that followed the IMF agreement did little to overcome the debt problem. The Paris Club agreement of September 1986 called for a rescheduling of 97.5 percent of the debt owed club members (the major donors) for five years. See *Daily News*, 27 July 1987, p. 3. Two years later, in a speech in Germany in September 1988, President Mwinyi asserted that during the fiscal year 1987/88, Tanzania got

$443 million in financial assistance and it spent $338 million for debt servicing. Had Tanzania complied with the Paris Club agreement and made all the debt payments to which it agreed, Mwinyi said, the country would have had to pay $603.4 million. It did not pay the 2.5 percent arrears it had agreed to pay. See *Daily News*, 17 September 1988, p. 4.

46. *Daily News*, 22 March 1990, p. 1.
47. *Daily News*, 8 July 1980, p. 1.
48. *Sunday News*, 10 November 1985, p. 3.
49. *Tanzania Economic Trends*, Vol. 4, Nos. 3 and 4 (October 1991 and January 1992), p. 63.
50. *Daily News*, 3 November 1988, p. 1.
51. Dean E. McHenry Jr., *Tanzania's Ujamaa Villages, The Implementation of a Rural Development Strategy* (Berkeley: Institute of International Studies, University of California, 1979), p. 68.
52. *Sunday News*, 21 July 1991, p. 1.
53. Amon Nsekela, "The Role of Public Sector in Tanzania: Performance and Prospects," in *The Role of Public Sector in the Economic Development in Tanzania, Proceedings of a Workshop Held in Arusha, Tanzania, on 27th to 29th of September 1983* (Dar es Salaam: Economic Research Bureau and Friedrich Ebert Stiftung, January 1984), p. 6; and *Daily News*, 27 November 1987, p. 3.
54. *Daily News*, 16 May 1990, p. 3.
55. *Daily News*, 27 December 1988, p. 3.
56. *Daily News*, 4 May 1989, p. 5.
57. *Daily News*, 2 April 1988, p. 3. The regional commissioner's response was to ask that the richer villages that could pay for the machines be given preference in any auction of the equipment. There was no discussion of the consequences in terms of the goals of Tanzanian socialism.
58. *Daily News*, 17 August 1989, p. 5.
59. *Daily News*, 22 March 1989, p. 3.
60. The move toward autonomy in 1991 was reflected in the new cooperative act that year and the effort to decrease direct CCM supervision. Incidentally, the title of the 1991 Cooperative College annual symposium was "Managing the Transition from State-Controlled Cooperatives to Member-Based Cooperative Societies." See *Daily News*, 14 August 1991, p. 3.
61. International Cooperative Alliance (ICA), "A Report of the ICA/FAO/ILO Inter-agency Mission to Tanzania, p. 38.
62. *Daily News*, 7 August 1989, p. 5; *Sunday News*, 12 February 1989, p. 1.
63. For example, see *Daily News*, 25 September 1989, p. 5; 21 March 1990, p. 3.
64. For example, CRDB impounded four vehicles belonging to the Mara union in late 1989 and said it would auction them if the loan was not repaid. See *Daily News*, 1 November 1989, p. 1.
65. *Daily News*, 15 September 1987, p. 3.
66. *Daily News*, 13 October 1989, p. 1; 16 November 1989, p. 1. Besides raising consciousness about the problem, the major outcome was an effort to collect on individual loans made by the unions.
67. *Daily News*, 20 October 1988, p. 3.
68. For example, *Daily News*, 24 August 1988, p. 3; 14 December 1988, p. 1; 13 February 1990, p. 3; 21 April 1990, p. 3.
69. *Daily News*, 2 April 1990, p. 5; 6 April 1990, p. 3; 12 May 1990, p. 3. Several political leaders felt that such deductions were inappropriate. They argued that since the debts were often caused by a corrupt few, the many should not have to pay for their thefts.
70. *Daily News*, 19 February 1990, p. 5.

71. *Daily News*, 14 April 1989, p. 3.
72. *Daily News*, 16 March 1989, p. 1.
73. Roy A. Medvedev, *Leninism and Western Socialism* (Worcester, United Kingdom: Verso Editions, 1981), pp. 168–189.
74. Christopher K. Chase-Dunn, "Socialist States in the Capitalist World-Economy," in Chase-Dunn, ed., *Socialist States in the World System* (Beverly Hills, Calif.: Sage, 1982), pp. 48–49.
75. Michael Lofchie, *The Policy Factor, Agricultural Performance in Kenya and Tanzania* (Boulder: Lynne Rienner Publishers, 1989), p. 47.
76. Julius Nyerere, "An Address by Julius K. Nyerere," *Development and Change,* Vol. 17 (1986), pp. 388–392.
77. *Daily News*, 24 June 1989, p. 4.
78. Pratt, "Tanzania's Transition to Socialism," p. 224.
79. *Daily News*, 4 June 1991, p. 1.
80. Lofchie, *The Policy Factor,* p. 64.
81. *Daily News*, 8 July 1980, p. 1.
82. Tanganyika African National Union, "Politics Is Agriculture," issued May 13, 1972, as a press release by the Information Services Division, Ministry of Information and Broadcasting, Dar es Salaam, p. 4.
83. Finn Kjaerby, *Problems and Contradictions in the Development of Ox-Cultivation in Tanzania* (Uppsala: Scandinavian Institute of African Studies, and Copenhagen: Centre for Development Research, 1983), p. 138.
84. Ibid., p. 74.
85. Crouch, *Western Responses to Tanzanian Socialism,* p. 170.
86. A.M. Babu, *African Socialism or Socialist Africa?* (Dar es Salaam: Tanzania Publishing House, 1981), pp. 46–47.
87. Samuel Wangwe, "Industrialization and Resource Allocation in a Developing Country: The Case of Recent Experiences in Tanzania," *World Development,* Vol. 11, No. 6 (1983), p. 490.

9

Subnationalism and Socialism

Pemba peremba.
"Visit Pemba carefully."

The pursuit of socialism in many parts of the world has been affected by nationalism, i.e., the sense of identity people feel with their nation.[1] Nations may be differentiated for analytical purposes into two types: those comprising the population of a country and those constituting a subset of the population of a country. In Africa, the sense of identity felt among the former group is usually called nationalism and that felt among the latter is usually called subnationalism. The impact of nationalism and subnationalism on socialist construction has long been the focus of intense discussion.[2]

To Marxists, there are several possibilities. Walker Connor suggested that these fall into three categories. First, "classical Marxism" involved the claim that nationalism/subnationalism (which emphasized vertical cleavages) was incompatible with socialism (which emphasized horizontal cleavages). In other words, nationalism/subnationalism was a form of false consciousness that had to be eliminated so that class consciousness, a requisite of Marxist socialist construction, might develop. Second, "strategic Marxism" involved the claim that support for national self-determination in a situation of imperialism was a progressive step toward socialism. That is, national liberation might be supportive of socialist construction. And third, "national Marxism" involved the claim that nations were "the principal instrumentality of historical forces." In other words, socialism and nationalism might foster each other.[3] Although these categories developed sequentially, they have come to form a complex of views drawn upon by both Marxist and non-Marxist socialists in debates over the relationship between nationalism/subnationalism and socialism.

To Tanzanian socialists, there are several possibilities, too. Unlike Marxists, Nyerere and most pragmatic socialists sought to avoid the formation of classes. To the extent that nationalism worked as classical Marxists thought it worked, it facilitated the construction of Tanzanian socialism. Once socialism had become a "national" objective, nationalism served as a carrier and protector of the ideals. Challenges to socialism became challenges to nationalism.

If nationalism became the protector of socialism in the Tanzanian context, what was the impact of subnationalism? In general, Tanzania has had more success than most African countries in containing subnationalism. Yet one case has persistently affected the Tanzanian socialist project—that of Zanzibar. Zanzibar is not simply a generic case of subnationalism: Federal structures have given it a constitutional base that distinguishes it from other subnationalisms. Zanzibar's impact on socialist construction is the focus of this chapter.

The Nature of the Relationship Between Tanzania and Zanzibar

There were two struggles for independence in Tanzania: one in Tanganyika, i.e., on the mainland, and one in Zanzibar, i.e., on the isles. On the mainland, TANU successfully united most Tanganyikans into a single nationalist movement, waged a relatively peaceful struggle against the British, and brought independence in December 1961. On the isles, the situation was quite different. An intense and sometimes violent struggle was waged among the Zanzibar National Party (ZNP), the Afro-Shirazi Party (ASP), and the Zanzibar and Pemba People's Party (ZPPP) in the period leading to independence in December 1963. Unlike the situation on the mainland, Zanzibari nationalism was subordinate to the subnationalisms of the Arabs, Shirazis, mainland Africans, and other subgroups during the struggle for independence. Following a bloody coup on January 12, 1964, many Zanzibaris fled and a major effort was made to create a new nationalism common to those who remained—a nationalism that became a subnationalism upon the union of Zanzibar and Tanganyika later in 1964.

Origin of the Union: What Purposes Would It Serve?

The People's Republic of Zanzibar existed as an independent country for about a hundred days. On April 22, 1964, the president of Tanganyika, Julius Nyerere, and the chairman of the Revolutionary Council of Zanzibar, Abedi Karume, signed the Articles of Union, which were immediately ratified by the National Assembly of Tanganyika and the Revolutionary Council of Zanzibar. The United Republic of Tanganyika and Zanzibar was formally established on April 26, 1964.[4] The reasons the union was formed are a matter of dispute.

Historical and Cultural Commonalities

There is least dispute over the presence of historical and cultural ties between Tanganyika and Zanzibar and their contributions to the union of the two. Both Nyerere and Karume suggested that the union was a natural consequence of such ties.[5] Most scholars accept these factors as contributory, though they debate their significance relative to other factors. Table 9.1 summarizes some of the similarities that facilitated the development of Tanzanian nationalist sentiments—and some of the differences that fostered the rise of subnationalism. Within Zanzibar the sense of separate identity felt by many who lived on Pemba had no real parallel on the mainland. A subnationalism had developed there before union, implicit in the old proverb, *Pemba peremba*—Visit Pemba carefully.[6] After union this "sub-subnationalism" sometimes served as a catalyst for the development of Zanzibari subnationalism, when government and party leaders blamed the mainland for causing Pemba's grievances, and other times as a catalyst for its suppression, when Zanzibari leaders used Tanzanian nationalism and mainland resources to curb Pemba's separatism.

Karume's Desire to Preserve His Leadership Position

Karume's motivation for union is widely attributed to his desire to preserve his leadership position. As soon as the revolution placed Karume in power, he was faced with severe challenges to his leadership. On the right were forces associated with the ZNP-ZPPP government, which had been overthrown; on the left were forces associated with militants in Karume's own party, as well as those of the Umma Party.[7] Union with the mainland had the potential of providing Karume and his associates with the support they needed to retain their positions and promote their policies.

Since the right was virtually destroyed by the revolution, self-preservation meant eliminating the power of the left. There is little dispute about this aspect of Karume's reasoning, though some writers suggest the primary motive was the destruction of the left and the secondary motive was self-preservation.[8] There is more dispute about whether this was a part of Nyerere's reasoning.[9]

The reaction of the left to the union was opposition. Karume got the approval of his Revolutionary Council when A.M. Babu, the leader of the Umma group, was out of the country. As Cranford Pratt wrote, "The Communist left generally received the news of the union as a defeat."[10] And a writer in the *New Left Review* remarked, "It seemed that the brightest spark in Africa had been snuffed when the news came through of the Tanganyika-Zanzibar *anschluss*."[11]

Concern over Consequences of International Rivalries

The significance of the left in the Zanzibari government following the revolution, including Babu's position as minister for external affairs and trade, facilitated quick recognition and assistance from communist countries. Expulsion of the British high commissioner and the American consul general and the demand that the American Mercury tracking station be dismantled

Table 9.1 Comparison of Historical, Cultural, and Political Features of Constituent Parts of Tanzania

	Tanganyika (mainland)	Zanzibar (islands)
Status prior to European colonization	Many (mostly Bantu-speaking) ethnic groups. Coast and parts of interior claimed by sultans after their establishment in Zanzibar.	A few Bantu-speaking ethnic groups who had come from the mainland. Arabs and a few Indian traders. Sultans originally from Oman ruled from about 1830.
European colonial status	German colony from 1891 to 1918. Germany purchased coast from Zanzibar about the time it assumed formal control of mainland. British mandate and then trusteeship.	British protectorate from 1890.
Status of dominant party at time of union	De facto single-party state.	De jure single-party state.
Ideological orientation of dominant party at time of union	Tentative socialist-nationalist.	Socialist-nationalist.
International orientation at time of union	Formally, nonaligned; informally, oriented toward the West.	Formally, nonaligned; informally, oriented toward the East.
Language	Swahili was the lingua franca.	Swahili.
Religion	Islam and Christianity each practiced by about 40 percent of population.	Islam practiced by about 90 percent of population.
Major ethno-territorial cleavage(s)	Among 125 ethnic groups.	Between people of Zanzibar and Pemba islands.

all indicated a significant shift in the role of international actors. The American government expressed its concern that Zanzibar would become an "African Cuba."[12]

Although some observers suggested that Nyerere sought through the union to avoid being trampled by an East-West struggle off Tanganyika's coast, others argued that his concern was more ideological. Colin Legum, after an interview with Nyerere, was reported to have said "that the union had been a brilliant manoeuvre to outwit the Babu faction which was seeking to move Zanzibar from a non-aligned position to a full orientation towards Communism."[13] B.P. Srivastava, while he was a law professor at the University of Dar es Salaam, argued that Nyerere's concern was not to protect his policy of nonalignment but rather to protect his embryonic socialist ideas:

> President Nyerere was concerned at protecting his ideas of African socialism in Tanganyika from being contaminated by communist doctrines through infiltration from a communist dominated state at its next door which post-revolution Zanzibar was likely to be as evidenced by the haste with which major communist powers rushed to establish relations with Zanzibar offering military and economic aid.[14]

There was also the fear that the Sino-Soviet conflict would be imported into East Africa because both the Soviet Union and China had become deeply and competitively involved in Zanzibar.

Nyerere's Desire to Promote African Unity

Nyerere's principal motivation probably was to promote African unity, long an important goal to him. By early 1964, his efforts to create a federation of Kenya, Uganda, and Tanganyika appeared likely to fail. Zanzibar offered the possibility of an initial step toward African unity. When Nyerere sought to persuade his parliament to adopt the Articles of Union that he and Karume had signed, he argued,

> Today, there is in Africa great enthusiasm for Unity.... We must remember that meaningful unity will not come simply by talking. Actions must demonstrate our determination, and show that a single Government in Africa is not an impossible dream, but something which can be realized.
> Countries which are friends and neighbours, and which have at some time in their history been united, have a special responsibility. If they fail to unite, their failure will be used to point the finger of scorn at our continent. But if they do unite, and make their unity into a living reality, they will be demonstrating that the hopes of our continent are not vain ones. If two countries can unite, then three can; if three can, then thirty can.[15]

In subsequent years Nyerere explained the continuation of the government in Zanzibar after union by saying it was to avoid the appearance that smaller Zanzibar was "swallowed" by the larger mainland. In other words, annexation and a unitary state were feasible alternatives to the kind of federalism that was established at the time the union was formed. Yet, because Nyerere saw the Tanganyika-Zanzibar union as a precedent or model for the evolution of a united Africa, he wanted to reduce the fears of small states that were concerned about the consequence of union with a larger state. Thus, to a considerable extent, the goal of African unity is responsible for the form of federalism in Tanzania.

The union between the mainland and the islands was not established to contain a subnationalist threat to Tanzanian socialism. Nevertheless, the structures that were established both stimulated the development of subnationalism and were used for the containment of subnationalism.

Form of the Union: What Degree of Unity?

In summarizing the relationship between Tanzania and Zanzibar, President Mwinyi has said it "was like marriage between two individuals in which both parties must of necessity surrender some of their sovereignty and interests for the common good."[16] Like the relationship in a marriage, that between Tanzania and Zanzibar has not been static: The constitutional arrangements, their interpretation, and the behavior of those governing Tanzania and Zanzibar have changed over the years. Tanzanian federalism should be understood as a dynamic mode of political organization attempting to contend with a dynamic subnationalism.

Formal Arrangement: Movement Toward Unification

The state constitutional documents that are relevant to the movement toward unification are the Articles of Union (1964), the Constitution of Tanganyika (1962), the Interim Constitution (1965), the Constitution of Tanzania (1977), the Zanzibar Constitution (1979), the Constitution of Tanzania (1984), the Zanzibar Constitution (1984), and occasional amendments of each. During the period between the adoption of the Articles of Union (1964) and the Interim Constitution (1965), the Constitution of Tanganyika (1962), as modified by the Articles, was the operative constitution of the United Republic.

The basic framework established in the Articles of Union has not been altered radically by subsequent constitutions or their amendments, except that the list of matters for which the union had sole authority grew substantially over the years. Initially, these matters included the constitution and government of the union; external affairs; defense; police; emergency powers; citizenship; immigration; external trade and borrowing; the union public service; income, corporation, customs, and excise taxes; and harbors, civil aviation, posts, and telegraphs.[17] Among the matters added to this list were currency, banks, and foreign exchange (1965); industrial licensing and statistics, higher education, and matters related to the Treaty for East African Cooperation (1967); oil, petroleum, and natural gas (1968); the National Examination Council of Tanzania and its functions (1977); and the Court of Appeal of the Union Republic (1984).[18] By implication, authority over other matters was the prerogative of the nonunion governments. Clearly, though, there has been a gradual increase in the formal powers of the union government over time.

In most federal systems, sole authority over union and nonunion affairs is assigned to the governments of the respective territorial units. In

Tanzania, the constitutional delegation of responsibility was complicated by the position of the political parties, which at the time of union were the Afro-Shirazi Party (ASP) on the islands and the Tanganyika African National Union (TANU) on the mainland. In order to describe the evolving constitutional form, it is necessary to consider both government and party as governing bodies.

In effect, the articles created a union government by adding together the existing governments of the Republic of Tanganyika and the People's Republic of Zanzibar. That is, the Revolutionary Council in Zanzibar was combined with the National Assembly in Tanganyika to create a new National Assembly for the union. The president of Tanganyika became the president of the union, and the president of the Revolutionary Council of Zanzibar became the first vice president of the union. The Constitution of Tanzania (1984) modified this allocation of executive positions, specifying merely that the president and vice president could not both be from the mainland or from the islands.

What was unusual about the union government was that it was assigned authority for nonunion matters in one of the two constituent parts of the union, the mainland. In effect, this meant that Zanzibar was involved in deciding nonunion matters for Tanganyika. A second government was established for Zanzibar. The fact that only two governments were established by the Articles of Union has been central to the arguments of those who view Tanzania as a unitary state with federal features rather than a federal one with unitary features.[19] Yet of even greater significance to this debate has been the constitutional position of the political party.

As long as the organs of the state were given constitutional supremacy over those of the party, the form of Tanzanian federalism was defined by the structures of government. The Articles made no mention of political parties. The Interim Constitution established a single-party state. It declared that until ASP and TANU were united, the former would constitute that part of the single party operating on the islands and the latter would be that part operating on the mainland. Yet the Interim Constitution exempted the organs of the state of the union and Zanzibar from party direction.

In 1975, though, an important amendment to the Interim Constitution made TANU and ASP constitutionally superior to all other institutions of state. As far as nonunion matters were concerned, the amendment did not affect the federal arrangement very much. It merely formalized what was the practice, i.e., for TANU to be the key decisionmaker on the mainland and ASP to be the key decisionmaker on the islands. But what of union matters? Either TANU or ASP or some combination of the parties had to be supreme. Yet there was no mechanism for joint decisionmaking.

The mechanism was supplied two years later with the merger of the two parties to form the Chama cha Mapinduzi (CCM). Although this merger solved the constitutional problem for union matters, it created a new one. If a unitary party was superior to what was supposed to be a federal polity, was anything left of federalism? What had happened was that the authority over all nonunion matters had been placed in a union-level institution, much as had been the case in the former Soviet Union. In other words, mainlanders, who because of the population imbalance dominated CCM, had been given the constitutional right to decide nonunion matters for the islands.[20] This situation constituted another deviation from traditional federal forms and produced a subnationalist reaction in Zanzibar.

As mainland-union authorities began denying that the union was a federal system, Zanzibari leaders responded with cries for formal guarantees that Zanzibar would not be "swallowed." The growing Zanzibari concern with the evolution of the union led to a major political upheaval in 1983/84.

The situation was this: In 1983, the National Executive Committee (NEC) of CCM issued proposals for changes in the union and Zanzibari constitutions. These proposals were prompted partly by the expectation that Nyerere would not be a candidate for president in 1985 and partly by a desire to "consolidate" the union. The position implied by the proposals aroused concern in Zanzibar. The NEC stated in the proposals that when the 1964 agreement between Tanganyika and Zanzibar was negotiated, union might have taken one of two forms: a federal system, consisting of a union government, a government for Zanzibar, and a government for Tanganyika; or a unitary system, which would have involved "the complete dissolution of the two previously existing Governments" and the creation of a union government. But, the NEC asserted, "It was decided that instead of having three Governments (the first method) or one Government only (the second method), we adopt the intermediate method of setting up two governments."[21] The NEC, noting the trend over the years, called for further consolidation. Consolidation meant making the union more unitary in character, i.e., more like that which would have been achieved through the second method.

The NEC's call for a public discussion of the proposals, in the words of Colin Legum, "unwittingly opened a Pandora's box." Legum observed,

> A number of Zanzibaris took the opportunity to vent their suspicions that Zanzibar was being swallowed by the mainland and proposed a federal Constitution with three separate governments for the mainland, Zanzibar and the union instead of the present situation where there is a single government for the mainland and union. At the same time, they argued that party supremacy should be rejected because, as the former Zanzibar Attorney-General, Wolf Dourado, said in a letter to the government-owned *Sunday News,* it would be a devious way of manipulating the creation of a unitary state. He also claimed that the 1964 Articles of Union have never been legally ratified on the mainland or islands.[22]

The party sought to close the "box" with the forced resignation of the president of Zanzibar, Aboud Jumbe, who took responsibility for the outpouring of antiunion feelings; the removal from leadership of Zanzibar's chief minister, Ramadani Haji Faki; and the forced resignations of other Zanzibari ministers. If anything, such action fueled antiunion feelings. Early in 1988, the succeeding chief minister, Seif Shariff Hamad, was removed by the NEC, fundamentally because of his independence from those who held power in CCM. He was arrested in 1989 after he made remarks questioning the legitimacy of the union.[23] Thus, the formal movement toward unification brought about a reaction against the union: a rise in subnationalism, which caused union intervention, which brought about a further rise in subnationalism. The introduction of the multiparty system in 1992 brought new pressures for a formal restructuring of the union that would provide greater autonomy for both Zanzibar and Tanganyika.

Informal Arrangement: Resistance to Movement Toward Unification

Although the formal extension of Tanzania's power over Zanzibar did occur, the actual supremacy of the union over Zanzibari affairs has tended to be exaggerated. Zanzibar often has been able to resist constitutional demands that it limit its scope of operations. This resistance was most pronounced under Karume, from the time of union to his assassination in 1972. As one observer put it, "Despite the union in 1964 of Tanganyika and Zanzibar, the latter essentially retained its complete internal political autonomy, with the result that two entirely separate administrations ruled different parts of the nominally united country."[24] But resistance was not confined to the Karume years. It has been a recurring theme of Zanzibar-union relations ever since, as illustrated by two examples, one dealing with foreign affairs and the other with union finances.

First, although external affairs were made a union matter by the Articles, Zanzibar continued to enter into economic, financial, and cultural agreements directly with foreign governments and international agencies.[25] And Zanzibar's international involvement on several occasions undermined Tanzania's foreign policy. Among the most "celebrated" examples during the Karume years was Zanzibar's refusal to accept the demotion of the East German embassy to a trade mission. In the end, the Federal Republic of Germany invoked the Halstein doctrine and withdrew all military aid from Tanzania. In early 1965 Zanzibar claimed there was a plot by the United States to overthrow its government; this claim ended in the withdrawal of the Tanzanian ambassador from the United States and the American ambassador from Tanzania. And, at a time when Tanzania had broken relations with Britain over its inaction following the Rhodesian Unilateral

Declaration of Independence, Karume was rebuilding his relations with the United Kingdom.[26]

For a few years following the merger of TANU and ASP in 1977, Zanzibar played a much less independent role in foreign affairs. Part of the reason for this change is Zanzibar's increasing financial dependence on the mainland, part is due to the increased control over Zanzibari leadership following the creation of CCM, and part has to do with a decline in foreign policy differences. Yet, as Zanzibar's economy declined, the need for external assistance grew. In late 1992, Zanzibar joined the Islamic Conference Organisation (OIC) as a means to gain access to such assistance. Although Zanzibar had a long history of acting independently in foreign affairs without significant resistance from the mainland, multipartyism, an opposition press, and the growth of Christian and Muslim subnationalism combined to make the issue a major threat to the union. Early in 1993, the parliamentary Constitutional and Legal Affairs Committee investigated the issue and reported to the National Assembly that Zanzibar had acted unconstitutionally. Before the matter could be debated, the National Assembly voted to refer the matter to the Tanzania and Zanzibar governments to be worked out within twelve months.[27]

Nevertheless, the underlying issue of mainland-Zanzibar relations festered. In August 1993 Zanzibar finally withdrew from the OIC, yet its action did not assuage mainlanders. Later that month the National Assembly unanimously passed a motion calling for the creation of a separate government for the mainland by 1995. Nyerere entered the fray, condemning both Zanzibar's OIC membership and the move for a government on the mainland. CCM's NEC responded in October 1993 by calling for a presidential commission, similar to the Nyalali Commission, to assess public feelings on restructuring the union. The OIC incident was only a symptom of the growing estrangement between Zanzibar and the mainland in the early 1990s.

Second, although formal agreements required the remittance to the union government of income, customs, and excise taxes collected in Zanzibar, the Zanzibar government resisted. In 1987, the Tanzanian government newspaper reported that for the four years from 1982/83 to 1986/87, Zanzibar had failed to remit TSh. 1,208,639,224 to the union government on the grounds that economic difficulties on the islands made it impossible to do so.[28] And, during the twenty-fifth anniversary celebrations of the union in 1989, the union's President Mwinyi observed that for several years the mainland had not only "met the whole bill for union matters like the Police Force, the Tanzania People's Defence Forces (TPDF) and other matters meant to be shared under the union setup" but also had met the budgetary deficit of the isles' government.[29]

Thus, though formally the ability of Zanzibar to act independently of Tanzania has been curtailed over the years, informally Zanzibar has been able to maintain considerable autonomy. By the early 1990s, pressures for structural changes in the union allowing greater autonomy not only for Zanzibar but also for Tanganyika were significant. When the Nyalali Commission recommended that a true federation be formed with three governments—one for Tanganyika, one for Zanzibar, and one for Tanzania—CCM rejected the suggestion, partly on the grounds that it would be a victory for subnationalism and a defeat for nationalism.[30] Yet by 1993 the OIC issue had made manifest latent mainland opposition to what was perceived as Zanzibar's privileged position in the union and led to a reconsideration of the structural relationship between the mainland and the islands.

Political Struggle in Zanzibar: How Did It Impact Unity?

Whereas Tanzania has been quite successful in suppressing subnationalism on the mainland, it has been much less successful in preventing its use by politicians in Zanzibar. Federalism provided Zanzibari politicians with a degree of insulation from the union government that made possible the use of subnationalism in political struggles. Whether it was used depended on two factors: first, the presence of grounds for believing that islanders were treated unfairly when compared with mainlanders; second, the belief by politicians that they would benefit from the use of subnationalism.[31] With regard to the first, Zanzibari leaders found numerous inequalities between the treatment of people on the islands and on the mainland that might arouse subnationalist feelings.[32] With regard to the second, subnationalism did not seem to become an issue because of its intrinsic value but rather because of its instrumental value in a particular situation; i.e., it was invoked when it served to facilitate the retention or acquisition of political office.

Political struggle in Zanzibar bred subnationalism. Despite Abeid Karume's role in creating the union, he was characterized often as a Zanzibari nationalist, i.e., in the context of Tanzania, a subnationalist.[33] He opposed unification of the ASP and TANU. And, as we have seen, he resisted transferring to the union government even those functions he agreed to transfer at the time of the merger. Such actions facilitated his political position. After his assassination in 1972, most of the group of leaders who had served with him on the Revolutionary Council or were closely associated with him in other ways became known as the Liberators. His successor, Aboud Jumbe, rose from that group but did not consistently support it. Sometimes he acted to favor a group of reform-minded challengers who became known as the Frontliners, and at other times he supported the Liberators.

After he became Zanzibar's president, according to Abdulwahid Mazrui, Ali Saleh, and Muhda Fadhid, Jumbe sought to reduce the power of the Liberators by engaging more actively in union affairs and cooperating with the Frontliners. He cooperated closely with Nyerere to facilitate the merger between the ASP and TANU in 1977.[34] Although motivation is difficult to determine, Mazrui, Saleh, and Fadhid claim that Jumbe's objective was to become president when Nyerere retired, but he became disillusioned when Sokoine was appointed prime minister and thereby became Nyerere's likely successor. In bitterness, they suggest, Jumbe turned back to the Liberators and to subnationalism in an attempt to "embarrass" the union. When his "plot" was revealed, he was forced to resign.[35]

Whether or not Jumbe's reasons are appropriately described by Mazrui, Saleh, and Fadhid, it is clear that following the party merger, there was a change in the character of the political leadership in Zanzibar. Muhammed Mzale argues that those who entered or reentered politics included former members of the ZNP and ZPP, rank-and-file ASP members who wanted to "untooth" the party, and idealists who saw the union as a step toward African unity. He suggests that those who supported the merger participated in CCM and came to play important roles in that party.[36] The appointment of Seif Shariff Hamad as the new chief minister and the selection of Mwinyi as the president of Zanzibar meant that what was known as the Third Phase government was dominated by Frontliners. In the short time they served together, significant changes took place that pushed the country toward economic liberalization.

In 1985, when Mwinyi was chosen to be Nyerere's replacement as union president, a struggle ensued over who should be nominated to be Zanzibar's presidential candidate. The decision came down to an NEC choice between Idris Abdul-Wakil, identified as a Liberator, and Hamad, who as we have seen was identified as a Frontliner. The NEC selected Wakil by a narrow margin. To many observers, the decision was puzzling, given the fact that Hamad had close ties with the leadership of CCM through his membership in the Central Committee and his position as head of the Economic and Planning Department of the National Executive Committee's secretariat.[37] One explanation for the decision was that the ideological socialists objected to the vehemence with which Hamad had pursued liberalization as chief minister and that they considered him too much a pragmatic socialist. The repercussions were significant.

Although Wakil was elected president of Zanzibar in 1985, it was by the smallest margin ever in a Zanzibari presidential contest, and opposition on Pemba was particularly strong. To heal the wounds, Nyerere strongly and successfully urged Hamad's reappointment as chief minister.[38] But the Frontliners had come to realize that the ideological socialists on the mainland acting for CCM were able to dominate the selection of leaders on Zanzibar in a way contrary to their interests. The basis was laid for a resurgence of subnationalism. Jan Kees van Donge and Athumani Liviga observed that "Hamad was . . . more and more identified with separatism and the ideals of further economic liberalisation: Zanzibar as a freeport; ties with the Arab world should replace the ties with the mainland."[39] Hamad's removal in May 1988 by the NEC was more fuel for the subnationalist fire.

With the approach of multipartyism early in 1992, a Zanzibari pressure group–cum–political party called Kamahuru emerged. Yet, fearful of a rise in subnationalism, CCM imposed a "national" conditionality on new political parties that were to be formed—that is, each party was required to show a following on both the mainland and the islands in order to be registered. Kamahuru lent its support to what became the Civic United Front (CUF), and Seif Shariff Hamad became vice-chairman of the party. Although Hamad favored reworking the constitutional arrangements over secession, the dynamics of multipartyism lent themselves to the rise of subnationalism.[40] Faced with the CUF challenge, the Zanzibar CCM leaders sought to undercut the opposition's use of subnationalism by using the OIC agreement and by fostering subnationalism on its own.[41] Tanzanian nationalism was weakened and Zanzibari subnationalism was strengthened by a new phenomenon: Several of the new political parties began to stress a Tanganyikan subnationalism, speaking out in opposition to the union on the grounds that it disadvantaged people on the mainland.[42]

It is apparent from this brief review that subnationalism was used as an instrument in the struggle for power. Virtually every leader in Zanzibar has at one time or another moved between being a nationalist and a subnationalist depending upon the situation, i.e., on whether the union was politically beneficial to him. Karume was a nationalist at union, then a subnationalist after removing Marxists from positions of power; Jumbe was a nationalist at the time of CCM's initiation, then a subnationalist following Sokoine's appointment; Hamad was a nationalist when he was appointed chief minister, then a subnationalist when he lost the nomination to Wakil. Although the causes for invoking nationalism and subnationalism may be more complex than these, the shifts in position suggest that support for subnationalism had more to do with the struggle for power in Zanzibar and on the mainland than with subnationalism per se. The nature of political struggle in Zanzibar tended to invoke subnationalist rhetoric.

The importance to this study of the use of nationalism and subnationalism in Zanzibar's political struggles lies in their impact on socialist construction. Nationalism was associated with support for socialism; subnationalism, therefore, tended to be associated with opposition to socialism.

The Impact of the Relationship Between Zanzibar and Tanzania on Socialist Construction

It is clear that asking a question about the impact of subnationalism on Tanzanian socialism is equivalent to asking how Zanzibar's association with Tanzania has affected the Tanzanian transition to socialism. In assessing Zanzibar's influence, I will focus on its role as an initiator, subverter, and innovator of Tanzanian socialism.

Adoption of Tanzanian Socialism

The union encouraged the adoption of Tanzanian socialism in two ways: First, it brought into mainland-union politics committed Zanzibari socialists, and second, it provided an example of the potentials of the socialist path.

The Zanzibari Marxists

In the wake of the Zanzibar revolution, committed socialists rose to power and socialist goals were adopted. Union brought Zanzibar and its socialist militants into closer association with the mainland and its leaders. Abdulrahman Muhammed Babu and Abdulla Kassim Hanga, the most significant socialist militants in the ASP, both became ministers in the union government shortly after the United Republic was formed. Other militants who were members of Zanzibar's Revolutionary Council became members of the National Assembly of the union, which, it will be recalled, made decisions on both union and nonunion affairs for the mainland. Thus, it is reasonable to suggest that the link between Zanzibar and Tanzania, by providing an entree to committed socialist leaders from Zanzibar, facilitated the adoption of Tanzanian socialism.

This hypothesis is supported by many scholars. Martin Bailey observed that "several of the leading Zanzibaris, particularly Babu and Hanga, were interested in the development of Socialist policies on the mainland."[43] Henry Bienen, in his seminal work on Tanzania published in 1967, argued that from the middle of 1964 the views of individuals who were more Marxist-Leninist than Nyerere were expressed in the official TANU newspaper:

> These individuals include men from Zanzibar who, since the union of Tanganyika and Zanzibar in April 1964, brought to their government posts a new language, a new rhetoric. They have infused a distinct ideology into the mainland.[44]

Bienen cited as an example a speech in the National Assembly by Hanga, who was then minister for industries and mineral resources, and suggested that "Hanga's style and his ideas echoed the Soviet Five Year Plans of the 1930's."[45] Yet mainlanders listened. William Tordoff, commenting on the same speech, said,

> Mr. Hanga's speech was punctuated by outbursts of loud applause from Tanganyikan (as well as Zanzibari) M.P.s, whose post-union euphoric mood blinded them to the sharp contrast between these policies and the

milder, less doctrinaire approach to socialism pursued by Mr. Nyerere's Government since September 1960.[46]

And a similar conclusion was reached by Sherman Kent, a Central Intelligence Agency (CIA) officer, in September 1964:

> Several of the principal Zanzibari pro-Communists were brought into a cabinet in Dar es Salaam composed mainly of moderate Tanganyikans. . . . Instead of restraining the expansion of Communist influence, URTZ [the United Republic of Tanganyika and Zanzibar] is probably facilitating the spread of this influence into Tanganyika."[47]

The first indication of this influence, according to many observers, was in the international arena. During 1964/65 relations with several socialist countries were enhanced, and relations with the West declined. The first military assistance from China was accepted in August 1964. As noted previously, under pressure the American ambassador was withdrawn as a consequence of an alleged plot against the Zanzibari government in November 1964. And West German military aid was withdrawn as a consequence of a dispute over an East German consulate during 1964/65. These events cannot be attributed solely to the influence of Marxist Zanzibaris in the union government, nor did they directly affect the evolution of Tanzanian socialism. Nevertheless, they were at least congruent with the notion of influence and furthered a mood supportive of the development of Tanzanian socialism.

There are, of course, alternative observations and arguments. Some conclude that union killed Marxist influence both in Zanzibar and on the mainland. The argument goes something like this: Marxists were the major challengers to Karume; union made possible the transfer of the most prominent Marxists to the mainland, where they lacked a political base; as a consequence, they were unable to influence policies to any great extent either in Zanzibar or on the mainland.

Looking back from a perspective of twenty years, Babu supported this argument:

> Nyerere used the appointments to weaken the progressive forces. With the assistance of the US he pinpointed specific people like myself, Hanga and Moyo. . . . We were sent to insignificant cabinet posts—for example, in my case, I was put in the Ministry of Economic Planning. But I was not in charge, there were three ministers of state. All three of us were under the President. There was nothing we could do. I could not plan policies or implement them. . . . The effect of this kind of cabinet was to incapacitate us. We were given big houses and cars but we had no function in Zanzibar and no function in the mainland.[48]

Babu's description of his complete powerlessness was probably an exaggeration. Hank Chase, a writer very sympathetic to him, had commented ten years earlier:

From 1964 through February 1972, Babu served continuously in some ministerial capacity, culminating in his heading the Ministry of Economic Affairs and Development Planning. Throughout this period, Babu was one of the leading supporters of Nyerere's various progressive measures, although he was also one of the major critics of the restricted character of these developments. Thus, for example, while supporting the vaguely socialist character of the Ujamaa orientation, Babu was sharply critical of its implications as regards industrial development.[49]

The implication of Babu's recollections and Chase's comments is that Babu did hold important union positions; he did voice his socialist views; yet he was unable to determine the precise character of Tanzanian socialism. It is true that Nyerere has explicitly attacked the scientific or dogmatic socialism of Marxist-Leninists.[50] But, as Zanzibar's chief minister, Omar Ali Juma, once said, quoting Babu, "A small amount of salt can influence the taste of a big amount of cooked rice."[51]

Obviously, it is difficult to determine the extent of the influence of the Zanzibari Marxists who joined the union government. Certainly, the seeds of much of Tanzanian socialism had already been sown on the mainland, and the form that socialism took in 1967 differed from what these Marxists had advocated.[52] Yet the evidence suggests two points. On the one hand, the Marxists' militant voices strengthened those leaders who supported the decision to commit their country to build a form of socialism. On the other hand, their voices found resonance with those of the mainland ideological socialists who believed it was possible to transform the ideas of the Arusha Declaration into a socialism more congruent with the ideas of the Zanzibari Marxists.

The Experiment's Experiment

Since the adoption of socialism in Tanzania, many writers have described it as an experiment, often to the displeasure of Tanzanians who looked upon it as more than that. What these writers meant was that, should Tanzania be successful, other countries might follow its path. In a sense, Zanzibar was the prototype for the Tanzanian experiment. Two influences are often mentioned: Zanzibar's policies and Zanzibar's treatment of the Marxist-Leninist left.

There is some evidence to support the validity of the first assertion: Most of the major socialist policies that Tanzania adopted following the Arusha Declaration, including nationalization, mass education, extending access to health facilities, state farms, and parastatal organizations with a monopoly over import and export, had been adopted previously by the revolutionary government in Zanzibar. Lucien Rey, just after the formation of the United Republic, expressed his optimism that "the Union will lead to the 'spreading' of the Zanzibar revolution in a much more effective way than could have been done by outside example."[53] And Martin Bailey has suggested that Rey's optimism was justified: "The union with Zanzibar was partially responsible for pushing Tanganyika away from the British model of development which the country shared with Kenya and Uganda toward socialism."[54]

There is little evidence to support the validity of the second assertion: As has been noted, one of the reasons Karume and Nyerere agreed to union was because they feared the consequences of the rise of a militant left in Zanzibar. Following union, the main leaders on the left were transferred to the mainland, assigned diplomatic posts, or executed, dissipating the Marxist-Leninist character of early postrevolutionary Zanzibar. To contend that Zanzibar's experience with the left affected the form socialism took on the mainland does not accord with most of the facts: The form socialism took in the Arusha Declaration is similar to that found in Nyerere's writings prior to the Zanzibar revolution. Since the Marxist-Leninist left never threatened those who led TANU and CCM, there was no need to act toward them as Zanzibar had. And, as we have seen, Tanzanian socialism was radicalized, not "deradicalized," for twenty years following the Arusha Declaration.

Decline of Tanzanian Socialism

Although, as we have seen, some evidence suggests that Zanzibar's association with the union encouraged the adoption of Tanzanian socialism, many argue that the association has been detrimental to socialism's realization in the long run. Among the principal arguments are the following: Zanzibar has acted in ways that have undermined international support for Tanzanian socialism; it has been an economic burden to the union, thereby reducing resources available to implement Tanzanian socialism; and it has allowed the development of internal opposition to Tanzanian socialism.

International Support

Although Zanzibar has attracted limited international attention since the assassination of Karume in 1972 and the subsequent treason trial, it was often an embarrassment to Nyerere during Karume's tenure. Tanzania was criticized repeatedly for Zanzibar's actions. A few examples are illustrative.

1. *The execution of Hanga and Shariff.* Both Hanga and Othman Shariff had been important leaders in ASP, and both had opposed Karume, Hanga on the left and Shariff on the right. Karume claimed they were involved in a plot against him. They were arrested on the mainland. Following assurances that they would receive a fair trial, Nyerere turned them over to Karume. Shariff was

a personal friend of Nyerere's and had served as the Tanzanian ambassador to the United States. No formal trial took place, yet Hanga and Shariff were executed toward the end of 1969. International condemnation of the incident was substantial.

2. *Justice under the early "people's courts."* The same year, 1969, Karume announced a major reform of the judiciary, which involved the establishment of "people's courts." At the lowest level, the three-member court was appointed by the local chairman of the Afro-Shirazi Party. In all courts, defendants were not to be allowed counsel. The prosecutor was also assigned the task of defense. Not until January 1985 were accused persons allowed to have a lawyer appear to defend them before the High Court and were they deemed innocent until proven guilty, changes brought about by the 1984 constitution, which went into effect January 12. The new constitution, besides introducing a high court, acknowledged the jurisdiction of the Tanzanian Court of Appeal.[55] Again, international criticism of the early people's courts was loud.

3. *Forced marriages.* Several girls of Asian descent, some under sixteen, were forcibly married to members of the Revolutionary Council. Protesting family members were arrested, and some were ordered to leave Zanzibar. Karume justified the acts by claiming that in colonial times Arabs took African concubines and now the shoe was on the other foot.[56] Nyerere was highly embarrassed, and the world press made much of the incident.[57]

4. *"Democracy" without elections.* Although Nyerere argued that democracy was a necessary condition for socialism, Karume argued that there should be no elections in Zanzibar for fifty or sixty years following the revolution. Indeed, it was not until 1980 that voters were given a chance to elect a legislature there. The slow pace of democratization has also been the subject of international criticism.

5. *Refusal to adhere to the leadership code.* Karume also resisted the Arusha Declaration's leadership code. He and other members of the Revolutionary Council found no contradiction between advocating socialism and earning income from renting houses. This problem was rectified by the Zanzibar Constitution (1979), under which Zanzibari officials became subject to the code. Nevertheless, Zanzibari defiance probably undermined the credibility of Tanzanian socialism.

6. *The treason trial.* Following Karume's assassination, there was a major treason trial. This time, although Nyerere arrested those said to be implicated by Zanzibar authorities who lived on the mainland (including Babu), he did not send them to Zanzibar. The trial was widely seen as a farce.[58] There were no defense lawyers; the cases were based on "confessions" that were recanted in court and were

said to have been made while the confessors were being tortured. Babu was sentenced in absentia to death. The international image of Tanzania was tarnished by the proceedings.

No direct connection between these six incidents and international support for Tanzanian socialism is apparent. Aid to Tanzania since the Arusha Declaration has been substantial, apparently regardless of Zanzibar's actions and despite the fact that those giving intellectual support knew enough to realize the absence of a connection between Tanzanian socialism and Zanzibari leaders' actions in these matters. Subtly and indirectly, though, international skepticism toward the Tanzanian undertaking might have been increased by Zanzibari actions.

Economic Burden

The decline in the Zanzibar economy, exacerbated by a sharp fall in the price of cloves in the late 1970s, had a much greater impact on the success of Tanzanian socialism than did the early Zanzibar embarrassments. First, Zanzibar became a financial burden on the union. Between 1982/83 and 1986/87, the Zanzibar government was unable to pay the union government over TSh. 1.2 billion it owed.[59] In July 1989 the deputy minister for finance told the House of Representatives that Zanzibar owed the union government TSh. 2.8 billion in arrears for contributions to union affairs such as defense, communications, home affairs, foreign affairs, and currency.[60] Clearly, during the 1980s and early 1990s, Zanzibar became a financial burden. Second, and more importantly, the economic decline fostered liberalization in Zanzibar, which both undermined and brought innovations to Tanzanian socialism.

Innovation in Tanzanian Socialism

Although Zanzibari Marxists may have facilitated the initiation of Tanzanian socialism and lent support to the ideological socialists in the 1960s, by the 1980s Zanzibari leaders were facilitating a major revision in the practice of that socialism and lending support to the pragmatic socialists. Indeed, part of the tension between Zanzibar and the union was due to the relatively greater importance of the ideological socialists in the union government and of the pragmatic socialists in the Zanzibar government.

We have seen how Zanzibar's refusal to hold elections under Karume embarrassed the union government and how elections were introduced only with the 1979 constitution. A strong case can be made to support the view that democratization in Zanzibar was the result of the creation of CCM and union-mainland actions. But in the last decade Zanzibar has taken the lead in important areas to democratize the polity. When the Bill of Rights was adopted in 1984, Zanzibar opted for its immediate implementation, whereas the mainland-union government delayed implementation for three years. Although President Nyerere initiated the debate over a multiparty system in 1990, Zanzibaris have been among its strongest advocates. The reasons are not simply due to a change in leadership or an increase in idealism. Rather, they are directly related to subnationalism. Many Zanzibaris feel that democratization would mean a diminution of CCM power and a return toward Zanzibar's control of Zanzibari affairs.

Economic liberalization has followed a similar pattern. As previously noted, the formal economy of the islands declined even more than that of the mainland during the early 1980s, despite the presence of some goods in Zanzibari shops that could not be found in Dar es Salaam. When the door to formal liberalization was opened with the 1984/85 budget, Zanzibar moved much more rapidly to seize the opportunity to use liberalization as a way out of its difficulties. This move was partly due to the fact that there were no equivalents of the ideological socialists with any significant power in Zanzibar, so there was no major resistance. Zanzibar took the lead in a wide variety of areas.

In April 1989 the chief minister, Omar Ali Juma, announced that Zanzibar had asked the United Nations Development Programme (UNDP) to finance studies on the possibility of turning the isles into a free port area to boost foreign exchange earnings, as suggested by British consultants who had drawn up a three-year economic recovery plan.[61] Later that year, in a talk before the British-Tanzania Society, Juma praised the private sector's increasing significance and the success of "own money" imports (i.e., imports using convertible currencies held abroad by the importer). And he reiterated the possibility of making Zanzibar into a free trade area with offshore banking facilities.[62] Still later that year, he spoke of "government's long-term plans to turn the Indian Ocean island into a duty free port to serve the . . . nations in east and central Africa, a task which Zanzibar undertook until early this century."[63] Discussions about the possibility of creating an African Hong Kong in a part of Tanzania were certainly a far cry from the socialism of CCM's Fifteen-Year Party Programme.

An array of actions followed that went much further than those being taken on the mainland at the time to liberalize the economy. In 1984 the government sold many of the old Stone Town houses it had seized after the revolution to private individuals, on condition that they be repaired.[64] A Private Investment Protection Act was passed in 1985 and was made more favorable to such investment subsequently.[65] In 1987 it was announced that Zanzibar would allow private clinics.[66] In 1989, Chief Minister Ali Omar Juma said that the foreign exchange crisis had led the government to consider allowing private traders in the clove market, and he spoke of plans to deconfine major foodstuffs.[67] In 1991 the principal secretary in the chief minister's office said marketing of cloves should be decontrolled.[68]

Early in 1991 a reporter interviewed several Zanzibaris about trade liberalization. The responses were all positive but quite varied. A mango hawker said the availability of bicycles and spares made it possible for him to sell on more streets; a taxi driver said the availability of more cars eased transport problems; a consumer said people could get products even when foreign exchange was exhausted; a traveler said sea transport liberalization made people less dependent on the government.[69] This was certainly not a random sample with any statistical meaning, but the responses suggested that Zanzibar was in the forefront of a major transformation in Tanzanian socialism.

Still, like union leaders, Zanzibar's leaders continued to stress that all these changes did not imply the abandonment of the effort to build socialism.

Conclusion

Although the case of Zanzibar exemplifies the impact of subnationalism on an effort to build a socialist society, it has been strongly affected by a variety of unusual factors. The union with Tanzania was born in part as an antisocialist undertaking: Karume sought to reduce the power of the Zanzibari Marxists, and Nyerere sought to reduce the power of the newly arrived representatives of Marxist states for he feared the probable consequences of a cold war struggle in East Africa. The initial result of the union was to shift the thrust toward socialism from Zanzibar to Tanzania. Although the Arusha Declaration rejected scientific socialism, many of the ideas of the Zanzibari Marxists became integrated into the beliefs of what have been identified as the ideological socialists.

The union's federal structure has provided Zanzibar with a level of autonomy much greater than that of any other region of Tanzania, partly accounting for the fact that subnationalism has been a more significant element of politics there than elsewhere. Zanzibari subnationalism has tended to be "unprincipled"; i.e., it is used not so much as an end as it is as a means to gain or retain political power. Nevertheless, as a subnationalism it challenges Tanzanian nationalism. Since the latter has been closely associated with Tanzanian socialism, the subnationalism has tended to be antisocialist. Yet its impact has been more complex than is implied by such a simple conclusion.

From the time of CCM's formation, the party has sought to suppress Zanzibari subnationalism by promoting or demoting leaders. When Jumbe and his chief minister sought to use it, they were forced to resign. In the aftermath, two union men were chosen, Mwinyi as president and Hamad as chief minister. Responding to serious economic decline on the islands, they pursued liberalization measures that went further than those on the mainland. In doing so, they linked themselves with the mainland's pragmatic socialists. A variety of circumstances led to Mwinyi's nomination to succeed Nyerere, circumstances that overcame the disadvantages of those links at a time when the ideological socialists still dominated CCM. But Hamad was rejected as Zanzibar's presidential candidate in 1985 by the ideological socialist–dominated NEC. In response, many of his supporters began to emphasize subnationalism in their opposition to the Zanzibar government. Although Mwinyi's succession to the presidency may have limited the development of Zanzibari subnationalism, it stimulated Tanganyikan subnationalism. With the advent of multipartyism, opposition leaders began to argue that Mwinyi had brought in a disproportionate number of Zanzibari and Muslim ministers, thereby capturing the "national" government from those on the mainland. The result was that Tanzanian nationalism, and what remained of the Tanzanian socialism that was linked to it, was challenged by a new subnationalism—that of Tanganyika.

Notes

1. Virtually all definitions of nationalism include the notion of a sense of identity with the nation as an essential element. Yet there is disagreement over the requisites of nationhood. The fundamental disagreement is over the necessity of a myth of common descent. On one side are writers like Walker Connor, who contend it is essential. See Connor, *The National Question in Marxist-Leninist Theory and Strategy* (Princeton, N.J.: Princeton University Press, 1984), p. xiv. On the other side are writers like Louis Snyder, who consider citizenship in a sovereign state as sufficient. See Snyder, *The Meaning of Nationalism* (Westport, Conn.: Greenwood Press, 1954), p. 72, or *The New Nationalism* (Ithaca, N.Y.: Cornell University Press, 1968), p. 2. James Coleman suggests that a nation need only be a "community destined to be an independent state." See Coleman, *Nigeria, Background to Nationalism* (Berkeley: University of California Press, 1960), p. 422. Anthony Smith suggests that the two views of nation and nationality might be called the "cultural" and the "political" varieties. He notes that the latter form best characterizes the use of the terms in Africa. See Smith, *Theories of Nationalism*, second edition (New York: Holmes & Meier, 1983), p. xiii.

2. See, for example, Connor, *The National Question;* Ronaldo Munck, *The Difficult Dialogue, Marxism and Nationalism* (London: Zed Books, 1986).

3. Connor, *The National Question*, pp. 19–20.

4. The name was changed to the United Republic of Tanzania toward the end of 1964. See Haroub Othman and L.P. Shaidi, "Zanzibar's Constitutional Development," *Eastern Africa Law Review,* Vols. 11–14 (1978–1981), p. 200.

5. Afro-Shirazi Party, *The Afro-Shirazi Party Revolution, 1964–1974* (Zanzibar: Afro-Shirazi Party, 1974), p. 27.

6. Historically, the island of Pemba differed from the island of Zanzibar in several ways: Its people had fewer ethnic links with the mainland, a greater sense of kinship with inhabitants of Arab descent, and a lower level of economic development. Traditionally, most of the cloves that provided most of the foreign exchange for the Zanzibar government were produced on Pemba.

7. The Umma Party was a radical Marxist-Leninist party led by A.M. Babu. Its popularity had grown rapidly in the months prior to the revolution.

8. That seems to be Babu's contention in the introduction to Amrit Wilson, *U.S. Foreign Policy and Revolution, The Creation of Tanzania* (London: Pluto Press, 1989), p. 2.

9. For example, Hank Chase says "yes" in his "The Zanzibar Treason Trial," *Review of African Political Economy,* No. 6 (May–August 1976), p. 18, whereas Lucien Rey says "no" in his "The Revolution in Zanzibar," *New Left Review,* No. 25 (May–June 1965), reprinted in Lionel Cliffe and John Saul, eds., *Socialism in Tanzania: Vol. 1, Politics* (Nairobi: East African Publishing House, 1972), p. 30.

10. Cranford Pratt, *The Critical Phase in Tanzania, 1945–1968, Nyerere and the Emergence of a Socialist Strategy* (Cambridge: Cambridge University Press, 1976), p. 139.

11. Rey, "The Revolution in Zanzibar," p. 29.

12. Wilson, *U.S. Foreign Policy and Revolution,* p. 66.

13. Cited in Pratt, *The Critical Phase in Tanzania,* p. 139.

14. B.P. Srivastava, "The Constitution of the United Republic of Tanzania 1977—Some Salient Features—Some Riddles," *Eastern Africa Law Review,* Vols. 11–14 (1978–1981), p. 91.

15. Julius Nyerere, "The Union of Tanganyika and Zanzibar," in Nyerere, *Freedom and Unity* (London: Oxford University Press, 1967), p. 292.

16. *Daily News* (Dar es Salaam), 25 April 1989, p. 1.

17. The Articles of Union can be found in S.G. Ayany, *A History of Zanzibar* (Nairobi: East African Literature Bureau, 1970), appendix J, pp. 181–183.

18. Othman and Shaidi, "Zanzibar's Constitutional Development," pp. 202–203; and Colin Legum, ed., *Africa Contemporary Record, 1984–1985* (New York: Africana Publishing Company, 1985), pp. B372–B373 (for 1984 change).

19. The crux of the academic debate has a definitional and an empirical component. It involves the *degree* of sovereignty each level must have for a state to be an instance of federalism and the *degree* of sovereignty that actually exists on each of those levels at any time in Tanzania. Ivo Duchacek, writing in 1970, considered Tanzania a federation; Preston King, writing in 1982, also identified Tanzania as a federation; but Daniel Elazar, writing in 1987, identified it as "a political system with federal arrangements" rather than as a federal system. Although he presented no data to indicate the basis of his determination, it appears to rest on his sense that the sovereignty of Zanzibar over nonunion affairs on the islands was too limited for it to be a federal system. See Duchacek, *Comparative Federalism, The Territorial Dimension of Politics* (New York: Holt, Rinehart and Winston, 1970), p. 196; King, *Federalism and Federation* (Baltimore: Johns Hopkins University Press, 1982), p. 71; and Elazar, *Exploring Federalism* (Tuscaloosa: University of Alabama Press, 1987), p. 46.

20. The population of the mainland in 1988 was approximately 23 million; that of the islands was about 450,000.

21. Colin Legum, ed., *Africa Contemporary Record, 1983–1984* (New York: Africana Publishing Company, 1984), p. C29.

22. Ibid., p. B272.

23. *Africa Confidential,* Vol. 30, No. 11 (May 1989), p. 8. It was not until late 1992 that the courts ruled in Hamad's favor.

24. Chase, "The Zanzibar Treason Trial," p. 14. Michael Lofchie makes the same point in his *Zanzibar: Background to Revolution* (Princeton, N.J.: Princeton University Press, 1965), p. 281.

25. *Daily News,* 12 March 1993, p. 4.

26. Anthony Clayton, *The Zanzibar Revolution and Its Aftermath* (London: Archon, 1981), p. 150.

27. *Daily News,* 26 February 1993, p. 1; and *Sunday News* (Dar es Salaam), 28 February 1993, p. 3.

28. *Daily News,* 24 July 1987, p. 3.

29. *Daily News,* 25 April 1989, p. 1.

30. Jamhuri ya Muungano wa Tanzania, Tume ya Rais ya Mfumo wa Chama Kimoja au Vyama Vingi vya Siasa Tanzania, 1991, *Kitabu cha Kwanza: Taarifa na Mapendekezo ya Tume Kuhusu Mfumo wa Siasa Nchini Tanzania* (Dar es Salaam: NPC-KIUTA, 1992), p. 6.

31. Jan Kees van Donge and Athumani Liviga have argued similarly, i.e., that the appeal to subnationalism in Zanzibar has not been a constant theme of politicians but rather a card they play in particular situations, especially when their power is threatened. See van Donge and Liviga, "The Democratisation of Zanzibar and the 1985 General Election," *The Journal of Commonwealth and Comparative Politics,* Vol. 28, No. 2 (July 1990), pp. 203–207.

32. Many issues were raised in this context. For example, a Zanzibari member of the National Assembly complained that when the Tanzania Posts and Telecommunications Corporation cut a coconut tree in Zanzibar it paid only TSh. 95, whereas on the mainland it paid a compensation of TSh. 500. See *Sunday News,* 28 June 1987, p. 1. Of course, the inequalities that benefited Zanzibaris were ignored.

33. By uniting with the mainland in 1964, Karume at least feigned a kind of Tanzanian nationalism. Yet even at the time he was characterized, in contrast to the Zanzibari Marxists, as a Zanzibari nationalist. Sengondo Mvungi has summarized a widely held view of his period of rule as follows: "The well intended revolution lost its way to its avowed goals of social justice, racial equality, economic prosperity and democracy and strayed into untold horizons of political persecution, liquidation of dissent, torture, and racial harassment." See Mvungi, "Recent Constitutional Developments in Zanzibar: Some Problems and Prospects," a paper presented at the Zanzibar Revolution Twenty-Fifth Anniversary Seminar, University of Dar es Salaam, January 1989, pp. 32–33.

34. Abdulwahid Mazrui, Ali Saleh, and Muh'da Fadhid, "The First Three Phases of Zanzibar Revolutionary Government," a paper presented at the Zanzibar Revolution Twenty-Fifth Anniversary Seminar, University of Dar es Salaam, January 1989, pp. 15 and 16.

35. Ibid., p. 16.

36. Muhammed M.H. Mzale, "Zanzibar, Where To—After Successful Class Struggle," a paper presented at the Zanzibar Revolution Twenty-Fifth Anniversary Seminar, University of Dar es Salaam, January 1989, p. 27.

37. Haroub Othman, "Zanzibar—Democracy in Transition?" a paper presented at the Zanzibar Twenty-Fifth Anniversary Seminar, University of Dar es Salaam, January 1989, pp. 32–33.

38. *Daily News,* 6 March 1989, p. 3. Earlier that month Nyerere said that after the 1985 elections the NEC would have expelled Hamad because of his instigation of the anti-Wakil vote, had it not been for the chairman's (Nyerere's) imposition. Nyerere said he engineered the endorsement of Hamad and his group to contest NEC membership "in the hope they would reform." See *Daily News,* 3 March 1989, p. 1.

39. Van Donge and Liviga, "The Democratisation of Zanzibar," p. 215.

40. *New African* (London), No. 298 (July 1992), p. 36.

41. *Africa Events* (London), Vol. 9, No. 2 (February 1993), p. 7.

42. Ibid. The rise of Tanganyikan subnationalism was fostered by politicians from several parties. Mwinyi was characterized as a Zanzibari who now ruled the mainland. His appointment of Muslim ministers was characterized by them as

indicative of the union government's favoritism toward Muslims and Muslim Zanzibar and estrangement from the Christian population on the mainland. The destruction by Islamic fundamentalists of pork butcheries in Dar es Salaam and the distribution of audiotapes on the mainland calling for support of Muslim politicians in early 1993 further strengthened the assertions of these opposition party leaders and weakened nationalism.

43. Martin Bailey, *The Union of Tanganyika and Zanzibar: A Study in Political Integration* (Syracuse, N.Y.: Program of Eastern African Studies, Maxwell School of Citizenship and Public Affairs, Syracuse University, 1973), p. 108.

44. Henry Bienen, *Tanzania, Party Transformation and Economic Development* (Princeton, N.J.: Princeton University Press, 1967), p. 208.

45. Ibid., p. 222.

46. William Tordoff, *Government and Politics in Tanzania* (Nairobi: East African Publishing House, 1967), p. 174.

47. Wilson, *U.S. Foreign Policy and Revolution*, p. 93.

48. Ibid., p. 83.

49. Chase, "The Zanzibar Treason Trial," pp. 25 and 26.

50. Julius Nyerere, "Introduction," Nyerere, *Freedom and Socialism* (Dar es Salaam: Oxford University Press, 1968), pp. 14–19.

51. *Daily News*, 22 July 1989, p. 3.

52. Julius Nyerere, "Ujamaa—The Basis of African Socialism," in Nyerere, *Freedom and Unity* (London: Oxford University Press, 1967), pp. 162–171.

53. Rey, "The Revolution in Zanzibar," p. 31.

54. Bailey, *The Union of Tanganyika and Zanzibar*, p. 34.

55. Legum, ed., *Africa Contemporary Record, 1984–1985*, pp. B372–B373.

56. Clayton, *The Zanzibar Revolution*, p. 124.

57. Nyerere commented on the problem in an interesting speech he gave in Zanzibar many years later, published in *Africa Events*, November 1987, pp. 24–33, under the title "Woe, Dereliction, Ruin and Decay."

58. Chase, "The Zanzibar Treason Trial," pp. 14–33.

59. *Daily News*, 24 July 1987, p. 3.

60. *Daily News*, 13 July 1989, p. 3.

61. *Daily News*, 15 April 1989, p. 1.

62. *Daily News*, 22 June 1989, p. 3.

63. *Sunday News*, 5 November 1989, p. 1.

64. *Daily News*, 25 April 1990, p. 4.

65. *Daily News*, 26 May 1989, p. 1.

66. *Daily News*, 27 January 1987, p. 3.

67. *Daily News*, 16 January 1989, p. 1.

68. *Daily News*, 9 May 1991, p. 1.

69. *Daily News*, 11 February 1991, p. 3.

10

Conclusion

Asiyekubali kushindwa si mshindani.
"One who does not admit defeat is not a fighter."

Tanzania has had an importance in Africa and the world disproportionate to that warranted by the size of its population and the extent of its wealth. Many of the most significant African and non-African scholars of African politics have taught at the University of Dar es Salaam and/or studied the country. Tanzania became a central focus of courses on African politics in universities outside the continent.[1] Much of the writing on African political change—especially that of scholars on the left—has used Tanzania as a surrogate for the continent as a whole. Certainly, Tanzanian leaders have played an active role in a variety of issues and in a variety of organizations within Africa and the Third World.[2] Yet Tanzania's importance derives more from the fact that it was known as *the* African experiment in socialist construction than from anything else.

The Arusha Declaration initiated a period of renewed idealism and hope in Tanzania, but the struggle for the realization of its tenets has brought pessimism and despair. This cycle of excitement and then disillusionment is evident in the response of expatriate scholars to the undertaking. Initially, socialist and Marxist intellectuals flocked to the country to share in the glow of socialism's birth and to nurture Tanzania's pilgrimage. But soon after their arrival, many—though not all—of the Marxist scholars became disillusioned with the ambiguous progress being made toward what was clearly a non-Marxist form of socialism and moved, both physically and intellectually, to new Marxist experiments elsewhere on the continent.

Democratic socialist scholars were not as quickly disillusioned nor as quick to turn their attention elsewhere. Nevertheless, following the onset of economic decline in the late 1970s, most academics of all orientations wrote off Tanzanian socialism either because of its slow progress or because of its deviations from a "true" socialist path. Long before people began to talk about the death of socialism in Eastern Europe and the former Soviet Union, the death of the Tanzanian experiment was widely proclaimed. Yet CCM remained formally committed to the pursuit of socialism despite the scholarly proclamation of its death and the numerous defeats described and analyzed in the preceding chapters. The question that remains is whether there will be a "resurrection," in other words, whether the setbacks are permanent or merely temporary.

This concluding chapter reviews briefly the substance of the preceding chapters; examines major explanations for what has happened; and then considers whether the factors contributing to the defeats might be overcome in the future.

Tanzanian Socialism

Although Tanzanian socialism differs in many respects from other socialisms, its doctrine falls within a broad-based definition of socialism: It shares the common starting point, which is "the assault on capitalism and its philosophy of individualism."[3] And it shares a vision of the good society in which there is equality, democracy, an attitude that places collective interest above individual interest, public ownership of the "commanding heights" of the economy, a gradually increasing standard of living, and self-reliance.[4] Although Nyerere was its initiator, he gave up proprietary rights to Tanzanian socialism when the NEC made it the party's objective. At that time, the "right" to further elaborate and define it was assumed by the collective political leadership.[5]

Tanzanian socialism is an instance of utopian, democratic socialism, despite its dynamism and ambiguities in implementation. First, during the 1970s and 1980s, party leaders significantly radicalized its means, though not its ends. Although these changes moved Tanzanian socialism toward "scientific" socialism, I have contended that it remained in the category of democratic socialism. In the early 1990s, leaders "deradicalized" the means, moving the ideology back toward its initial utopian social democratic form. Second, state actions often diverged from the means and ends of Tanzanian socialism, leading some observers to deny that it is an instance of socialism, let alone an instance of utopian social democracy. I have contended that Tanzanian socialism is a body of ideas, rather than a set of state actions. The empirical question addressed in this book involves the relationship between the vision of the good society embodied in Tanzanian socialism and the reality of Tanzanian society; i.e., How effective have state actions been in moving Tanzania closer to the vision?

In a sense, socialist construction and development have the same meaning. At least at the time it was adopted, Tanzanian socialism reflected societal aspirations. The volitional, as distinct from the determinist, notion of development may be defined as the process of moving society toward the achievement of its aspirations. Therefore, the effort to build Tanzanian socialism and to develop are identical. If one disaggregates the variety of goals embedded in Tanzanian socialism, one may identify the experience as an instance of many other general concepts, including the more narrow notions of economic development, democratization, the plight of a neocolonial country, and the struggle for equality.

The Experiences

I have argued that Tanzania's experiences with socialist construction have been deeply affected by a fundamental political cleavage among those who have dominated the state since the time of the Arusha Declaration, i.e., that between the ideological and pragmatic socialists. The distinction between the groups is not class based, since each is composed of a mixture of sections of the petty bourgeoisie; it is not ethnicity based, since each has contained a cross-section of ethnic groups; it *is* based on differences in the form of Tanzanian socialism advocated. Although some leaders have persistently advocated socialist positions that are ideological or pragmatic, more have followed Nyerere's lead and moved between these positions. The motivation for leaders to side with those articulating ideological or pragmatic socialist positions probably comprises a mixture of factors, including patron-client considerations, a set of personal beliefs, an assessment of what is best for the leader's constituency and/or the country, the leader's class position, and many others. Whatever the motivation for joining one faction or the other, this cleavage has repeatedly affected the effort to realize socialism. The difference between ideological and pragmatic socialists is found primarily in the issue of the means to be employed in socialist construction. The ideological socialists have looked to the experiences of "more advanced" socialist states as a model; the pragmatic socialists have argued that there is no model and that Tanzania must find its own way. In the dispute between the two, each tends to deny the socialist character of the other; i.e., the former are called by the latter "dogmatists" and the latter are called by the former "pragmatists."

Pragmatists are concerned with what works, i.e., what achieves immediate goals rather than fundamental ones. This focus is reflected in the comments of many scholars. W.Y. Elliott wrote more than a half century ago,

> Pragmatism professes to accept a single test: 'By their fruits shall ye know them.' The fruits of the pragmatic attitude have only the criteria of arrival and survival, however, to tell us what it is lawful and good to eat. ... Pragmatism can offer no normative program.[6]

Charles Anderson recently wrote, "Pragmatism can be understood as sheer instrumental rationality, the mutual adjustment of means and ends, resources and values. This is taken as a general conception of method: the aim can be anything."[7] And, in a Marxist appraisal of pragmatism, George Novack wrote,

> Pragmatic people rely not upon laws, rules, and principles which reflect the determinate features and determining factors of objective reality, but principally upon makeshifts, rule-of-thumb methods, and improvisations based on what they believe might be immediately advantageous.[8]

Each of these authors suggests not only that pragmatism focuses on means but also that such instrumental thinking can be harmful. Elliott blamed pragmatism for the rise of syndicalism on the left and Fascism on the right in the 1920s. He said, "The pragmatic attitude toward the state offers an easy, popular apology for the attacks on constitutional and representative government that dominate contemporary political phenomena."[9] Anderson argued that "pragmatism needs liberalism if it is to have moral and political significance."[10] And Novack saw it as challenging the Marxist argument that there are social laws governing the means by which a socialist society comes into being.[11]

These arguments are echoed in Tanzania. Ideological socialists have claimed that pragmatic socialists forget the ends, the purposes of socialist construction, whereas pragmatic socialists have claimed that ideological socialists will never reach the ends because of their fear of trying alternative means. The many policy changes that have followed the temporary "victories" of one faction over the other have adversely affected sectors such as agriculture, industry, and the cooperatives.[12] As we have seen, the *tendency* was for the ideological socialists to dominate the party from about 1967 to about 1990, while the pragmatic socialists dominated the government. During this period, the ideological socialists successfully moved Tanzanian socialist *ideas* toward a less pragmatic form, whereas the pragmatic socialists successfully moved Tanzanian *policies* toward a less ideological form. The pragmatic socialists came to dominate both forums in the early 1990s. Without the restraint imposed by the ideological socialists, those who led the state increasingly tended to move from being pragmatic socialists to mere pragmatists.

The Pragmatic Origins of Ujamaa

In his seminal work on the emergence of socialism in Tanzania, Cranford Pratt contended that the Arusha Declaration was a consequence of Nyerere's concern over the development of two attitudes among Tanzanian leaders: a belief that "major and sustained foreign capital assistance" was a requisite for economic development and a belief in the appropriateness of "self-seeking acquisitiveness."[13] The declaration was a practical response to these problems. Pratt contended that Nyerere cleverly combined nationalizations, which leaders enthusiastically approved, with a leadership code, which leaders were reluctant to accept. Enthusiasm for the former facilitated acceptance of the latter.[14] Nyerere's pragmatism was evident not only in the adoption of socialism as a goal but also in the discussion of the distinction between ujamaa and "dogmatic socialism."

Nyerere's criticism of "dogmatic socialism" was made basically on pragmatic grounds; i.e., he argued that there was no single means by which socialism might be constructed. Instead, he argued, "The task of a socialist is to think out for himself the best way of achieving desired ends under the conditions which exist now. Africa's conditions are very different from those of the Europe in which Marx and Lenin wrote and worked."[15] He continued, "For if 'scientific socialism' means anything, it can only mean that the objectives are socialist and you apply scientific methods of study in working out the appropriate policies."[16] He suggested that in the Tanzanian context, "one could well finish up with the Arusha Declaration and the policies of ujamaa!"[17] Clearly, Nyerere was pitting dogmatism against pragmatism and associating the latter with ujamaa, and he was arguing that it was really the "scientific" thing to do.

If Nyerere urged the adoption of the Arusha Declaration and criticized "dogmatic socialism" on pragmatic grounds, then ujamaa and pragmatism must not be in opposition. What seems to have happened is that the means he suggested often did not "work." If pragmatic socialists ran Tanzania alone, one would expect that the means would be altered until a set was found that "worked." But for years the only changes in Tanzanian socialism seemed to be in the direction of dogmatism.

The "Radicalization" of the Ideology of Ujamaa

The explanation of this situation hinges on the fact that those who redefined ujamaa following the Arusha Declaration in 1967 through the Fifteen-Year Party Programme in 1987 were dominated by ideological socialists, who were more dogmatic than pragmatic. As we have seen, this redefinition can be traced through the major party documents, "TANU Guidelines, 1971" and *CCM Guidelines, 1981,* culminating in the *Programu ya Chama cha Mapinduzi, 1987 hadi 2002.*[18] When one compares the latter with the Arusha Declaration, one finds a socialism much more like the "dogmatic socialism" Nyerere criticized twenty years before: It called for a vanguardlike party; emphasized the importance of class struggle; decried capitalist proclivities of peasants; stressed industrialization; attacked the idea of a mixed economy; and urged Tanzanians to pay more attention to historical models of socialism in the USSR and Mongolia.[19] In the Tanzanian context, these changes toward dogmatism were seen as a "radicalization" of ujamaa.

The question of why Tanzanian socialism became progressively more dogmatic until about 1990 is essentially the question of why the ideological socialists increasingly dominated the pragmatic socialists within CCM. There are several partial answers. First, the ideological socialists' call for "more radical" action in the face of the frustrations facing Tanzanians was more appealing. The pragmatic socialists were too easily associated with a comprador or international bourgeoisie, which was characterized as the cause of the frustrations. Second, once in high positions, the ideological socialists used a patron-client–like system to muffle opposition. Higher party officials had power to approve candidates for lower party positions or to remove lower party officials from office. An implicit exchange occurred: Lower party officials got positions; higher party officials got ideological support. Approval of the Fifteen-Year Party Programme in 1987 at the Kizota Party conference, I would suggest, was partly a consequence of the operation of this system. Third, pragmatic socialists could use the government to do what they wanted anyway. Although the party was de facto supreme until the mid-1970s and de jure supreme in succeeding years, the pragmatic socialists found mechanisms that allowed them considerable room for maneuver within the government. As a result, "victory" within the party was not a necessity. Fourth, the moderately ideological and moderately pragmatic socialists may have seen control of the party by "radical" ideological socialists as necessary for progress toward socialism. With a bureaucracy ready to borrow policies from the "bourgeois" West, a strong pull to the left was required if any socialist content was to remain. Thus, for moderate socialist policies to be implemented, the ideological socialists needed to control the party. Whatever the causes, it is clear that the "radicalization" occurred.

The ideological socialists did not win every battle within the party during the first twenty years following the Arusha Declaration, but they did win a majority of them. Although the IMF agreement in 1986 signaled their vulnerability, their loss of dominance within the party occurred sometime between the end of 1987, when the Fifteen-Year Party Programme was adopted, and early 1990, when Nyerere called for a major debate on whether Tanzania should give up its single-party system. This loss of dominance corresponded with a period of rapid disillusionment with socialism in Eastern Europe and elsewhere. To borrow ideas from the experiences of successful socialist countries was no longer a way out. Discredited, the ideological socialists lost legitimacy and began to question their own positions. The way was open for pragmatic socialists to come to the fore. This is a major turning point, but it is unlikely to be the last one.

Although the "radicalization" of Tanzanian socialism did not *prevent* implementation of more pragmatic policies by the bureaucracy, it did have an impact on them: (a) It probably restrained some government officials from ignoring socialist ends as they implemented policy; (b) it probably undermined state legitimacy when the party forced the government to radically alter policies, such as it did with rural cooperatives; and (c) it probably diminished party support among those who saw radicalization as an indication that the party was out of touch with reality.

The "Pragmatization" of the Practice of Ujamaa

Tanzania's experience with the "old" transition mechanisms was not very positive. In a famous review of the accomplishments of the first ten years after the Arusha Declaration, Nyerere said that in 1967 he was asked how long it would take Tanzania to become socialist: "I thought 30 years. I was wrong. . . . I am now sure that it will take us much longer!"[20] A brief summary of Tanzanian experiences in pursuing major socialist ends is illustrative of the problems that have arisen and of the pragmatic response to those problems.

Democracy

When the commitment to socialist construction was made in 1967, the expectation was that the single party would be the principal instrument for the achievement and enhancement of democracy. At first the goal was defined in terms of liberal democracy. Nyerere argued that though a single party system *appeared* to violate liberal democratic procedures, it did not do so in reality so long as the overriding societal objective was development, the party was a mass one, and competition, periodic elections, and participation were encouraged.[21]

By the 1980s, though, the party was "sick"; i.e., it was not functioning as envisioned under one-party democracy. Membership was stagnant or declining; party branches were atrophying; disillusionment was widespread. Two approaches to getting the party back on track were suggested by party leaders. The first approach, a "vanguardization" of the party, was championed by the ideological socialists. They did not argue against using the party to promote democracy. But they sought to shift the definition of democracy from a liberal to a popular one, i.e., from one that equated democracy with a set of procedures thought to make the party act in accord with the popular will to one that equated democracy with control by leaders thought to embody the popular will. To the ideological socialists, the party should be a vanguard one like that in many other socialist states. A vanguard party was one in which there was ideological purity, achieved by indoctrination and by weeding out dissident elements. As far back as the mid-1970s for TANU and 1977 for CCM, the ideological socialists had made the leadership code applicable to all members. A three-month period of ideological training was introduced prior to membership being granted. The Fifteen-Year Party Programme called for further efforts to attain ideological purity in accord with practices in many other socialist states. Despite efforts at "vanguardization," popular disillusionment with the party grew.

The second approach, a revitalization of the party, was championed by both pragmatic and ideological socialists. When Nyerere retired as president in 1985, he accepted as one of his principal responsibilities as chairman of CCM the task of party "consolidation," i.e., reviving a party that was then languid. Yet he was unsuccessful. In response, in February 1990 he proposed consideration of a new mechanism for linking society and state in a democratic fashion—a multiparty system. There is considerable evidence to support the view that Nyerere had not given up on the old mechanism, i.e., CCM. Rather, he saw a multiparty system as a means of reviving CCM. Clearly, it was a call for pragmatism, for exploring alternative means to foster democracy—at least, alternative means to make the "old" mechanism "work."

Equality

Equality was sought through a variety of methods, including distributive policies in education and health, public ownership of the means of production, collective production, and government regulation of wages and salaries. Initially, there were many more successes than failures. Health centers were opened throughout the country; Tanzania's Universal Primary Education (UPE) and adult education programs were seen as among the most successful in Africa; following nationalizations, the public sector grew substantially; collective production gained a foothold in some of the initial ujamaa villages; and the gap between the highest-paid and the lowest-paid workers narrowed considerably. Yet the economic decline beginning in the late 1970s doomed many of these policies. The government could not properly fund them.

The response has been pragmatic, sometimes sacrificing one kind of equality for another. Examples abound. Private imports have been allowed and private production encouraged for the sake of increased employment and increased taxes that the government might use to support distributive policies. Fees have been introduced for public health and education services so that more centers and more schools might remain operative. Nongovernmental groups and individuals have been encouraged to enter the services sector; e.g., so many private secondary schools have been established that they now outnumber the public ones. Slow but measurable progress has been made in closing some money-losing public enterprises, freeing funds that might be used to support distributional policies. To keep professionals on the job, special perquisites are given to them, supplementing their salaries. Collective production has been virtually abandoned, following abortive efforts during the 1980s to convert marketing-oriented cooperatives into real production-oriented ones. Many of these new mechanisms appear to move the country away from, rather than toward, equality. Apologists contend that they are short-run detours, necessary retreats so that advances might be made later. They evidence, though, considerable movement away from the earlier approaches to socialist construction.

Cooperatives

Neither cooperative marketing organizations nor cooperative production organizations have "worked," i.e., have promoted the achievement of socialist goals effectively. The former have been closed, replaced, reopened, restructured, drained of resources, and "cleansed" in a fashion that did more to weaken than to strengthen them. The latter were even less successful. When voluntary movement into ujamaa villages became mandatory in 1973, communal production that had been initiated was inundated by the influx of peasants not convinced of its likely benefit. Efforts by the party to require villages to have substantial communal farms in the late 1970s and to promote production-oriented cooperatives in the 1980s similarly faltered.

The response has been pragmatic. Communal production has been virtually abandoned as unworkable, and crop marketing has been opened to private traders. Although the cooperatives have not been abandoned, the state no longer supports them as though they constituted the only route to rural socialism. Indeed, the major thrust of cooperative policy in the early 1990s is to make the cooperatives autonomous—like cooperatives in capitalist countries—so that they can resist being used for the kinds of purposes they were used for in the 1960s, 1970s, and 1980s.

Parastatals

The Arusha Declaration brought both the seizure of private industries and assurances that private industries had a future. As we have seen, these contradictory policies were referred to by Jeannette Hartmann as stemming from two "Arusha Declarations," one proclaiming the party's position and one proclaiming the government's position.[22] For twenty years following the declaration, except for a brief period in the late 1970s, the party's position dominated; i.e., the public sector was encouraged and the private sector was discouraged. Initially, the public sector's role in the economy grew substantially in trade, state farming, and industrial production. Manufacturing, most of which was in the public sector, grew to contribute 13 percent of GDP in 1978, but it fell to 4.7 percent by 1984 as foreign exchange became very tight.[23] When Mwinyi succeeded to the presidency in 1985 he promised to use an "iron broom" to eliminate malfunctioning parastatals. The following year, IMF conditionalities were accepted, which hastened the move away from public enterprise. The party continued to resist the trend: The Fifteen-Year Party Programme, adopted in 1987, decried the idea of a mixed economy under socialism. By the late 1980s, though, public enterprises were in retreat and encouragement had shifted to the private sector.

Symbolically, the shift of policies to favor private over public production has been the most momentous of all policy changes. Mwinyi summarized the state's position in September 1993, stating that

> the ultimate objective of the current economic reforms in Tanzania is to reduce Government's participation in trade and industry in favour of private operators in a free market environment. . . . It had been found out over the years that the Government was not a very good trader or industrialist."[24]

In other words, public ownership had not "worked." The new emphasis, though, was not meant to be an abandonment of Tanzanian socialism, according to Mwinyi: "The Government would continue to regulate and referee the economic activities to guard local industries and maintain fair play in favour of the majority of poor Tanzanians."[25]

Self-Reliance

Tanzanian leaders tended to view self-reliance as additive; i.e., the self-reliance of an individual would promote that of a group of which the individual was a member, and the self-reliance of one group would promote that of a larger group of which it was a member. National self-reliance was regarded as both a means to and a goal of socialist construction. Freed from the negative impact of the world system, Tanzanian leaders foresaw their chances of successfully promoting development and socialist construction increased. Ironically, the commitment to self-reliance led to high levels of aid, which, in turn, undermined self-reliance. When donors responded to Tanzania's economic decline by reducing assistance pending "structural readjustment" and agreement to IMF conditionalities, Tanzania was forced to accept the latter in 1986. Since then, Tanzania's self-reliance has declined further. Foreign debt has nearly doubled to almost U.S.$7 billion. Imports are approximately three times exports (U.S.$1.2 billion verses U.S.$400 million). The pragmatism demonstrated when Tanzania acceded to the IMF accords has continued.

Self-reliance at various levels *within* the country has been interpreted more and more in individual rather than in group terms since the late 1970s. Yet, as has been noted, individual self-reliance is almost equivalent to the capitalist notion of possessive individualism. Party and government leaders decry the loss of the "self-reliant spirit." Yet survival has required this. As long as individuals cannot attain their aspirations through group action, one might expect this "retreat" to be likely to persist.

Once again, the pragmatic response is clear. When the effort to keep the IMF out meant no oil and all that that implied, Tanzania let the IMF in. When the choice was between great individual hardship and individual entrepreneurship, Tanzania allowed the latter. In both cases, former socialist policies were being abandoned. Yet those policies had not "worked," i.e., made it possible for individuals and Tanzanians as a group to improve, or to sustain, their livelihood—at least under the conditions that then prevailed.

Subnationalism

Tanzanian leaders tend to rank relative peace and unity as the foremost achievement of the first twenty-five years of socialist construction. Part of this peace has been a result of their ability to mesh Tanzanian socialism with Tanzanian nationalism, and part of it has been a result of their ability to contain subnationalism. The cost of this containment, though, has been the reduction of liberal democratic rights. Ethnic and religious groups have been banned from participation in Tanzanian politics. Yet the federal status of Zanzibar has allowed subnationalism to occasionally develop there. Without such protection, subnationalism would have remained hidden or latent. Although initially a spur for the adoption of socialism on the mainland, Zanzibar has become a kind of socialist Achilles' heel. That is, the logic of a subnationalism is an appeal that opposes nationalism. Even though appeals to subnationalism may be merely means by which a politician gains political power, they tend to become anti–whatever is held sacred by those who rule the nation. In Tanzania that meant opposition to socialism—or at least the way Tanzanian socialism was pursued.

Zanzibar responded more quickly to economic liberalization than did the mainland for two reasons: Its economy had suffered more, and its subnationalism made it easier to move away from policies closely associated with Tanzanian nationalism. Yet that subnationalism combined with multipartyism and a freer press to ignite other subnationalisms that posed serious threats to Tanzanian nationalism.

Thus, in the years since the Arusha Declaration, Tanzania has shifted many of the means it uses to attain socialist goals. The reasons are clear: CCM was not operating effectively to promote democracy; distributive policies could not promote equality if there was nothing to distribute; collective and public-sector production was not producing economic progress; and neither national nor group self-reliance seemed appropriate in the face of intense economic hardship. As a result, there were changes of policy and practice. By the early 1990s, pragmatism had become the modus operandi of the state to such an extent that many observers concluded that power had passed from both ideological and pragmatic socialists to pure pragmatists. Why has Tanzania's effort to build socialism faced such difficulties?

The Explanations

Explanations for Tanzania's failure to make rapid progress toward socialism may be divided into two categories: First, many explanations have been employed to account for the difficulties of Africa and other Third World countries to achieve economic goals regardless of whether these are associated with socialism; second, explanations have been employed to account for the specific case of Tanzania's problems in achieving its socialist objectives.

General Obstacles to the Realization of Development and Socialist Construction

As we have seen, problems with the economy are at the heart of the difficulties Tanzania has experienced. Yet similar problems have been experienced by most African countries. Although the statistical representation of what has happened to the economies of African countries is imperfect, Figure 10.1 indicates that the downturn in Tanzanian GNP per capita in the early 1980s was paralleled by downturns elsewhere in Africa. These data also suggest that under Tanzanian socialism there was economic progress during the 1970s and that the decline came later than that elsewhere in Africa. The steep continued decline during the late 1980s under IMF conditionalities is disputed by other sources.[26] Nevertheless, the broad similarity of the Tanzanian trend to that of Kenya, which was not seeking to build socialism, and to that of other countries in Africa suggests that the presence or absence of socialism in a country is of limited significance to the economic difficulties experienced. Generic explanations, i.e., those not specific to socialist-aspiring countries, have been offered to account for the continent's problems. Examples of such explanations are those focusing upon economic policy proferred by the IMF and those focusing upon the spacial distribution of political power suggested by some political scientists.

The IMF's list of conditionalities, applied with minor variations throughout Africa, identified certain economic policies as the culprit. The initial conditionalities applied to Tanzania included devaluation and limits on credit to the government, on bank credits to parastatals, on debt, on budget deficits, and on new external borrowing.[27] These and subsequent conditionalities led to the increase of prices paid for agricultural products, the end of subsidies on basic foodstuffs, greater commercial and industrial competition, the closure of unprofitable parastatals, and the extension of the market. Each conditionality aimed at correcting what the IMF considered to be policies that had brought about the economic decline. The fact that similar conditionalities were applied to African countries not pursuing socialism suggests that socialist construction was not a critical factor.

A second generic explanation focuses on the centralized state. James Wunsch suggests that "a strong central government was regarded as essential to the national unity and modernization of African societies" for several reasons:

> It was consistent with the structure and habits of the colonial-administrative state, it was selected in an era when both Eastern and Western models of development emphasized central direction and planning, it complemented nicely the expectations of international assistance organizations for "rational" planning, management, and negotiation of assistance programs, it emphasized the relatively stronger *juridical* claim to

Conclusion 227

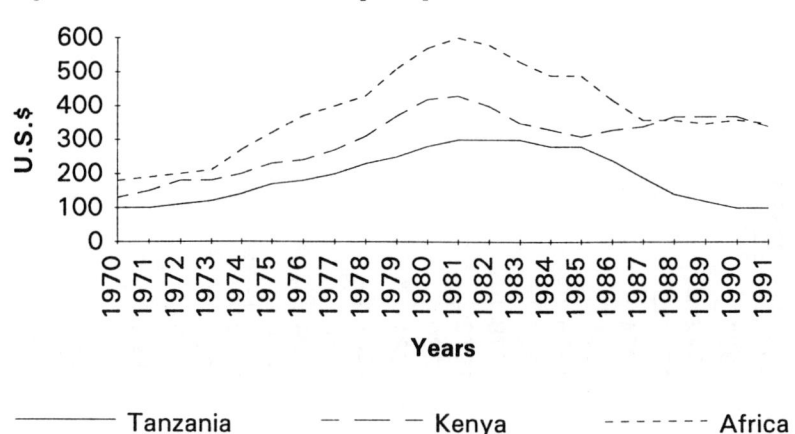

Figure 10.1 Gross National Product per Capita

```
         Tanzania    — — —  Kenya    - - - - - -  Africa
```

Source: World Bank, *World Tables, 1993* (Baltimore: Johns Hopkins University Press for World Bank, 1993), pp. 2–3. The Africa figures are for sub-Saharan Africa.

international recognition above the somewhat tenuous *de facto* reality of sovereignty, it was encouraged by the hierarchical and centralist leaning of post-enlightenment rationalism in the West, and it provided an apparently possible solution for the real challenges African leaders faced.[28]

Yet, Wunsch contends, the major aspects of the centralized state—the establishment of one- or no-party systems, "national" planning, limited local government, the maximization of executive authority, and the use of the national budget as the primary source of funds for development—have failed to bring about the modernization envisioned.[29] Implicit in this argument is the contention that the state's role in the economy became much greater than that of society's. That this was the case or that it had much to do with the effort to build socialism is contradicted by Figure 10.2, which shows that the ratio of private to government consumption in Tanzania has been higher throughout the last twenty years than that of either Kenya or Côte d'Ivoire, two more capitalist-oriented countries. In other words, private consumption has been relatively greater in socialist-oriented Tanzania than in major capitalist-oriented African countries.

The solution Wunsch proposes is self-governance: "By self-governance we mean, essentially, the institutionalized empowerment of the people, and the expansion of their ability to engage in collective choice and action at a variety of scales of human organization."[30] This solution is

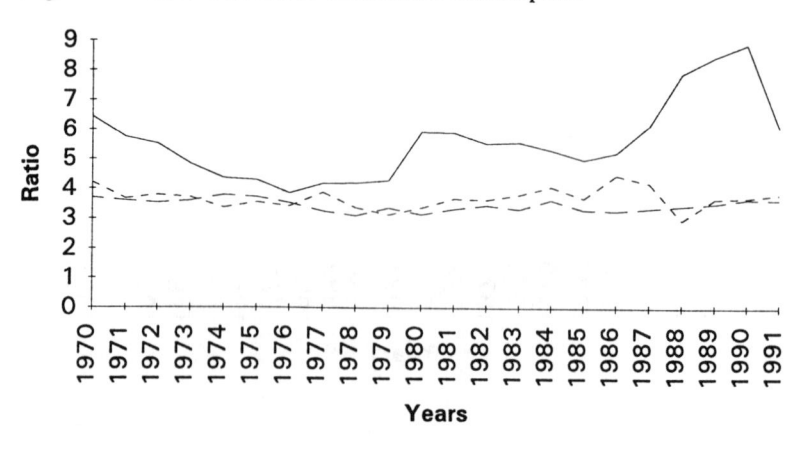

Figure 10.2 Ratio of Private to Government Consumption

Source: World Bank, *World Tables, 1993* (Baltimore: Johns Hopkins University Press for World Bank, 1993), pp 588–589, 356–357, and 204–205, respectively. The figures are based on domestic absorption of GDP at market prices.

much like an important aspect of the theory of ujamaa. Ironically, it implies that one of Africa's problems may be a *lack* of socialism.

A wide variety of additional factors have been used to explain Africa's economic problems, including declining world prices for raw materials; increasing prices for imported goods; rapidly growing population; rapid urbanization; lack of oil; limited skills; corruption; and a lack of capital. Tanzanian leaders seeking to explain why the move to create a socialist society has stagnated often invoke such explanations because they are factors not directly related to Tanzania's pursuit of socialism.

There are noneconomic, generic explanations as well—for example, those attributing the problems to "one-partyism" or "tribalism." Yet most nonsocialist states in Africa were one-party states, and ethnic conflict has been much greater in most nonsocialist states than in Tanzania, at least until the early 1990s. Thus, neither the economic nor these noneconomic problems are intrinsic to a country pursuing socialism. These data suggest that the difficulties Tanzania has faced have little to do with the fact that it sought to realize a socialist vision.

Specific Obstacles to the Realization of Tanzanian Development and Socialist Construction

Just as there is an array of explanations for the general difficulties with development and socialist construction, so there is an array of explanations for the specific difficulties Tanzania has faced. Among the most important are those related to the character of the ruling class, representation, the nature of the peasant mode of production, institutions, incentives, political conflict, and units of action.

Class Explanation

Issa Shivji has argued that ujamaa was a kind of fraud; i.e., it was not really socialism. Rather, the Arusha Declaration was a means by which a state or bureaucratic section of the petty bourgeoisie gained a foothold in the economy. At the time, Tanzania was a neocolony; i.e., the petty bourgeoisie that came to power at independence was "a *ruling class* albeit in a subordinate place to the international bourgeoisie."[31] For ten years the state bourgeoisie retained its hegemony over other sections of the petty bourgeoisie and the private bourgeoisie. Subsequent rises in oil prices, drought, world recession, and the war with Amin brought on an economic crisis that threatened that hegemony. In response, the state bourgeoisie sought to sustain itself by extracting greater wealth from the peasantry; the peasantry consequently withdrew from the market; and the crisis deepened.

From the mid-1980s, the state bourgeoisie's hegemony was so seriously undermined that it accepted IMF conditionalities and the enhanced position of the private bourgeoisie that they implied.[32] According to Howard Stein, those who controlled the Tanzanian state welcomed the IMF agreement as a savior.[33] He contends that Nyerere and other "critics" are really supporters because they "have compelling unifying class interests to ensure the hegemony of the state and the bureaucratic class."[34] The bottom line of this class argument is that Tanzanian socialism was not a "real" socialism but only a set of ideas used by a ruling group to consolidate its power. The implementation of "real" socialism requires the removal of the state bourgeoisie and its replacement by a group with "proletarian consciousness."[35] Real, rather than symbolic, steps toward democratization are the key to putting socialist construction on track.

The contention that Tanzanian socialism is not socialism, I would argue, is based on an overly restrictive conceptualization of socialism. Its classification of Tanzania as a neocolony accurately reflects an absence of self-reliance but is not very sensitive to variations in dependence and oversimplifies the nature of the country's subordination to an "international bourgeoisie." Its assertion that the IMF was welcomed by those who controlled the state is incomplete: Nyerere and the pragmatic socialists reluctantly accepted the conditionalities as the least harmful of a set of alternatives, all of which were considered injurious. Its neglect of conflict within the "state bourgeoisie" and of the units problem limits its comprehensiveness. Its view that individual volition is severely constrained by economic factors is strongly supported by our findings. And its general description of the shift of power among groups is insightful.

Representational Explanation

Associated with the class explanation is one that suggests that faulty policy is the consequence of the failure of the productive sectors, especially agriculture, to be represented in the state. Michael Lofchie found that this is a major cause of the poor agricultural performance of Tanzania as compared with Kenya.[36] Similarly, Oda van Cranenburgh argues that "common" farmers were not really represented either in the party or in the government and that this omission contributed to "a structural disarticulation of state and rural society."[37] Without policies reflecting the interests of the farmers, she contends, the policies could not be properly implemented.[38] Van Cranenburgh suggests that "Tanzanian political culture exhibited a degree of ideological hegemony, but under a layer of nominal adherence to the party ideology, differences of opinion and criticism were expressed within the party."[39] Such disagreement among the central leadership meant that "regional government and party officers could allow a divergence of practices in their regions from the official goals formulated in the center."[40] In a sense, the inability of the party to implement socialist policies was both the result of a lack of democratic representation and a manifestation of democratic behavior.

The representational explanation parallels the class explanation in locating the principal problem in the absence of a critical group within the ruling coalition, though it is the absence of the peasantry (or, at least, a part of the peasantry) rather than of the proletariat (or, at least, those with "proletarian consciousness") that is deemed causal. Yet peasants were represented in Tanzania in the sense that most leaders came from peasant backgrounds, were chosen by peasants, and/or were patrons of peasants. What was not represented well were the interests of the "rich" peasants, often referred to as the kulak farmers. Their role has been the subject of considerable debate, with ideological socialists tending to support their suppression and pragmatic socialists tending to support their co-optation—with the two points of view exemplified by the struggle over whether they should be "cleansed" from cooperative leadership. The debate involves a struggle over the ranking of potentially conflicting goals in Tanzanian socialism, e.g., the desire for greater production (hence the encouragement of kulaks) and greater equality (hence the discouragement of kulaks).

There is a problem in the representational explanation related to a narrow view of representation. On the one hand, the pursuit of development and socialism is said to have been undermined by the discrepancy in policymaking between the centrality—those who hold power—and the marginality—those who are productive. The result has been policies that are detrimental to the latter. On the other hand, van Cranenburgh implies that development and socialism have been undermined by the ability of rich peasants and others to distort policy in the process of implementation. The result has been implementation that is not in accord with policy intent. If van Cranenburgh is right, then "representation" in policymaking is not likely to interfere with the activities of kulak farmers.

Peasant Mode of Production Explanation

In contrast to Shivji and others, who account for many of Tanzania's problems by reference to the country's neocolonial status, Goran Hyden contends that

> the problems of underdevelopment do not stem from an excessive penetration by world capitalism. Rather they stem from the inability of capitalism to produce the same dynamic transformation of the material base as it once did in Europe and America.[41]

This inability is brought about by a peasant mode of production that produces an "economy of affection." Hyden argues that the Arusha Declaration appealed to the peasantry because of its populist content. He says of Nyerere,

> In trying to turn his country away from market criteria he has enjoyed spontaneous support of many since it is characteristic of all pre-capitalist societies that non-economic performance excites popular admiration. What Tanzania has achieved in the years after the Arusha Declaration is to replace an essentially capitalist-inspired superstructure with an institutional formation that more directly reflects the pre-capitalist realities of the country.[42]

Hyden contends that the "economy of affection" protects the peasantry from the demands for resources of those who dominate the state. Because the bureaucratic bourgeoisie is dependent on the peasant, it is forced to "mitigate this structural constraint" by collaborating "with the agencies of outside capital and expertise."[43] He argues that the ruling classes "can only reduce their dependence on the metropolitan bourgeoisie by forcing the peasants into more effective relations of dependence"[44]—in other words, by "turning the tables" on the peasantry. And "where small retains his exit option, socialism, at least in its modern form, is impossible."[45] How can the peasantry be made more dependent on the state? Hyden suggests two ways: "the provision of reliable services by the various organs that are necessary to serve modern agriculture" and the provision of a range of consumer and capital goods that appeal to the peasant's needs.[46] In other words, he says, socialists must encourage capitalism![47]

In a sense, the early 1990s found some former pragmatic socialists doing just that, having "evolved" to become pure pragmatists or pragmatic capitalists. Hyden's contention that capitalism is a prerequisite for socialism was a part of orthodox Marxism, challenged by the early architects of Tanzanian socialism. Yet, if socialist construction was made impossible by the "economy of affection," how does one explain the substantial economic and social achievements of the first post-Arusha decade?

Hyden's point of view, manifested by his focus on the "economy of affection," that the choices underlying economic behavior vary with culture and environment, is an important assertion that scholars frequently ignore. His contention that peasants are basically self-sufficient, i.e., that they can easily move into or out of producing for the money economy, has produced the strongest critique. Nelson Kasfir, for example, has claimed that Hyden's assertion is exaggerated.[48] Peasants may be able to survive in an "economy of affection," but they may have appetites that cannot be satisfied in such an economy. Whether peasants opt out probably depends upon whether the state or private traders extract more resources from their product than the peasants deem warranted. The extraction rates during the 1970s were so high that there was a consequent decline in production. Rather than contend that a prerequisite of socialism is a situation in which peasants cannot opt out, one might argue that the prerequisite is a level of extraction that does not surpass peasants' willingness to sell crops.

Institutional Conflict Explanation

Institutional conflict leading to policy ambiguity is another explanation for the problems with socialist construction. As has previously been noted, Jeannette Hartmann contends that the "Party and the Government held conflicting ideologies of development because they were occupied with different problems."[49] The result of these differences was policy ambiguity, and policy ambiguity interfered with socialist construction. In a sense, Hartmann is arguing that the party was more socialist and the government was more pragmatist:

> The Party's view of development has always been distribution-oriented and has relied more on human mobilisation to achieve results.... On the other hand, the Government's view of development has been influenced over the years by problems of implementation, and it has evolved its own policies on a *de facto* basis to solve them.[50]

One way to avoid these dysfunctional conflicts would be to harmonize government and party positions.[51] What has happened in the post-1990 period is that the party positions have accommodated themselves to the government positions; i.e., the "more socialist" party has given in to the "less socialist" government. A problem with an explanation of this sort is that it does not account for the divisive struggles and contradictory behavior *within* the party and government over policy.

Matthew Costello has sought to deal with this difficulty. Like Hartmann, he suggests that the party's effort to use the bureaucracy for development purposes created "policy ambiguity," i.e., room for the bureaucracy to implement policies in ways the party had not intended.[52] The bureaucracy responds to its particular "resource context" in carrying out the party's directives—bureaucrats in different contexts respond differently. Some, such as those in the Ministry for Agriculture, who were relatively more dependent upon state funding, responded more in accord with the party's wishes than others, such as those working for the National Development Corporation, who were relatively more dependent on international funding and so responded more to such donors. Yet by the mid-1980s the economy had so declined as a result of the conflict between the party and administrators that the country as a whole became vulnerable to its "resource context." With the acceptance of IMF conditions, "the party was forced to relinquish its control of policy formation."[53] A fundamental shift of power within the state from the politicians to the administrators followed.[54]

Costello's view that the key to institutional behavior is its "resource context," i.e., the sources of funds that will allow it to carry out policy, is a "He who pays the piper calls the tune" argument. It is basic to many explanations, such as those identifying self-reliance as a necessary condition for socialist construction. Why Tanzanian socialists could not pay the piper after the late 1970s is not addressed by this view. Nevertheless, the idea that an institution's "resource context" affects institutional support for, and resistance to, socialism is both reasonable and insightful.

Incentives Explanation

In addition to the macro explanations like class conflict and the middle-level explanations like institutional conflict, there are micro explanations like that of Louis Putterman. Putterman argues that the problems with socialist construction in rural areas are caused by a faulty incentive system. He contends that "it is not socialism or rural cooperation, but rather statism and ideological 'anti-incentivism', that were responsible for the failure of rural cooperation."[55] Putterman suggests that with appropriate incentives, instead of bureaucratic state control, it might have been possible to implement rural socialist ideals.[56]

An important incentive for agricultural production is the price paid for crops. The basic contention of much of the work of Frank Ellis is that the producer prices set for crops did not provide sufficient incentive to sustain production.[57] Hyden would contend that it nudged peasants back into the "economy of affection." As many observers have noted, the relative decline in agricultural exports contributed to the balance-of-payments problems that undermined socialist construction.[58] Thus, the incentives explanation is a basic part of many other explanations.

Incentives are often divided into two dichotomous categories: (1) moral and material and (2) group and individual. Many socialists have tended to consider moral incentives provided to groups to be more in accord with the values of socialism than material incentives provided to individuals, despite the socialist dictum "to each according to his work." The effectiveness of different types of incentives depends upon the context in which they are used. Putterman is justified in his criticisms that types of incentives have been used in contexts that make them ineffective. In general, though, the problem in Tanzania has been less that of inappropriate use and more that of an insufficiency of material incentives.

Political Conflict Explanation

I have argued throughout this book that part of the explanation for the problems faced in the pursuit of socialism is the struggle between ideological and pragmatic socialists. I have defined the membership of these factions in terms of whether an individual supports a cluster of ideas about socialist construction identified as that of the ideological socialists or that of the pragmatic socialists. Membership in these factions has been fluid and, at times, instrumental. That is, self-interest has played a role in determining whether a leader supported the ideological socialist path or the pragmatic socialist path. Nevertheless, conflict between these two groups has played an important role in determining the success of the effort to achieve most socialist goals.

The detrimental effect of this struggle on socialist construction is best illustrated by the case of rural cooperatives, described in Chapter 6. Policy changes stemming from the alternating success of the ideological and pragmatic socialists so weakened the movement that its ability to serve socialist ends has been severely undercut. Sometimes the result of the seesaw political struggle has been policy ambiguity that allowed people or institutions to pursue nonsocialist paths; other times it was the destruction of institutions that might have contributed to socialist construction, as in the case of cooperatives. I do not argue that this factional political struggle was determinative of, only that it was contributory to, Tanzania's lack of success in its pursuit of socialism.

Units of Action Explanation

Socialism focuses on groups and group action; it criticizes capitalism for its focus on individuals and individual action. Yet there are several problems associated with the implementation of group-oriented socialist policies. First, ascertaining group wants in a situation in which the constituents of the group are urged to be selfless poses severe problems. The normal method of summing individual wants and taking the mean as a measure of group wants does not provide a meaningful measure when some individuals seek to be selfless. The selfless individual opts out of playing a role in determining group interest. That may leave the decision to those not acting in accord with the selflessness of a good socialist, a situation unlikely to lead to actions for the good of all.

Second, overlapping group memberships pose severe problems. Even if one could determine group interest, individuals are members of many different groups. To behave in accord with the wishes of all of them at the same time is virtually impossible. Almost every goal of ujamaa would take on different practical meanings for different groups. Actions to achieve self-reliance, development, democracy, and equity would involve contradictory actions for each group of which one is a member. For example, among the Chagga the syndication method of selling coffee for oil would be an undemocratic policy, i.e., one not supported by a majority of Chagga people. Yet among all Tanzanians it might be a democratic one; i.e., most Tanzanians would accept the loss of wealth of the Chagga for a more assured supply of petroleum. Or, if villages were fully self-reliant, there would be no internal source of food for urban areas; i.e., the country as a whole might be less self-reliant than would have been the case if the villages had not been so self-reliant.

Third, the "free rider" poses severe problems. In a situation in which selflessness is emphasized, those who work for the good of all may be supporting many who do not contribute to the collective good. Day-rate remuneration systems for work on communal farms meant that the return to individuals depended on the number of days they appeared and not on the work put in. The incentive system made it rational for peasants who were not imbued with socialist selflessness to appear at the farm but put in as little work as possible, saving energy for work on their private farms. The burden fell on those who sought to enhance the well-being of the group as a whole.

The several problems that are exacerbated by socialism's focus on the group and on individuals as selfless parts of groups have contributed to, but not determined, the difficulties Tanzania has faced in socialist construction.

The Future

The degree to which the goals of ujamaa are attained in the future will be determined by whether new means can be developed that will "work," i.e., will overcome the causes of the failure of the old means. The task is compounded both by the wide range of factors adversely affecting socialist construction and by disagreement over what the "real" causes of failure were. The current turn toward pragmatism provides hope—and real danger.

Just as socialism without a means to attain it is irrelevant to the real world, pragmatism without a purpose beyond solving the immediate problem is hazardous. The danger is that what "works" in the short run may have harmful consequences for most people in the long run. The opportunity is that, if harnessed by a vision, such as ujamaa, pragmatism may result in finding means that facilitate the achievement of the ends sought.

In the short run, the trend is away from socialism: The means being adopted are more associated with individualism than with collectivism. With the internal situation demanding a "correction"; with the IMF and World Bank pushing for a liberal economy; and with the major models of socialist construction lying in ruins, it is not unreasonable that the party would begin to try new means. Yet the new means it has tried are basically those of Western capitalist countries. To proceed with privatization, encourage the profit motive, open the economy to a "free" market, and so on, is unlikely to encourage the selflessness that is at the heart of socialism.

In the long run, the current trend may reverse itself: It is not unreasonable to predict that the new means will fail to produce a vibrant economy. As we have seen, many of the causes of socialism's plight are not unique to socialism. That is, they adversely affect most Third World nations regardless of the vision of the good society they seek to pursue. If the new means fail to "work," one might expect disenchantment and the possible future development of alternative means more conducive to the realization of socialism.

The Tanzanian experience makes one lesson starkly clear: Human volition has limits. Stirred by their victory over British colonialism six years earlier, Tanzanian leaders declared in the Arusha Declaration their independence from a tradition of fatalism. They asserted that the grand vision of a good society embodied in Tanzanian socialism might be crafted by Tanzanians for Tanzanians. Their pride and self-confidence attracted the attention and admiration of much of the world. Their break with the traditional belief that human choice was limited by forces not under their control was a revolutionary one. Twenty-five years later, the wisdom embedded in the tradition is more clear. The real choices that the leaders of a state like Tanzania can make are quite limited. Not only nature constrains those choices but also the world system, leaders with alternative visions, the character of the productive system, and a myriad of other factors. This does not mean that those who have led the state have abandoned the vision of Tanzanian socialism. It does mean that they are more aware of the difficulties and constraints they face in finding the path to that vision.

Notes

1. In a 1973 survey, Tanzania was found to be the most "emphasized" country by scholars in African politics courses at American universities. See Henry Kenski and Margaret Corgan Kenski, "Teaching African Politics at American

Universities: A Survey" (Institute of Government Research, University of Arizona, Tucson, March 1974, mimeographed), p. 6. In a survey five years later, Tanzania was found to be the country about which there was the most self-proclaimed expertise and the country with the second "most stressed" political system. See Mark DeLancey and Christopher Herrick, "African Politics at American Universities and Colleges: A Survey of Purposes, Methods, and Materials," a paper presented at the annual meeting of the African Studies Association, Baltimore, 1978.

2. Nyerere's leadership in the struggle for the New International Economic Order, the Frontline States, and the South-South Commission, and Salim Ahmed Salim's work as Tanzania's ambassador to the United Nations and as secretary general of the Organization of African Unity are illustrative.

3. Anthony Wright, *Socialisms, Theories and Practices* (Oxford: Oxford University Press, 1986), p. 23.

4. Julius Nyerere, *Freedom and Socialism* (Dar es Salaam: Oxford University Press, 1968), pp. 1–32.

5. This assertion runs contrary to the claim by many writers that Nyerere's ideas on socialism can be equated with Tanzanian socialism. See, for example, Robert Fatton Jr., "The Political Ideology of Julius Nyerere: The Structural Limitations of 'African Socialism,'" *Studies in Comparative International Development*, Vol. 20, No. 2 (Summer 1985), pp. 3–24.

6. W.Y. Elliott, *The Pragmatic Revolt in Politics* (New York: Macmillan, 1928), p. 42.

7. Charles Anderson, *Pragmatic Liberalism* (Chicago: University of Chicago Press, 1990), p. 2.

8. George Novack, *Pragmatism Versus Marxism* (New York: Pathfinder Press, 1975), p. 17.

9. Elliott, *The Pragmatic Revolt*, p. 495.

10. Anderson, *Pragmatic Liberalism*, p. 2.

11. Novack, *Pragmatism Versus Marxism*, p. 13.

12. Joel Samoff has argued, somewhat differently, in "Bureaucrats, Politicians, and Power in Tanzania: The Institutional Context of Class Struggle," *Journal of African Studies*, Vol. 10, No. 3 (Fall 1983), p. 86, that policy ambiguity was due to "the temporary dominance of the capitalist or the socialist tendencies within this governing class. "

13. Cranford Pratt, *The Critical Phase in Tanzania, 1945–1968, Nyerere and the Emergence of a Socialist Strategy* (Cambridge: Cambridge University Press, 1976), p. 231.

14. Ibid., pp. 238–239.

15. Nyerere, *Freedom and Socialism*, p. 15.

16. Ibid., p. 16.

17. Ibid., p. 17.

18. Tanganyika African National Union, "TANU Guidelines on Guarding, Consolidating and Advancing the Revolution of Tanzania and of Africa," in Andrew Coulson, ed., *African Socialism in Practice: The Tanzanian Experience* (Nottingham: Spokesman, 1979), pp. 36–42; Chama cha Mapinduzi, *The CCM Guidelines, 1981* (Dar es Salaam: Printpak, for CCM, n.d.); and Chama cha Mapinduzi, *Programu ya Chama cha Mapinduzi, 1987 hadi 2002* (Dodoma: CCM, 1987). An unofficial English translation was published in the *Daily News* (Dar es Salaam) over several weeks in January and February 1988.

19. *Daily News*, 5 January 1988, p. 4; 6 January 1988, p. 4; and 14 January 1988, p. 4.

20. Julius K. Nyerere, *The Arusha Declaration, Ten Years After* (Dar es Salaam: Government Printer, 1977), p. 1.

21. Julius Nyerere, *Freedom and Unity* (London: Oxford University Press, 1967), pp. 195–203.

22. Jeannette Hartmann, "The Two Arusha Declarations," a paper presented at the International Conference on the Arusha Declaration, Arusha, December 1986.

23. Calculated from United Republic of Tanzania, Ministry of Finance, Planning and Economic Affairs, Bureau of Statistics, *Statistical Abstract, 1984* (Dar es Salaam: Bureau of Statistics, February 1986), p. 77.

24. *Daily News*, 1 September 1993, p. 1.

25 Ibid.

26. The decline in Tanzania's GNP per capita during the late 1980s, shown by Figure 10. 1, which is based on figures in World Bank, *World Tables, 1993* (Baltimore: Johns Hopkins University Press for World Bank, 1993), pp. 2–3, is contradicted by IMF, *International Financial Statistics Yearbook, 1992* (Washington, D.C.: IMF, 1992), pp. 148–149, which shows that Tanzania's annual growth in GDP at constant prices from 1984 to 1990 averaged 3.64 percent (Africa averaged 3.34 percent), which is above the population growth rate of 2.7 percent.

27. Howard Stein, "Economic Policy and the IMF in Tanzania: Conditionality, Conflict, and Convergence," in Horace Campbell and Howard Stein, eds., *Tanzania and the IMF: The Dynamics of Liberalization* (Boulder: Westview, 1992), pp. 71–72.

28. James S. Wunsch, "Centralization and Development in Post-Independence Africa," in James S. Wunsch and Dele Olowu, eds., *The Failure of the Centralized State, Institutions and Self-Governance in Africa* (Boulder: Westview, 1990), p. 44.

29. Ibid., p. 45.

30. Dele Olowu and James S. Wunsch, "Conclusion: Self-Governance and African Development," in Wunsch and Olowu, eds., *The Failure of the Centralized State*, p. 294.

31. Issa Shivji, *Class Struggles in Tanzania* (Dar es Salaam: Tanzania Publishing House, 1976), p. 22.

32. Issa Shivji, "Introduction: The Transformation of the State and the Working People," in Shivji, ed., *The State and the Working People in Tanzania* (Dakar: Codesria, 1985), pp. 4–5.

33. Stein, "Economic Policy," p. 59.

34. Ibid., p. 81.

35. Shivji, *Class Struggles in Tanzania*, p. 23.

36. Michael Lofchie, *The Policy Factor, Agricultural Performance in Kenya and Tanzania* (Boulder: Lynne Rienner Publishers, 1989).

37. Oda van Cranenburgh, *The Widening Gyre* (Delft, Netherlands: Eburon, 1990), p. 216.

38. Ibid., p. 220.

39. Ibid., p. 218.

40. Ibid.

41. Goran Hyden, *Beyond Ujamaa in Tanzania, Underdevelopment and an Uncaptured Peasantry* (Berkeley: University of California Press, 1980), pp. 3–4.

42. Ibid., pp. 138–139.

43. Ibid., p. 124.

44. Ibid., p. 232.

45. Ibid., p. 152.

46. Ibid., p. 232.

47. Ibid., p. 233.

48. Nelson Kasfir, "Are African Peasants Self-Sufficient?" *Development and Change*, Vol. 17 (1986), pp. 335–357.

49. Hartmann, "The Two Arusha Declarations," p. 1.

50. Jeannette Hartmann, "Development Policy-Making in Tanzania, 1962–1982: A Critique of Sociological Interpretations," Ph. D. thesis, University of Hull, United Kingdom, April 1983, p. 441.

51. Kimse Okoko suggests that harmonization of the relationship between the political leadership and the bureaucratic bourgeoisie requires two changes: "a more systematic, clear and coherent ideological framework" and the forfeiture of Western aid. See Okoko, *Socialism and Self-Reliance in Tanzania* (London: KPI Press, 1987), p. 228.

52. Matthew Costello, "The Divided State: Coherence and Transformation in Contemporary Tanzania," Ph.D. dissertation, Department of Political Science, University of North Carolina, Chapel Hill, 1992, p. 139.

53. Ibid., p. 225.

54. Ibid., p. 148.

55. Louis Putterman, "Tanzanian Rural Socialism and Statism Revisited: What Light from the Chinese Experience?" a paper presented at the International Conference on the Arusha Declaration, Arusha, December 1986, p. 5.

56. Ibid., pp. 13 and 14.

57. Frank Ellis, "Agricultural Price Policy in Tanzania," *World Development*, Vol. 10, No. 4 (1982), pp. 263–283, and "Agricultural Marketing and Peasant-State Transfers in Tanzania," *Journal of Peasant Studies*, Vol. 10, No. 4 (July 1983), pp. 214–242.

58. For example, Rune Skarstein and Samuel Wangwe, *Industrial Development in Tanzania: Some Critical Issues* (Uppsala: Scandinavian Institute of African Studies, 1986), p. 271.

Appendix

Table A.1 Official Exchange Rate of Tanzanian Shilling (TSh.) (number of TSh. per U.S.$)

Year	Official Rate (end of year)
1967	7.14
1968	7.14
1969	7.14
1970	7.14
1971	7.14
1972	7.14
1973	6.90
1974	7.14
1975	8.26
1976	8.32
1977	7.96
1978	7.41
1979	8.22
1980	8.18
1981	8.32
1982	9.57
1983	12.46
1984	18.11
1985	16.50
1986	51.72
1987	83.72
1988	125.00
1989	192.30
1990	196.60
1991	233.90
1992	335.00
1993	479.87

Sources: International Monetary Fund, *International Financial Statistics Yearbook, 1992* (Washington, D.C.: IMF, 1992), pp. 674–675, for 1967–1991 figures; and International Monetary Fund, *International Financial Statistics,* Vol. 47, No. 3 (March 1994), p. 526, for 1992 and 1993 figures.

Bibliography

Adelman, Kenneth. "The Great Black Hope, Richard II of Tanzania." *Harper's*, vol. 263 (July 1981), pp. 14–19.
Africa Confidential (London).
Africa Demos (Atlanta).
Africa Events (London).
Afro-Shirazi Party. *The Afro-Shirazi Party Revolution, 1964–1974*. Zanzibar: Afro-Shirazi Party, 1974.
Agricultural Cooperative Development International (ACDI). "Review of Cooperative Development in Tanzania as It Relates to Agriculture." Dar es Salaam: ACDI, December 1982. Mimeographed.
Ake, Claude. *Revolutionary Pressures in Africa*. London: Zed Press, 1978.
Almond, Gabriel, and James Coleman, eds. *The Politics of Developing Areas*. Princeton, N.J.: Princeton University Press, 1960.
Anderson, Charles. *Pragmatic Liberalism*. Chicago: University of Chicago Press, 1990.
Anderson, Mary Baughman. "Self-Reliant Development: A Comparison of the Economic Development Strategies of Mohandas Gandhi, Mao Tse Tung and Julius Nyerere." Ph.D. thesis, Department of Economics, University of Colorado, Boulder, 1978.
Ayany, S.G. *A History of Zanzibar*. Nairobi: East African Literature Bureau, 1970.
Babu, A.M. *African Socialism or Socialist Africa?* Dar es Salaam: Tanzania Publishing House, 1981.
———. "Twenty Years After Arusha." A paper presented at the International Conference on the Arusha Declaration, Arusha, December 1986.
Bagachwa, M.S.D., and S. Chandrasekhar. "Performance of the Manufacturing Parastatal Enterprises in Tanzania." In *The Role of Public Sector in the Economic Development in Tanzania, Proceedings of a Workshop Held in Arusha, Tanzania, on 27th to 29th of September 1983*. Dar es Salaam: Economic Research Bureau/Friedrich Ebert Stiftung, 1984. Pp. 51–69.
Bailey, Martin. *The Union of Tanganyika and Zanzibar: A Study in Political Integration*. Syracuse, N.Y.: Program of Eastern African Studies, Maxwell School of Citizenship and Public Affairs, Syracuse University, 1973.
Bank of Tanzania. *Tanzania: Twenty Years of Independence (1961–1981), A Review of Political and Economic Performance*. Dar es Salaam: Bank of Tanzania, n.d.
Barkan, Joel, ed. *Beyond Capitalism and Socialism in Kenya and Tanzania*. Boulder: Lynne Rienner Publishers, 1993.
———. "Comparing Politics and Public Policy in Kenya and Tanzania." In Joel Barkan, ed., *Politics and Public Policy in Kenya and Tanzania*. Revised edition. New York: Praeger, 1984. Pp. 3–42.
Barker, C.E., M.R. Bhagavan, P.V. Mitschke-Collande, and D.V. Wield. *African Industrialisation, Technology and Change in Tanzania*. Aldershot, United Kingdom: Gower, 1986.
Bavu, I.K. "Proliferation of Parastatals and the Efficacy of Government." A paper presented at the International Conference on the Arusha Declaration, Arusha, December 1986.

———. "Some Issues in the 1982 Party Electoral Process: The National Conference." *Maji Maji*, no. 44 (September 1984), pp. 1–17.
Bay, Edna, ed. *Women and Work in Africa*. Boulder: Westview, 1982.
Beckman, Bjorn. "Whose Democracy? Bourgeois Versus Popular Democracy." *Review of African Political Economy*, no. 45/46 (Winter 1989), pp. 84–97.
Berg-Schlosser, Dirk, and Rainer Siegler. *Political Stability and Development: A Comparative Analysis of Kenya, Tanzania, and Uganda*. Boulder: Lynne Rienner Publishers, 1990.
Bgoya, Walter. "Thoughts on 1982 Party Elections and People's Participation in Tanzania." *Maji Maji*, no. 44 (September 1984), pp. 39–45.
Bienefeld, Manfred. "Evaluating Tanzanian Industrial Development." In Martin Fransman, ed., *Industry and Accumulation in Africa*. London: Heinemann, 1982. Pp. 104–141.
———. "Trade Unions, the Labour Process, and the Tanzanian State." *The Journal of Modern African Studies*, vol. 17, no. 4 (1979), pp. 553–595.
Bienen, Henry. "The Party and the No Party State: Tanganyika and the Soviet Union." *Transition* (Kampala), no. 13 (March–April 1964), pp. 25–32.
———. *Tanzania, Party Transformation and Economic Development*. Princeton, N.J.: Princeton University Press, 1967.
Biermann, Werner. "The Problems of Industrialization in Tanzania." *Journal of African Studies*, vol. 14 (Fall 1987), pp. 127–140.
———. "Tanzanian Politics Under IMF Pressure." In Michael Hodd, ed., *Tanzania After Nyerere*. London: Pinter Publishers, 1988. Pp. 175–183.
Biermann, Werner, and Jumanne H. Wagao. "The IMF and Economic Policy in Tanzania: 1980–84." *Journal of African Studies*, vol. 14 (Fall 1987), pp. 118–126.
———. "The IMF and Tanzania—A Solution to the Crisis?" In Peter Lawrence, ed., *World Recession and the Food Crisis in Africa*. London: Review of African Political Economy and James Currey, 1986. Pp. 140–147.
Biersteker, Thomas. "Self-Reliance in Theory and Practice in Tanzanian Trade Relations." *International Organisation*, vol. 34, no. 2 (Spring 1980), pp. 229–264.
Blaustein, Albert, and Gisbert Flanz, eds. *Constitutions of the Countries of the World*. Dobbs Ferry, N.Y.: Oceana Publications, 1979.
Blaut, James. *The National Question, Decolonizing the Theory of Nationalism*. London: Zed Books, 1987.
Blomstrom, Magnus, and Bjorn Hettne. *Development Theory in Transition*. London: Zed Books, 1984.
Bobbio, Norberto. "The Upturned Utopia." *New Left Review*, no. 177 (September/October 1989), pp. 36–37.
Boesen, Jannik, Birgit Storgard Madsen, and Tony Moody. *Ujamaa—Socialism from Above*. Uppsala: Scandinavian Institute of African Studies, 1977.
Bolton, Dianne. *Nationalization—A Road to Socialism? The Lessons of Tanzania*. London: Zed Books, 1985.
Bradford, Colin, Jr. "Policy Interventions and Markets: Development Strategy Typologies and Policy Options." In Gary Gereffi and Donald Wyman, eds., *Manufacturing Miracles, Path of Industrialization in Latin America and East Asia*. Princeton, N.J.: Princeton University Press, 1990. Pp. 32–51.
Bryceson, Deborah Fahy. "Household, Hoe and Nation: Development Policies of the Nyerere Era." A paper presented at "Tanzania After Nyerere," an international conference on the economic, political, and social issues facing Tanzania, London, June 1986.

———. *Second Thoughts on Marketing Co-operatives in Tanzania, Background to Their Reinstatement.* Plunkett Development Series 5. Oxford: Plunkett Foundation for Cooperative Studies, 1983.
Buganga, J.K. "The Registration, Management and Development of Cooperatives in Tanzania Mainland: The Future of Their Past." A paper presented at the Annual Symposium, Cooperative College, Moshi, 29 September–4 October 1986.
Bujra, Janet. "Taxing Development in Tanzania: Why Must Women Pay?" *Review of African Political Economy*, no. 47 (Spring 1990), pp. 44–63.
Bukuku, Enos S. "Twenty Years of the Arusha Declaration: Issues of Equity and Income Distribution." A paper presented at the International Conference on the Arusha Declaration, Arusha, December 1986.
Bulletin of Tanzanian Affairs (London).
Burnell, Peter. *Economic Nationalism in the Third World.* Boulder: Westview, 1986.
Business Times (Dar es Salaam).
Carnoy, Martin, and Joel Samoff, eds. *Education and Social Transition in the Third World.* Princeton, N.J.: Princeton University Press, 1990.
Castells, Manuel, and Alejandro Portes. "World Underneath: The Origins, Dynamics, and Effects of the Informal Economy." In Manuel Castells, Alejandro Portes, and Lauren A. Benton, eds., *The Informal Economy, Studies in Advanced and Less Developed Countries.* Baltimore: Johns Hopkins University Press, 1989. Pp. 11–37.
Chachage, C.L.S. "The Arusha Declaration and Developmentalism." A paper presented at the International Conference on the Arusha Declaration, Arusha, December 1986.
Chaligha, Amon. "Taxation and the Transition to Socialism in Tanzania." Ph.D. dissertation, Claremont Graduate School, Claremont, Calif., 1990.
Chama cha Mapinduzi (CCM). *CCM Constitution.* Dar es Salaam: Tanganyika Standard (Newspapers) Ltd., n.d.
———. *The CCM Guidelines, 1981.* Dar es Salaam: Printpak for CCM, n.d.
———. *The Constitution of Chama cha Mapinduzi, 1982.* Dar es Salaam: Printpak for CCM, n.d.
———. "1985 Uchaguzi Mkuu, Mapendekezo ya Kamati Kuu Kuhusu Wagombea Nafasi ya Ubunge, Mkutano wa Halmashauri Kuu ya Taifa, Agenda." Dar es Salaam: CCM, n.d. Mimeographed.
———. *Programu ya Chama cha Mapinduzi, 1987 hadi 2002.* Dodoma: CCM, 1987.
Chama cha Mapinduzi. Idara ya Uenezi wa Siasa na Ushirikishaji Umma. *Ushirika wa Uzalishaji Mali Vijijini, Utekelezaji wa Maamuzi ya Halmashauri Kuu ya Taifa.* Dar es Salaam: CCM, April 1985.
Chambua, S.I. "The Nature of Tanzania's Development: A Critical Approach to the Development Debates After the Arusha Declaration." A paper presented at the International Conference on the Arusha Declaration, Arusha, December 1986.
Chande, Girish. "Role of Private Capital in the Context of the Arusha Declaration." A paper presented at the International Conference on the Arusha Declaration, Arusha, December 1986.
Chase, Hank. "The Zanzibar Treason Trial." *Review of African Political Economy*, no. 6 (May–August 1976), pp. 14–33.
Chase-Dunn, Christopher K. "Socialist States in the Capitalist World-Economy." In Christopher K. Chase-Dunn, ed., *Socialist States in the World System.* Beverly Hills, Calif.: Sage, 1982. Pp. 21–55.
Cheru, Fantu. "Adjustment Problems and the Politics of Ecomomic Surveillance: Tanzania and the IMF." A paper presented at the 1987 annual meeting of the African Studies Association, Denver, November 1987.

———. *The Silent Revolution in Africa, Debt, Development and Democracy.* London: Zed Books, 1989.
Chossudovsky, Michel. *Towards Capitalist Restoration? Chinese Socialism After Mao.* New York: St. Martin's Press, 1986.
Chuo cha Elimu ya Ushirika, Moshi. *Uongozi wa Uende wa Vyama vya Ushirika.* Dar es Salaam: Swala Publications, 1984.
Clark, W. Edmund. *Socialist Development and Public Investment in Tanzania.* Toronto: University of Toronto Press, 1978.
Clarkson, Stephen. *The Soviet Theory of Development.* Toronto: University of Toronto Press, 1978.
Clayton, Anthony. *The Zanzibar Revolution and Its Aftermath.* London: Archon, 1981.
Cliffe, Lionel, and John Saul, eds. *Socialism in Tanzania: Vol. 1, Politics.* Nairobi: East African Publishing House, 1972.
Coleman, James. *Nigeria, Background to Nationalism.* Berkeley: University of California Press, 1960.
Collier, Paul, Samir Radwan, and Samuel Wangwe. *Labour and Poverty in Rural Tanzania.* Oxford: Clarendon Press, 1986.
Connor, Walker. *The National Question in Marxist-Leninist Theory and Strategy.* Princeton, N.J.: Princeton University Press, 1984.
Costello, Matthew. "The Divided State: Coherence and Transformation in Contemporary Tanzania." Ph.D. dissertation, Department of Political Science, University of North Carolina, Chapel Hill, 1992.
Coulson, Andrew, ed. *African Socialism in Practice, The Tanzanian Experience.* Nottingham: Spokesman, 1979.
———. "The Silo Project," "The Automated Bread Factory," and "Tanzania's Fertilizer Factory." In Andrew Coulson, ed., *African Socialism in Practice, The Tanzanian Experience.* Nottingham: Spokesman, 1979. Pp. 175–178, 179–183, and 184–190, respectively.
———. "The State and Industrialization in Tanzania." In Martin Fransman, ed., *Industry and Accumulation in Africa.* London: Heinemann, 1982. Pp. 60–76.
———. *Tanzania, A Political Economy.* Oxford: Clarendon Press, 1982.
Crouch, Susan. *Western Responses to Tanzanian Socialism, 1967–1983.* Aldershot, United Kingdom: Avebury, 1987.
Cunningham, Frank. *Democratic Theory and Socialism.* Cambridge: Cambridge University Press, 1987.
Daily News (Dar es Salaam).
DeLancey, Mark, and Christopher Herrick. "African Politics at American Universities and Colleges: A Survey of Purposes, Methods, and Materials." A paper presented at the annual meeting of the African Studies Association, Baltimore, 1978.
De Wilde, John C. *Agriculture, Marketing, and Pricing in Sub-Saharan Africa.* Los Angeles: African Studies Center, UCLA, and African Studies Association, 1984.
Diamond, Larry. "Crisis, Choice and Structure: Reconciling Alternative Models for Explaining Democratic Success and Failure in the Third World." A paper presented to the 1989 annual meeting of the American Political Science Association, Atlanta, 31 August–3 September, 1989.
———. "Sub-Saharan Africa." In Robert Wesson, ed., *Democracy, A Worldwide Survey.* New York: Praeger, 1987. Pp. 73–111.
Duchacek, Ivo. *Comparative Federalism, The Territorial Dimension of Politics.* New York: Holt, Rinehart and Winston, 1970.

Dumont, René, and Marie-France Mottin. *Stranglehold on Africa*. London: André Deutsch, 1983.
Economist (London).
Elazar, Daniel. *Exploring Federalism*. Tuscaloosa: University of Alabama Press, 1987.
Elliott, W.Y. *The Pragmatic Revolt in Politics*. New York: Macmillan, 1928.
Ellis, Frank. "Agricultural Marketing and Peasant-State Transfers in Tanzania." *Journal of Peasant Studies*, vol. 10, no. 4 (July 1983), pp. 214–242.
———. "Agricultural Price Policy in Tanzania." *World Development*, vol. 10, no. 4 (1982), pp. 263–283.
———. "Prices and the Transformation of Peasant Agriculture: The Tanzanian Case." *Bulletin* (Sussex), vol. 13 (1982), pp. 66–72.
Ergas, Zaki. "The State and Economic Deterioration: The Tanzanian Case." *Journal of Commonwealth and Comparative Politics*, vol. 20, no. 3 (November 1982), pp. 286–308.
Evans, Ruth. "Pride and Prejudice." *Focus on Africa*, vol. 4, no. 3 (July–September 1993), pp. 33–37.
Express (Dar es Salaam)
Family Mirror (Dar es Salaam).
Fatton, Robert, Jr. *The Making of a Liberal Democracy, Senegal's Passive Revolution, 1975–1985*. Boulder: Lynne Rienner Publishers, 1987.
———. "The Political Ideology of Julius Nyerere: The Structural Limitations of 'African Socialism.'" *Studies in Comparative International Development*, vol. 20, no. 2 (Summer 1985), pp. 3–24.
Fortmann, Louise. "Women's Work in a Communal Setting: The Tanzanian Policy of Ujamaa." In Edna Bay, ed., *Women and Work in Africa*. Boulder: Westview, 1982. Pp. 191–205.
Freund, W.M. "Class Conflict, Political Economy and the Struggle for Socialism in Tanzania." *African Affairs*, vol. 80, no. 321 (October 1981), pp. 483–499.
Fukuyama, Francis. "The End of History?" *The National Interest*, no. 16 (Summer 1989), pp. 3–18.
———. *Moscow's Reassessment of the Third World*. Santa Monica, Calif.: RAND, 1986.
Galtung, Johan. "The Politics of Self-Reliance." In Johan Galtung, Peter O'Brien, and Roy Preiswerk, eds., *Self Reliance: A Strategy for Development*. London: Bogle-L'Ouverture Publications for Institute of International Development Studies, Geneva, 1980. Pp. 355–383.
———. *The True Worlds: A Transnational Perspective*. New York: Free Press, 1980.
Ghai, Dharam, Eddy Lee, Justin Maeda, and Samir Radwan, eds. *Overcoming Rural Underdevelopment*. Geneva: International Labour Organisation, 1979.
Glickman, Harvey. "Frontiers of Liberal and Non-Liberal Democracy in Tropical Africa." *Journal of Asian and African Studies*, vol. 23 (July and October 1988), pp. 234–254.
Goulbourne, Harry. "The Role of the Political Party in Tanzania Since the Arusha Declaration." In Harry Goulbourne, ed., *Politics and State in the Third World*. London: Macmillan, 1979. Pp. 201–221.
Gould, Carol. *Rethinking Democracy: Freedom and Social Cooperation in Politics, Economy, and Society*. Cambridge: Cambridge University Press, 1988.
Green, Reginald Herbold. "Agricultural Crises in Sub-Saharan Africa: Capitalism and Transitions to Socialism." *Bulletin* (Institute of Development Studies, Sussex), vol. 13, no. 4 (1982), pp. 73–80.

———. "A Guide to Acquisition and Initial Operation: Reflections from Tanzanian Experience, 1967-74." In Julio Faundez and Sol Picciotto, eds., *The Nationalisation of Multinationals in Peripheral Economies*. London: Macmillan, 1978. Pp. 17-70.

———. "Industrialization in Tanzania." In Martin Fransman, ed., *Industry and Accumulation in Africa*. London: Heinemann, 1982. Pp. 80-102.

———. "Political-Economic Adjustment and IMF Conditionality: Tanzania, 1974-81." In John Williamson, ed., *IMF Conditionality*. Washington, D.C.: Institute for International Economics, 1983. Pp. 347-380.

Grindle, Merilee, "Policy Content and Context in Implementation." In Merilee Grindle, ed., *Politics and Policy Implementation in the Third World*. Princeton, N.J.: Princeton University Press, 1980. Pp. 3-39.

Gromyko, Anatoly. *Africa, Progress, Problems, Prospects (An Analysis of the 1960s and 1970s)*. Moscow: Progress Publishers, 1983.

Hartmann, Jeannette. "Development Policy-Making in Tanzania, 1962-1982: A Critique of Sociological Interpretations." Ph.D. thesis, University of Hull, United Kingdom, April 1983.

———. "The Two Arusha Declarations." A paper presented at the International Conference on the Arusha Declaration, Arusha, December 1986.

Havnevik, Kjell. *Tanzania: The Limits to Development from Above*. Uppsala, Sweden: Nordiska Afrikainstitutet, 1993.

Held, David, and John Keane. "Socialism and the Limits of State Action." In James Curran, ed., *The Future of the Left*. Cambridge: Polity Press and New Socialist, 1984. Pp. 170-181.

Hill, Frances. "Ujamaa: African Socialist Productionism in Tanzania." In Helen Desfosses and Jacques Levesque, eds., *Socialism in the Third World*. New York: Praeger, 1975. Pp. 216-251.

Holmquist, Frank. "Correspondent's Report: Tanzania's Retreat from Statism in the Countryside." *Africa Today*, vol. 30 (1963), pp. 23-35.

Hopkins, A.G. "On Importing Andre Gunder Frank into Africa." *African Economic History Review*, vol. 1 (Spring 1975), pp. 13-21.

Hopkins, Raymond. "The Influence of the Legislature on Development Strategy: The Case of Kenya and Tanzania." In Joel Smith and Lloyd Musolf, eds., *Legislatures in Development: Dynamics of Change in New and Old States*. Durham, N.C.: Duke University Press, 1979. Pp. 155-186.

Hughes, Helen. "Industrialization and Development: A Stocktaking." In Pradip Ghosh, ed., *Industrialization and Development: A Third World Perspective*. Westport, Conn.: Greenwood, 1984. Pp. 5-29.

Huntington, Samuel. "No Exit, The Errors of Endism." *The National Interest*, no. 17 (Fall 1989), pp. 3-11.

———. "Will More Countries Become Democratic?" *Political Science Quarterly*, vol. 99, no. 2 (Summer 1984), pp. 193-218.

Hyden, Goran. *Agriculture and Development in Africa: The Case of Tanzania*. University Field Staff International Field Staff Reports, No. 5, 1988/89, Africa/Middle East.

———. *Beyond Ujamaa in Tanzania, Underdevelopment and an Uncaptured Peasantry*. Berkeley: University of California Press, 1980.

———. *No Shortcuts to Progress*. Berkeley: University of California Press, 1983.

———. "The Politics of Cooperatives." In Goran Hyden, ed., *Cooperatives in Tanzania, Problems of Organisation Building*. Dar es Salaam: Tanzania Publishing House, 1976. Pp. 7-20.

International Cooperative Alliance (ICA). "A Report of the ICA/FAO/ILO Interagency Mission to Tanzania in Support of Cooperative Development." Moshi: ICA, May 1986. Mimeographed.
International Labour Organisation (ILO). *Basic Needs in Danger: A Basic Needs Oriented Development Strategy for Tanzania*. Addis Ababa: Jobs and Skills Program for Africa, ILO, 1982.

———. *Cooperatives, A Review of Cooperative Development in the African Region: Scope, Impact and Prospects*. Report III. Seventh African Regional Conference, Harare, November-December 1988. Geneva: International Labour Organisation, 1988.

———. *Distributional Aspects of Stabilisation Programmes in the United Republic of Tanzania, 1979–84*. Geneva: International Labour Organisation, 1988.

International Monetary Fund. *International Financial Statistics*, vol. 47, no. 3 (March 1994).

———. *International Financial Statistics Yearbook, 1991*. Washington, D.C.: IMF, 1991.

———. *International Financial Statistics Yearbook, 1992*. Washington, D.C.: IMF, 1992.

Jackson, Dudley. "The Disappearance of Strikes in Tanzania: Incomes Policy and Industrial Democracy." *The Journal of Modern African Studies*, vol. 17, no. 2 (1979), pp. 219–251.

Jackson, Robert, and Carl G. Rosberg. "Democracy in Tropical Africa: Democracy Versus Autocracy in African Politics." *Journal of International Affairs*, vol. 38 (Winter 1985), pp. 293–305.

Jacoby, Henry. *The Bureaucratization of the World*. Berkeley: University of California Press, 1973.

Jamhuri ya Muungano wa Tanzania. *Jumuiya ya Muungano wa Vyama vya Ushirika Act, 1979*, no. 9. Dar es Salaam: Mpiga Chapa wa Serikali, 1979.

———. *Majadiliano ya Bunge, 27 Aprili–5 Mei, 1982*. Dar es Salaam: Mpiga Chapa wa Serikali, 1984.

———. *Majadiliano ya Bunge, 20–25 Juni, 1984*. Dar es Salaam: Mpiga Chapa wa Serikali, 1984.

———. "Taarifa ya Kamati ya Waziri Mkuu na Makamu wa Pili wa Rais ya Kuchunguza Vyama Vikuu vya Ushirika Tanzania Bara." Dar es Salaam: Office of the Prime Minister and First Vice President, May 1975. Mimeographed.

Jamhuri ya Muungano wa Tanzania. Ofisi ya Waziri Mkuu na Makamu wa Pili wa Rais. *Sheria ya Kuandikisha Vijiji na Vijiji vya Ujamaa*. Dar es Salaam: KIUTA, 1975.

Jamhuri ya Muungano wa Tanzania. Ofisi ya Waziri Mkuu na Makamu wa Pili wa Rais. Idara ya Maendeleo ya Ujamaa na Ushirika. *Maendeleo ya Ujamaa na Ushirika Tanzania*. Dodoma: Office of the Prime Minister and First Vice President, June 1976.

Jamhuri ya Muungano wa Tanzania. Ofisi ya Waziri Mkuu na Makamu wa Pili wa Rais. Idara ya Maendeleo ya Ujamaa na Ushirika. Sehemu ya Maendeleo ya Siasa na Utafiti. "Utaratibu wa Kupendekeza na Kuamua Kijiji Kuwa Kijiji Cha Ujamaa." Dodoma: Office of the Prime Minister and First Vice President, December 1978. Mimeographed.

Jamhuri ya Muungano wa Tanzania. Ofisi ya Waziri Mkuu na Makamu wa Pili wa Rais. Kamati ya Kuchunguza Vyama Vikuu vya Ushirika Tanzania Bara (M.M. Massomo, chair). "Taarifa." Dar es Salaam: Office of the Prime Minister and First Vice President, May 1975. Mimeographed.

Jamhuri ya Muungano wa Tanzania. Tume ya Rais ya Mfumo wa Chama Kimoja au Vyama Vingi vya Siasa Tanzania, 1991. *Kitabu cha Kwanza: Taarifa na Mapendekezo ya Tume Kuhusu Mfumo wa Siasa Nchini Tanzania.* Dar es Salaam: NPC-KIUTA, 1992.

———. *Kitabu cha Pili: Majedwali ya Matokeo ya Uratibu wa Maoni ya Wananchi.* Dar es Salaam: NPC-KIUTA, 1992.

Jamhuri ya Muungano wa Tanzania. Tume ya Tabia ya Viongozi. *Taarifa ya Miaka Mikumi, 1974–1984.* Dar es Salaam: Kiwanda cha Uchapaji cha Taifa, n.d.

Kabudi, Pala J.A.M. "Freedom of Religion in Tanzania." A paper presented at a seminar held to commemorate twenty-five years of the Faculty of Law, University of Dar es Salaam, October 1986.

Kabudi, Pala J.A.M., and Sengondo E.A. Mvungi. "The Party System and Socialism in Tanzania: A Backlash of Populist Socialism?" A paper presented at the International Conference on the Arusha Declaration, Arusha, December 1986.

Kambona, Oscar S. *Crisis of Democracy in Tanzania.* London: TDS Ltd., 1968.

———. *Tanzania and the Rule of Law.* London: Africa News Services, n.d.

Karioki, James. *Tanzania's Human Revolution.* University Park: Pennsylvania State University Press, 1979.

Karume, Abeid Amani. *Karume na Siasa, Uchumi na Maendeleo ya Kimapinduzi.* Zanzibar: Shirika la Upigaji Chapa, 1973.

Kasfir, Nelson. "Are African Peasants Self-Sufficient?" *Development and Change,* vol. 17 (1986), pp. 335–357.

Kenski, Henry, and Margaret Corgan Kenski. "Teaching African Politics at American Universities: A Survey." Institute of Government Research, University of Arizona, Tucson, March 1974. Mimeographed.

King, Preston. *Federalism and Federation.* Baltimore: Johns Hopkins University Press, 1982.

Kitching, Gavin. *Development and Underdevelopment in Historical Perspective, Populism, Nationalism and Industrialization.* London: Methuen, 1982.

Kjaerby, Finn. *Problems and Contradictions in the Development of Ox-Cultivation in Tanzania.* Uppsala: Scandinavian Institute of African Studies, and Copenhagen: Centre for Development Research, 1983.

Kjekshus, Helge. "Socialism and Participation: Some Concluding Remarks." In Election Study Committee, ed., *Socialism and Participation, Tanzania's 1970 National Elections.* Dar es Salaam: Tanzania Publishing House, 1974. Pp. 365–378.

Konde, Hadji S. *Press Freedom in Tanzania.* Arusha: Eastern Africa Publications Limited, 1984.

Kuuya, Masette. "Import Substitution as an Industrial Strategy: The Tanzanian Case." In J.F. Rweyemamu, ed., *Industrialization and Income Distribution in Africa.* Dakar: Codesria, 1980. Pp. 69–91.

Legum, Colin, ed. *Africa Contemporary Record, 1983–1984.* New York: Africana Publishing Company, 1984.

———. *Africa Contemporary Record, 1984–1985.* New York: Africana Publishing Company, 1985.

Leonard, David. "Class Formation and Agricultural Development." In Joel Barkan, ed., *Politics and Public Policy in Kenya and Tanzania.* Revised edition. New York: Praeger, 1984. Pp. 141–170.

Lipumba, Nguyuru H.I. "The Arusha Declaration and the Economic Development of Tanzania." A paper presented at the International Conference on the Arusha Declaration, Arusha, December 1986.

Lipumba, Nguyuru H.I., Lucian A. Msambichaka, and Samuel M. Wangwe, eds. *Economic Stabilization Policies in Tanzania.* Dar es Salaam: Economics Department and Economic Research Bureau, University of Dar es Salaam, 1984.

Lofchie, Michael. *The Policy Factor, Agricultural Performance in Kenya and Tanzania*. Boulder: Lynne Rienner Publishers, 1989.
———. "The Roots of Economic Crisis in Tanzania." *Current History*, vol. 84 (April 1985), pp. 159–163 and 184.
———. *Zanzibar: Background to Revolution*. Princeton, N.J.: Princeton University Press, 1965.
Loxley, John, and John Saul. "Multinationals, Workers and Parastatals in Tanzania." *Review of African Political Economy*, no. 2 (January–April 1975), pp. 54–88.
Lwaitama, A.F. "Social Democracy and the Politics of the Arusha Declaration." A paper presented at the International Conference on the Arusha Declaration, Arusha, December 1986.
Maeda, Justin H.J. "Peasant Organisation and Participation in Tanzania." In Amit Bhaduri and M.D. Anisur Rahman, eds., *Studies in Participation*. New Delhi: Oxford University Press, 1982. Pp. 15–33.
Magani, P.A. "Tanzania Rural Development Bank Recovery of Seasonal Inputs Loans." A paper presented at the Seminar on Credit for the Development of Agriculture in Tanzania, Arusha, May 1979.
Maganya, Ernest. "Democratic or Socialist Transformation of the Rural Areas, A Comparative Review of the Experiences of Tanzania, Mozambique and Zimbabwe." A paper presented at the International Conference on the Arusha Declaration, Arusha, December 1986.
Magoti, Charles K. *Peasant Participation and Rural Productivity in Tanzania, The Case of Mara Cotton Producers, 1955–1977*. Hamburg: Institut fur Afrika–Kunde, 1984.
Malima, Kighoma. "The IMF and World Bank Conditionality: The Tanzanian Case." In Peter Lawrence, ed., *World Recession and the Food Crisis in Africa*. London: Review of African Political Economy and James Currey, 1986. Pp. 129–139.
Maliyamkono, T.L. "Research in Education." In H. Hinzen and V.H. Hundsdorfer, eds., *Education for Liberation and Development, The Tanzanian Experience*. London: Evans Brothers Ltd. for United Nations Educational, Scientific, and Cultural Organization (UNESCO) Institute for Education, 1979. Pp. 205–228.
———. "Ulanguzi: Emergence of a Second Economy in Tanzania." A paper presented at an Economic Research Bureau Seminar, University of Dar es Salaam, October 1985.
Maliyamkono, T.L., and M.S.D. Bagachwa. *The Second Economy in Tanzania*. London: James Currey, 1990.
Mapolu, Henry, ed. *Workers and Management*. Dar es Salaam: Tanzania Publishing House, 1976.
Martin, Robert. *Personal Freedom and the Law in Tanzania, A Study of Socialist State Administration*. Nairobi: Oxford University Press, 1974.
Mascarenhas, Ophelia, and Marjorie Mbilinyi. *Women in Tanzania, An Analytical Bibliography*. Uppsala: Scandinavian Institute of African Studies, 1983.
Mayer, Lawrence C. *Redefining Comparative Politics: Promise Versus Performance*. Newbury Park, Calif.: Sage Publications, 1989.
Mayer, William P. "Planning for Self-Reliance." *Taamuli, A Political Science Forum*, vol. 4, no. 2 (July 1974), pp. 17–33.
Mazrui, Abdulwahid, Ali Saleh, and Muh'da Fadhid. "The First Three Phases of Zanzibar Revolutionary Government." A paper presented at the Zanzibar Revolution Twenty-Fifth Anniversary Seminar, University of Dar es Salaam, January 1989.

Mazrui, Ali. "Socialism as a Mode of International Protest: The Case of Tanzania." In Robert Rotberg and Ali Mazrui, eds., *Protest and Power in Black Africa.* New York: Oxford University Press, 1970. Pp. 1139–1152.

———. "Tanzaphilia: A Diagnosis." *Transition* (Kampala), no. 31 (June/July 1967), pp. 20–26.

Mbunda, L.X. "Limitation Clauses in the Bill of Rights." A paper presented at a seminar held to commemorate twenty-five years of the Faculty of Law, University of Dar es Salaam, October 1986.

McHenry, Dean E., Jr. "A Measure of Harmony/Disharmony in a One-Party State: Low-Level Party Leaders' Choices for Members of Parliament Compared with Those of Both High-Level Party Officials and the People in Tanzania, 1965–1975." *Journal of Developing Areas*, vol. 17, no. 3 (April 1983), pp. 337–348.

———. "Socialist Morality: The Changing Character of Leadership in Tanzania." A paper presented at the annual meeting of the African Studies Association, Chicago, October 1988.

———. *Tanzania's Ujamaa Villages, The Implementation of a Rural Development Strategy.* Berkeley: Institute of International Studies, University of California, 1979.

Medvedev, Roy A. *Leninism and Western Socialism.* Worcester, United Kingdom: Verso Editions, 1981.

Meghji, Ramadhani, and Elizabeth Minde. "Historia, Mafanikio na Matatizo ya Vyama vya Ushirika Tanzania." Semina na Mkutano wa Vyama vya Ushirika, Mbeya, September 1986. Mimeographed.

Mihyo, Paschal. *Industrial Conflict and Change in Tanzania.* Dar es Salaam: Tanzania Publishing House, 1983.

Minde, Elizabeth M. "The Changing Nature of Cooperatives and the Law in Tanzania (Mainland)." LLM dissertation, University of Dar es Salaam, 1982.

———. "Cooperative Union of Tanzania and Cooperative Development." A paper presented at the Annual Symposium, Cooperative College, Moshi, 29 September–4 October 1986.

Miti, Katabaro. "Capitalism or Socialism: A Review of Candid Scope, Honest to My Country." *Maji Maji*, no. 44 (September 1984), pp. 46–51.

———. "Continuity and Change in Tanzania's Economic Policy Since Independence." E.R.B. Paper 81.2. Dar es Salaam: Economic Research Bureau, University of Dar es Salaam, 1981. Mimeographed.

Mkonyi, E.S. "Registration of Multipurpose Production Cooperative Societies in Arusha Region, Problems and Prospects." A paper presented at the Annual Symposium, Cooperative College, Moshi, 29 September–4 October 1986.

Mlimuka, Aggrey K.L.J. "The Party and the Arusha Declaration." A paper presented at the International Conference on the Arusha Declaration, Arusha, December 1986.

Mlimuka, A.K.L.J., and P.J.A.M. Kabudi. "The State and the Party." In Issa Shivji, ed., *The State and the Working People in Tanzania.* Dakar: Codesria, 1985. Pp. 57–86.

Mlowe, L.H.K. "Multi-Purpose Cooperative Development in Tanzania, Prospects and Problems." A paper presented at the Annual Symposium, Cooperative College, Moshi, October 1984.

Mmuya, Max, and Amon Chaligha. *The Anticlimax in Kwahani, Zanzibar.* Dar es Salaam: University of Dar es Salaam Press, 1993.

———. *Towards Multiparty Politics in Tanzania.* Dar es Salaam: University of Dar es Salaam Press, 1992.

Mohan, Jitendra. "Varieties of African Socialism." In Ralph Miliband and John Saville, eds., *The Socialist Register, 1966*. New York: Monthly Review Press, 1966. Pp. 220–266.

Mporogomyi, Kilonsi. "Industry and Development in Tanzania: The Origins of the Crisis." In Michael Hodd, ed., *Tanzania After Nyerere*. London: Pinter Publishers, 1988. Pp. 51–63.

Msanga, I.R.E.M. "Cooperatives, Policy and Law in Tanzania with Special Reference to Multi-Purpose Cooperative Societies: The Case Study of Same District." LLM dissertation, University of Dar es Salaam, November 1981.

———. "The Impact of Cooperative Legislations on the Development of Cooperatives in Tanzania with Special Reference to the Cooperative Societies Act, 1982." Cooperative College, Moshi, n.d. (ca. 1986). Mimeographed.

Msekwa, Pius. "The Quest for Workers' Participation in Tanzania." In N.S.K. Tumbo, J.M.M. Matiko, A.P. Mahiga, Pius Msekwa, and Helge Kjekshus, eds., *Labour in Tanzania*. Dar es Salaam: Tanzania Publishing House, 1977. Pp. 68–86.

———. "Towards Party Supremacy: The Changing Pattern of Relationships Between the National Assembly and the National Executive Committee of TANU Before and After 1965." Department of Political Science, University of Dar es Salaam, M.A. program, 1973/74. Typescript.

Msekwa, Pius, and T.L. Maliyamkono. *The Experiments, Education Policy Formation Before and After the Arusha Declaration*. Dar es Salaam: Black Star Agencies, 1979.

Mudoola, Dan. "The Pathology of Institution Building—The Tanzanian Case." In Fassil G. Kiros, ed., *Challenging Rural Poverty*. Trenton, N.J.: Africa World Press, 1985. Pp. 117–125.

Mueller, Susanne. "Retarded Capitalism in Tanzania." In Ralph Miliband and John Saville, eds., *The Socialist Register, 1980*. London: Merlin Press, 1980. Pp. 203–226.

Mukandala, Rwekaza. "The Nurture of Power and Torture of Parastatals in Africa." A paper presented at the annual meeting of the African Studies Association, Denver, November 1987.

Munck, Ronaldo. *The Difficult Dialogue, Marxism and Nationalism*. London: Zed Books, 1986.

Munishi, Gaspar. "The Ideological Basis of the Arusha Declaration: Nationalism, Populism or Socialism?" A paper presented at the International Conference on the Arusha Declaration, Arusha, December 1986.

Mushi, S.S. "Tanzania Foreign Relations and the Policies of Non-Alignment, Socialism and Self-Reliance." In K. Mathews and S.S. Mushi, eds., *Foreign Policy of Tanzania, 1961–1981: A Reader*. Dar es Salaam: Tanzania Publishing House, 1981. Pp. 34–66.

Mushokolwa, L. "The Political Economy of Tanzania." *Maendeleo* (Institute of Development Studies, University of Dar es Salaam), no. 1 (January 1985), pp. 36–65.

Mutahaba, G.R. "Organization for Development: Tanzania's Search for Appropriate Local Level Organizational Forms." In Fassil G. Kiros, ed., *Challenging Rural Poverty*. Trenton, N.J.: Africa World Press, 1985. Pp. 127–145.

Muungano wa Vyama vya Ushirika Tanganyika. Idara ya Elimu na Utangazaji. *Ushirika Wetu*. Dar es Salaam: CUT Press, 1977.

Mvungi, Sengondo. "Freedom of Expression and the Law in Tanzania." A paper presented at a seminar held to commemorate twenty-five years of the Faculty of Law, University of Dar es Salaam, October 1986.

———. "Recent Constitutional Developments in Zanzibar: Some Problems and Prospects." A paper presented at the Zanzibar Revolution Twenty-Fifth Anniversary Seminar, University of Dar es Salaam, January 1989.

Mwaga, D.Z., B.F. Mrina, and F.F. Lyimo, eds. *Historia ya Chama cha TANU, 1954 Hadi 1977.* Dar es Salaam: Chuo cha CCM, Kivukoni, 1981.

Mwakyembe, H.G. "Bill of Rights in Tanzania, A General Overview." A paper presented at a seminar held to commemorate twenty-five years of the Faculty of Law, University of Dar es Salaam, October 1986.

Mwansasu, Bismarck. "The Changing Role of the Tanganyika African National Union." In Bismarck Mwansasu and Cranford Pratt, eds., *Towards Socialism in Tanzania.* Toronto: University of Toronto Press, 1979. Pp. 169–192.

Mwase, Ngila R.L. "Cooperatives and Ujamaa: A Case Study of the Arusha Region Cooperative Union Limited (A.R.C.U.)." In Goran Hyden, ed., *Cooperatives in Tanzania, Problems of Organisation Building.* Dar es Salaam: Tanzania Publishing House, 1976. Pp. 78–90.

Mwinyi, Ali Hassan. "Opening Address by H.E. President Ali Hassan Mwinyi to the International Conference on the Arusha Declaration, 16-12-1986." Mimeographed.

Mzale, Muhammed M.H. "Zanzibar, Where To—After Successful Class Struggle." A paper presented at the Zanzibar Revolution Twenty-Fifth Anniversary Seminar, University of Dar es Salaam, January 1989.

Nationalist (Dar es Salaam).

Ndulu, B.J. "The Role of the Public Sector in Tanzania's Economic Development." In *The Role of Public Sector in the Economic Development in Tanzania, Proceedings of a Workshop Held in Arusha, Tanzania, on 27th to 29th of September 1983.* Dar es Salaam: Economic Research Bureau and Friedrich Ebert Stiftung, January 1984. Pp. 14–37.

Nellis, John. *Public Enterprises in Sub-Saharan Africa.* Washington, D.C.: World Bank, 1986.

New African (London).

Ngombale-Mwiru, Kingunge. "Keynote Address." Delivered at the International Conference on the Arusha Declaration, Arusha, December 1986.

———. "The Policy of Self-Reliance." In Lionel Cliffe and John Saul, eds., *Socialism in Tanzania: Vol. 2, Policies.* Nairobi: East African Publishing House, 1973. Pp. 66–70.

Nguluma, A.T. "The Right of Association in Tanzania: Its Origins and Development." A paper presented at a seminar held to commemorate twenty-five years of the Faculty of Law, University of Dar es Salaam, October 1986.

Ng'wanakilala, Nkwabi. *Mass Communication and Development of Socialism in Tanzania.* Dar es Salaam: Tanzania Publishing House, 1981.

Nnauye, Col. M. "Uimarishaji wa Chama na Jumuiya za Wananchi." A paper presented at a seminar of the members of the Central Council of WASHIRIKA, Mbeya, September 1986.

Novack, George. *Pragmatism Versus Marxism.* New York: Pathfinder Press, 1975.

Nsekela, Amon. "The Role of Public Sector in Tanzania: Performance and Prospects." In *The Role of Public Sector in the Economic Development in Tanzania, Proceedings of a Workshop Held in Arusha, Tanzania, on 27th to 29th of September 1983.* Dar es Salaam: Economic Research Bureau and Friedrich Ebert Stiftung, January 1984. Pp. 2–13.

Nursey-Bray, P.F. "Consensus and Community: The Theory of African One-Party Democracy." In Graeme Duncan, ed., *Democratic Theory and Practice.* Cambridge: Cambridge University Press, 1983. Pp. 96–111.

———. "Tanzania: The Development Debate." *African Affairs*, vol. 79, no. 314 (January 1980), pp. 55–78.
Nyerere, Julius. "An Address by Julius K. Nyerere." *Development and Change*, vol. 17 (1986), pp. 387–397.
———. *Address by Mwalimu J.K. Nyerere, Chairman of Chama cha Mapinduzi at the Opening of the National Conference, Dodoma, 22nd October, 1987.* Dodoma: Chama cha Mapinduzi, n.d.
———. *Africa—Hunger and Debt*. An address given at the Royal Commonwealth Society in London, 20 March 1985, pamphlet.
———. "The African and Democracy." In Julius Nyerere, *Freedom and Unity*. London: Oxford University Press, 1967. Pp. 103–106.
———. "After the Arusha Declaration." In Julius Nyerere, *Freedom and Socialism*. Dar es Salaam: Oxford University Press, 1968. Pp. 385–409.
———. "The Arusha Declaration." In Julius Nyerere, *Freedom and Socialism*. Dar es Salaam: Oxford University Press, 1968. Pp. 231–250.
———. "The Arusha Declaration Ten Years After." In Andrew Coulson, ed., *African Socialism in Practice, The Tanzanian Experience*. Nottingham: Spokesman, 1979. Pp. 43–71. (Also published as *The Arusha Declaration, Ten Years After*. Dar es Salaam: Government Printer, 1977.)
———. "Convocation Address of the Chancellor." University of Dar es Salaam, 29 August 1980, quoted in "Politics of the Constitution Debate," by Mzirai Kangero, *Maji Maji*, no. 44 (September 1984), pp. 18–38.
———. "Decentralisation." In Julius Nyerere, *Socialism and Development*. Dar es Salaam: Oxford University Press, 1973. Pp. 344–350. (Also published as *Decentralisation*. Dar es Salaam: Government Printer, 1972.)
———. *Democracy and the Party System*. Dar es Salaam: Tanganyika Standard Limited, n.d. (Also in Julius Nyerere, *Freedom and Unity*. London: Oxford University Press, 1967. Abridged. Pp. 195–203.)
———. "Economic Development Through Self-Reliance: The Tanzanian Experience." In K. Mathews and S.S. Mushi, eds., *Foreign Policy of Tanzania, 1961–1981: A Reader*. Dar es Salaam: Tanzania Publishing House, 1981. Pp. 295–300.
———. "Education for Self-Reliance." In Julius Nyerere, *Freedom and Socialism*. Dar es Salaam: Oxford University Press, 1968. Pp. 267–290.
———. "Freedom and Development." In Julius Nyerere, *Freedom and Development*. Dar es Salaam: Oxford University Press, 1973. Pp. 58–71.
———. *Freedom and Development*. Dar es Salaam: Oxford University Press, 1973.
———. *Freedom and Socialism*. Dar es Salaam: Oxford University Press, 1968.
———. *Freedom and Unity*. Dar es Salaam: Oxford University Press, 1967.
———. "Inaugural Address at the Third Conference of Financial Institutions in Tanzania." In *Report of Proceedings*. Dar es Salaam: National Printing Company for Bank of Tanzania, 1983. Pp. 1–14.
———. "Introduction." In Julius Nyerere, *Freedom and Socialism*. Dar es Salaam: Oxford University Press, 1968. Pp. 1–32.
———. "President's Inaugural Address." In Julius Nyerere, *Freedom and Unity*. London: Oxford University Press, 1967. Pp. 176–187.
———. "The Principles of Citizenship." In Julius Nyerere, *Freedom and Unity*. London: Oxford University Press, 1967. Pp. 126–129.
———. "Public Ownership in Tanzania." In Julius Nyerere, *Freedom and Socialism*. Dar es Salaam: Oxford University Press, 1968. Pp. 251–256.
———. "The Purpose Is Man." In Julius Nyerere, *Freedom and Socialism*. Dar es Salaam: Oxford University Press, 1968. Pp. 315–326.

———. "The Rational Choice." In Julius Nyerere, *Freedom and Development*. Dar es Salaam: Oxford University Press, 1973. Pp. 379–390.

———. "Socialism and Rural Development." In Julius Nyerere, *Ujamaa, Essays on Socialism*. Dar es Salaam: Oxford University Press, 1968. Pp. 106–144. (Also in Julius Nyerere, *Freedom and Socialism*. Dar es Salaam: Oxford University Press, 1968. Pp. 337–366.)

———. "Socialism Is Not Racialism." In Julius Nyerere, *Freedom and Socialism*. Dar es Salaam: Oxford University Press, 1968. Pp. 257–261.

———. "Stability and Change in Africa." In Julius Nyerere, *Freedom and Development*. Dar es Salaam: Oxford University Press, 1973. Pp. 108–125.

———. "Ujamaa—The Basis of African Socialism." In Julius Nyerere, *Freedom and Unity*. London: Oxford University Press, 1967. Pp. 162–171. (Also in Julius Nyerere, *Ujamaa, Essays on Socialism*. Dar es Salaam: Oxford University Press, 1968. Pp. 1–12.)

———. "The Union of Tanganyika and Zanzibar." In Julius Nyerere, *Freedom and Unity*. London: Oxford University Press, 1967. Pp. 291–304.

———. "The Varied Paths to Socialism." In Julius Nyerere, *Freedom and Socialism*. Dar es Salaam: Oxford University Press, 1968. Pp. 301–310.

———. "Woe, Dereliction, Ruin and Decay." *Africa Events* (London), November 1987, pp. 24–33.

Okema, Michael. "The International Response to the Arusha Declaration." A paper presented at the International Conference on the Arusha Declaration, Arusha, December 1986.

Okoko, Kimse. *Socialism and Self-Reliance in Tanzania*. London: KPI Press, 1987.

Olowu, Dele, and James S. Wunsch. "Conclusion: Self-Governance and African Development." In James S. Wunsch and Dele Olowu, eds., *The Failure of the Centralized State, Institutions and Self-Governance in Africa*. Boulder: Westview, 1990. Pp. 293–317.

Othman, Haroub. "Zanzibar—Democracy in Transition?" A paper presented at the Zanzibar Revolution Twenty-Fifth Anniversary Seminar, University of Dar es Salaam, January 1989.

Othman, Haroub, and L.P. Shaidi. "Zanzibar's Constitutional Development." *Eastern Africa Law Review*, vols. 11–14 (1978–1981), pp. 181–224.

Payer, Cheryl. *Tanzania and the World Bank*. Development Research and Action Program, Working Paper A 285. The Chr. Michelsen Institute, Department of Social Science and Development, Bergen, Norway, December 1982.

Perkins, F.C. "Technology Choice, Industrialisation and Development Experiences in Tanzania." *Journal of Development Studies*, vol. 19, no. 2 (January 1983), pp. 213–243.

Pratt, Cranford. *The Critical Phase in Tanzania, 1945–1968, Nyerere and the Emergence of a Socialist Strategy*. Cambridge: Cambridge University Press, 1976.

———. "Tanzania's Transition to Socialism: Reflections of a Democratic Socialist." In Bismarck Mwansasu and Cranford Pratt, eds., *Towards Socialism in Tanzania*. Toronto: University of Toronto Press, 1979. Pp. 193–236.

Preiswerk, Roy. "Introduction." In Johan Galtung, Peter O'Brien, and Roy Preiswerk, eds., *Self Reliance, A Strategy for Development*. London: Bogle-L'Ouverture Publications, Ltd., for Institute of International Development Studies, Geneva, 1980. Pp. 11–15.

Przeworski, Adam. *Capitalism and Social Democracy*. Cambridge: Cambridge University Press, 1985.

Putterman, Louis. "Tanzanian Rural Socialism and Statism Revisited: What Light from the Chinese Experience?" A paper presented at the International Conference on the Arusha Declaration, Arusha, December 1986.
Raikes, Philip. "Socialism and Agriculture in Tanzania." A paper presented at "Tanzania After Nyerere," an international conference on the economic, political, and social issues facing Tanzania, London, June 1986.
Resnick, Idrian N. *The Long Transition, Building Socialism in Tanzania*. New York: Monthly Review Press, 1981.
Rey, Lucien. "The Revolution in Zanzibar." *New Left Review*, no. 25 (May–June 1965). Reprinted in Lionel Cliffe and John Saul, eds., *Socialism in Tanzania: Vol. 1, Politics*. Nairobi: East African Publishing House, 1972. Pp. 29–31.
Riggs, Fred. "Development." In Giovanni Sartori, ed., *Social Science Concepts, A Systematic Analysis*. Beverly Hills, Calif.: Sage, 1984. Pp. 125–203.
Riker, William. *Federalism, Origin, Operation, Significance*. Boston: Little, Brown, 1964.
———. *Liberalism Against Populism, A Confrontation Between the Theory of Democracy and the Theory of Social Choice*. San Francisco: W.H. Freeman & Co., 1982.
Rotberg, Robert. "Modern African Studies, Problems and Prospects." *World Politics*, vol. 18, no. 3 (April 1966), pp. 565–578.
Rothchild, Donald, ed. *Politics of Integration, An East African Documentary*. Nairobi: East African Publishing House, 1968.
Rweyemamu, J.F., ed. *Industrialization and Income Distribution in Africa*. Dakar: Codesria, 1980.
———. "The Silent Class Struggle in Retrospect." In *The Silent Class Struggle*, Tanzanian Studies No. 2. Dar es Salaam: Tanzania Publishing House, 1973. Pp. 129–138.
Samoff, Joel. "Bureaucrats, Politicians, and Power in Tanzania: The Institutional Context of Class Struggle." *Journal of African Studies*, vol. 10, no. 3 (Fall 1983), pp. 84–96.
———. "The Facade of Precision in Education Data and Statistics: A Troubling Example from Tanzania." *The Journal of Modern African Studies*, vol. 29, no. 4 (December 1991), pp. 669–689.
———. "'Modernizing' a Socialist Vision: Education in Tanzania." In Martin Carnoy and Joel Samoff, eds., *Education and Social Transition in the Third World*. Princeton, N.J.: Princeton University Press, 1990. Pp. 209–273.
———. "Single-Party Competitive Elections in Tanzania." In Fred Hayward, ed., *Elections in Independent Africa*. Boulder: Westview, 1987. Pp. 149–186.
Sartori, Giovanni. *The Theory of Democracy Revisited*. Chatham, N.J.: Chatham House, 1987.
Saul, John. "From Marketing Cooperative to Producer Cooperative." In Rural Development Research Committee, ed., *Rural Cooperatives in Tanzania*. Dar es Salaam: Tanzania Publishing House, 1975. Pp. 287–307.
Savage, Job, Newton Guderyon, and Harold P. Jordan. "Review of Cooperative Development in Tanzania as It Relates to Agriculture." Dar es Salaam: Agricultural Cooperative Development International (ACDI), December 1982. Mimeographed.
Scheven, Albert. *Swahili Proverbs, Nia Zikiwa Moja, Kilicho Mbali Huja*. Washington, D.C.: University Press of America, 1981.
Scope, Candid. *Honest to My Country*. Tabora: TMP (Tanganyika Mission Press) Book Department, ca. 1981.
Seers, Dudley. *The Political Economy of Nationalism*. Oxford: Oxford University Press, 1983.

Semakula, G.J. "The Role of Washirika in Promoting Productivity in Cooperatives in Tanzania." A paper presented at the Annual Symposium, Cooperative College, Moshi, September 29–October 4, 1986.

Shao, John. "Politics and the Food Production Crisis in Tanzania." In Stephen Commins, Michael Lofchie, and Rhys Payne, eds., *Africa's Agrarian Crisis, The Roots of Famine.* Boulder: Lynne Rienner Publishers, 1986. Pp. 84–102.

Shaw, Timothy M., and Ibrahim S.R. Msabaha. "Tanzania and the New International Economic Order." In K. Mathews and S.S. Mushi, eds., *Foreign Policy of Tanzania, 1961–1981: A Reader.* Dar es Salaam: Tanzania Publishing House, 1981. Pp. 67–93.

Shepherd, George W., Jr. *The Trampled Grass, Tributary States and Self-Reliance in the Indian Ocean Zone of Peace.* Westport, Conn.: Greenwood Press, 1987.

Shivji, Issa. *Class Struggles in Tanzania.* Dar es Salaam: Tanzania Publishing House, 1976.

———. "Introduction: The Transformation of the State and the Working People." In Issa Shivji, ed., *The State and the Working People in Tanzania.* Dakar: Codesria, 1985. Pp. 1–15.

———. "Notes on the Status of Legal Rights in Tanzania: A Jurisprudential Treatment." A paper presented at a seminar held to commemorate twenty-five years of the Faculty of Law, University of Dar es Salaam, October 1986.

———. "The Silent Class Struggle." In *The Silent Class Struggle*, Tanzanian Studies No. 2. Dar es Salaam: Tanzania Publishing House, 1973. Pp. 1–60.

———. "The State of the Constitution and the Constitution of the State in Tanzania." *Eastern Africa Law Review,* vols. 11–14 (1978–1981), pp. 1–34.

———. "Tanzania: The Debate on Delinking." In Azzam Mahjoub, ed., *Adjustment or Delinking: The African Experience.* London: Zed Books, 1990. Pp. 49–68.

Simmons, Reginald. "Tanzanian Socialism: A Critical Assessment." Ph.D. dissertation, Howard University, Washington, D.C., December 1984.

Singh, Ajit. "Tanzania and the IMF: The Analytics of Alternative Adjustment Programmes." *Development and Change,* vol. 17 (1986), pp. 425–454.

Skarstein, Rune, and Samuel Wangwe. *Industrial Development in Tanzania: Some Critical Issues.* Uppsala: Scandinavian Institute of African Studies, 1986.

Sklar, Richard. "Beyond Capitalism and Socialism in Africa." *The Journal of Modern African Studies,* vol. 26 (1988), pp. 1–21.

———. "Democracy in Africa." In Patrick Chabal, ed., *Political Domination in Africa, Reflections on the Limits of Power.* Cambridge: Cambridge University Press, 1986. Pp. 17–29.

———. "Obituary of Chief Obafemi Awolowo." *ASA News,* vol. 20, no. 3 (July/September 1987), p. 6.

Smith, Anthony. *Theories of Nationalism.* Second edition. New York: Holmes & Meier, 1983.

Snider, Lewis. "Identifying the Elements of State Power." *Comparative Political Studies,* vol. 20 (October 1987), pp. 324–337.

Snyder, Louis. *The Meaning of Nationalism.* Westport, Conn.: Greenwood Press, 1954.

———. *The New Nationalism.* Ithaca, N.Y.: Cornell University Press, 1968.

Sokoine, Edward Moringe. *Public Policy Making and Implementation in Tanzania.* Pau, France: Université de Pau et des Pays de l'Adour, Centre de Recherche et d'Etude sur les Pays d'Afrique Orientale, 1986.

Sosna, S.A. *Public Enterprises in Developing Countries: Legal Status.* Moscow: Progress Publishers, 1983.

Srivastava, B.P. "The Constitution of the United Republic of Tanzania 1977—Some Salient Features—Some Riddles." *Eastern Africa Law Review*, vols. 11–14 (1978–1981), pp. 73–127.
Standard (Dar es Salaam).
Stein, Howard. "Economic Policy and the IMF in Tanzania: Conditionality, Conflict, and Convergence." In Horace Campbell and Howard Stein, eds., *Tanzania and the IMF: The Dynamics of Liberalization*. Boulder: Westview, 1992. Pp. 59–83.

———. "The Economics of the State and the IMF in Tanzania." A paper presented at the annual meeting of the African Studies Association, Chicago, October 1988.
Stren, Richard. "Urban Policy." In Joel Barkan, ed., *Politics and Public Policy in Kenya and Tanzania*. Revised edition. New York: Praeger, 1984. Pp. 233–264.
Sunday News (Dar es Salaam).
Tandon, Yash, ed. *The Debate*. Dar es Salaam: Tanzania Publishing House, 1982.

———. "The Food Question in East Africa: A Partial Case Study of Tanzania." *Africa Quarterly*, vol. 17 (April 1978), pp. 5–45.
Tanganyika. *Development Plan for Tanganyika, 1961/62—1963/64*. Dar es Salaam: Government Printers, 1962.
Tanganyika African National Union. *Election Manifesto 1960*. Dar es Salaam: Thakers, Ltd., n.d.

———. *Katiba ya TANU, 1969*. Dar es Salaam: National Printing Co., n.d.

———. *Mwongozo Wa TANU, 1971*. Dar es Salaam: Mpigachapa Mkuu wa Serikali, n.d. (for English translation, see Coulson, *African Socialism in Practice*).

———. "Politics Is Agriculture." Press release by the Information Services Division, Ministry of Information and Broadcasting, Dar es Salaam, May 13, 1972.

———. "TANU Constitution." In William Tordoff, ed., *Government and Politics in Tanzania*. Nairobi: East African Publishing House, 1967. Pp. 236–251.

———. "TANU Guidelines on Guarding, Consolidating and Advancing the Revolution of Tanzania and of Africa." In Andrew Coulson, ed., *African Socialism in Practice, The Tanzanian Experience*. Nottingham: Spokesman, 1979. Pp. 36–42.
Tanganyika Standard (Dar es Salaam).
Tanzanian Economic Trends (Dar es Salaam).
Tenga, R.W. "Land Law and the Peasantry in Tanzania, A Review of the Post-Arusha Period." A paper presented at the International Conference on the Arusha Declaration, Arusha, December 1966.
Thomas, Clive. "Class Struggle, Social Development and the Theory of the Non-Capitalist Path." In Mai Palmberg, ed., *Problems of Socialist Orientation in Africa*. Uppsala: The Scandinavian Institute of African Studies, 1978. Pp. 17–37.

———. *Dependency and Transformation*. New York: Monthly Review Press, 1974.

———. *The Rise of the Authoritarian State in Peripheral Societies*. New York: Monthly Review Press, 1984.
Throup, David. "Zanzibar After Nyerere." A paper presented at the "Tanzania After Nyerere," an international conference on the economic, political, and social issues facing Tanzania, London, June 1986. (Also in Michael Hodd, ed., *Tanzania After Nyerere*. London: Pinter, 1988. Pp. 184–192.)
Tibaijuka, A.K., and L.A. Msambichaka. "The Role of Large Scale Farming in Tanzania." In L.A. Msambichaka and S. Chandrasekhar, eds., *Readings of*

Economic Policy of Tanzania. Dar es Salaam: Economic Research Bureau, University of Dar es Salaam, 1984. Pp. 68–84.
Tickner, J. Ann. *Self-Reliance Versus Power Politics.* New York: Columbia University Press, 1987.
Tordoff, William. *Government and Politics in Tanzania.* Nairobi: East African Publishing House, 1967.
———. "Residual Legislatures: The Case of Tanzania and Zambia." *Journal of Commonwealth and Comparative Politics,* vol. 15, no. 3 (November 1977), pp. 235–249.
Tumbo, J.M.M. Matiko, A.P. Mahiga, Pius Msekwa, and Helge Kjekshus. *Labour in Tanzania.* Dar es Salaam: Tanzania Publishing House, 1977.
United Republic of Tanzania. *Cooperative Societies Act, 1982* (Act No. 14 of 1982, dated 28 June 1982), Section 4. Published as Supplement to the *Gazette of the United Republic of Tanzania,* vol. 43, no. 30, 23 July 1982, pp. 273–342.
———. *Cooperative Societies Act, 1991* (Act No. 15 of 1991). Published as Supplement to the *Gazette of the United Republic of Tanzania,* vol. 72, no. 33, 16 August 1991, pp. 165–219.
———. *Government Paper No. 4 (Wages, Incomes, Rural Development, Investment and Price Policy).* Dar es Salaam: Government Printer, 1967.
———. "Interim Constitution of Tanzania." In William Tordoff, ed., *Government and Politics in Tanzania.* Nairobi: East African Publishing House, 1967. Pp. 205–235.
———. *Jumuiya ya Muungano wa Vyama vya Ushirika (Establishment) Act, 1979* (Act No. 9 of 1979).
———. "The Permanent Constitution, 1977." In Albert Blaustein and Gisbert Flanz, eds., *Constitutions of the Countries of the World.* Dobbs Ferry, N.Y.: Oceana Publications, 1979.
———, *Report of the Presidential Special Committee of Enquiry Into Cooperative Movement and Marketing Board.* Dar es Salaam: Government Printer, 1966.
———. *Report on Rules for the Nomination Process and Conduct of Election Campaigns for the National Assembly.* Dar es Salaam: Government Printer, 1965.
———. *Tanzania, Second Five-Year Plan for Economic and Social Development, 1st July 1969–30th June 1974, Volume I: General Analysis.* Dar es Salaam: Government Printer, 1969.
———. *Written Laws (Miscellaneous Amendments) Act, 1985* (Act No. 8 of 1985).
United Republic of Tanzania. Ministry of Agriculture and Livestock Development. Marketing Development Bureau. *Price Policy Recommendations for the 1985 Agricultural Price Review, Summary.* Dar es Salaam: Marketing Development Bureau, 1985.
United Republic of Tanzania. Ministry of Finance, Planning and Economic Affairs. Bureau of Statistics. *Statistical Abstract, 1984.* Dar es Salaam: Bureau of Statistics, February 1986.
———. Ministry of Planning and Economic Affairs. Bureau of Statistics. *Statistical Abstract, 1982.* Dar es Salaam: Bureau of Statistics, 1983.
United Republic of Tanzania. Office of the Prime Minister, Ujamaa and Cooperative Development Department. "Report on Village Data System, 1980." Dodoma: Nordic Project for Cooperatives and Rural Development in Tanzania, December 1980.
United Republic of Tanzania, Ofisi ya Waziri Mkuu, "Registrar's Circular No. 4 of 1985." Dodoma: Registrar of Cooperatives. 1985. Mimeographed.

United Republic of Tanzania. Registrar of Cooperatives. "Registrar's Circular No. 1 of 1982." Dodoma: Registrar of Cooperatives. 1982. Mimeographed.
United Republic of Tanganyika and Zanzibar. *Tanganyika, Five-Year Plan for Economic and Social Development, 1st July, 1964–30th June, 1969. Vol. I: General Analysis*. Dar es Salaam: Government Printer, 1964.
Valentine, Theodore. "Wage Adjustments, Progressive Tax Rates, and Accelerated Inflation: Issues of Equity in the Wage Sector of Tanzania." *The African Studies Review*, vol. 26, no. 1 (March 1983), pp. 51–71.
van Cranenburgh, Oda. *The Widening Gyre*. Delft, Netherlands: Eburon, 1990.
van Donge, Jan Kees, and Athumani J. Liviga. "In Defence of the Tanzanian Parliament." *Parliamentary Affairs*, vol. 39, no. 2 (April 1986), pp. 230–240.
———. "The Democratisation of Zanzibar and the 1985 General Election." *The Journal of Commonwealth and Comparative Politics*, vol. 28, no. 2 (July 1990), pp. 201–218.
———. "The 1985 Tanzanian Parliamentary Elections: A Conservative Election." *African Affairs*, vol. 88 (January 1989), pp. 47–62.
Van Velzen, H.U.E. Thoden, and J.J. Sterkenburg. "The Party Supreme." In Lionel Cliffe and John Saul, eds., *Socialism in Tanzania. Vol. 1: Politics*. Nairobi: East African Publishing House, 1972. Pp. 257–264.
———. "The Party System." In Lionel Cliffe and John Saul, eds., *Socialism in Tanzania. Vol. 1: Politics*. Nairobi: East African Publishing House, 1972. Pp. 248–253.
Von Freyhold, Michaela. *Ujamaa Villages in Tanzania: Analysis of a Social Experiment*. New York: Monthly Review Press, 1979.
Wall Street Journal (New York).
Wallerstein, Immanuel. "The Decline of the Party in Single-Party African States." In Joseph La Palombara and Myron Weiner, eds., *Political Parties and Political Development*. Princeton, N.J.: Princeton University Press, 1966. Pp. 201–214.
Wambali, Michael K.B. "The Enforcement of the Bill of Rights Against the Government." A paper presented at a seminar held to commemorate twenty-five years of the Faculty of Law, University of Dar es Salaam, October 1986.
Wanambisi, Saulo Busolo. "National Liberation or Socialism in East Africa? Some Theoretical Considerations." A paper presented at the International Conference on the Arusha Declaration, Arusha, December 1986.
Wangwe, Samuel. "Factors Influencing Capacity Utilisation in Tanzanian Manufacturing." *International Labour Review*, vol. 115, no. 1 (January–February 1977), pp. 65–77.
———. "Industrialization and Resource Allocation in a Developing Country: The Case of Recent Experiences in Tanzania." *World Development*, vol. 11, no. 6 (1983), pp. 483–492.
WASHIRIKA. *Kanuni na Muundo wa Jumuiya ya Muungano wa Vyama vya Ushirika*. Dar es Salaam: WASHIRIKA, 1983.
Watzal, Ludwig. "Ujamaa—The End of a Utopia?" Munich, 1982.
Weaver, James, and Alexander Kronemer. "Tanzanian and African Socialism." *World Development*, vol. 9, nos. 9/10 (1981), pp. 839–849.
Wemu, Bob. "Zanzibar's Reluctant Brides." *Drum* (Nairobi), no. 237 (January 1971).
Wilson, Amrit. *U.S. Foreign Policy and Revolution, The Creation of Tanzania*. London: Pluto Press, 1989.
Wiseman, John A. *Democracy in Black Africa, Survival and Revival*. New York: Paragon House, 1990.

World Bank. *World Debt Tables, 1993–94, Vol. 2 (Country Tables)*. Washington, D.C.: World Bank, 1993.
———. *World Tables, 1991*. Baltimore: Johns Hopkins University Press for the World Bank, 1991.
———. *World Tables, 1993*. Baltimore: Johns Hopkins University Press for the World Bank, 1993.
Wright, Anthony. *Socialisms, Theories and Practices*. Oxford: Oxford University Press, 1986.
Wunsch, James S. "Centralization and Development in Post-Independence Africa." In James S. Wunsch and Dele Olowu, eds., *The Failure of the Centralized State*. Boulder: Westview, 1990. Pp. 43–73.
Yeager, Rodger. *Tanzania, An African Experiment*. Boulder: Westview, 1982.
———. *Tanzania, An African Experiment*. Second edition. Boulder: Westview, 1989.
Young, Crawford. "Political Systems Development." In John Paden and Edward Soja, eds., *The African Experience*. Evanston, Ill.: Northwestern University Press, 1970. Pp. 452–472.
Zanzibar. *Revolutionary Council Decree No. 3, 1979*.

Abbreviations

ADC	Annual District Conference
ARCU	Arusha Cooperative Union
ASP	Afro-Shirazi Party
BIS	Basic Industrial Strategy
BORA	Tanzania Shoe Company
CC	Central Committee
CCM	Chama cha Mapinduzi
CIA	Central Intelligence Agency
COASCO	Cooperative Audit and Supervision Corporation
CPI	consumer price index
CRDB	Cooperative and Rural Development Bank
CUF	Civic United Front
CUT	Cooperative Union of Tanganyika/Tanzania (see WASHIRIKA)
DOWICO	Dodoma Wine Company
ERP	Economic Recovery Programme
GDP	gross domestic product
GNP	gross national product
ICA	International Cooperative Alliance
ILO	International Labour Organisation

IMF	International Montary Fund
ISI	import substitution industrialization
JUWATA	Union of Tanzania Workers
KILTEX	Kilimanjaro Textile Corporation, Ltd.
KIUTA	Kiwanda cha Uchapaji cha Taifa
MP	member of parliament
MRCU	Morogoro Region Cooperative Union
MUTEX	Musoma Textile Mills, Ltd.
MWATEX	Mwanza Textile Mills, Ltd.
NBC	National Bank of Commerce
NDC	National Development Corporation
NEC	National Executive Committee
NESP	National Economic Survival Programme
NHC	National Housing Corporation
NMC	National Milling Corporation
NPC	National Printing Company
NUTA	National Union of Tanganyika Workers
NUWA	National Urban Water Authority
OIC	Islamic Conference Organisation/Organisation of Islamic Conference
OTTU	Organisation of Tanzania Trade Unions
PMSAC	Parastatal Management Services Agreement Committee
POLYTEX	Morogoro Polyester Mills, Ltd.

PSRC	Presidential Parastatal Reform Commission
ROB	Registrar of Buildings
RPC	regional political committee
RTC	regional trading company
SAP	Structural Adjustment Programme
SCOPO	Standing Committee on Parastatal Organisations
SIRECU	Singida Region Cooperative Union
SPM	Southern Paper Mills
STAMICO	State Mining Corporation
SUNGURATEX	Tanganyika Dying and Weaving Mills, Ltd.
TANESCO	Tanzania Electrical Supply Company or Tanganyika Electrical Supply Company
TANU	Tanganyika African National Union
TAPO	Tanzania Association of Parastatal Organisations
TCA	Tanzania Cooperative Alliance
TDFL	Tanzania Development Finance Limited
TES	Tanzania Elimu Supplies
TEXCO	National Textile Corporation
TFL	Tanganyika Federation of Labour
THB	Tanzania Housing Bank
TIB	Tanzania Investment Bank
TLAI	Tanzania Leather Associated Industries
TMP	Tanganyika Mission Press

TPDF	Tanzania People's Defence Forces
Tsh	Tanzanian shillings
TYL	TANU Youth League
UDI	Unilateral Declaration of Independence
UNDP	United Nations Development Programme
UNESCO	United Nations Educational, Scientific, and Cultural Organization
UNICEF	United Nations International Children's Emergency Fund
UPE	Universal Primary Education
URAFIKI	Friendship Textile Mills, Ltd.
URT	United Republic of Tanzania
URTZ	United Republic of Tanganyika and Zanzibar
USAID	United States Agency for International Development
UWT	Union of Tanzanian Women
VIJANA	Tanzania Youth Organisation
WASHIRIKA*	Jumiya ya Muungano wa Vyama vya Ushirika/Union of Cooperative Societies/Cooperative Union of Tanzania
WAZAZI	Tanzania Parents Association
WHO	World Health Organization
ZNP	Zanzibar National Party
ZPPP	Zanzibar and Pemba People's Party

*Between the time of the passage of the Jumiya ya Muungano wa Vyama vya Ushiriki Act in 1929 and the Cooperative Societies Act in 1982, the apex organization was known in law as WASHIRIKA. The name was commonly used interchangeably with the name CUT after that.

Index

Acquisition of Buildings Act, 1971, 90
African socialism, 10, 23–24, 193. *See also* Tanzanian socialism
African unity, 193–194. *See also* Union of Tanganyika and Zanzibar, reasons for
Afro-Shirazi Party (ASP), 113, 190, 206
Agricultural cooperatives, 7, 105–127
   autonomy of, 54, 117, 118–119, 126(n76), 176–177, 186(n60)
   closure of, 110–112
   conversion to villages, 107–110. *See also* Ujamaa villages; Villages
   debt of, 119, 126–127(n82)
   debt to, 177
   economic viability of, 113, 114
   expansion of, 106–107
   explanations for problems with, 110–112, 119–121
   number of, 115(table), 117
   problems with, 107, 118, 126(n77), 177
   reestablishment of, 112–115
   reorganization of, 115–118
   types of: marketing, 105–106, 108, 121, 222; production-oriented, 22, 115–117; multipurpose, 108–109, 111, 113, 118; multivillage, 114–115(table), 117, 118
   socialist construction and, 105–106
   See also Apex organization; Cooperatives; Corruption; Self-reliance, subnational
Agriculture
   explanations for decline of, 145–146
   importance of, 22, 105, 129
Aid
   aid and help, relation between, 185(n44)
   debt forgiveness, 169
   periods of, 170
   self-reliance, impact on, 181
   size of, 169
   See also Self-reliance, national
Ake, Claude, 16
Annual District Conference of party (ADC), 36
Apex organization, 113–115, 117–119, 125(n53). *See also* Cooperative Audit and Supervision Corporation; Cooperative Union of Tanzania; National Apex Organisation of Tanzania (Formation) Act, 1990; Tanzania Cooperative Alliance; WASHIRIKA

Articles of Union. *See* Union of Tanganyika and Zanzibar, Articles of Union
Arusha Declaration, 19
   cooperatives, 105–106, 107–108
   decentralization of industry, 137
   expansion of public sector, 130
   priority of agriculture, 129
   self-reliance, 162, 163, 182
   See also Leadership code
Arusha Resolution. *See* Leadership code
Asians, 106–107, 119, 153
Autonomy of organizations. *See* Agricultural cooperatives, autonomy of; Democracy, character of people-party link, mass organizations; Self-reliance, meaning of, degree of autonomy

Babu, A.M.
   as leader of Umma party, 191, 210(n7)
   power of, 203–204
   on reason for dependence, 181
   on social democratic character of ujamaa, 24
   as a socialist militant, 202
   treason trial of, 206–207
Bagachwa, M.S.D., on second economy, 78
Bailey, Martin, on impact of A.M. Babu and A.K. Hanga on Tanzanian socialism, 202, 205
Bank of Tanzania, gold purchases of, 93. *See also* Banks
Banks. *See* Bank of Tanzania; National Bank of Commerce; Tanzania Housing Bank; Tanzania Investment Bank; Self-reliance, subnational
Barkan, Joel, on wage gap, 76, 99(n25)
Barker, C.E., et al., on socialist rhetoric and capitalist action concerning parastatals, 144
Basic Industrial Strategy (BIS), 136
   distortion of initial idea, 137–138
   See also Thomas, Clive, on basic industries; Iron and steel industry; Rweyemamu, Justinian, on basic industries; Paper and pulp industry
Bata Shoe Company
   nationalization of, 131
   renamed BORA, 142

267

Bavu, I.K., on parastatals, 130
Berg-Schlosser, Dirk, and political factions, 10
Bienen, Henry
  on persistence of party autonomy from state, 56
  on Zanzibar's Marxist-Leninist influence on the mainland, 202
Biermann, Werner, on technocracy's role in IMF agreement, 185(n42)
Biersteker, Thomas, on stages in a self-reliance strategy, 164
Boesen, Jannik, on utopian character of ujamaa, 23
BORA. *See* Tanzania Shoe Company
Bryceson, Deborah, on cooperative problems, 120
Bryceson, Derek, on middleman role of cooperatives, 109
Bujra, Janet, on reasons for gender inequality, 96
Bureaucratization, 56
  technocracy's support for IMF agreement, 185(n42)
  See also Ngombale-Mwiru, Kingunge, on bureaucratization
Burnell, Peter, on meaning of economic nationalism, 165

Capacity utilization
  explanation for low level of, 141–142, 145–146, 157(n95)
  as goal of Second Union Five-Year Plan, 138
  in textile industries, 140
  variations among industries, 157(n95)
  See also Foreign exchange; Industrial parastatals, capacity utilization and efficiency
Capital goods industries. *See* Industrial parastatals, intermediate and capital goods industries
CCM. *See* Chama cha Mapinduzi
CCM Extraordinary National Party Conference, 1992, approval of multiparty system, 66
CCM Fifteen-Year Party Programme
  ideological socialists' apogee, 38
  on industry, 93, 129
  on leadership, 31
  Nyerere's vision, comparison with, 21–22
CCM Guidelines, 1981, 20–21
  on leadership, 31, 41
Central Committee of party (CC)
  and supervision and direction of WASHIRIKA, 113
  and vetting candidates, 33–36, 70(n31)

See also National Executive Committee
Centralization, 226–227. *See also* Explanations, applied to Africawide problems, centralization
Chama cha Mapinduzi (CCM)
  dependence on government subvention, 173
  formation of, 195
  growth of public cynicism toward, 46(n42)
  and ideology, 31
  and mass organizations, 53
  as a vanguard, 20
  See also Party; Self-reliance, subnational
Chande, Girish, on private sector, 4
Chase, Hank, on Babu's influence, 203–204
Chase-Dunn, Christopher, on inhospitality of international capitalist system, 178
China
  emphasis on cooperatives, 7
  importance of leader, 6
  and involvement in Zanzibar, 203
  potential conflict with Soviet Union, 193
  transformation of socialism in, 2
Civic United Front (CUF), 201
Civil rights, 60–61
  Zanzibar and the Bill of Rights, 207–208
  See also Democracy, character of people-government link
Clark, W. Edmund, on nationalization of industry, 131
Class struggle, 9–10, 21
  cooperatives and bureaucratic bourgeoisie–kulak conflict, 112
  cooperatives and petty bourgeoisie–commercial bourgeoisie conflict, 106–107
  explanation for problems of parastatals, 147–148
  state bourgeoisie or state class, 9, 42
  See also Asians; Explanations, applied to Tanzania's problems, class
Clove market, 208
Collier, Paul, on problems with communal production, 95
Commission Act No. 6 of 1973, 38
Communal production, 20. *See also* Equality, production policies for communal production
Connor, Walker, on relation between nationalism and socialism, 189
Consumer goods industries. *See* Industrial parastatals, consumer goods industries
Consumer prices
  index of, 77(table)
  problems with, 80, 146
  supplemental charges, 149
  variation in, 98(n19)

See also Equality, consumer price policies for; Price Commission
Cooperative Audit and Supervision Corporation (COASCO), 119
Cooperative College, Moshi
 cooperative autonomy, symposium on, 126(n76)
 national cooperative policy, call for, 126(n79)
Cooperative and Rural Development Bank (CRDB)
 provision of loans with conditionalities by, 176–177
 seizure of property by, 175, 186(n64)
 See also Banks
Cooperatives, 222–223
 government officers concerned with, 116, 117
 legislation affecting: Cooperative Societies Act, 1968, 113; Cooperative Societies Act, 1982, 111, 112–113, 114, 116, 118, 124(n45), 125(n53); Cooperative Societies Act, 1991, 118, 126(n76); Jumuiya ya Muungano wa Vyama vya Ushirika (Establishment) Act, 1971, 113, 114. *See also* National Apex Organisation of Tanzania (Formation) Act, 1990
 national cooperative policy, need for, 126
 objectives of, 113
 principles of, 105, 112–113, 118, 121(n2)
 and state, 186(n60)
 and state farms, 7
 and units of action problem, 11, 106
 See also Agricultural cooperatives; Cooperatives; Tanzania Cooperative Alliance; Tanzanian socialism
Cooperative Union of Tanzania (CUT)
 abolition of, 113, 119, 126(n74) autonomy of, 53–54
 legality of, 113, 118
 as mass organization, 113
 replacement by Tanzania Cooperative Alliance, 54
 on ujamaa villages: assistance to, 110; opposition to assistance, 109
 See also Apex organization; National Apex Organisation of Tanzania (Formation) Act, 1990; WASHIRIKA
Corporatism, 52. *See also* Mass organizations
Corruption, 4, 5
 in cooperatives, 107, 109, 117–118, 120, 186(n69)
 in education, 87–88
 in land allocation, 92, 146
Costello, Matthew, on explaining policy ambiguity, 233

Coulson, Andrew, self-reliance as a multipurpose strategy, 163
Crop authorities
 debts to banks and cooperatives, 112, 177
 as "higher forms" of socialism, 11
Crop prices, 78–80, 233
 decline and rise, 79(table), 112
 See also Equality, income policies for, crop prices
Crouch, Susan, 11
 on aid disbursements undermining development, 181
 on compromises in self-reliance for sake of other goals, 166

Dar Tadine Tanzania (DTT), 93
Data problems, 4–5
 generalizing from a regional study, 13(n17)
 interpreting vetting process, 44–45(n18)
 "soft" and anecdotal evidence, 40
Debt, 170–171(table)
 repayment problems, 185–186(n45)
 written off, 169
 See also Self-reliance, national; Zanzibar, Tanzanian socialism, impact on
Decentralization, 62. *See also* Democracy, character of people-government link
Defensive radicalism. *See* Ake, Claude
Democracy, 221–222
 character of party-government link, 56–60: constitutional supremacy of party, 57; *kofia mbili*, 58–59; National Assembly, 57–58
 character of people-government link, 60–62: civil rights, 60–61, 64. *See also* Fifth Constitutional Amendment Act, 1984
 character of people-government link, decentralization, 62
 character of people-government link, local government, 61–62
 character of people-party link, 51–56: elections, 54–55; mass organizations, 52–54; mass vs. vanguard party, 51–52; party consolidation, 55–56
 definitions of liberal democracy, 47–48, 68(n6)
 definitions of popular democracy, 47–48
 economic democracy as a prerequisite for political democracy, 48
 multiparty means to, 62–67
 one-party means to, 48–49, 62
 "racist" opposition to liberal democracy, 69(n10)
 reasons for variations in assessments, 49–50
 variations in assessments, 50

See also One-party system
Dependence
 of breweries, 179
 changing character of, 170, 172(table)
 on food, 170–171(table), 172(table)
 on fuel, 172–173
 need for, 231
 on tractors, 180–181
 water development, 89, 102(n96)
 See also Neocolonialism
Development
 as choice, 184(n24)
 demand for, 181
 and socialism, 24
 See also Tanzanian socialism,
  categorization of, developmentalism
Development plans
 First Five-Year Plan (1964–1969), 136
 First Union Five-Year Plan
  (1981/82–1985/86), 138
 Second Five-Year Plan (1969–1974),
  136–137: on cooperatives as midwife to
  ujamaa villages, 108; on voluntaristic
  development, 27–28(n38)
 Second Union Five-Year Plan
  (1988/89–1992/93), 138
 Third-Five-Year Plan (1976–1981),
  137–138
 Three-Year Plan (1961/62–1963/64),
  136
District Councils. *See* Local government
Dodoma Wine Company (DOWICO),
 174–175
Dumont, René, on utopian character of
 ujamaa, 24

East African Community, 161
Economic decline, 139
 and acceptance of IMF conditionalities,
  168
 and cooperatives, 121
 and education, 86–88 and health policies,
  83–84
 and leadership code, 31–32, 41
 and party, 52
 and peasant income, 124(n43)
 and self-reliance, 167
 See also Economic Recovery Programme;
  Explanations, applied to Africawide
  problems; National Economic Survival
  Programme
Economic liberalization, 26, 200, 207–208,
 236
 hard currency demand as a consequence,
  93
 and parastatals, 148
 revenue decline, response to, 84
 in Zanzibar, 200, 207–209

See also Zanzibar, Tanzanian socialism,
 impact on
Economic Recovery Programme (ERP), 91,
 139
Economy of affection, 231–232
Education. *See* Equality, services policies
 for education
Elections
 Karume's opposition to, 206
 manifestos for, 54–55
 vetting of candidates for, 32–36, 54, 61,
  70(n31)
 See also Democracy, character of people-
  party link, elections
Ellis, Frank, on extraction of resources from
 peasantry, 233
Equality, 7, 186(n57)
 consumer price policies for, 80
 group status policies for, 96–97:
  gender, 96–97. *See also* Peasants;
  Subnationalism; Workers
 income policies for, 76–80, 99(n25),
  99(n28): crop prices, 78–80; wages and
  salaries, 76–78
 inverse relation with production, 97
 meaning of, 75
 ownership policies, 91–94, 132
 ownership policies for land, 91–92, 102–
  103(n113). *See also* Land Tenure
  (Established Villages) Act, No. 22 of
  1992, Shivji Commission on Land
  Issues
 ownership policies for minerals, 92–94.
  See also Bank of Tanzania; Dar Tadine
  Tanzania; Kwira coal mine; Liganga
  iron ore complex; Mwanza Regional
  Miners Association; State Mining
  Corporation
 ownership policies for nationalization, 94.
  See also Nationalizations
 production policies, 94–95
 production policies for communal
  production, 95. *See also* Parastatals
 services policies, 82–91
 services policies for education, 84–88,
  100(n58, n59, n64), 101(n74, n82). *See
  also* Sokoine University; Universal
  Primary Education; University of Dar
  es Salaam
 services policies for health, 82–84,
  100(n52). *See also* Private Hospitals
  (Regulation) Act, 1977
 services policies for housing, 89–91,
  102(n97, n102, n108, n109). *See also*
  National Housing Corporation;
  Registrar of Buildings; Rent Restriction
  Act of 1984; Tanzania Housing
  Bank

Index

services policies for water, 88–89, 101(n87). *See also* National Urban Water Authority
socialism and, 75–103
tax policies, 80–82
Ergas, Zaki, on failure of Tanzanian socialism, 3
Explanations
  applied to Africawide problems, 226–228: centralization, 227–228; economic failure, 226–227; IMF role, 226
  applied to Tanzania's problems: class, 229; incentives, 233–234; institutional conflict, 232–233; mode of production, 231–232; political conflict, 234; representational, 230–231; units of action, 234–235
  for industrial parastatals problems, 145–149. *See also* Industrial parastatals, explanations for performance
  for leadership problems, 42–43
  for self-reliance problems, 178–182
External pressures, 167
  for autonomous cooperatives, 126(n74)
  for democratization, 65
  hypocrisy of, 72(n88)
  impact of, 147, 178–179
  Mwinyi's observations on, 66
  for privatization, 151, 152. *See also* IMF agreement; International Monetary Fund; World Bank

Factional political struggle, 9–10, 17–19, 234
  in Zanzibar, 199–201
  See also Explanations, applied to Tanzania's problems; Ideological socialists; Pragmatic socialists; Self-reliance, explanations for lack of
Faki, Ramadhani Haji, forced removal of, 197
Federalism, 8, 193, 194–199, 211(n19). *See also* Union of Tanganyika and Zanzibar, structure of
Fifth Constitutional Amendment Act, 1984, 61
Food dependence. *See* Self-reliance, national, food dependence
Foreign exchange
  explanations for lack of, 145–146
  rates of, 241(table)
Freund, William, on utopian character of ujamaa, 24
Frontliners. *See* Factional political struggle, in Zanzibar
Fundikira, Abdullah, support for multipartyism, 64

Gender. *See* Equality, group status policies for, gender
Global General Merchandise, 142
Government officers
  authoritarian relation to peasants, 61
  bureaucratic bourgeoisie core, 109, 112, 147, 231
  cooperatives, working with, 116–118, 121
  corruption, and, 92
  leadership code's definition of, 38
  parastatals, working with, 30
  party, link to through kofia mbili, 58–59
  restraints upon, 220
Government-party interaction, 18, 56–60, 116–117, 173, 232–233, 239(n51)
Grindle, Merilee, on policymaking, 56
Gross domestic product–gross national product (GDP–GNP), 238(n26)

Halstein doctrine, 197
Hamad, Seif Shariff
  appointment and reappointment as chief minister, 200
  call for release of, 65
  expulsion from CCM, 40
  on mass organizations, 53
  and Nyerere, 212(n38)
  removal from office of, 197
  as vice-chair of CUF, 201
Hanga, Abdulla Kassim, 202–203, 205–206
Hartmann, Jeannette
  on institutional explanation of socialism's problems, 232–233
  on leadership code, 30
  on political causes of cooperative problems, 107
  on private sector, 19, 223
Health. *See* Equality, services policies, for health
Holela, David, on cooperative autonomy, 53–54
Housing. *See* Equality, services policies for housing
Hyden, Goran
  on contradictions in self-reliance, 162
  on cooperatives as arena for political struggle, 110
  on peasant mode of production, 231–232
  on socialism and development, 25

Ideological socialists
  communal production, 94–95
  cooperatives, 112–113, 114, 115, 119
  democratic theory and practice, 50
  dependence, 181
  government, 58
  IMF agreement, 169

industrial parastatals, 136, 137, 138, 144, 148, 152
industry, 129
iron and coal, 93
kofia mbili, 59
leadership code, 30–32, 43
leadership training, 36–38
mass organizations, 53
pragmatic socialists, 17–19, 218–220
self-reliance, 160, 165–166
University of Dar es Salaam, 101(n69)
vanguard party, 51–52
Wakil's selection over Hamad, 200
worker militancy, 134, 135–136
Zanzibari Marxists' impact on, 204
IMF agreement, 159, 167–170, 173, 185, 226, 229, 233. *See also* Explanations, applied to Africawide problems, IMF role; International Monetary Fund; Self-reliance, national, IMF accord
IMF conditionalities. *See* IMF agreement; International Monetary Fund, conditionalities of
Import substitution industrialization (ISI), 146, 157(n93)
Incentives, 233–234. *See also* Explanations, applied to Tanzania's problems, incentives
Income policies. *See* Equality, income policies for
Industrial parastatals
  capacity utilization and efficiency, 138–139
  consumer goods industries, 136–139
  control of, 130–136: through limitations on private sector, 131–133; through nationalization, 130–131; through restrictions on workers, 133–136
  explanations for performance of, 145–149: technical, 145–147; political, 147–149
  intermediate and capital goods industries, 137–138
  losses of, 143
  performance of, 139–144: shoes, 142–143; textiles, 139–142
  Presidential Parastatal Reform Commission, 151
  reform of, 149–152
  socialist construction's impact on, 143
  Tanzania Association of Parastatal Organisations, 143, 151
Industry
  growth and decline of, 129–130, 133
  importance of, 21–22
  industrialization, definition of, 153(n1)
  manufacturing contribution to GDP, 140(table)

Institutional conflict. *See* Explanations, applied to Tanzania's problems, institutional conflict
Instrumentalism. *See* Self-reliance, meaning of, strategy vs. goal issue; Subnationalism, instrumentalism of
Interim Constitution, 194, 195
Intermediate goods industries. *See* Industrial parastatals, intermediate and capital goods industries
International Cooperative Alliance (ICA)
  on contradiction between national and cooperative self-reliance, 162
  on demand for cooperative autonomy, 126(n74), 176
International influences. *See* International Monetary Fund; Union of Tanganyika and Zanzibar, reasons for international rivalries and; Zanzibar, Tanzanian socialism, impact on
International Labour Organisation (ILO)
  income differentials, estimate of rural-urban gap, 79
  real income, decline of wage earners', 78
  secondary school enrollments, limited, 84
International Monetary Fund (IMF)
  conditionalities of, 23, 119, 121, 179, 180
  consumer prices decontrol, 80, 99(n28)
  privatization, encouragement of, 151
  production, emphasis on, 97
  public employment, contraction of, 78
  See also IMF agreement
Iron and steel industry, 138. *See also* Equality, ownership policies for minerals
Islamic Conference Organisation (OIC), 198, 201

Juma, Omar Ali, 204, 208
Jumbe, Aboud, 197, 199–201, 209
Jumuiya ya Muungano wa Vyama vya Ushirika (Establishment) Act, 1979. *See* Cooperatives, legislation affecting; WASHIRIKA
JUWATA. *See* Union of Tanzania Workers

Kabudi, P.J.A.M., 3
  on Fabian character of ujamaa, 24
  on the "left" in party, 25
  on violations of leadership code, 41
Kahama, George, 17
Kamahuru. *See* Steering Committee for Free Political Parties in Zanzibar
Karume, Abedi
  agreement on union, 190
  assassination of, 197
  embarrassment to Nyerere, 205–207
  as nationalist and subnationalist, 199, 201, 212(n33)

See also Union of Tanganyika and Zanzibar, reasons for Karume's position in Zanzibar and
Kasfir, Nelson, on the economy of affection, 232
Kawawa, Rashidi
  on cooperatives and ujamaa villages, 109–110
  on mass organizations, 53
Kawawa, Sophia, 63
Kibo Paper Industries, Ltd., 146
Kilimanjaro Native Cooperative Union (KNCU), 123(n33)
Kilimanjaro Region
  democracy in, 10–11
  reorganization of cooperatives in, 116–117
Kilombero Sugar Company, 146
Kitching, Gavin, on Tanzanian socialism as a form of populism, 24
Kivukoni College, 36–37
Kjaerby, Finn, 180–181
Kofia mbili, 58–59, 61. *See also* Democracy, character of party-government link, *kofia mbili*
Kolimba, Horace
  on avoiding theoretical socialism, 67
  on decision to introduce multiparty system, 66
  on relaxation of leadership code, 22, 32
Kronemer, Alexander, on failure of Tanzanian socialism, 3
Kulaks
  cooperatives, controlled by, 109
  and representational explanations for problems, 230
Kwira Coal Mine, 93

Labor. *See* Workers
Labor unions. *See* National Union of Tanganyika Workers; Organisation of Tanzania Trade Unions; Self-reliance, subnational, labor unions; Tanganyika Federation of Labour; Union of Tanzania Workers
Land. *See* Equality, ownership policies for land
Land Tenure (Established Villages) Act, No. 22 of 1992, 92, 103(n115)
Leadership, 6
  assessment of, 40–42
  democracy and, 49
  exclusion of leadership code violators from, 32–36
  explanation of problems with, 42–43
  expulsion of leadership code violators from, 38–40
  socialism and, 29–46

  training for, 36–38
  See also Leadership code
Leadership code, 22, 29–32
  constitutional incorporation of, 31
  criticisms of, 41
  definition of leaders in, 30, 38
  economic decline, impact on, 31–32
  enforcement of, 32–40: Commission for the Leadership Code, 38–39; Control and Disciplinary Commission, 39
  explanation for problems with, 41–42
  extension of applicability to party members, 38–39
  loopholes in, 39
  Nyerere's support for, 32
  principles of, 30
  relaxation of, 22, 30, 32
  society's response to violations of, 42
  teaching of, 36–38
  on Zanzibar, applicability of, 38–39, 206
  See also Commission Act No. 6 of 1973; Political clientelism; Zanzibar Declaration, 1991
Leonard, David, 76
Liberalization. *See* Democracy, multiparty means to; Economic liberalization
Liberators. *See* Factional political struggle, in Zanzibar
Liganga iron ore complex, 94
Liviga, Athumani
  on Hamad's economic liberalization, 200
  on subnationalism as instrumentalism, 212(n31)
Local government
  debts of, 176
  debts owed to, 176
  decline of, 61
  district councils, 87
  reestablishment of, 62
  self-reliance, absence of, 175–176
  See also Democracy, character of people-government link; Self-reliance, subnational, local government
Lofchie, Michael
  on agricultural policy errors, 180
  on impact of world system, 178
  on insufficiency of foreign exchange, 145
  on problems of Tanzanian socialism, 3
  on representational explanation of problems, 230
Lwaitama, A.F., on social democratic character of ujamaa, 24

Madsen, Birgit Storgard, on utopian character of ujamaa, 23
Malima, Kighoma
  on new colonialism of IMF, 167–168
  on restructuring parastatals, 151

Maliyamkono, T.L, on the second economy, 78
Manley, Michael, 1
Manufacturing. *See* Industry
Marketing cooperatives. *See* Agricultural cooperatives, types of
Marketing policies, problems involving
  commerce, 87
  cooperatives, 110–121
  minerals, 93
  parastatal industries, 146–147
  See also Crop authorities; Regional trading companies; Tanzania Hides and Skins Company; Zana za Kilimo
Marxists, 215
  democracy and, 50
  factional political struggle among, 9–10
  ideological socialists and, 17
  industrial workers and, 7–8
  on leadership, 6
  on leadership code, 41–42
  and nationalism, 189
  on priority of industry, 129, 137
  on radicalization of Tanzanian socialism, 25
  on socialism in one country, 178
  and University of Dar es Salaam, 86
  Zanzibari Marxists, 202–204
  See also Zanzibar, Tanzanian socialism, impact on
Mass organizations, 52–54
  autonomy of, 53–54, 70(n29)
  as means to subordinate special interests to general will, 52
  non–party members' access to party and vice versa, 53
  See also Cooperative Union of Tanzania; Democracy, character of people-party link, mass organizations; Organisation of Tanzania Trade Unions; Tanzania Cooperative Alliance; Tanzania Parents Association; Tanzania Youth Organisation; Union of Tanzanian Women; Union of Tanzania Workers
Mass party
  Nyerere's support for, 21
  persistence of, 56
  and vanguard party, 52–53
  See also Democracy, character of people-party link, mass vs. vanguard party
Mayer, William, on self-reliance as strategy for development, 164
Mazrui, Ali, on impact of Zanzibari Marxists, 16
Mbeya Ceramic Company, 174
Members of parliament (MPs)
  benefits to, 46(n52)
  candidate selection, 32–36, 44–45(n18)
  dilemma of, 58
  expulsion of, 39–40
  See also National Assembly; Political clientelism
Minde, Elizabeth
  on absence of cooperatives in villages, 111
  on party control of WASHIRIKA, 114
Minerals. *See* Equality, ownership policies for minerals
Minimum wage
  ameliorating decline for the better paid, 78
  changes in, 77(table)
  fall in real wages, 76–78
  reduction in range of, 76
  See also Equality, income policies for, wages and salaries; Population
Mlimuka, A.K.L.J
  on capitalist expansion, 4
  on "left's" role in party, 25
  on punishment inequities for leadership code violators, 41
Mode of production. *See* Explanations, applied to Tanzania's problems, mode of production
Mongela, Gertrude, 102–103(n113)
Mongolia, as model for Tanzanian socialism, 21, 219
Moody, Tony, on utopian character of ujamaa, 23
Morogoro Region Cooperative Union (MRCU), thwarted attempt to force reorganization of, 117–118
Morogoro Shoe Company, 142–143, 156(n79)
Mottin, Marie-France, on utopian character of ujamaa, 24
Mount Carmel Rubber Factory, 134–135
Mrema, Augustine, on cost of imprisoning defaulters of development levy, 82
Msanga, I.R.E.M., on political interference in cooperatives, 107
Msekwa, Pius, on workers' committees and councils, 133–134
Msuya, Cleopa
  on credit default problems, 179
  on taxes, 80
  on textile industry problems, 141
Mtikila, Reverend Christopher, inciting anti-Asian sentiment, 158(n124)
Mueller, Susanne
  on ujamaa as vehicle for pauperization, 3
  on utopian character of ujamaa, 24
Mukandala, Rwekaza, 148–149
Multiparty system
  external pressures and, 65
  leaders' initial reaction to proposal for, 63–64

Index

Nyerere's call for debate on, 55, 62
opposition to, 65
political consequences of, 42–43, 56, 66–67
reasons for, 62–63, 65–66
support for, 64–65
See also CCM Extraordinary National Party Conference, 1992; Democracy, multiparty means to
Multipurpose cooperatives. *See* Agricultural cooperatives, types of
Multivillage cooperatives. *See* Agricultural cooperatives, types of
Mutahaba, Gelase, on local government, 61–62
Mvungi, S.E.A
on Fabian character of Tanzanian socialism, 24
on leadership code violations, 41
on socialist progress, absence of, 3–4
on Zanzibar revolution's problems, 212(n33)
Mwanza Regional Miners Association, 93
Mwase, Ngila R.L., on cooperative union assistance to ujamaa villages, 110
MWATEX, 140, 141
Mwinyi, Ali Hassan
and IMF accord, explanation for acceptance of, 168–169
on lack of self-reliance of subnational institutions, 177
on leadership code revision, 43
on mass organizations' autonomy, 70(n29)
on meeting people, need for, 56
on multipartyism: announcing acceptance of, 66; channeling debate on, 64; initial reaction to, 63
on parastatal problems, 150
and president of Zanzibar's selection, 200
on social service, inadequate expenditures for, 91
union and marriage analogy, 194
on Western pressure for multipartyism, 66

National Apex Organisation of Tanzania (Formation) Act, 1990, 118–119
National Assembly
and cooperative legislation, 118 formation of Tanzania's, 195
impotence of, 40, 57–58
Tanganyika's ratification of Articles of Union, 190
votes to give Tanganyika separate government, 198
See Democracy, character of party-government link, National Assembly
National Bank of Commerce
autonomy, lack of, 174
interest rates of, 141
loans with conditionalities of, 176–177
National Development Corporation (NDC), 135, 233
National Economic Survival Programme (NESP), 139
National Executive Committee of the party (NEC)
Arusha Declaration, adoption by TANU of, 19
candidates, role in vetting of, 33–36, 44–45(n18)
constitutional supremacy, 1974 decision on, 57
cooperative apex organization, direction of, 113–114, 125(n53)
cooperative union general managers, call for explanation for losses, 177
Hamad's removal, 200–201
IMF agreement, acceptance of, 168–169
leadership code, acceptance by, 30
multipartyism, approval of, 66
National Assembly, role in, 58
party leaders, expulsion of, 39–40
union structure, 1983 proposal to change, 196
Wakil as Zanzibar presidential candidate, selection of, 200
See also Central committee of party; Party secretariat; Zanzibar Declaration
National Housing Corporation (NHS), 89–91
Nationalizations
companies acquired, 131
sectoral proportions, 154(n11)
small businesses, 155(n23)
See also Acquisition of Buildings Act, 1971; Equality, ownership policies for nationalizations; Industrial parastatals, control of, through nationalization
National Milling Corporation (NMC), 174
National Textile Corporation (TEXCO), 140–141, 174
National Union of Tanganyika Workers (NUTA), 133–135
National Urban Water Authority (NUWA), 89
Nellis, John, on number of parastatals, 130
Neocolonialism
situation of Tanzania, 160, 184(n29)
socialist progress, obstacle to, 42
Ngombale-Mwiru, Kingunge
on bureaucratization, 62
on cadre training abroad, 37
on democracy, need for economic and social justice in, 48
as ideological socialist leader, 17
Kivukoni college work of, 37

on one-party system, dissociating socialism from, 63
party and government positions held by, 116, 125(n59)
on producer-oriented, single-village cooperatives, 116
on self-reliance, 162–163, 164, 183(n4)
Novack, George, on pragmatism, 217–218
Nsekela, Amon, on parastatals, failure to achieve social or economic objectives, 154(n5)
Nursey-Bray, P.F., on utopian character of ujamaa, 23–24
Nyalali Commission. *See* Presidential Commission on the Party System
Nyerere, Julius
and Arusha Declaration, 19
on cooperatives, 106, 109
on corrupt officials, call for confrontation of, 92
on decentralization, 62
and democracy, 47, 48–49, 72(n88)
on development levy defaulters, cost of imprisoning, 82
on education, 19
on elitism in the university, 85
on external factors, harm by, 178
on Hamad, 212(n38)
and IMF, 168–169, 184–185(n33)
on individualism and communalism, relation between, 73(n101)
on International Monetary Fund, 184–185(n33): conditionalities, opposition to, 168; IMF agreement, reasons for accepting, 168–169
on *kofia mbili*, problems with, 58–59
on leadership code, 32, 41
on management-worker relations, 134
mantle of, 37–38
and mass party, support for, 51
on multipartyism, 48–49, 55, 62–63, 65
on parastatal problems, 150
popularity of transferred to party, 57
pragmatism of, 218–219
private sector, reassurance of, 131–132
on Second Five-Year Plan, 27–28(n38)
on self-reliance, 162, 163, 165
on socialism: and CCM's Fifteen Year Party Programme, 21–22; and cooperatives, 11; and education, 84, 88; and equality, 75; and rural socialism, 19–20; and scientific socialism, 23; in traditional society, 11
on union to promote African unity, 193
on wage gap, 76

OIC. *See* Islamic Conference Organisation

Oil dependence, 168, 172–173. *See also* IMF agreement; Self-reliance, national, oil dependence
Okema, Michael, 3
One-party system
elections in, 54–55, 57
kofia mbili, effectiveness of, 58–60
mass organizations, role of, 52–54
mass vs. vanguard struggle in, 51–52
National Assembly, subordination to party, 58
organized opposition, need for, 48–49
party, evaluation of democracy in, 51–56
party-government relation, 56–60
people-government link in, 60–62
See also Bureaucratization; Democracy, one-party means to; Local government; Presidential Commission on the Party System
Organisation of Islamic Conference. *See* Islamic Conference Organisation
Organisation of Tanzania Trade Unions (OTTU), 54, 70(n30), 177
OTTU. *See* Organisation of Tanzania Trade Unions

Paper and pulp industry, 138. *See also* Southern Paper Mills
Parastatals
autonomy, lack of, 174–175
definition of, 130
number of, 130
Parastatal Management Services Agreement Committee (PMSAC), 151
socialism and, 129–158
Standing Committee on Parastatal Organisation (SCOPO), 151
See also Industrial parastatals; Self-reliance, subnational
Parliament. *See* National Assembly
Party
branches in industries, establishment of, 134
decline of, 52, 57
expulsion: decentralization of responsibility for, 45–46(n36); of leaders, 38–40
the "left" in, role of, 25, 53, 70
mass vs. vanguard, 36–38, 51–52
multivillage cooperatives and, 114
party conference, 1987, 55
party supremacy, efforts to establish, 57–60
relation to government, 55–60
revitalization of, 45(n23), 55–56
size of, 52
WASHIRIKA and, 124(n49)
See also Afro-Shirazi Party; Annual District Conference of party; Central

Index

Committee of party; Chama cha Mapinduzi; Civic United Front; Mass Organizations; National Executive Committee of the party; Party secretariat; Presidential Commission on the Party System; Tanganyika African National Union
Party secretariat
 contraction of, 56, 60
 creation of, 60
 departments and commissions of, 70(n58)
 Hamad's position in, 200
 reorganization of, 125(n59)
 See also Democracy, character of party-government link
Party supremacy
 constitutional entrenchment of, 195
 expulsion of MPs and, 39–40
 and *kofia mbili*, 58–60
 National Assembly, subordination of, 57–58
 See also Democracy, character of party-government link, constitutional supremacy of party
Patron-client system. *See* Political clientelism
Peasants/peasantry
 authoritarian treatment of, 61
 centrality in Tanzanian socialism of, 19–21, 30, 105–106
 communal production and, 223
 cooperatives, disillusionment with, 119, 177
 extraction of resources from, 232
 frustration with, 42
 gender division within, 96–97
 income decline of, 124(n43)
 reasons for withdrawing from market, 229–232
 trampled by political struggle, 105, 110
 and ujamaa villages, 20
 See also Kulaks
Pemba
 expulsion of North Pemba party leaders, 40
 subnationalism, basis for, 191
 and Wakil's narrow election, 200
 and Zanzibar, differences between, 210(n6)
Perkins, F.C., contradiction between parastatal theory and practice, 144
Policies, pragmatization of, 23
 See also Equality: consumer price policies for; group status policies for; ownership policies; production policies; services policies
Political clientelism
 cooperatives and, 120
 evidence for in candidate vetting process, 34, 36

as explanation for public commitment to and private violation of leadership code, 42
Population
 growth rate of, 238(n26)
 of mainland and isles, 211(n20)
 wage and salary earners, number of, 78, 98–99(n21)
Populism. *See* Tanzanian socialism, categorization of, as populist
Portland Cement Company, 146
Pragmatic socialists
 communal production and, 95
 cooperatives: abolition of, 112; form of cooperatives, 113, 115; reintroduction of, 112
 democratic theory and practice, discrepancy between, 50
 equality and production, shift of emphasis on, 97
 government, relation to, 60
 ideological socialists and, 17, 18(table), 19, 218
 IMF agreement, acceptance of, 169
 industry, deemphasis by, 129
 iron and coal, struggle over, 93
 leadership code, position on, 30–32
 leadership training, struggle over, 36–38, 43
 mass organizations, role of, 53
 mass party, support for, 51–52
 modernization, demand for quick, 181
 parastatals, 136–138, 144, 148, 152
 and self-reliance, 160, 166
 University of Dar es Salaam and, 101(n69)
 worker militancy, relation to, 134, 135–136
 Zanzibar governments, relation to, 207
Pragmatism
 Charles Anderson on, 217, 218
 W.Y. Elliott on, 217, 218
 meaning of, 217
 George Novack on, 217, 218
 and purpose, 218, 236
Pratt, Cranford
 on cooperatives, party-government interference in, 107
 on self-reliance, compromises with, 166
 on socialism, commitment to, 16
 on ujamaa, social democratic character of, 24
Presidential Circular No. 1 of 1970, 134
Presidential Commission on the Party System (Nyalali Commission)
 chairperson, appointment of Judge Nyalali as, 64

discontent with party system, popular expression before, 49, 51
formation of, 64
recommendation of, 65
union, recommendation on restructuring, 199
Price Commission, 146, 151. *See also* Equality, consumer price policies for
Private Hospitals (Regulation) Act, 1977, 83
Private sector, 21
  insecurity of, 132
  persistence of, 133
  reassurances to, 131–132
  resurgence of, 152
  status, ambiguity of, 131–133
Private traders
  and breakdown of cooperatives, 112
  clove market and, 208
  cooperative monopoly's end, impact on, 119
  and multifunctional cooperatives, 109
Privatization
  Asian and foreign control of resources, consequences of, 153
  progress, rate of, 151
  reason for, 87, 151
  socialist intent of, 152
  worker reaction to, 158(n116)
  See also Industrial parastatals, reform of
Production-oriented cooperatives. *See* Agricultural cooperatives, types of, production-oriented
Public Corporations Act, 1992, 151–152, 158(n122)
Putterman, Louis, 233–234

Radwan, Samir, on communal production, problems with, 95
Raikes, Philip, on cooperative unions becoming like parastatals, 120
Regional political committees of the party (RPCs)
  composition of, 44(n17)
  vetting of potential candidates, 33
Regional trading companies (RTCs), 147
Registrar of Buildings (ROB)
  buildings controlled by, 102(n105)
  debts owed to, 102(n106)
  See also Acquisition of Buildings Act, 1971
Registrar of Cooperatives
  Circular No. 4 of 1985, 116
  union management committees, thwarted efforts to dissolve, 117–118
Rent Restriction Act of 1984, 102(n109). *See also* Equality, services policies for housing

Representation. *See* Elections; Explanations, applied to Tanzania's problems, representational
Resnick, Idrian, on self-reliance strategy, stages of, 164
Rey, Lucien, on Zanzibar revolution, spread through union with Tanganyika, 204
Rubber Industries, Ltd., 135
Rural cooperatives. *See* Agricultural cooperatives
Ruvuma Development Association, 175
Rwegasira, Joseph, on IMF agreement, acceptance of, 169
Rweyemamu, Justinian, on basic industries, 137–138

Salaries. *See* Equality, income policies for, wages and salaries
Salim, Salim Ahmed, 237(n2)
Samoff, Joel, 10, 100(n58), 237(n12)
Saul, John, on cooperatives as potential danger to socialism, 109
Second economy, 78
Security of Employment Act, 1964, 133
Self-reliance, 8, 11, 224
  capitalism and, 11, 165
  development and, 164
  economic nationalism and, 165
  explanations for lack of, 178–182: factional struggle, 180–182; units of action, 178–180
  independence and, 165
  levels of, 182–183(n2)
  meaning of, 159–165: degree of autonomy, 159–160; strategy vs. goal issue, 163–165; unit-specific character, 161–163
  Mwinyi calls lack of subnational "cancerous chain," 177
  national: aid, 169; debt, 170, 171, 176; food dependence, 168, 170–172(table); IMF accord, 167–170; oil dependence, 172–183
  phases of, 164, 183(n15)
  power through, 160, 164
  socialism and, 159–187
  subnational: banks, 174; CCM, 173; cooperatives, 176–177; labor unions, 177; local government, 175–176; parastatals, 174–175; ujamaa villages, 175
  tractors and, 180
  See also Aid; Debt; Dependence; Food dependence; International Monetary Fund; Neocolonialism; Oil dependence
Senegal, on multipartyism in, 73(n97)
Shariff, Othman, on execution of, 205–206

Shepherd, George W., Jr., on Tanzania as part of a "subimperial tributary system," 184(n29)
Shivji, Issa
  on cooperative problems, class explanation for, 107, 229
  on leadership code, breaches of, 41
  on OTTU, government powers over, 70(n30)
  on parastatal problems, class explanation of, 147–148
  on self-reliance, 167
Shivji Commission on Land Issues, 103(n113, n114)
Shoe industry, 142–143
  government assistance to, 142
  privatization of, 143, 156(n80)
  production decline, 142
  and Tanzania Leather Associated Industries, 142–143
  See also Industrial parastatals, performance of, shoes
Siegler, Rainer, on political factions, 10
Singh, Ajit, on IMF, political motives of, 167
Skarstein, Rune
  on foreign exchange, explanations for insufficiency of, 145
  on steel and paper and pulp industries, inefficiencies of, 138
Sklar, Richard, social democratic character of ujamaa, 24
Social democracy. *See* Tanzanian socialism, categorization of, as social democractic
Socialism
  demise of, 1, 12(n5)
  democracy and, 68–69(n7)
  forms of: deterministic, 6; voluntaristic, 6
  transformation of, 2
  See also African socialism; Tanzanian socialism; Third World socialisms
Socialist morality, as prerequisite for socialist transition, 29. *See also* Leadership code
Sokoine, Edward, 200–201
Sokoine University, 86
Solarz, U.S. Representative Stephen, on "aid" to Tanzania, 185(n44)
Southern Paper Mills (SPM)
  inefficiency of, 138
  Kwira coal, problems with, 93
  partial privatization sought for, 156(n55)
  price coordination, problems of, 146
  temporary closure of, 156(n55)
South-South Commission, 161
Soviet Union
  example to emulate, 21, 37, 219

federalism: impact of one-party system, 196; as a solution to subnationalism, 8
state farms, 7
Zanzibar, involvement in, 193
Special Committee of Enquiry into the Cooperative Movement and Marketing Boards, 107
Srivastava, B.P., on purpose of union of Tanganyika and Zanzibar, 192–193
State farms, 7
State Mining Corporation (STAMICO), 93
Steering Committee for Free Political Parties in Zanzibar, 73(n94), 201
Stein, Howard
  class explanation, 229
  IMF agreement, 185(n42)
Sterkenburg, J.J., expulsion of MPs in 1968, 39–40
Stren, Richard
  on housing policy, 90
  on wage gap, 76
Structural Adjustment Programme (SAP), 139
Subnationalism, 224–225
  definitions of nationalism, 210(n1)
  growth of, 67
  instrumentalism of, 201, 209
  Islam's rise, 210
  and Karume's Tanzanian nationalism, 212(n33)
  Marxist views on socialism and, 189
  meaning of, 189–190
  multipartyism, impact on, 212–213(n42)
  and "national" conditionality for party registration, 66, 73(n94), 201
  nationalism and, 189
  and nationalization of socialism, 189
  Pemba's impact on Zanzibar's subnationalism, 191
  political struggle, impact on, 199
  privatization, impact on, 153, 158(n24)
  Tanganyika, case of, 210
  unification, impact of movement toward, 197
  Zanzibar, case of, 190–201
  See also Mtikila, Reverend Christopher, inciting anti-Asian sentiment; Pemba; Sykes, Ali, and anti-Asian sentiment; Union of Tanganyika and Zanzibar; Zanzibar, Tanzanian socialism, impact on; Zanzibar, politics in
Sungusungu, autonomy, subversion of, 179
Sykes, Ali, and anti-Asian sentiment, 158(n124)

Tanganyika
  increased autonomy from union, 197, 199

independence struggle: impact on socialism, 16; impact on unity, 190 and subnationalism, 210, 212–213(n42) union with Zanzibar, 190
  See also Subnationalism, Tanganyika, case of; Union of Tanganyika, and Zanzibar
Tanganyika African National Union (TANU), 16
  merger with ASP, 195–196
  See also Party
Tanganyika Electrical Supply Company (TANESCO). *See* Tanzania Electrical Supply Company
Tanganyika Federation of Labour (TFL), 133
TANU. *See* Tanganyika African National Union
TANU Constitution, 75
TANU Creed
  cooperatives, role of, 107–108
  and equality, 75
  See also TANU Constitution
TANU Guidelines, 1971, 20
  labor militancy, 53, 134
  leadership, 41
Tanzania Association of Parastatal Organisations (TAPO). *See* Industrial parastatals
Tanzania Audit Corporation (TAC). *See* Industrial parastatals
Tanzania Breweries, lack of self-reliance of, 179
Tanzania Cooperative Alliance (TCA), formation of, 54, 119, 126(n74)
Tanzania Electrical Supply Company (TANESCO), power cuts to force payments to, 174, 176
Tanzania Elimu Supplies (TES), 87
Tanzania Hides and Skins Company, 147
Tanzania Housing Bank (THB), 90
  debt owed by, 176
  debt owed to, 102(n100)
  See also Banks
Tanzania Investment Bank (TIB). *See* Banks
Tanzania Leather Associated Industries (TLAI). *See* Industrial parastatals, performance of, shoes
Tanzania Legal Education Trust. *See* Democracy, multiparty means to
Tanzanian Court of Appeal, 206
Tanzania News Agency Act of 1976. *See* Democracy, character of people-government link, civil rights
Tanzanian socialism, 2–4, 15–28
  categorization of, 23–26: as developmentalist, 24–25; as populist, 24; as social democratic, 24; as utopian, 23–24

commitment of state to, 16
cooperatives and, 105–106
defensive radicalism, 16
development, form of, 27–28(n38)
disputes over, 4–5
dynamic character of, 26
failure of, 3–4
formulation of, 16–17
and human volition, 3, 9, 16, 159, 182, 216, 229, 236
leadership code and, 22
models for, 21
problems of, explanations for, 8–12, 225–235
radicalization of, 19–23, 25, 219–220
scholarly study of, 2–3, 4–5
top-down character of, 29
training of leaders in, 36–38, 42
unit-specific goals of, 10
as vision rather than reality, 15
Tanzania Parents Association (WAZAZI), 53
  party, relation to, 54
  See also Mass organizations
Tanzania People's Defence Force (TPDF), 198
Tanzania Shoe Company (BORA), 142–143
Tanzania Tanneries, Ltd., 176
Tanzania Youth Organisation (VIJANA), 53, 54. *See also* Mass organizations
Tanzaphilia. *See* Tanzanian socialism, scholarly study of
Tanzaphobia. *See* Tanzanian socialism, scholarly study of
Tax policies
  development levy, 81–82, 99(n37, n38)
  income tax on capital and labor, 81
  ineffectiveness of, 80, 98(n16)
  trade and sales taxes, 80–81
  See also Equality, tax policies
TEXCO. *See* National Textile Corporation
Textile industries
  capacity of, 156(n57)
  declining production of, 139, 141(table): explanations for, 141–142
  See also Industrial parastatals, performance of, textiles
Third World socialisms, 3–4. *See also* Tanzanian socialism
Thomas, Clive, on basic industries, 137–138
Tobacco, 149
Tordoff, William, on Zanzibari Marxists, 202–203
Tractors, 180
Trotsky, Leon, 8
Tumbo, Kasanga, support for multipartyism of, 64
Twiga Cement Factory, 146

Ujamaa. *See* Tanzanian socialism
Ujamaa villages
  cooperative help in formation of, 107–110
  producer cooperative form of, 22
  registration as cooperatives, 122(n23)
  self-reliance and, 175
  Tanga region and, 13(n17)
  See also Self-reliance, subnational; Villages
Umma Party, 191, 210(n7)
Union of Tanganyika and Zanzibar
  Articles of Union, 190, 193–196
  foreign affairs, Zanzibar independence in, 198
  party(ies), impact on, 195, 197
  reasons for, 190–194: African unity and, 193–194; international rivalries and, 191–193; Karume's position in Zanzibar and, 191
  size difference, problem of, 193
  structure of, 194–197: flexible character of, 194; Nyalali Commission recommendations on, 199; separate government for Tanganyika issue, 198
  subnationalism of, encouraged by federal insulation, 199
  unification, resistance to, 197–199
  union powers, growth of, 194
  See also Federalism
Union of Tanzanian Women (UWT), 53
  IMF agreement, acceptance of, 169
  multipartyism, chairperson's reaction to, 63
  party, relation to, 54
Union of Tanzania Workers (JUWATA), 52
  autonomy of, 54
  replacement of, 54, 70(n29)
  See also Organisation of Tanzania Trade Unions
United Nations Development Programme (UNDP), 208
United Republic of Tanzania (URT), 210(n4)
United Republic of Tanzania and Zanzibar (URTZ)
  formation of, 190
  reaction of the "left" to, 191
  reasons for, 190–194
  See also Union of Tanganyika and Zanzibar
Units of action, 10–12, 180, 234–235
  cooperatives and, 11, 106, 120
  democracy and, 10–11, 67–68, 72(n88)
  district council problems and, 62
  "law of larger units," 179
  overcoming by tempering individualism with communalism, 73(n101)
  Ruvuma Development Association and, 175
  selfishness and, 11–12
  self-reliance and, 11, 161–163, 178–180
  socialism in traditional society and, 11
  See also Explanations, applied to Tanzania's problems, units of action; Self-reliance, explanations for lack of, units of action; Tanzanian socialism, problems, explanations for
Unit specificity. *See* Self-reliance, meaning of, unit-specific character
Universal Primary Education (UPE), 84, 86, 166
University of Dar es Salaam, 4, 85–86
  authoritarianism in dealing with, 101(n69)
  cost of, 100(n66)
  enrollment in, 100(n65)
  ideological socialists at, 101(n69)
University of Dar es Salaam Legal Aid Society, 90
URAFIKI, 140–141
USSR. *See* Soviet Union
Utopian socialism. *See* Tanzanian socialism, categorization of, utopian
UWT. *See* Union of Tanzanian Women

Valentine, Theodore, on real wages, decline of, 76
Van Cranenburgh, Oda, 230–231
Van Donge, Jan Kees
  on economic liberalization, Hamad's policy of, 200
  on subnationalism as instrumentalism, 212(n31)
Vanguard party
  dispute over mass vs. vanguard character, 51–52
  ideological socialists and, 53, 63
  mass organizations and, 53
  "vangardization" of party, 20, 221
  See also Democracy, character of people-party link, mass vs. vanguard party
Van Velzen, H.U.E. Thoden, expulsion of MPs in 1968, 39–40
VIJANA. *See* Tanzania Youth Organisation
Villages
  cooperatives and, 114–115
  number per cooperative, 114–115(table)
  Villages and Ujamaa Villages Act, 1975, 110–111
  See also Ujamaa villages
Villagization. *See* Ujamaa villages; Villages
Von Freyhold, Michaela, on ujamaa villages in Tanga region, 13(n17)

Wages. *See* Equality, income policies for, wages and salaries

Wakil, Idris Abdul-
  multipartyism, initial reaction to, 63
  on teachers' lack of training, 101(n74)
  on Zanzibar president, election of, 200
  on Zanzibar presidential candidate, selection of, 200
Wallerstein, Immanuel, on party autonomy from the state, 56
Wall Street Journal, 3
Wangwe, Samuel
  on communal production, problems with, 95
  on foreign exchange insufficiency, 145
  on idle industries, 181
  on steel and paper and pulp industries, inefficiency of, 139
WASHIRIKA
  autonomy of, 54
  leadership of, 114
  party and, 124(n49)
  replacement by Tanzania Cooperative Alliance, 54
  See also Apex organization; Cooperative Union of Tanzania; Jumiya ya Muungano wa Vyama vya Ushirika; Mass organizations
Water. *See* Equality, services policies for water
Watzal, Ludwig, on "individual" and "family" individuality, 11
WAZAZI. *See* Tanzania Parents Association
Weaver, James, 3
Women. *See* Equality, group status policies for, gender
Workers
  control by state, 133, 136
  labor aristocracy, 135
  militancy of, 134–136
  supression of at Mt. Carmel Rubber Factory, 135
  pauperization of, 136
  quiescence of, 135
  See also Industrial parastatals, control of, through restrictions on workers;
    Security of Employment Act, 1964; Workers' Committees; Workers' Councils
Workers' Committees, 133–134. *See also* Security of Employment Act, 1964
Workers' Councils, 134. *See also* Presidential Circular No. 1 of 1970
World Bank, 167
  conditionalities of, 23
  and inappropriate technology, 181
  shoe industry, support of, 142–143
World Health Organization (WHO), 83
Wunsch, James, 226–228

Young, Crawford, on party's mass character, persistence of, 56

Zana za Kilimo, 146
Zanzibar
  CUT's demise, resistance to, 126(n74)
  economic burden of mainland, 198, 207
  mainland, historical ties to, 190–191, 192(table)
  1979 constitution of, 206, 207
  politics in, 199–201
  prototype of socialism, 204–205
  Revolutionary Council, 195, 206
  subnationalism, an example of, 8, 189–213
  Tanzanian socialism, impact on, 201–209
  unequal treatment of, 212(n32)
  See also Hamad, Seif Shariff; Pemba; Subnationalism; Union of Tanganyika and Zanzibar
Zanzibar Bottling Plant, 149
Zanzibar Declaration, 1991, 22–23, 32, 41, 43
Zanzibar House of Representatives, 149
Zanzibar National Party (ZNP), 190, 200
Zanzibar and Pemba People's Party (ZPPP), 206–207
Zanzibar Treason Trial, 206–207

About the Book and Author

Tanzania, with its policies of socialism and self-reliance, was looked upon as Africa's greatest hope in the 1960s—and its greatest disappointment by the 1980s. Beset with problems, Tanzania ultimately accepted the capitalist world's prescriptions of IMF conditionalities and Western-style democratization. Still, unlike other African countries, it did not formally abandon the goal of building a socialist society in the future.

The purpose of this study is to contribute to an understanding both of Third World attempts to build socialist societies and of Tanzania's postindependence political evolution.

McHenry sets Tanzania's continually evolving form of government in the context of the family of socialisms. He then examines the country's efforts to create leadership able to contribute to socialist construction; to secure democracy during the transition to socialism; to achieve social and economic equality; to use agricultural cooperatives and urban industrial parastatals as vehicles for socialism; to foster self-reliance; and to contain Zanzibari subnationalism, which threatened the socialist project. Central to his account of the Tanzanian experience is the political tension between two leadership factions, the ideological and the pragmatic socialists.

Dean E. McHenry Jr. is associate professor of political science at the Center for Politics and Economics, Claremont Graduate School. His extensive work on Tanzania includes *Tanzania's Ujamaa Villages: The Implementation of a Rural Development Strategy.*